THE ROLE OF THE COMPUTER IN ECONOMIC AND
SOCIAL RESEARCH IN LATIN AMERICA

Financial support for the conference was supplied by the IBM World Trade Corporation, the National Science Foundation, and the National Bureau of Economic Research.

THE ROLE OF THE COMPUTER IN ECONOMIC AND SOCIAL RESEARCH IN LATIN AMERICA

Edited by

NANCY D. RUGGLES
National Bureau of Economic Research

A CONFERENCE REPORT OF THE NATIONAL BUREAU
OF ECONOMIC RESEARCH

NATIONAL BUREAU OF ECONOMIC RESEARCH
New York 1974

Distributed by
COLUMBIA UNIVERSITY PRESS
NEW YORK AND LONDON

Copyright © 1974 by the National Bureau of Economic Research, Inc.
All Rights Reserved
Library of Congress Card Number: 73–81540
ISBN: 0-87014-260-7
Printed in the United States of America

RELATION OF THE NATIONAL BUREAU DIRECTORS TO
PUBLICATIONS REPORTING CONFERENCE PROCEEDINGS

Since the present volume is a record of conference proceedings, it has been exempted from the rules governing submission of manuscripts to, and critical review by, the Board of Directors of the National Bureau.

*(Resolution adopted July 6, 1948,
as revised November 21, 1949,
and April 20, 1968)*

CONTENTS

FOREWORD

The computer is changing the technology of economic and social research. The ability of the computer to process large bodies of data makes possible new methods of research, employing highly disaggregated, or "micro," data. Not only are such methods more powerful in testing hypotheses, but they make possible entirely new kinds of research applicable to a broadened range of economic and social problems.

With the aim of bringing together social scientists from both North and Latin America who are currently engaged in quantitative research, a conference on the role of the computer in economic and social research in Latin America was held at Cuernavaca, Mexico, October 25–29, 1971. This volume contains some of the papers presented at that conference.

The sponsors and organizers of the conference were the National Bureau of Economic Research, the Colegio de Mexico, the Instituto Brasileiro de Economia of the Fundaçao Getulio Vargas, and the Instituto Torcuato di Tella, Argentina. The Latin American Social Science Council (CLACSO) also collaborated in the conference. The organizing committee for the conference consisted of Richard Ruggles, chairman; Roberto Cortes Conde, di Tella; Janes de Souza, Vargas; Nancy Ruggles, National Bureau; and Victor Urquidi, Colegio de Mexico. Financial support for the conference was supplied by the IBM World Trade Corporation, the National Science Foundation, and the sponsoring organizations. The conference was one of a new series established by the National Bureau on the role of the computer in economic and social research.

The conference was designed to include both papers dealing with computer methodology and papers reporting on substantive projects making significant use of the computer. A list of all of the papers presented appears at the end of this volume. The conference was organized into nine sessions, as follows:

1. The computer and government statistical systems
2. Data banks and computer centers
3. Computer simulation models
4. Macroeconomic models
5. Round table on the computer and society
6. Demography, manpower, employment, and education
7. International comparisons of income, consumption, and prices
8. International trade problems and commodity markets
9. Summary session on the role of the computer.

The first two sessions, on government statistical systems, data banks, and computer centers, dealt with the impact of the computer on the gathering, processing, maintenance, and use of large data systems. Government statistical offices have altered both their methods of processing information and the types of output which they produce. It is increasingly possible to relate different bodies of information to one another, and the central question now becomes how to organize and integrate the data base so that it is most useful for economic and social research and for policy guidance. Changing computer technology means that new devices and new techniques are continually becoming available. The first paper in this volume, by Ivan P. Fellegi and Simon Goldberg of Statistics Canada, addresses the problems of the impact of the computer on government statistics. The next two papers describe presently existing data banks—the time-series data bank of the National Bureau of Economic Research and the collection of census samples of the Latin American Center for Demographic Studies (CELADE). The next paper, by Harold Watts, discusses the problems that arose in the collection, processing, and use of a specific microdata set, the Survey of Economic Opportunity.

The next two sessions centered about the use of specific techniques of analysis: simulation and macroeconomic modeling. Simulation of economic and social phenomena as a method of analysis became feasible only with the advent of large-scale computers. The three papers by Okner and Pechman, Schulz, and the Urban Institute team describe microsimulations of specific economic and social problems, and the following paper by Naylor and associates presents a macrosimulation model of Brazil. With the increasing sophistication of macroeconomic modeling, this methodology, too, requires the computer. Growth models, planning models, short-term forecasting models, and dynamic multisectoral models have been constructed for a number of Latin American countries. De Souza's paper presents a summary of several such models constructed for Brazil; those of Beltran del Rio and Klein, Foxley, and Manne each present an individual model for a particular country.

Sessions 6, 7, and 8 each dealt with the application of the computer to problems relating to a particular subject-matter area. The paper by Schiefelbein is an example of the use of the computer for the analysis of a particular educational-planning problem. The next five papers discuss problems arising in handling large data files of material relating to international comparisons as encountered in the UN-Pennsylvania International Comparison Project, the Brookings-ECIEL project, and the European Economic Community. The papers by Balassa and Schydlowsky and the CENDES group deal with international trade problems.

The final session was devoted to an attempt to bring together the methodological conclusions developed in the individual sessions, and to consideration of the information needs for policy formation in developing countries and the role of the computer in meeting them. The final paper by Richard Ruggles summarizes the conference and presents these conclusions.

The work begun at this conference is being continued through a series of workshops to be held over the next five years. The IBM World Trade Corporation has made available a continuing grant for this purpose. Our thanks are due to Ruth Ridler, who prepared the proceedings for press, and to H. Irving Forman for his charting.

Nancy D. Ruggles
National Bureau of Economic Research

The Role of the Computer in Economic and Social
Research in Latin America

THE COMPUTER AND GOVERNMENT STATISTICS

I. P. FELLEGI AND S. A. GOLDBERG*

Statistics Canada

INTRODUCTION

Technological barriers to the effective realization of many of the overly enthusiastic pronouncements of the sixties in regard to the utilization of the computer are being removed, while the cost of hardware is actually declining. Yet one can sense in the literature on computer utilization a tendency toward greater caution. This tendency is presumably the result of the failure of many automation projects to realize fully their promised goals, and to complete their implementation within anything like their scheduled times, and is undoubtedly a healthy one. This paper is an attempt to present some views in regard to automation in the light of our recent experience in Statistics Canada. It draws upon and updates an earlier paper presented at the London meetings of the International Statistical Institute, which dealt with the theme of the present session; namely, government statistics and the computer.[1]

We shall concentrate here on problems associated with automation in a statistical office. In so doing, our intention is to promote the cause of automation, rather than to inhibit it. By identifying problems and facing them squarely, we should be able to cope with them more effectively.

Three classes of problems are discussed in this paper: data problems; problems related to the implementation of projects for automation; and problems arising from the overriding need to maintain confidentiality. The discussion of these problems is preceded by some reflections on the goals of the statistical office and of automation. We end the paper with some remarks on issues confronting management.

SOME REFLECTIONS RELATED TO GOALS OF A STATISTICAL OFFICE AND OF AUTOMATION

Clearly the goals of automation must derive from the goals of the statistical office, which in turn must derive from the goals of society. It is appropriate then to start with the question, Why should a statistical office aim to automate its operations?[2] This should provide perspective to the subsequent discussion.

The statistical office, like other organizations, must strive to become more efficient; that is, to increase its output per dollar spent. If analysis indicates that

---

* The views expressed in this paper are the personal views of the authors and may not be shared by other officers of Statistics Canada.

[1] I. P. Fellegi and S. A. Goldberg, "Some Aspects of the Impact of the Computer on Official Statistics," *Bulletin*, ISI, Vol. 43. 1969.

[2] In our usage, the word *automation* consists of more than mere conversion of existing operations to the computer. Rather, we understand by the automation of surveys their complete redesign—taking into account the full impact of the possibilities opened up by computer processing—with the aim of rendering efficient the survey as a whole, given its objectives, not just its parts.

the increase in timeliness, quality, or volume of useful output exceeds the cost of the conversion to automated procedures, this is a good and sufficient reason for conversion.

However, output per dollar is not the only relevant factor to consider in deciding whether or not to automate. Thus, we may find that the satisfaction, without automation, of a sharply rising demand for statistical information would involve substantial increases in manpower, rendering the management of the statistical office more difficult and unwieldy. In such a case, even elementary considerations of efficiency and effectiveness might well make automation desirable.

However, considerations of effectiveness become much more prominent when we consider the basic goals of society, which should be reflected in the goals and programs of the statistical office. The goals of society are seldom defined unambiguously. Some "traditional" goals relating to economic growth can, it is true, be quantified and monitored, though even this is far from simple. However, the more recently formulated social goals have so far been articulated in most societies only in broad, vague terms, such as the elimination of poverty, abatement of pollution, a more egalitarian society in terms of income and asset distribution, better control of crime and socially maladjusted behavior, less congestion in urban areas, participatory democracy, reduction of social tensions, and a better quality of life. Precise definitions of these notions and measurable concepts are still to be worked out and a great deal of experimentation will be involved, by both users and producers of statistics—not only to devise appropriate measurements but to evolve appropriate analyses of the data. Thus, the statistical agency finds itself facing a multiplicity of goals not fully defined in advance, and the traditional cycle of statistical operations—collection, processing, and publication—is becoming insufficiently flexible. What is required, in addition, is the storage of the most detailed data cells and a capacity for retrieval of an almost infinite variety of unanticipated cross-classifications and aggregations, consistent with confidentiality requirements.

There is also a growing requirement to be able to interrelate data collected in a variety of surveys or through other sources. In fact, policies and programs are frequently interrelated so that the formulation of any single one must take into account its effect on the others. The dangers of formulating policies in isolation and on the basis of partial knowledge are being recognized increasingly, as reflected in the following quotation from the Report of the Special Commission on the Social Sciences of the National Science Board of the United States.

> Partial policies, based upon some narrow band within the whole spectrum of relevant knowledge, may cause more indirect harm than direct good, and will always require costly modification, improvisation and patching, when unexpected and unwanted results appear. We need only mention insecticides, irrigation, mass transport, and urban housing to bring to mind a host of striking examples of the pitfalls of narrow approaches to *broad* problems.[3]

Broad approaches to the analysis of problems require a great deal of detailed data and highly flexible retrieval capability, facilitating their joint and interrelated

---

[3] *Knowledge Into Action: Improving the Nation's Use of the Social Sciences*, National Science Foundation, 1969, pp. 51–52.

use. The more widespread utilization of economic and social models based on a large number of equations, and the development of simulation models designed to study the behavior of persons, businesses, and governments—as well as society as a whole—under alternative assumptions, clearly require massive data storage and quick and flexible retrieval capability in addition to an unprecedented level of data cleanliness (editing).

Finally, we quote from a recent paper on "The Elusive Management Information System."

> Those who have delved into the Management Information System problem from a management viewpoint soon discover that the classical systems methodology for identifying output requirements simply doesn't work in a Management Information System environment. Conventional requirements analysis, as a prelude to systems design, is based on the assumption that user needs can be adequately defined in advance, whereas experience has shown that management's need for information is largely *ad hoc* in nature and cannot be predicted even by the most thoughtful and articulate of managers.[4]

What Head has said about management information systems applies equally well to statistical information systems. Increasingly, we must treat the data we have collected as a capital which can be drawn upon repeatedly to satisfy a variety of user needs. Implicit in this approach is the requirement of fast, flexible, and inexpensive access to such data.

While the preceding section suggests the goals that the statistical office should try to reach through automation, the attainment of these goals is enormously difficult, so that they are probably best regarded for the moment as merely indicating the *direction* in which the statistical office should strive to go. Here, we can no more than hint at the prerequisites for achieving the goals, and at the immensely complex obstacles which lie in the way, before turning our attention to the more *immediate* problems which must be coped with in order to carry forward successfully a practical program of automation.

First, as already suggested, the statistical office must develop facilities for storing the data collected in highly disaggregated form (to be referred to as "microdata sets"), and for retrieving quickly a large variety of unanticipated, as well as anticipated, tabulations. Clearly, if only aggregates are stored or retained, this limits the flexibility for subsequent reaggregation and cross-classification. The storage of microdata has major implications for processing: the microdata must be particularly well edited, adjusted for nonresponse, weighted in the case of sampling, and so on—and these operations must be carried out in relation to individual records. Thus, statistical standards related to concepts, classification, edits, and imputations must be much more rigorous than formerly when the statistical end products were, by comparison, much fewer in number, more highly aggregated, and largely preconceived.

Second, statistical standards related to collection (coverage, fieldwork, and so forth) must be tighter than they have been previously in order to ensure that the large variety of detailed tabulations and cross-classifications will have predictable (and acceptable) margins of error. Without elaborating on this point, what

[4] R. V. Head, *Datamation*, Sept. 1, 1970.

is involved is an increasing responsibility to follow up the nonrespondents (probably necessitating a greater role for the field function) and greater integration of follow-up procedures for different surveys, which in turn requires careful scheduling and planning. Put differently, our thesis is that the integrity of the data must increasingly be assured during its collection and processing at the level of the individual observations, since we can no longer design our surveys with a view to minimizing the error of a few predetermined aggregates only.

Third, the more data is accumulated in the statistical office, the more important it is for the statistical office to carry out analyses of the data in order to identify the relationships existing between the data derived from different surveys and other sources, with a view to providing users "guided tours" of the character, limitations, and potentials of the data. Without such "guided tours," the abundance of data can be just as confusing as the lack of it. Such "guided tours," and the analyses on which they are based, can have major beneficial feedbacks into the statistical system: the more data is available, the more it is important to standardize concepts, to study and weed out inconsistencies, to structure the data base in a coherent manner and, in general, to carry forward what is known as the function of statistical integration. In sum, the statistical office should strive to provide an analytical information service, rather than just a data-collection facility—a very challenging task.

The last problem we shall point out is that of privacy and confidentiality. Previous practices of publishing only predetermined aggregates lent themselves more easily to confidentiality checks than does the retrieval flexibility mentioned above. The latter carries with it dangers of inadvertently disclosing confidential information, which must be overcome. Moreover, the very process of storing individual returns in machine-readable form and building up facilities to interrelate them creates fears in the public mind in regard to privacy. These fears must not be disregarded on the grounds that they are unfounded, since statistical offices merely require individual observations as raw material to produce aggregations which remove identifiable events.

Later we shall discuss in more detail some of the points raised above. Now we turn to the first of our immediate practical problems in regard to automation; namely, data problems.

DATA PROBLEMS

As indicated above, the storage of individual data (microdata sets) and the facility for retrieving unanticipated tabulations necessarily put an increased strain on data reliability. The whole theory of survey sampling and census-taking evolves around the minimization of the error of a particular statistic for a given overall cost. While some attempts have already been made to generalize this theory to multipurpose surveys, this generalization still refers only to a set of *anticipated* needs. It is difficult to conceive how any theory could be developed to guide us in the face of completely unanticipated retrieval requirements. At the very least, however, we have to strive toward flexibility in systems and operations and experienced staff to adapt the allocation of effort in the light of emerging needs.

At the heart of most automated survey-processing systems is a subsystem to accomplish the editing of individual returns, their correction, and the imputation for nonrespondents. We believe that the proper utilization of the edit and imputation subsystem in an automated survey is vital in overcoming the data problems referred to above. However, this subsystem is typically the most complex of the automated survey-processing system and great care must be taken that its implementation does not get out of control (in terms of time, resources, testing the results, and so on). We shall return to this matter later on. Here we want to emphasize the role of automatic editing and imputation with respect to the quality of the stored data.

It appears to us that automatic editing and imputation must have a dual role in the processing system. The first role is the most visible one; namely, the identification of inconsistencies in the reported data and their elimination, and the identification of nonrespondents with the creation of some imputed data for them. This must, however, be an iterative process. The computer is not only capable of carrying out the necessary edits and imputations. It is also capable of providing print-outs indicating in summary form the impact of the changes in the data due to computer processing. Whenever this impact (in terms of both gross and net changes) is small, there is no point in attempting to overrule the computer through subsequent manual corrections. Where the impact is large, however, this can be interpreted as a danger signal. The input data in such cases can be examined and external manual corrections can be made (thereby overruling the original computer corrections). This strategy facilitates the utilization of human intervention in areas where it is most beneficial. At the same time, by reducing the scale of the human intervention required, it facilitates a more careful and considered intervention.

The most important intervention probably relates to nonrespondents. It is unrealistic to assume a 100 percent response rate even though we aim to approximate it. Computer editing and imputation and the resulting summary measures can focus the follow-up effort in the areas where it can have the most important impact.

In this connection, it is important to emphasize that the storage of microdata and the availability of flexible retrieval systems should have an impact on what are considered to be important, or unimportant, cases of nonresponse. Traditionally, when we were aiming to produce only a few major aggregates from a survey, we identified as the most important nonrespondents the large units; or, in the case of repetitive surveys, units which had a volatile pattern of reporting from survey to survey, thus making imputation on the basis of historical data difficult. This strategy needs to be reassessed in the era of microdata-set storage. Some of the unanticipated retrieval requirements may well relate to small survey units for which we have traditionally tended to allow a higher nonresponse rate. At the very least, in addition to following up the "important" nonrespondents, we should also follow up a sample of the remainder in order to evaluate the impact of imputations on all types of nonrespondents.

Increased flexibility of retrieval may expose data weaknesses not only within individual surveys, but also between surveys. One of the objectives of automation of individual surveys is the creation of a data base permitting easy retrieval of information from the files resulting from the particular survey. In a sense, therefore, we are in the process of developing a multitude of small data banks whose subject-matter scopes overlap. As more such data banks are developed, they can create incompatibility problems of immense complexity. Integration tools are urgently needed to overcome these problems. One important integration tool is a central register, containing the universe of units included in individual surveys. Such a register can facilitate an unambiguous definition of the scope of different surveys; it can provide a high-quality frame for the selection of samples; it can provide a tool for the consistent classification of identical units in different surveys; and it can facilitate the comparison of microdata collected in different surveys. Statistics Canada is in the process of establishing a central register covering all business (and other, e.g., institutional) reporting units, taking into account the many complexities in the identification of respondents in different business surveys.

At least as important as a uniform frame for related surveys is the problem of uniform concepts. What is needed with increasing urgency is a data-element dictionary identifying the statistical concepts underlying each data element (e.g., "hours worked," "total retail sales"), which can serve as a standard convention enabling the unique referencing of identical data elements with identical terms and different data with different terms. Such a data-element dictionary would also serve as the foundation for an overall system of file descriptions of all machine-readable files. Clearly, such an overall file-description system is a necessary part of the strategy of flexible retrieval and other statistical manipulations: we must be able to reference identical data by the same terms for the convenience of users.

One of the most important data problems facing the statistical office is that of drawing users' attention to the degree of reliability of the statistics released. This was difficult enough in the era of preconceived tabulations. It will be exponentially more difficult in the period of flexible retrievals. We must develop general models incorporating the contribution to the total mean squared error of sampling error and reporting errors, as well as conceptual, classification, and processing errors. While it might not be possible to estimate the mean squared error of each individual retrieved aggregate, this should be estimated for a sufficient variety of such aggregates to enable the development of general models of the mean squared error which could provide guidance to users of the order of magnitude of the errors associated with the data.

Statistics Canada has developed a very flexible retrieval system which is being implemented in connection with the 1971 Population Census. We are in the process of developing generalized tables which will be provided to any user who obtains a retrieval of census data, and which will show, for each of several broad classes of estimates, the size of the mean squared error as a function of the size of the estimate. Similarly, we have developed such general tables for the sampling error of Labour Force Survey data. However, these efforts must be considered as only the very beginning of a program to develop tools which will enable users to identify and appraise errors.

An important part of controlling data problems and of developing the necessary error models referred to above is the conduct of a rigorous program of *evaluation* of surveys. Traditionally, we are used to computing sampling errors, and the formulas used in the past for these computations incorporate the impact of the random reporting and processing errors. Such formulas, however, do not measure the bias which may arise from any of a number of possible sources. Starting with the 1961 Census, we began to conduct, as part of our quinquennial population censuses, extensive evaluation programs aimed at measuring the different components of the mean square error. These evaluation studies had far-reaching impact on the methodology employed in the 1971 Census. Several of our other surveys incorporate control features which provide as a by-product some evaluation information. However, we have a very long distance to travel before we can claim to understand with the necessary clarity the sources of errors in surveys and the complex forces at work in generating them.

PROJECT IMPLEMENTATION PROBLEMS

While data problems are probably the most fundamental of those underlying the automation of statistical processes, the most immediate and frustrating problems relate to project implementation.

Several of our surveys now utilize machine-readable files to accomplish the mailing out of questionnaires, the checking in of respondents, the identification of nonrespondents and the corresponding follow-up actions, the editing and correction of the returns and imputations for nonrespondents, tabulations, and variance tabulations. As indicated above, we are in the process of automating a comprehensive central register of business units. We have automated the data processing of the 1971 Census, including the editing, correction, sample weighting, and production of predetermined tabulations, as well as the creation of a general retrieval system to permit the retrieval of any cross-tabulation for any area based on the census data. We also have established a general time-series data bank capable of storing tens of thousands of time series and retrieving any number of them for print-out or subsequent manipulation. However, with a few notable exceptions, our accomplishments to date have been accompanied by considerable frustrations and delays. We have made a conscious effort to learn from our own experience but there are still many lessons ahead of us.

In the London paper referred to above, we articulated five important lessons we learned from our previous automation experience. Although, in the light of our subsequent experience, these lessons need to be supplemented, they are, as far as they go, as valid today as they were two years ago. It might be worth reproducing these five points here in summary form.

1. We emphasized the importance of developing an overall design for the automation project, identifying its individual components and specifying in detail at least some of them before programming begins. We emphasized that the development of such an overall design may go through several iterations and that a number of areas of functional responsibility are necessarily involved in it: subject matter, survey operations, survey methodology, computer systems analysis, computer operations, and so on.

2. The ultimate system implied by the overall design should be split up into fairly self-contained modules made up of subsystems and program packages, with minimum interaction between them, to make it possible to lift out and replace

any one as necessary. The modules should be small enough for the implementation to be carried out in a reasonably short time. Whenever possible, the systems and subsystems should be capable of being broken down into programs simple enough for an *average* programmer to implement.

3. Specifications for the corresponding computer systems have to be developed in collaboration between experts in survey methodology, computer systems, and subject matter.

4. While the importance of working in an interdisciplinary milieu was emphasized, it was also felt that it is individuals, rather than committees, who produce the most efficient work. Therefore, it was stressed that individual responsibilities must be assigned within a working team, and that a project manager must be designated, whose particular responsibility it is to ensure adherence to objectives and budgets, to monitor and coordinate the implementation, and to ensure communication between areas of functional responsibility involved in the project.

5. Finally, the vital importance of effective communication between members of a project team was emphasized.

Even though we were trying to live by the prescriptions that we have just outlined, we nevertheless encountered some difficult problems of implementation during the last two years. One of these is that the stress on the necessity for an overall design and the need for complete and unambiguous specifications resulted in some unduly long gestation periods. Having emphasized that computer systems, once implemented, are difficult to change, having emphasized the need for complete and unambiguous specifications, we tended to inculcate a sense of finality in those who had the task of writing such specifications. Yet, in spite of this, we did not succeed in eliminating the need for changes in specifications after programming began, or even after some of the subsystems were developed and tested. This was due to the fact that the ultimate systems we were aiming at could not be thought through in complete detail in advance of their implementation. The full impact of some complex subsystems like editing and data correction could not be anticipated in advance. Moreover, if one took sufficient time to think out and specify in advance all the requirements of the system, the time consumed would likely be so long that the environment would change in the meantime, and the requirements of the system also. So, even where detailed specifications were prepared and were successfully implemented, it turned out that the specifications resulted in some unanticipated impact on the data and changes to the systems had to be made. Given the complexity of the ultimate systems we were aiming at, changes in specifications resulted in considerable delays and they often had unanticipated effects on other parts of the system (due to the interaction of the various subsystems).

While modular programming helps when changes to programs have to be made, it appears that we have to extend the concept of modularity from programming to implementation. In fact, what we may need is a phasing of implementation. By phased implementation, we mean one of two possible alternatives: either the implementation of a subset only of the overall system, with additional subsystems added to it gradually as required; or the initial implementation of a skeletal version of the whole system, with provisions for its subsequent expansion and refinement. The latter is the one we now favor. We want to emphasize that we are not advocating compromising the ultimate objectives. Rather, we advocate, where feasible, their attainment through several generations of gradually more complex systems.

The process of phased (or gradual) implementation just outlined has several advantages. First of all, it reduces the complexity of design testing and implementation, since *at any point in time* one would be aiming at a more modest incremental goal. The achievement of the more modest goals provides a convenient checkpoint for everyone participating. The particular features of the new systems can be tested thoroughly in a real application (rather than just using test data). Shorter implementation periods also give us a better sense of achievement.

This point is more important than it may at first appear. Personnel responsible for the operation of the survey are typically faced with an overwhelming task at the time of automation. They are required to learn all the complexities of operating a major new system, and they are also required to monitor and test the data produced by the new system and to compare them with the results of the old one. (This is necessary both as a system test and as part of the effort to monitor and control historical continuity of series.) Since this kind of testing of a new system cannot be accomplished using test data alone, the personnel in question are often faced with the parallel running of the old system and the new. They seldom have sufficient skilled resources to do this, since the publication of statistics (usually based on the old system) assumes priority, while the testing of the new system and the analysis of the data produced by it must take second place. The consequences of this, in terms of a long period of double work load, inadequate testing, acceptance on the basis of insufficient evidence, and so on, are obvious enough. By contrast, in a phased implementation of a mail survey, for example, the mail out and check in can be automated and implemented after a relatively short period of testing. The implementation of automatic mail out might immediately save some resources, which could then be available for the testing of subsequent subsystems. The next module to be implemented might, for example, be the tabulation module (leaving editing and data collection a manual operation for the time being). Finally, a simple version of editing and imputation might be implemented, which could gradually be refined to more sophisticated versions.

Thus, the first major advantage of phased implementation is that it reduces the impact of automation on the operating personnel (or, rather, it phases this impact over time in a more realistic fashion). It minimizes the problem of running a dual operation and minimizes the management problem which arises when one has to accept or reject the end result of what might be several years of development. A second advantage of phased implementation is psychological. The successful implementation of each new generation of the automated system and its acceptance for operational use provides a psychological boost, not only to members of the developmental team, but also to the receiving division: it provides them with tangible benefits.

The third advantage of phased implementation is that the implementation of each phase provides management with a checkpoint at which a decision can be made as to whether additional features of the intended overall system should be proceeded with eventually, proceeded with immediately, or abandoned altogether.

It is very difficult to make a rational judgment concerning the end result of a major developmental project which, after the investment of many man-years, runs into serious problems: the temptation is inevitably to try to fix up such systems and salvage as much as possible. In the case of phased implementation, an earlier version of the same system is always available as a backup to meet current operational needs, and problems with newer versions of the system can be resolved without major crises.

There may seem to be an inconsistency between the concept of phased implementation presented here and our earlier views, presented in our paper in London:

> The computer is more than a hardware equivalent of a host of clerks. The application of computer processing is a fundamental parameter which must be taken into account in the design of surveys with the aim of rendering efficient the survey as a whole, given its objectives, not just its parts. In addition, it is our view that in order to derive the full benefits of computer processing, one should in general actually plan to go all the way: to comprehensive automation of all phases of the survey.[5]

The danger of piecemeal implementation is that it might tend to lock us into the framework of what exists. The danger is real. We must emphasize that modular implementation is no substitute for an overall system; rather, it should be looked upon as a way of accomplishing a comprehensive change with as little pain as possible. The *outlines* of the overall system embodying the final automated survey must not be shortchanged. The modules that are selected for implementation must be consistent with the overall design. *Moreover, they have to be conceived in a general enough fashion to be capable of expansion and change.* To the extent, however, that these modules are required to be compatible with the existing survey (or with some relatively small modifications of it), this may undoubtedly be the source of some conflicts. As additional modules are implemented, previous modules may have to be changed somewhat. We believe that so long as these changes are anticipated, their impact can be minimized. Even so, it is probable that if one were to compare the cost of implementing the ultimate system at once with the cost of implementing it in a gradual fashion, phased implementation might well be the more expensive of the alternatives. However, such a simplistic cost calculation would be based on the assumption that the systems are successfully implemented on schedule. This may not be the case. Thus, one should look at the incremental cost of phased implementation as insurance money. It may well be worth *planning* to spend, say, 50 percent more on the implementation of the ultimate system in order to ensure that we do not have to pay an *unplanned* 300 percent more.

Fortunately, important tools are being developed to assist us with the problem of modular implementation. A series of generalized programs have been developed in Statistics Canada (and elsewhere) capable of coping with a particular phase of processing of a variety of surveys. For example, we have a generalized program to produce address labels for mail-out purposes; another generalized program for the comparison of two files, for example in preparation for historical editing;

---

[5] Fellegi and Goldberg, *op. cit.*, Book 1, p. 158.

another generalized program for editing and data correction (embodying a variety, though certainly not all, of commonly used editing and correction techniques); and retrieval programs capable of producing tabulations (including weighted tabulations) from a number of files.

We believe that these generalized programs and their extensions will play an increasing role in the automation of our surveys. They have several major advantages over special custom-made systems. First, because they are generalized and widely used, they soon become reasonably well debugged. Secondly, because they are widely used, they must be well documented. Thirdly, their application reduces the implementation time in that it avoids the time-consuming process of program design, coding, testing, and debugging. Fourthly, and most important of all, they facilitate experimentation and relatively easy subsequent changes.

This last point requires elaboration. When specifications are prepared for a complex custom-made program, the consideration of alternatives is of necessity a theoretical exercise. Because of the complexity of what is to be implemented, assessing and testing its impact would require very large volumes of test data and almost impossible amounts of manual calculations. Thus, very often one finds out the full impact of such programs on the data only after they have been implemented at a considerable cost and with considerable effort. The most fundamental advantage of generalized programs is that because of their ease of implementation, they facilitate the testing of alternatives at a reasonable cost.

While generalized programs may not have precisely all of the features required for the implementation of the ultimate system, they may have an exceedingly important role to play in the scheme of modular implementation: they provide an easy means of implementing skeletal versions of the ultimate system, which may subsequently be replaced, if necessary, with custom-made programs at a later date. In fact, as successive versions of generalized programs are developed, they may be capable of coping with very complex and sophisticated processing requirements as well.

One final point on project implementation. It is essential that the anticipated benefits of automated surveys, as well as their cost and time of implementation, be estimated in advance, and that these estimates be checked out after implementation in the form of post-implementation audits. This is an important feedback of the automation process, enabling all concerned to improve gradually their ability to estimate both costs and benefits, as well as enabling the management of the statistical office to derive general lessons regarding policy that can be applied to future projects.

CONFIDENTIALITY PROBLEMS

It is a salient feature of statistical information that it always relates to a well-defined population, rather than to a particular respondent. However, if a population of interest is sufficiently narrowly defined, it may contain only one respondent. If this respondent can be identified on the basis of the statistics, their release would violate statistical confidentiality. Undoubtedly, this type of potential disclosure is not overly difficult to detect, although a manual process of checking each retrieved tabulation prior to its release may be expensive and time consuming. Much more difficult is the problem of so-called residual disclosure. Residual disclosure occurs when a number of tabulations are released, none of which violates confidentiality in itself, but which together enable a user to deduce information about a single identifiable respondent. The simplest example of residual disclosure occurs when one statistical aggregate is based on all but one of the respondents involved in another published aggregate and, consequently, the difference between the two aggregates discloses information about that one respondent. Unlike direct disclosure, residual disclosure is notoriously difficult to detect, even in the case of preconceived tabulations. Obviously, a policy of flexible retrievals exponentially increases the problems of checking for residual disclosure, since each new retrieval must be checked against all the previous retrievals.

In a recent article, one of the authors has developed a precise mathematical theory dealing with tests of residual disclosure. In all but the simplest situations, the practical implementation of this theory would involve prohibitive amounts of calculation. How, therefore, can the overriding objective of protecting the confidentiality of statistical returns be reconciled with the need to utilize the data that has been collected as extensively as possible?

In connection with the general retrieval system mentioned earlier, which is being implemented on the 1971 Census data base, we have developed a general approach to the solution of the confidentiality problem. As far as direct disclosure is concerned, the retrieval system automatically checks each tabulation cell to ensure that it satisfies the predetermined requirements of statistical confidentiality. (This test is generally based on the requirement that each aggregate must relate to more than a predetermined minimum number of respondents.)

In order to avoid the more complex problem of residual disclosure, each *ad hoc* tabulation will be subjected to a small amount of random disturbance. This will involve a random reallocation of a small proportion of selected respondents within the table. The particular strategy of reallocation is so designed as to minimize the impact of this random disturbance on the accuracy of the data. This random disturbance will prevent users from manipulating the retrieved statistics in order to derive other statistics which were not tabulated. In the case of the simple example above, if let us say, someone took the difference between two published statistics and observed that the difference appeared to relate to a single respondent, he could not be sure whether this was a real event, or rather the result of a random disturbance on one or the other of the tabulated aggregates.

While, undoubtedly, the strategy of random disturbances will increase somewhat the mean square error of the statistics, this may well be a necessary price for making the data available at all in the detail requested. The procedure can be automated and, thus, it can be fast and inexpensive. Even apart from this consideration, however, the strategy of random disturbances appears to be a "necessary evil," since a rigorous checking for residual disclosure is impossibly complex even with our modern computers; it is simply unmanageable using manual methods. Statisticians are well used to making compromises between the often conflicting requirements of cost, reliability, and timeliness. It now appears that a new dimension of the compromise must involve confidentiality and reliability.

As we have seen, the requirement for retrieval flexibility sharpens the need for rigorous procedures to safeguard against statistical disclosure. Another methodological and technological development which also reemphasizes the fundamental importance of safeguarding confidentiality relates to record linkage. The association of information with particular respondents was traditionally of no substantive interest to the statistical office; identification has traditionally been only a means of control during the collection of data. More recently, with the advent of computer technology and some relevant statistical methodology, the identification of respondents has assumed an added importance to statistical offices: they may wish to compare information collected in different surveys, either for editing purposes or to enrich the information content of one or the other of the surveys through record linkage.

While the interest of the statistical office in record linkage is entirely statistical, the process of linkage aggravates the confidentiality problem. Linkage usually involves the identification of respondents through a unique number, or through descriptive information—name, address, and so forth. It appears that society is not only concerned about the ends but also about the means as far as privacy is concerned. The statistical office must emphasize at every opportunity that the data it collects are not available to other government agencies for any purpose whatsoever; that the data are made available as *statistics* in the form of tabulated aggregates. This assurance, must, however, be followed up by a consistent policy of ensuring the security of data both physically (in the sense that the schedules collected are secure and accessible only to employees of the statistical office) and in its publication policy. The development of precise rules for disclosure testing and their implementation is, therefore, of paramount importance.

Given the concern of society regarding record linkage, we believe that this is not the right time to engage in it on a massive scale. At any rate, even from a substantive statistical point of view, record linkage may have serious limitations. First, it is hardly of benefit when the records involved are obtained from two independent sample surveys. After all, the probability that the same person is involved in both surveys is approximately equal to the product of the sampling fraction in the respective surveys: typically a rather small quantity. Hence, for maximum benefit, at least one of the surveys involved in record linkage should be a census or an administrative file with no sampling, or little sampling, in its coverage.

In the case of administrative files other problems may be present: the scope of their coverage is usually determined by the administrative requirements for which they were set up, rather than by any statistically meaningful definition. Also, the concept underlying the information recorded in administrative files might well be different, or it might be differently coded, differently edited, and so on. The problem of scope of coverage may diminish as the major administrative files involved in our modern state become more and more universal. The problems of concepts and care of processing, however, can only be reduced through close collaboration between the statistical and administrative agencies involved.

Finally, the dual problem of error of record linkage should also be noted: some records which should be linked will not be linked (in a broad sense, this is not dissimilar to the problem of nonresponse in surveys) and some records which should not be linked might be linked (in the same broad sense, this phenomenon is somewhat similar to the problem of response errors). Assuming the absence of a unique identifier, these two problems can only be controlled if there is adequate information recorded in the two files for carrying out the record linkage with an acceptable standard of precision, and if the resulting linked file, as well as the residual unlinked files, are subjected to careful editing and, if necessary, follow-up.

While most of the technological and methodological problems have been solved, record linkage is seen to present real conceptual problems and problems related to public concern. An alternative method of bringing together the information content of two files has recently been proposed. This pseudolinkage method consists essentially of allocating information from one file to another on the basis of some common core of information and a set of assumptions. For example, if both surveys contain age-sex and labor-force information, and one file contains, in addition, some expenditure data, while the other contains some income data, then the distribution of expenditure within an age, sex, labor force cross-classification cell can be estimated from one survey, and this same distribution of expenditure can then be imputed randomly to the other survey file within the same age, sex, labor-force cell. Clearly, any such activity would be based on the assumption that the distribution of the substantive characteristic which is to be imputed from one file to another is entirely determined by the characteristics which are common to the two files. This is equivalent to assuming that whatever correlation exists between the characteristics that are not common to the files is entirely explained by the common information which is the basis of the imputation. In the case of the example above, the imputation would be based on the assumption that whatever correlation exists between income and expenditure is entirely explained by age, sex, and labor-force status (or, put differently, that within an age, sex, labor-force-status cell, there is independence between income and expenditure). In this example, such an assumption would clearly not be reasonable. The trouble is that even in situations where the assumption does not appear to be blatantly unreasonable, one can never be sure of its validity without testing. In important applications, one should not assume independence in the sense explained above, but rather should take a special survey to test for it. The hypothesis is, of course, capable of being tested if a survey is appropriately designed for it.

In conclusion, we assume a very cautious posture with respect to record linkage. At present, we are applying it, for example, in situations where two lists have to be made free of duplication in order to arrive at a single comprehensive mailing list. We have not applied it as yet for the actual bringing together of substantive data from different surveys. We have some plans for applying the pseudolinkage outlined above in relation to data collected in two recent surveys on incomes and expenditures, and the 1971 Census. The validity of the pseudo-linkage techniques, however, must be tested again and again, probably separately for each application. We believe that we have a long way to go before we can claim to have created adequate data bases from each of our surveys individually. We would attach a much higher priority to developing uniform statistical standards between surveys, uniform concepts where applicable, standard codes, and flexible retrieval systems. At any rate, it appears that these would be prerequisites for record linkage as well: it is hardly worthwhile to bring together data between surveys if deficiencies in the concepts involved, and in the standards of collection, coding, and so forth, would render the linked information of dubious validity.

CONCLUDING REMARKS: SOME ISSUES CONFRONTING MANAGEMENT

In spite of a somewhat cautious tone throughout this paper, a logical analysis of what has been said will lead to the conclusion that the process of automation is, in spite of the frustrations involved, desirable and essential. The fundamental reasoning that leads to this conclusion starts with the fact that the extensive utilization of data already collected (together with the collection of additional series as required) is the only conceivable way of satisfying the variety of information requirements of society. As indicated above, this information need cannot be fully predicted in advance and, therefore, the posture adopted by the statistical office should be one of readiness. Thus, there is a compelling need for storing microdata and creating automated, flexible retrieval systems.

Starting from this premise, and considering the strain that such extensive utilization of data puts on data reliability, the cleanliness of the stored microdata becomes an essential consideration. Thus, we are inexorably led to the necessity of automated editing and correction at the microdata level. We are also led to other considerations of statistical standards, such as the necessity for complete and up-to-date frames for surveys and censuses, which in the case of economic surveys, renders the requirement for a central register of business units almost unavoidable. An important source for the updating of such a register is the surveys which are currently using it. Accordingly, we are led to the desirability and necessity of using the central register of business units either in the form of a central mailing list or as a coordinating device with which individual survey lists are kept fully in parallel (at least in the respective subject-matter fields in which the particular surveys operate).

We have more than a decade of experience to indicate that the mere existence of a central register does not ensure that the mailing lists of individual business surveys conform to it or feed it in a systematic fashion with respect to the updating of information. In the heat of current operations, the emphasis is on completing the survey—and often the liaison with the central register falls by the wayside. This problem can only be remedied by automating the information flows between the central register and the user surveys. As a consequence, we are led to the necessity both of creating a machine-readable central register and of creating machine-readable mailing lists for individual surveys, the two to be connected by an automatic process of information flows. Starting from the nature of information utilization, we are thus led inexorably to the full process of automating individual surveys and creating coordinating devices. One of the challenges involved in the management of statistical offices is the recognition of this fundamental unavoidability of automation.

Another challenge, which, of course, is at the heart of most management problems, is how far and how fast we should go. We have no magic solutions to offer. Individual decisions will have to be made according to individual circumstances. However, a few important considerations basically related to costs and benefits are sufficiently general to be applicable to almost any situation.

Short-term costs are very real and highly visible (although not necessarily accurately predicted at the beginning of development). For example, the total cost of developing the generalized retrieval system we mentioned earlier, which will be implemented in connection with the 1971 Census, was estimated to be in the neighborhood of two and a half million dollars. About a third of this figure was expended in systems analysis, programming, and computer testing. The cost of the time-series data bank, also mentioned earlier, is estimated at about $750,000, of which somewhat more than half a million dollars involved systems analysis; programming; and management, professional, technical, and clerical staff.

However, once such systems are developed, the cost of effective data dissemination through them is relatively small in comparison to the costs involved in the collection of statistics. We are firmly convinced that the benefits of these two systems will be far in excess of the costs. The precise estimation of these benefits in advance is, however, exceedingly difficult. Given the long developmental time required for such systems, any advance estimation of their benefits would necessarily involve forecasting the information requirements of users some years in advance—a very knotty problem. In the case of the census information system, one can speculate, however, that a relatively few significant uses of the system would repay its entire development cost. A single bridge that will not be built at the wrong place, the more precise delineation of one or two urban renewal areas, a single instance of a more precise identification of poverty areas which might receive economic aid from the government, a few small-scale household surveys that need not be taken because the data will be available from the census through the system—any one of these applications might repay the development cost of the system.

The estimation of benefits to users is rendered particularly difficult because users are a heterogeneous group, both with respect to their requirements and to their own capability of utilizing large amounts of information. It is relatively safe to forecast that user requirements will increase in respect to the amount of data required, the type of disaggregations, the kinds of manipulations, the format and medium of the retrieved data, and the desired retrieval response time. However, users have a wide variety of requirements and varying levels of computer sophistication. For example, a few users may genuinely require, and be able to take advantage of, access to speeds approaching "real time," while other users might be satisfied with overnight, or even longer, turnaround. If the statistical office wants to keep in step with the users having the most advanced requirements, then it must be prepared to take greater risks in terms of development costs. Given the rapid changes in computer hardware and the software industry, forecasting the requirements of advanced users several years in the future might appear to be a visionary process. Yet, again given the long development time required by automation, we believe that only a general policy commitment to attempt to *keep ahead* of the information requirements of users will succeed in ensuring that the statistical information service does not *fall seriously behind* the demands put on it.

Although it is not overly difficult to argue about the ultimate benefits of automation in relation to its cost, this fact by itself does not necessarily guarantee a green light for automation. There are too many other activities that the statistical office can undertake which have impressive cost-benefit ratios. Thus, cost-benefit considerations, while they might reaffirm the ultimate need for automation, do not necessarily provide generally applicable guidelines with respect to the question of how fast we should proceed with it in comparison with other activities—for example, the alternative of undertaking several new surveys. Here again, we believe that the development and utilization of generalized programs should have a high priority because of the broad facilitating nature of such programs. The automation in a one-by-one fashion of individual surveys in a large statistical office like Statistics Canada, having hundreds of surveys under way, is a gigantic task. Moreover, if one takes into account that custom-made programs which are parts of complex systems are difficult to change—while at the same time, due to alterations in technology, in methodology, and in user needs, various changes to these systems are unavoidable—one can foresee a situation where the updating of earlier automated systems could keep one-half to two-thirds of a large programming staff occupied. Modular programming can diminish this ratio. Nevertheless, we believe that only through extensive development and utilization of generalized programs will this ratio be significantly improved in favor of new developments as against changes to existing systems.

In our paper delivered in London, we dealt extensively with the problems of management involved in the reorientation of personnel to the era of automation and its implications: the initial fear of the computer, the fear of loss of control, the difficulties of infusing a genuine spirit of interdisciplinary cooperation, the role of training to alleviate some of these problems, and the need for documentation and systematic follow-up of the progress of the various projects. We shall not repeat this material here, although we believe it is still relevant. However, we do want to add two additional points. First, it is difficult enough to overcome the initial fears when they relate to the unknown. It is particularly difficult to overcome such fears successfully when they are based on actual unpleasant experience with automation. It is, therefore, essential to try to achieve a few notable successes at the beginning. This points, once again, to a strategy of modular implementation of automated systems. No amount of abstract indoctrination can take the place of the impact of success, and this applies not only to the management of subject-matter divisions but also to all the staff involved in operating surveys, including technical and clerical personnel. The second point concerns the difficulty of incorporating personnel involved in the operation of current surveys in inter-disciplinary development teams, due to the lack of spare resources which can be devoted to new developments. Again, phased implementation and generalized systems might help (since they reduce the scope of dual operations). Ultimately, however, it may be necessary to have a special group of personnel which could be seconded to operating divisions for the duration of developmental projects and their implementation.

THE DATA BANK OF THE LATIN AMERICAN DEMOGRAPHIC CENTER

JULIO MORALES VERGARA

Latin American Demographic Center

1. BACKGROUND INFORMATION

In the past few years, several institutions devoted to social research in Latin America have shown their interest in the formation of records of scientific data which may be placed at the disposal of persons or institutions concerned with social phenomena in the region. The need for such records has become more evident with the marked increase of interest in such phenomena and also because existing empirical information is scarce and, as a rule, difficult and expensive to obtain.

In addition, it should be taken into consideration that some of these records have become feasible thanks to the level of development attained by cybernetics within the past ten to fifteen years. In fact, storing and processing of material gathered was possible with conventional equipment for mechanical data processing, but treatment of large volumes of data—such as are often handled in population censuses, for example—was only made possible, both in terms of space devoted to the storage of records and of the broad possibilities of exploitation of data, by means of computers.

For the purpose of taking steps toward "the creation, development and modernization of Latin American records of data in social sciences,"[1] the Latin American Council of Social Sciences (CLACSO) appointed a special commission, which has been active since 1967. At its meetings in Lima (1968) and Caracas (1969), decisions were taken for promoting contacts between institutions with the aim of establishing an inventory of available data, promoting the creation and preservation of records, establishing uniform classification standards, and making possible a widespread access to the information incorporated into these records. The goals which have been established are ambitious, and therefore it is anticipated that they will be attained only on a long-term basis.

On the other hand, the Latin American Demographic Center (CELADE), at approximately the time when the CLACSO Commission initiated its activities, decided to form its own data bank—naturally, of an exclusively demographic nature—on the basis of the considerable amount of numerical data which the institution had obtained from its own investigations, as well as from a program initiated in 1960 for the purpose of collecting data from population censuses taken in Latin America during the 1960s.

As with other records of scientific information, the fundamental aim of CELADE's data bank is to permit demographers, and social researchers in general, to carry out their studies on the basis of empirical data. Available material not only permits a better knowledge of different demographic variables in Latin

[1] Jorge García-Bouza, "El archivo latinoamericano de datos de CLACSO." *Revista Latinoamericana de Sociología*, 69/3, Buenos Aires.

America, but also allows the formulation or verification of theories of demographic change and the establishment of interrelationships with variables from other social disciplines. Moreover, it will serve as background for historical studies to be carried out in the future.

Material incorporated into the bank is at the disposal of all researchers or agencies concerned in the study of Latin America, with the sole limitations occasionally imposed by statistical secrecy or, eventually, by preparation costs of given data.

This report contains a description of material incorporated into the bank and of several aspects connected with it. Finally, present plans for the future development of this data bank are presented.

2. MATERIAL GATHERED AND ITS CHARACTERISTICS

So far, data on Latin American countries available at the bank come from six different sources:
1. samples from population censuses taken in the 1960s;
2. experimental censuses;
3. experimental demographic survey in Cauquenes (Chile);
4. Program of Comparative Fertility Surveys (Urban and Rural PECFAL);
5. Program of Comparative Studies on Induced Abortion and Use of Contraceptives; and
6. surveys of migration to metropolitan areas.

The following is a brief description of origin, type of data kept, and bibliography, with additional background information on the above material. The table presents some of the relevant facts in concise form.

A. Population Census Samples from the 1960s (OMUECE)

This project was initiated following a recommendation of the Seminar on Evaluation and Utilization of Results from Population Censuses in Latin America, held in Santiago, Chile, at the end of 1959. This seminar specifically recommended selecting samples from population censuses, at a national level, for the purpose not only of advancing census figures (the complete processing of censuses as a rule takes rather a long time) but also of preparing special tabulations, not requiring complete census information, in order to ensure future availability of data for studies of a historic-demographic nature.

CELADE received this recommendation with great interest, urging governments to select such samples, at the same time offering—and, in fact, providing—technical assistance in the designing and selection of samples. The sampling unit was the individual or the household and for each person complete information was gathered, as it had been obtained in the census.

In most cases CELADE obtained a copy of the selected samples, which were subsequently incorporated into the data bank. Among Latin American countries, only Peru and Nicaragua—in addition to those countries where no censuses were taken in the 1960s: Bolivia, Cuba and Haiti—did not provide copies of these samples. Furthermore, it was also possible to obtain a sample for Puerto Rico and

CONTENT OF THE DATA BANK

Title of the Research	Dates	Countries or Regions Covered	Approximate Size (number of persons)
Population census sample (OMUECE)	1960 and 1964	Argentina, Brazil, Colombia, Costa Rica, Chile, Ecuador, El Salvador, Guatemala, Honduras, Mexico, Panama, Paraguay, Dominican Republic, Uruguay, Venezuela, and Puerto Rico	From 20,000 (Honduras) to 900,000 (Brazil); total, 3.5 million
Experimental censuses	1968 and 1969	Cantón Grecia (Costa Rica) and Belén (Argentina)	11,000 (Grecia) and 6,000 (Belén)
Experimental demographic survey	1964 and 1966	Cauquenes Hospital Area (Chile)	12,000
Program of Comparative Fertility Surveys (PECFAL):			
Urban	1963–64	Bogota, Buenos Aires, Caracas, Mexico City, Panama, Rio de Janeiro, and San Jose (subsequently, Quito, Guayaquil, and Guatemala City)	From 2,000 to 2,500 each (Quito and Guayaquil, about 1,000 each)
Rural	1968–70	Colombia, Costa Rica, Mexico, and Peru	From 2,000 to 3,000 each
Program of Comparative Studies on Induced Abortion and Use of Contraceptives (PEAL)	1967–69	Bogota, Buenos Aires, Lima, and Panama	1,500 each
Surveys of migration to metropolitan areas	1962–67	Caracas, Lima, Santiago	From 11,000 to 14,000 (some 2,000 households)

another for the United States. For Latin America, information is available on nearly 3.5 million persons in seventeen geographical units.

The different samples gathered show a great deal of variation with regard to size. The number of individuals selected ranges from 18,818 (Honduras) to 900,000 (Brazil), while in relative terms, the sampling rate varies from 0.63 percent (Argentina) to 6.61 percent (Dominican Republic) and 10.21 percent (Puerto Rico).

Because of the different absolute sizes of the samples, it has been difficult to prepare tabulations with the same degree of breakdown for all the countries; in addition, tabulations can be prepared at the regional level only for the countries with large samples. Such limitations will have to be taken into account in similar programs undertaken in the future.

Material received at CELADE includes complete individual information, as processed in the censuses of each country; only Puerto Rico and the United States suppressed some information in relation to geographical location.

Census questionnaires from the different countries contain only certain variables (questions) in common, and thus the comparative analysis of the different variables cannot always include all the countries. Moreover, some variables which have been investigated in all the countries present different categories of classification. Thus, for example, under marital status, consensual unions or divorced persons may or may not have been considered as separate categories. To a certain extent, this lack of uniformity imposes limitations on a comparative analysis of information from the different countries.

Variables investigated in every one of the censuses of the 1960s are:

1. Geographical characteristics
   (a) Place of enumeration
   (b) Place of birth
   (c) Condition of urban-rural residence
2. Personal characteristics
   (d) Sex
   (e) Age
   (f) Relationship to head of household
   (g) Marital status
3. Cultural characteristics
   (h) Literacy
   (i) Educational level
   (j) Years of schooling
4. Economic characteristics
   (k) Type of activity (active or inactive)
   (l) Principal occupation
   (m) Branch of industry
   (n) Occupational status

In relation to internal migration, eleven countries provided data on "time of residence" in addition to information included under "geographical characteristics." Only El Salvador, Honduras, the Dominican Republic, and Venezuela did not provide this information.

With regard to fertility, the question on "children ever born" was asked in Argentina, Brazil, Chile, Guatemala, Mexico, Paraguay, and Venezuela, and also in Puerto Rico.

Additional information on characteristics of these samples and of the OMUECE program may be found in the *Boletines Informativos del Banco de Datos de CELADE*. These bulletins, of which a total of four have been published, include information on contents of national samples, classification of variables, tabulations anticipated in the OMUECE program, stage attained by the project, and other useful information concerning the samples.

B. Experimental Censuses

According to a recent CELADE publication, the experimental censuses in which the Center participates are an attempt "to test procedures for obtaining data in relation to population, capable of contributing to the improvement of the quality of the information gathered in Latin American countries."[2] These, then, are field studies carried out mainly for methodological purposes. Therefore, these experimental censuses may eventually omit investigating certain topics which raise no doubts with regard to definition of concepts, formulation of questions, or other aspects of a general nature.

[2] *Censo Experimental de Costa Rica*, CELADE, Series A, No. 108, Santiago, Chile, 1971, p. 1.

So far, the data bank includes information from two experimental censuses: one carried out in Canton Grecia (Province of Alajuela), Costa Rica, March 15–19, 1968, and the other in Belen village (Province of Catamarca), Argentina, taken in April 1969. Information from an experimental census carried out in Nicaragua during 1970 is expected to be incorporated soon.

In the Grecia census three different aspects were approached methodologically: (a) investigation of new topics; (b) changes in the formulation of some questions; and (c) analysis of the quality of information obtained, according to the person providing the information. In addition, an analysis was made of the household, based on the question about relationship.

From the point of view of the potential user of this information from the data bank, it should be noted that in the Grecia census the following subjects, which are not usually included in population censuses of the region, were investigated: (i) condition of orphanage (of father and mother, separately); (ii) size of establishment where economically active person works; (iii) number of principal occupations of different kinds carried out in the last six months; and (iv) number of live-born children borne by women during the last year.

The incorporation of the first and last of these subjects is an attempt to establish a procedure for collecting new antecedents or substitute information on mortality and fertility; while questions (ii) and (iii) are aimed at investigating indirectly the degree of modernization of economic activities carried out by the population, and also underemployment. Eventually, cross-tabulations of these variables with all the others investigated in this experimental census may be programmed.

In the Belen Census, in Argentina, special emphasis was placed on the question on orphanage, but in this case only in relation to the mother. This experimental census did not take special consideration of other methodological aspects, since it was programmed principally with a view to broadening general census procedures for the Population Census of Argentina, taken in September 1970.

For further information on part of the material covered by this section of the data bank, see *Censo Experimental de Costa Rica*,[3] which includes a chapter analyzing the main subjects investigated.

C. Experimental Demographic Survey in Cauquenes (Chile)

Through this survey, CELADE planned to investigate the economic feasibility (reasonable cost) of obtaining information about the level of some simple demographic indicators in predominantly rural areas where continuous registration of vital events is either unsatisfactory or nonexistent. The same methodology had already been tested previously in an urban area, in the State of Guanabara, Brazil.

The final report of the Cauquenes Survey includes the following:

The aim of the investigation was fundamentally to test a procedure for collecting data which would permit the preparation of the more elemental demographic indices. . . .

The operation was initiated towards the middle of 1964 and field work continued until the middle of 1966. A registration was made of some twelve

[3] *Ibid.*

thousand persons residing in dwellings selected in the region (Cauquenes Hospital Area, Province of Maule) and who were visited on four occasions. During these visits, an investigation was made of changes occurring from one visit to the next in relation to a series of events under study: births, deaths, changes in marital status, and migration.[4]

By means of information gathered in the questionnaire it was possible to establish "time of exposure to risk" for each of the phenomena studied, which, together with the observed frequency of such events, led to the establishment of the level of the respective rates. In addition, the survey collected data on sex, age, marital status, schooling, relationship to head of household and economic characteristics of the latter, and of members of households interviewed. These variables led to the establishment of differentials in the level of rates.

For detailed information on the field investigation itself, on methodology and results, and also for an analysis of the latter, see CELADE's publication: *Encuesta Demográfica Experimental de Cauquenes*.[5] Other CELADE documents have also been published containing accounts and a report presented by persons responsible for the investigation to the World Population Conference, held in Belgrade in 1965. In addition, an article has been published in *Demography*.[6]

D. Program of Comparative Fertility Surveys (PECFAL)

Background for this program was a fertility survey initiated in Santiago, Chile, at the end of the 1950s. On the basis of experience gathered in this survey, CELADE promoted in 1963 the carrying out of similar studies in other major cities of the region and subsequently also in rural areas.

These surveys are known as KAP-Surveys (Knowledge, Attitude, and Practice) and their objective was to obtain information on: (a) levels and trends of fertility, according to different socioeconomic characteristics; (b) attitudes and opinions on desired family size, family planning, and socioeconomic factors associated with it; and (c) use of contraceptives, attitudes toward their use and means of information about them.

The questionnaires employed contain a great deal of information on explanatory variables such as religiousness, traditionalism, and personal characteristics of interviewees and of their spouses, pregnancy histories constituting the base of the investigation.

Fieldwork was executed by local institutions in the respective countries, with technical assistance—especially in the designing of the sample—from CELADE staff members. Thus, it was possible to ensure that investigations would be basically similar and also that comparative analyses of the surveys would be feasible.

Urban PECFAL Surveys were carried out from 1963 to 1964 in Bogota, Buenos Aires, Caracas, Mexico City, Panama City, Rio de Janeiro, and San Jose; subsequently Quito and Guayaquil (Ecuador) and Guatemala City were incorporated into the program.

The study was limited to women aged 20–49 years, of any marital status, selected in a probability sample. In each of the two cities of Ecuador, the number

[4] *Encuesta Demográfica Experimental de Cauquenes*, CELADE, Santiago, Chile, 1968, p. 1.
[5] *Ibid.*
[6] Vol. II, 1965.

of women interviewed was approximately 1,000; in the others, the size of the sample ranged from 2,000 to 2,500.

The Rural PECFAL Surveys were carried out in Colombia, Costa Rica, Mexico, and Peru. The age range of women interviewed was broadened to 15–49 years and the self-weighting samples were probabilistically drawn from areas with scattered population or from localities of less than 20,000 inhabitants. The size of the samples ranged from 2,000 to 3,000 in the different countries.

Local institutions responsible for the surveys have been preparing the respective analytical reports. CELADE, in its turn, is responsible for the comparative analysis of the different surveys.

So far, available literature on the PECFAL program refers to the following: (a) methodological aspects (CELADE documents, Series A, Nos. 40 to 45); (b) national reports prepared by Brazil, Colombia, Costa Rica, Panama, and Venezuela (see Appendix); (c) comparative analyses (CELADE documents, Series A, Nos. 47, 49 and 56); and (d) rural PECFAL documents, Nos. 1–37.

E. Program of Comparative Studies on Induced Abortion and Use of Contraceptives in Latin America (PEAL)

Various investigations on trends and levels of fertility in Latin America have shown that, together with the use of contraceptives, induced abortion has contributed substantially to the reduction of biological levels of fertility in the different countries. In view of this, during the past five years CELADE has carried out a program of studies similar to the PECFAL, the principal objective of which was investigating fundamental aspects in the practice of induced abortion and in the use of contraceptives in different capital cities of the region.

The questionnaire prepared for this program is composed of 156 basic questions, in addition to two annexes. Its concrete purpose is to find out the influence of each of these two factors (abortion and family planning) on the reduction of fertility or on its differentials; to find out attitudes of women toward these alternatives for the limitations of their fertility; and to determine what are the consequences of the practice of abortion for women that use it.

Due to the very nature of the subject investigated, obstacles encountered in fieldwork are easy to understand. It is thus possible that notwithstanding all precautions taken to overcome these obstacles, and the elimination of defective information, the degree of validity of information may not be as great as that of other material gathered by CELADE.

The first survey was initiated in Bogota toward the middle of 1967; subsequently this was followed by surveys in Panama (1968), Buenos Aires (1968), and Lima (1969). Fieldwork was in all instances executed by local agencies, while the necessary technical assistance in its different stages was rendered by members of CELADE's staff.

The number of women at fertile ages (15–49 years) interviewed in each instance is approximately 1,500, selected in two stages: in the first, through a self-weighting random sample a selection of some 750 women was made; in the second, after classifying these women into three socioeconomic strata with different characteristics, the number of women originally obtained was increased until there were 500 in each of these strata. In this manner, then, the sample permits direct conclusions to be drawn for the local area under study, and also, comparisons between groups of equal size from different strata—or from the same strata—may be made for the different cities.

The bibliographical material available so far is composed solely of internal publications of CELADE, of a methodological nature. Nine of these documents have been prepared, known as PEAL 1, PEAL 2, and so on, covering the different stages of the investigation, from "Presentation of the Study and Its Objectives" to "Supervision Handbook."

F. Migration Surveys to Metropolitan Areas

The mass movement of population from rural areas toward the large urban centers, together with the high rate of population growth, comprise the two most characteristic demographic phenomena of our times, requiring careful attention from social scientists. The field of internal migration, of special importance in Latin American countries, thus could not remain outside the scope of investigations carried out by CELADE.

In view of the above, explorations were initiated as early as 1961 in regard to taking a survey in the metropolitan area of Greater Santiago, the main purposes of which were:

(a) estimating the volume and historical trends of migration towards the metropolitan area;

(b) investigating differential demographic and social characteristics of the migrant population, in relation to the city-born population;

(c) investigating the demographic and socioeconomic factors which appear to be linked with the movements; and

(d) studying the degree and conditions of adjustment of in-migrants to the economic and social environment, taking into consideration time of residence and certain characteristics of in-migrants (sex, age on arrival, region of origin, educational level, etc.).[7]

This survey was carried out in 1962, with the valuable collaboration of the Instituto de Sociología of the Universidad de Chile. Subsequently, similar surveys were carried out in Lima (1965–1966) and in Caracas (1967) with the participation of the respective National Bureaus of Statistics. The content of questionnaires for these two surveys is quite similar to that of the Santiago survey; except that in the two later ones the status of migrant is applicable only to those persons aged 14 years or over who arrived in Lima or Caracas during the ten years prior to the survey.

In each of the three capital cities, the survey covered a total of approximately 2,000 households that included from 11,000 to 14,000 persons.[8] There were two types of questionnaire in each survey: one aimed at gathering general information, both on migrants and nonmigrants, and the other aimed at investigating more specific aspects of the migrant and characteristics of migration. Information from both questionnaires has been incorporated into the data bank.

[7] *Encuesta de Inmigración Lima Metropolitana No. 1*, Dirección Nacional de Estadística y Censos, Lima, 1966, p. 3.

[8] In Lima 2,000 households were added later, for certain segments of the city.

Different methodological aspects of the Santiago and Lima surveys, as well as an analysis of their findings, may be found in:

CELADE, *Encuesta sobre Inmigración en el Gran Santiago*, General Report, Series A, No. 15, Santiago, 1964.

Juan C. Elizaga, *Migraciones a las Areas Metropolitanas de América Latina*, CELADE, Series E, No. 6, Santiago, 1970.

Dirección Nacional de Estadística y Censos, Perú: *Encuesta de Inmigración. Lima Metropolitana* (3 volumes), Lima, 1966 and 1968.

So far there is no literature available oñ the Caracas survey.

3. Record Keeping

Information available in the data bank is stored principally in the form of magnetic tapes or punched cards.

In the case of the Urban-PECFAL, in addition to tapes and cards, there is a series of over 1,000 already-processed tabulations for each of the cities included in the program, thus making it possible to answer requests for information in a short space of time and at a reduced cost.

The punch cards are IBM cards, which may be processed by means of conventional systems of mechanical processing or computing equipment. On the other hand, magnetic tapes have a nine-channel recording with a density of 800 bytes per inch. The computer equipment used by CELADE is an IBM 360/40, from the Computing Center of the Universidad de Chile.

The system for storage of data from each project is as follows:

OMUECE-60:	Magnetic tapes
Experimental censuses:	
Belen:	Magnetic tapes
Grecia:	Punched cards
Cauquenes Survey:	Punched cards
Urban-PECFAL:	Magnetic tapes and cards (for each city)
Rural-PECFAL:	Magnetic tapes
PEAL:	Punched cards
Migration survey:	
Santiago:	Punched cards
Lima:	Magnetic tapes
Caracas:	Magnetic tapes

With regard to the OMUECE project, it should be noted that for standardization purposes, original material from each of the countries was transferred to a single code for the recording of the necessary information for tabulations planned in the OMUECE. However, original samples are also kept, either in cards or tapes with their original codes, including the different variables investigated in national censuses which are not included in the OMUECE tabulations.

For purposes of comparative analysis, the OMUECE tabulations, a total of 34, cover the different fields of demography which are investigated through censuses: geographical distribution, sex, age and marital-status structure, characteristics of the economically active population, cultural characteristics, internal migration, and fertility. For programming reasons, these tables have appeared in three successive generations, the first covering aspects of a general nature in the population, including economic activity and cultural characteristics; the second, the area of migration; and the third, fertility.[9]

So far, the three generations of tables have been completed for Chile and Paraguay; for Colombia, Costa Rica, and Panama, the first two generations have been prepared; while for Ecuador, El Salvador, Guatemala, Honduras, Mexico, and the Dominican Republic, only the first generation of tables is available. For the remaining countries (Argentina, Brazil, Puerto Rico, Uruguay, and Venezuela), for a variety of reasons, not even coding for the eventual transfer of material to tapes has been carried out.

4. SOME PROBLEMS

Most of the studies incorporated into the data bank correspond to investigations carried out by CELADE in collaboration with national institutions. On this account, interpretation and processing of data have presented no difficulties. Codes were processed internally and opportunely, for the purpose of allowing standard tabulations to be processed for the different geographical units in question so that comparative analysis would be feasible.

In the case of the OMUECE project, however, in view of the fact that national statistical units applied their own individual criteria to the programming and execution of their population censuses and to the processing of data collected in these censuses, the necessary standardization was not possible. This, together with other negative circumstances, led to numerous difficulties in the processing of tabulations anticipated for the program.

The standardization of codes, an indispensable task in view of the large number of countries involved and the number of tabulations designed, presented difficulties in two respects: there were divergences between national coding manuals and codes registered in the cards of samples received (punching of codes not appearing in manuals, and so on), and there were samples which did not register certain characteristics (e.g., educational level and occupation) for certain groups of persons (women, in many instances) in some geographical areas. Numerous consultations with responsible national institutions, necessarily time consuming, led as a rule to the satisfactory solution of these difficulties.

On the other hand, it should be noted that data processing carried out by CELADE has shown that some samples are subject to errors (apparently the norms for selection are not always followed strictly) leading to wide differences between censual and sample tabulations. Actually, for this reason, and also because no reliable antecedents existed on the designing and selection of the sample, at least one of the national samples had to be eliminated.

Finally, it should be recognized not only that the small size of some samples prevents the preparation of tabulations for medium-sized geographical areas, much less for the smaller ones, but that the degree of breakdown possible is very limited. In view of this, in at least one instance (Costa Rica) it was possible to increase the size of the sample originally obtained. At present, it is considered that for the OMUECE program tabulations, a minimum sample of some 200,000

[9] See *Boletín Informativo No. 4 del Banco de Datos.*

persons would be required, and that a sample of some 500,000 persons would be necessary if the same tabulations are to be processed for broad geographical areas.

5. Costs

It is very difficult to estimate real costs of the data bank, since many of the items are in common with other CELADE projects. Moreover, in strict justice, at least a small part of the cost of the original projects (PECFAL, PEAL, and so on) should be included under bank costs.

Since it is not possible to make even a rough estimate of these indirect expenditures, for illustrative purposes, only direct expenditures (computing hours, cards, magnetic tapes, purchase of processed material, and so forth) incurred between 1967 and 1970 and the respective sources of financing are shown:

Source	Fiscal Year	Total
Agency for International Development (AID)	1967	U.S. $ 1,500
Agency for International Development (AID)	1968	5,000
Agency for International Development (AID)	1969/70	6,798
Population Council	1969/70	2,225
Ford Foundation	1969/70	41,940

At first glance, it is to be noted that nearly 90 percent of total expenditures, amounting to almost U.S. $57,500, were made in the fiscal year 1969/70. This is due to the fact that during this period the OMUECE project was in its tabulating stage and, in addition, the demand for information from the different projects incorporated into the bank had become greatly intensified.

It should be emphasized that direct data bank expenses are financed exclusively by contributions from different institutions, which, in consideration of the importance of each of the projects, have been most generous. On the other hand, the salaries of personnel responsible for the data bank—one analyst and three programmers—are included in CELADE's ordinary budget. In addition, an international expert and a research assistant work half-time at the bank.

6. Use of the Stored Information

Notwithstanding the short existence of the bank, the information stored has been profusely used in different research projects. Users may be classified into three types: (a) CELADE researchers; (b) researchers outside CELADE; and (c) students from CELADE's Basic and Advanced Courses. Since it is impossible to provide a detailed description of each of the studies carried out with the material of the bank, only the major ones will be indicated and their basic characteristics underlined.

The group responsible for interrelationships between demography and economics within CELADE initiated a study of the level of underemployment, using census information. Underemployed persons were defined as those persons who, being economically active, work in given occupations in some specified branches of economic activity, the productivity of which may be estimated as very low.

Using information from the OMUECE project available at the time (Central American countries, mainly), relevant tabulations were prepared. Thus, it was established that the level of underemployment obtained through this procedure for the area under study was approximately the same as estimates obtained through complicated methods for the handling of extracensual statistical information, not always at the disposal of the researcher. This would be a proof that the above phenomenon may be measured with satisfactory approximation through census information habitually gathered.

Another CELADE researcher used OMUECE data in a study of the principal educational characteristics of the Latin American countries. His findings and conclusions will be published in the near future by CELADE.[10]

Officials from the Economic Commission for Latin America (ECLA) have also requested special tabulations with OMUECE data, in order to investigate characteristics of internal migration (in Colombia) and the standardization of geographical units (in Ecuador). Their results have been summarized in two publications.[11]

CELADE students are among those who have most benefited from the data bank, through the use not only of data from the OMUECE project but, most especially, of data from the Urban-PECFAL and from experimental censuses. Results of these studies, carried out under the guidance of members of CELADE's staff, have been included in research reports which the students have to present at different stages of their training period. Undoubtedly, the most interesting studies are those referring to an in-depth analysis of fertility in the city of Buenos Aires; to methodological aspects; and to examination of results from experimental censuses in relation to family units.

Finally, it should be pointed out in this section that with due authorization from the respective statistical bureaus, copies of some of the census samples have been made available to the University of Florida in Gainesville, Florida (United States), as part of an exchange program. This university has established its own data bank, part of which is composed of samples from some censuses taken in the region.

7. FUTURE PROGRAM

The OMUECE tabulations for those countries with satisfactory samples should be completed in the very near future, and a program of publications will be initiated, with different series of subjects, covering given geographical units. These publications will include, in addition to tabulations, simple comparative analyses between the different countries in each region, thus permitting an adequate interpretation of figures. The different volumes in these series will be of not more than five hundred pages each. The subjects to be covered are: (a) economic characteristics; (b) educational characteristics; (c) fertility; (d) internal migration; and (e) family.

On the other hand, samples from censuses being taken during the present decade in Latin America have already been requested. Coverage of countries is

[10] Thomas Frejka, *Trabajo sobre la educación en América Latina*, CELADE, Series E, No. 10.
[11] George Martine, *Volume and Characteristics of Internal Migration in Colombia*, and Aníbal Quijano, *El proceso de urbanización en Ecuador*, ECLA internal documents.

expected to be as good as that of the OMUECE-60, or even better. In addition, experience gained previously will permit accelerating the preparation of tabulations, and what is more important, will lead to a broadening of the range and validity of the tabulations programmed.

OMUECE-70 will give rise to the need for revising tabulations made for OMUECE-60 to ensure that the analysis between both groups of censuses is compatible.

CELADE is also at present in the process of collecting data on international migration of Latin Americans. For this purpose, the Center has requested from the institutions responsible for censuses in the region the information on all foreigners, Latin Americans or not, or nonnatives of the country, who have been enumerated in their censuses. This will permit the study of intraregional movements as well as of the contribution of extraregional flows.

In addition, action has been taken with some European countries, and with the United States, for the purpose of obtaining similar information on all Latin Americans enumerated in those countries. Negotiations with many of the countries are in an advanced stage and obtaining such data will lead to the broadening of the scope of the studies of migratory movements of Latin Americans.

All this information will, of course, be incorporated into the data bank, as will be that from any other research undertaken by CELADE for which empirical data on demographic characteristics of the population of the region are gathered, either directly or through the action of third parties.

8. SUMMARY

Throughout its almost fifteen years of existence, the Latin American Demographic Center (CELADE) has been carrying out numerous investigations on demographic aspects of the population of the region, many of which are based on empirical data collected through fieldwork.

With data from many of these studies, CELADE has formed a data bank, thus making it possible for information gathered to be useful not only to the originally planned investigation, but also to any future scientific study requiring new tabulations—not initially programmed—either for the investigation of trends or to verify or reject theories in relation to certain interrelationships.

Information kept by this bank is essentially of a numerical nature and refers to demographic, economic, and social characteristics of individuals who have been under study in each investigation.

Samples from the population censuses taken in the 1960s in fifteen countries of the region, plus Puerto Rico, which were gathered at CELADE for the purpose of making a comparative demographic analysis, have also been incorporated into the data bank.

The present report presents a brief description of the different studies, data from which have been included in the bank, with background information about their purpose, volume of data, and other characteristics, as well as bibliographical material. (The Appendix presents an additional bibliography.)

In the final part of the report, other general aspects of the data bank are discussed, such as storing of data from each investigation, direct costs, utilization of information, and so on. Finally, a brief reference is made to future expansion plans for the data bank.

Lastly, it should be noted the data bank has been created not only as an answer to research requirements of CELADE personnel and students, but likewise to answer requests for information from different institutions or researchers concerned with social, economic, and demographic studies in Latin American.

APPENDIX

Reports of the Countries on the Results of Urban-PECFAL

1. Brazil

   Centro Latinoamericano de Pesquisas em Ciencias Sociais: *Fecundidade da Populaçao Urbana do Rio de Janeiro.*

2. Colombia

   Universidad de Los Andes, Centro de Estudios sobre Desarrollo Económico (CEDE): *Análisis de la Encuesta de Fecundidad.* Informe Preliminar, Bogotá, 1965.

   Rafael Prieto Durán y Roberto Cuca Tolosa: *Análisis de la Encuesta de Fecundidad.* Centro de Estudios sobre Desarrollo Económico (CEDE), Monografía 19.

   Universidad de Los Andes, Centro de Estudios sobre Desarrollo Económico (CEDE): *Encuesta de Fecundidad en Bogotá, Anexo Estadístico.* Bogotá, 1965.

3. Costa Rica

   Gómez B. Miguel: *Informe de la Encuesta de Fecundidad en el Area Metropolitana.* Universidad de Costa Rica, Instituto Centroamericano de Estadística. San José, 1968.

   Universidad de Costa Rica, Instituto de Estadística, Dirección General de Estadística y Censos: *Algunos Resultados de la Encuesta de Fecundidad en el Area Metropolitana de San José, Costa Rica, abril-mayo, 1964.* San José, Costa Rica, 1966.

4. Panama

   Hildebrado Araica: *Informe de la Encuesta de Fecundidad en el Area Metropolitana de la Ciudad de Panamá. Año 1964.* Dirección de Estadística y Censos. Panamá, 1964.

5. Venezuela

   República de Venezuela, Ministerio de Fomento, Dirección General de Estadística y Censos Nacionales: *Encuesta de Fecundidad en el Area Metropolitana de Caracas.* Año cuatricentenario de Caracas, 1967.

THE NBER TIME SERIES DATA BANK

CHARLOTTE BOSCHAN*

National Bureau of Economic Research

1. INTRODUCTION

One of the favorite occupations of practicing economists is forecasting aggregate economic activity and its components. Many of these forecasts involve short-term predictions of major indicators of aggregate economic activity, either as final products or as inputs to a "dependent" forecast of other, disaggregated minor variables. The methods used vary widely. Some base their forecasts on the indicator approach, some on econometric models, ranging from single equations to very complicated and elaborate multi-equation models, some on a sectorial approach, some on intuition, and some on a combination of different approaches. Whatever the methods, almost all forecasters use time series of economic variables, which are collected, maintained, and published by a wide variety of government and private agencies. If each individual economist had to keep track of these data—of their revisions and updates, changes in definition, lack of comparability, new information and discontinuances—the resources spent on such housekeeping tasks would be enormous.

For a large number of time series these tasks were facilitated by the data collections and analyses published in the *Survey of Current Business* which, for many years, provided the main source of current economic and business information. Since 1961 the Census Bureau's monthly publication *Business Cycle Developments*—now named *Business Conditions Digest*—has provided numeric and graphic information for the analysis and forecasting of current business conditions. The organization and the approach of this publication is an extension of the National Bureau's work on indicators, diffusion indexes and recession-recovery analysis. BCD contains adjusted numerical information for the three most recent calendar years, graphs from 1950 to date, certain statistical summary measures and some analytic measures. This publication serves a very useful purpose and is indeed very popular among business economists and other forecasters. However, it still has several shortcomings. Publication and distribution of such a data collection necessarily involves delay, and thus some time series may be out-of-date by the time BCD reaches the economist's desk. Also, the number of time series published is severely limited and may not include time series important for given users. Finally, the data are not immediately in machine readable form, ready for input into computer programs. A data bank residing in a time sharing system, in which series are updated and revised as soon as new data are available from the publishing agency, is free of many of these shortcomings. The latest data are always in the bank and available to users. Series important to users can be stored, listed, plotted, and used as input into canned general purpose programs, or into the user's own

* It gives me pleasure to acknowledge the many helpful comments and suggestions I received from Gerhard Bry and Peggy Cahn. I am also grateful to Peggy for the large amount of thought and energy she unstintingly puts into the operations of the data bank.

special ones. Such a time series data bank, operated and maintained by the National Bureau of Economic Research, is the subject matter of this paper.

The most interesting aspect of maintaining a data bank is the number and variety of problems that arise and must be solved. Hence this paper is largely problem oriented. First, there are problems arising in connection with the selection of series to be included, their time coverage, periodicity, and seasonal adjustment status. Second, the National Bureau has a special problem in having to deal with several time sharing systems simultaneously and to fulfill a unique obligation of being scrupulously nondiscriminatory between the small and the large, the good and the bad, the wise and the foolish. A third set of problems are operational and revolve around checking and updating, having the very latest information at the very earliest moment, and generally maintaining time series on-line. After discussing the documentation for such a system (the minimum requirements as well as the ideal envisaged for the future) we will give an overview of the economics of running the venture. We hope that a description of the problems we faced and are still facing, as well as an indication of how we tried to solve them, may be helpful to others who want to set up, maintain, and use similar banks. We also hope that readers who can suggest better solutions than the ones we tried will give us the benefit of their thoughts.

Before we start with the description of the specific problems, a short explanation of the historical and institutional background of the particular data bank is in order. Early in 1967 a group of economists from about twenty large New York firms, all engaged in short term forecasting, became aware of the extent of duplication in their efforts. Therefore, they started an experimental cooperative venture, called "Project Economics," consisting of a time series data bank on General Electric's Mark I system. Each member was assigned a set of time series to be maintained in the bank, with updates and revisions as published by the respective government agencies. Manipulative computer programs, largely written by General Electric, were pooled and kept in common storage. This scheme worked tolerably well for a while; but problems arose: data handling expertise varied among members, quality control of the data in the bank was never fully developed, large revisions became too cumbersome for members to enter, and the quality of the data deteriorated.[1] This is when the National Bureau of Economic Research entered the picture. The provision of economic data to economists has long been an accepted function at the National Bureau. Data developed and selected by the Bureau play a prominent role in such government publications as *Historical Statistics*, *Business Conditions Digest*, and *Indicators of Economic Growth*. The Bureau has published several source books, such as the second volume of *Business Cycle Indicators* (1958) and a volume on construction statistics (1966), and has always made its unpublished material freely available to other economists. Also, we felt that, in the long run, nobody else could insure the standard of accuracy that we think appropriate. Thus it was a natural step for the Bureau to develop and maintain a machine readable data bank. In 1969 the Bureau took over the maintenance of the Project Economic's data bank, expanded its coverage and made it available to other time sharing systems and user groups.

[1] For a description of the original Project Economics see Robert E. Lewis, "Operating a Cooperative Economic Data Bank on a Time Sharing System," *Business Economics*, May 1970.

2. CONTENT OF THE DATA BANK

The two main purposes for which the data bank was designed are the analysis of current business conditions and short-term forecasting. These purposes have several implications for the content of the bank: the bank contains practically all indicators, aggregates, and other time series which may be considered important in evaluating current business conditions; most series are either monthly or quarterly, with a few annual ones included for the convenience of model builders; all time series start in 1946 or later, whenever they become available (none are carried before 1946); all series which have a seasonal component are carried on a deseasonalized basis; the series in the bank are updated as soon as new or revised estimates become available from the primary source.

Time Series Included

In the pursuit of the broad goals outlined above a number of problems arose and a number of decisions had to be made.

(a) What size should the data bank be? For instance, should all or most available time series be included? To the uninitiated user there may seem to be definite advantages in having a large number of series in the data bank: a bank which has twice as many series appears to be twice as good. However, a smaller collection of series is not only less costly to store and easier to update but it also takes less time to access and is more economical to use. Thus we decided to include only series which are clearly useful and which would, in fact, be used. It turned out that this was one decision which was easier to make than to implement—which leads directly to the next question:

(b) How should series be selected for inclusion in the bank? During the first stage of its existence, time series to be included in the data bank were chosen by a committee of users. Later, for a short period of time, we included almost anything anybody wanted, as long as it could be called a cyclical indicator or was part of the National Income and Product Accounts. This procedure had several obvious disadvantages. We could not make any use of the economies involved in updating a number of series from the same source. Code names were determined on an ad hoc basis, without reference to names for other series, let alone a systematic nomenclature. Worse than that, we might find ourselves maintaining esoteric regional or industrial subclassifications, which some user may regularly need (or may have needed for a special purpose in the past), without carrying the more important aggregates in the bank. We, therefore, soon became very careful about inclusion of further series. At present we are working with a "dictionary" or "directory" of significant time series which contains, in addition to all the series presently in the bank, many series we consider to be important enough to warrant inclusion, provided enough users express an interest in them. These series are already ordered by source. Also, orderly and meaningful code names have been determined for all of them.

During the past year we have continuously added new series. Now that we think we have a fairly reasonable selection, we will only add new series if new statistics are compiled and published by issuing agencies (job vacancy statistics of the BLS, for example, and the new production series by the FRB) or if we think that existing series, or series which can be constructed, have become important (deflated indicators are a good example or, if many users need them, the flow of funds series may be a case in point).

(c) How should series, now in the bank, be selected for deletion? This problem is difficult to handle. Since none of the systems we are using is designed to keep track of how often a particular series has been accessed, it is quite likely that some of the series which we painstakingly bring up-to-date have never been used and will never be used at all. In order to avoid this waste we are planning to experiment with several schemes such as transitory second class storage (where a user must request series before he can use them and where one can monitor the rate of usage), low priority updating, announcement of plans for discontinuance, and perhaps some others. Users would be invited to comment and we hope that their reactions would give us some clues to the importance they attach to individual series.

(d) What should subscribers do if they need series which are not of general interest and, therefore, not included in the bank? This problem is not difficult since in all the systems we are using—and probably in all time sharing systems in which one can use a data base—it is possible to maintain private files of series and use them in conjunction with data in the bank. As a special service, we sometimes provide subscribers with exact source information for data they want to keep on line and update privately; occasionally we even give them the actual figures.

At present the bank contains some 2000 time series, covering all U.S. series shown in the Census Bureau's publication *Business Conditions Digest*, almost all series shown in the Council of Economic Advisers' *Economic Indicators*, and all series included in the Bureau of Economic Analysis' "National Income and Product Accounts" as published monthly in the *Survey of Current Business* as well as most of the national income series published only in July. The series can be roughly classified as follows:

	Number of Series
National Income and Product Accounts	950
Manufacturers' Shipments, Inventories, Orders	140
Retail and Wholesale Trade and Inventories	30
Construction and Housing	30
New Plant and Equipment Expenditures	30
Industrial Production	70
Population, Labor Force, and Employment	120
Productivity and Unit Labor Cost	30
Prices	80
Financial Series	220
Balance of Payments	30
Federal Fiscal Operations	20
Miscellaneous	250
	2,000

Time Coverage and Reporting Span of Data

Since the data bank was originally conceived to be a tool of current conditions analysis and forecasting, none of the time series start before 1946. For an on-line time sharing data bank this is probably sufficient, and longer series might be difficult to handle. However, there is no compelling reason why the Bureau's collection of pre-World War II data should not be available on magnetic tape, to supplement data bank information. Many of these series provide back data for series presently included in the bank, and may constitute the best available time series for the earlier years. They could be used for longer period analysis, for an analysis of the stability of relationships, for comparisons of pre- and post-war cyclical and other behavior, and for a variety of other research purposes.[2]

At the moment the data bank contains 1350 monthly series, 500 quarterly, and 150 annual ones. Most annual series are part of the National Income Accounts, some 25 series are population and labor force data. For many purposes it is desirable to work with data of uniform periodicity. The software provided by time sharing companies usually includes functions which take quarterly averages or totals from monthly series, and annual averages from quarterly or monthly series. We are providing straight line interpolation subroutines and are in the process of incorporating a spline function interpolation. This function has the property that the arcs, on which the interpolation is performed, join smoothly.

Seasonal Adjustment

For the analysis of current business conditions, particularly if the "indicator approach" is used, one obviously needs time series which are free of seasonal fluctuations. We are, therefore, carrying almost all series which have a seasonal component in seasonally adjusted form. However, model builders often prefer to use unadjusted data, with dummy variables to represent the seasons; and for current business conditions analysis it is desirable to know the magnitude of the seasonal fluctuations, their variability, and the reliability of seasonal indexes and seasonal adjustments. But the inclusion of all original data and major analytical measures would, of course, more than double the amount of work and space needed. Hence, we decided, early in the life of the bank, that the cost of carrying all original data on line is too high and included only a few series in their unadjusted form. (Whenever only original data are published by the primary source, we usually provide our own seasonal adjustment and carry both versions in the bank.)

This decision does not mean, however, that we are not searching for some solution of the problem. The question of the reliability of seasonal adjustments occurs too often to be ignored. Perhaps we should include original data for all important series which have a large seasonal component and for all those whose seasonal factors are unreliable, fluctuate much or are in any other way problematic. Another possibility would be to include recent seasonal factors and confidence ranges or other variability measures of the seasonal factors in the description of

---

[2] If enough internal and external demand exists to make key punching and other chores worthwhile, we would certainly consider such a venture. The data would not need to be brought up-to-date and the probability of revisions is extremely small. Thus, the production of a machine readable tape would be a one-time task.

series. Such variability measures are, of course, quite problematic when we deal with moving seasonal patterns.

We cannot ignore the needs of model builders either, since TROLL,[3] one of the systems which uses our data bank, was especially designed to facilitate model estimation and simulation. We will probably provide them with a selection of unadjusted series on a low-priority update basis.

Confidential and Proprietary Data

Our bank includes several "confidential" series, originating in the Bureau of Economic Analysis, which may be used for analytic purposes in combination with other series, but may not be published. Before we release the code names and thus permit retrieval of these series to individual users, they must agree not to publish these data. We also carry several sets of proprietary data of Dun and Bradstreet, the Conference Board and the F. W. Dodge Corporation. We have permission to carry these series but, again, users must not publish them.

Discontinuities, Overlaps, and Missing Observations

Economic time series frequently contain discontinuities of various kinds. The underlying sample may change from one period to the next, concepts are improved or updated, the geographic coverage changes, or the method of collection varies. Statistical agencies sometimes carry these data with an overlap, sometimes with a footnote indicating the break and including perhaps a few observations on both bases; sometimes two separate series are published. As far as carrying these series in the data bank is concerned, we have conflicting goals. On the one hand we want to preserve data in the "purest" possible form, that is without any manipulation. On the other hand, we want to make time series easy to use in statistical analyses of various kinds, and for this purpose they must be continuous over the period of analysis. We could, of course, let each user do his own splicing, estimating, and manipulating of segments, but we prefer to avoid duplication of effort, use of several, slightly different, spliced versions by different subscribers, and waste of time we might have to spend in advising people. We therefore decided to compromise. Whenever possible we carry both segments: the old segment to the latest available date, and the new segment from the earliest available date. Continuous with the new segment we carry the old one, spliced and "adjusted" to the level of the new. The particular splicing method used is, of course, fully documented. A sophisticated user can do his own thing, while the analyst in a hurry has a ready-made adjustment.

Our treatment of missing observations is somewhat less exemplary. In the few cases of this kind we provide interpolations. However, because of the inability of our software to deal with flags and footnotes, a user has to consult the source notes before he can tell that a particular value represents our estimate rather than an original observation.

---

[3] For a brief description of the TROLL system see Mark Eisner, "TROLL—An Interactive Computer System for Economic Research," *Annals of Economic and Social Measurement*, Vol. 1, Number 1, January 1972.

3. OPERATIONAL PROBLEMS

Any data bank run by the National Bureau, a non-profit publicly supported organization, must be accessible to anybody who wants to use it. Since we do not have a large enough computer system of our own—or, at least, did not have one at the time the data base was set up—and since we cannot give an exclusive franchise to any one computer manufacturer or time-sharing service, it follows that the data bank has to be accessible through different time sharing systems; and it must be available on magnetic tape in a "standard" easy-to-read format, for batch processing in any kind of system.

Participating Time-Sharing Systems

At the present time our data base can be accessed through three time sharing systems: Rapidata, General Electric MAP; and TROLL. A fourth one, Interactive Science Corporation's PDP-10 system, is in the process of developing software for using and updating our time series efficiently. Other groups are planning to participate.

The problem of dealing with several not always compatible systems may be unique to our particular set-up, since producers of data banks usually deal with one system only. It is obviously very expensive and time consuming to enter additions and revisions by hand via a system's editor, for each of the varying systems. We have solved this problem by writing "update" programs for each system, which can interpret the same paper tape input. Thus, the paper tape is punched once and read into each system. Once it has been read, the update program in each system takes care of the rest. The provision of an update program able to interpret our standard paper tape is now a condition for the participation of any new time sharing system in our data bank. One other condition for adding a new system is that there be at least ten paying users, since it would otherwise be too costly to update—even with the same paper tape input.

Series Code Names

Historical accidents sometimes determine how systems will operate in the future. In the General Electric Mark I time sharing system, the first system in which our data bank was used, each time series constituted a file and each file was retrievable with a six-letter file name. This is the origin of our system of six-digit code names for each series. Since most computers can handle six characters in a word, there has been no reason to change.

In naming our time series we have attempted to attain some hierarchical order and some consistency, apart from mnemonic considerations. Thus, all series starting with G are part of the GNP—National Income Accounts. All financial series start with F, all industrial production series with I, all labor series with L, and so forth. All annual series have the letter A in the second position and most series which are not deseasonalized, the number 6. Whenever possible, industrial subclasses carry the SIC code number.

Although the six letters obviously do not permit a lot of flexibility or a really useful structure, at least our naming conventions insure a certain amount of orderliness and facilitate manipulation : When the data bank became so large that the Rapidata system had trouble accommodating all series in one "library," we simply put all National Income Account series into a separate library, and changed the software to look in the second library for all series starting with G. This principle can, of course, be carried further if necessary. Since, in the Rapidata System, individual time series form individual files on a disk which are accessed directly by the system looking through a table to find their address on a disk, access time can also be cut by using several separate "libraries."

The TROLL system permits a much more sophisticated explicit hierarchical structure, which should not only speed up retrieval but also permit the user to locate series whose code names he does not know.[4] Time series in TROLL can be stored, referred to, and retrieved by using an explicit decision tree. One can have as many "nodes" as one wants. Obviously, the system will not be better than we design it, and we plan to work on this as soon as more people use our data base on TROLL.[5]

Internal File Organization

Originally, the last lines of each file contained the name of the time series, the units of measurement, and some other information. Later on these last lines were dropped so that each time series could be read entirely, to the last available figure, by a retrieval program, without explicit specification of the length of the series (which was not always known by the user). Instead, a "directory" or "dictionary" was provided which contained the code name of the series and other pertinent information and which could be accessed on line. We have since had occasion to regret the decision to have files which contain nothing but numerical information. When we wanted to "export" the bank from one system to another, for example, we were unable to just dump the contents of the disk on a magnetic tape, since the name of the file would not be dumped and there would have been no way to identify the numbers. Instead we had to write a program which first read a file name from the index, then searched for that file on the disk, and copied it on magnetic tape—together with the pertinent information from the index. Also, for listing and plotting time series it is more convenient to have the title together with the numerical information.

Fortunately, Rapidata is now in the process of changing its software, so that it can read several lines of non-numeric information (including the number of such lines) in the beginning of a file. This means that identifying information can now be carried in the beginning of each series. We hope that other systems will follow suit.

On the Rapidata system, the numerical information within each file is organized as follows: Monthly series are stored and listed six items per line with 3-digit identifying line numbers. The first two digits of the line number indicate the year and the last digit (1 or 2) indicates whether the data refer to the first or second

---

[4] For a description of how this can be accomplished on the Rapidata system see *NBER Data Bank for Project Economics*, National Bureau of Economic Research and Rapidata, 1971.

[5] For a description of the theoretical background of the methods and algorithms used in the estimation capability in the TROLL/1 system see Mark Eisner and Robert S. Pindyck, "A generalized approach to estimation for the TROLL/1 system," April 1971, mimeo., NBER.

half of the year. For example, the line number of January–June, 1956 would be 561. July–December of 1956 would appear on line 562. Quarterly data are stored four items per line with a 2-digit line number indicating the year, and annual data are stored one item per line with a 4-digit line number.

Routine Updating and Checking Procedures

Up-to-dateness is a very important aspect of our data bank. Our contract specifies that all new and revised data be incorporated into our bank within two working days of their official release. We are located in New York City and most governmental data are generated and published in Washington, D.C. This creates some problems. If we relied on ordinary mail service we would sometimes receive a release several days later than some of the data bank users. We therefore employ a "press service" which picks up specified releases from government offices and sends them by airmail. During any particular month we may use as many as a hundred different source documents.

Once the release is received, figures have to be entered into the different time sharing systems. A paper tape[6] is produced, which contains the name of the series, the date for which an addition or revision is made, and the new figures to be used. For each of the systems there exists a program which can take the information from that tape and make the necessary changes and additions to the affected time series.

Entries are checked from a print-out of the paper tape and then again from a listing produced by the update program. This listing is cut up and pasted on the time series listing, which is kept on file for each series. Periodically, new listings are obtained and checked against primary and secondary sources. The secondary sources we use are mainly the *Survey of Current Business*, the *Federal Reserve Bulletin*, *Business Conditions Digest*, and some others. Whenever one of these appears, print outs are again checked against these sources. (This is one way in which we find errors in Government publications!) Consistency checks and checks for the adequacy of seasonal adjustments are made frequently and, if necessary, the source agencies are informed of their outcome. In many instances inconsistencies can be resolved (or at least explained) and bad seasonal adjustments can be improved.

Major Revisions

At the present time, government agencies do not release machine readable revisions in advance of or concurrently with printed revisions. It seems that revisions are still computed by long hand and key punched afterwards. The Bureau of Labor Statistics is a possible exception, but their tapes are incompatible with our time sharing systems and very difficult to read. Until such time as procedures are modernized and communications standardized we have to enter all revisions by hand—punching paper tape, punch cards or magnetic tape casette. This is time consuming and error prone, and we hope it will soon be a thing of the past.

---

[6] We may switch from paper tape to a magnetic tape cartridge, which is easier to edit and to handle.

Software for Statistical Analysis

The analytical software available to the user of the data bank is, of course, different for the different systems. We added to the software offered by the various time-sharing companies only if we needed something for our own updating procedures or if generally useful programs (such as the X-11 seasonal adjustment program) could be incorporated.

We also have several FORTRAN programs which are specifically designed for the analysis of current business conditions, such as a Recession-Recovery analysis program, a program which determines cyclical turning points, and several diffusion index programs.[7] These programs, being written in minimum FORTRAN, are compatible with most time sharing systems and can be made available to users.

In the case of Rapidata, we were involved in the development of their language PLEA (Prototype Language for Economic Analysis) from its very beginning. We cooperated with Rapidata's programmers on specification, documentation and testing. They now have a very useful language and they are continuing to make improvements and refinements. PLEA deals with time series as vectors, which can be taken either from our data bank or a user's own files for a specified time period. It contains (1) a simple but powerful data manipulation section, including arithmetic operations, averaging, concatenation, deviations, extractions, mathematical functions, creations of dummy variables, (2) a facility to shift series in time, (3) the ability to perform a variety of statistical tasks, such as seasonal analysis, correlations, regressions, analysis of variance and factor analysis, and (4) several ways to output results, including plotting and the generation of new data files. These features are described in two manuals: "PLEA for Statistical Analysis," Rapidata, 1971 and "The PLEA*ECO Statistical Library," Rapidata, August 1970.

General Electric's MAP (Management Analysis and Projection) System runs on a GE 605 under the Desk-Side Time-Sharing System. It consists of a collection of programs that allow easy manipulation of data, analysis and forecasting. Input to those programs can be obtained from our data bank or from the user's own data. MAP includes various types of display of data—lists, tabulations, graphs, and a transformation package which can compute arithmetic operations, moving averages, leads and lags, various mathematical functions, growth triangles, curve fits, correlation matrixes, auto-correlations, and so forth. The mainstay of the system is GE's factor analysis forecasting system. All these programs can be used interactively if desired. In addition, several FORTRAN subroutines are available to interact with the data base. The system is described in "MAP, An Information Management Analysis and Projection System, Economic Data Base," General Electric Manual, November 1970.

Tape for Academic Institutions

Colleges and universities are interested in using the time series data bank for various purposes. Courses in econometrics, economic statistics, forecasting, business cycle analysis and model building can all use a data bank of time series,

---

[7] For a description of some of these programs see Gerhard Bry and Charlotte Boschan, *Cyclical Analysis of Time Series: Selected Procedures and Computer Programs*, NBER Technical Paper 20, 1971.

particularly if it is accessible by their computer. Some of the research may also utilize some of the time series included in the bank. For all these purposes it is usually not necessary that the data be very current and updated to the very last month. Therefore, we are providing some universities with magnetic tapes containing our data base. The format of these tapes is a compromise between the new "data transmission standards" set up by Ruggles and Sadowsky[8] and cost considerations in producing the tape from the existing data bank. (For format see Exhibit 1 in the Appendix.)

4. DOCUMENTATION

This is one of the most problematic areas. How much documentation should there be? How much of it should be on-line, how much hard copy? Is it necessary to document each figure in the bank? Can other source descriptions be used without actually being reproduced?

Hard Copy

The primary document describing the content of our data bank is a printed dictionary or directory consisting of four major parts: The main part lists all series included in the bank, with the six letter code name assigned to it, its starting date, periodicity, units, seasonal adjustment status, and a list of the source documents from which it was taken. Whenever possible, documentation is presented in tabular form, with a table showing all series from one source pertaining to a particular subject matter. Exhibit 2 is a sample page containing manufacturing and trade inventory and sales series published by the Department of Commerce. The series code names are shown in capital letters next to the descriptions and the starting years next to the names. Footnotes, including cross references, and source notes are shown at the bottom of the page. If the material is not easy to put in tabular form, it is just listed sequentially, as in Exhibit 3. It will be noted that the source documentation is somewhat unusual. The numbers on the extreme right hand side indicate the successive source documents from which the data were obtained. Thus, on line #09688, for "Number of Job Vacancies in Manufacturing" #45 refers to "U.S. Department of Labor, Bureau of Labor Statistics," *Employment and Earnings*, and #45B to the monthly news release from the same agency; "Job Vacancies, Hires, Quits and Layoffs in Manufacturing." (The key to these source code numbers is, of course, also included in the dictionary.) Thus, the source documentation in the dictionary refers to the printed releases which underlie the data shown in the bank. It does not, unfortunately, contain any economic or statistical description of the series, informing the user whether, for instance, it is based on a full count or a sample, when, where, and how data are collected, how reliable the data are and what their coverage is. Nor does it, at the present time, refer the user to the publication in which these characteristics of the time series are discussed and explained. This is a serious shortcoming of our documentation and we are in the process of correcting it. As a first step we will add code number and

[8] See Richard Ruggles and George Sadowsky, "Standards for Time Series Interchange." Mimeograph, NBER.

date of the document containing the description (or descriptions) to the source part of the index for each series or for entire sections of series. Since this is not a trivial task, it will take some time and effort. We have started to collect this information and to write up our own descriptions when none are published anywhere. Strangely enough very few users have ever asked us for this type of information. The reason is probably that we are dealing primarily with well known macro economic time series and most users know what they represent or at least where they are described.

The second part of the printed dictionary consists of a facsimile reproduction of the tables contained in *Economic Indicators* published by the Council of Economic Advisers. Instead of data, the associated code names are shown. The third and fourth parts consist of similar reproductions of the "Series Finding Guide" and "Titles and Sources of Series" of *Business Conditions Digest* and of the National Income and Product Accounts as published in *The Survey of Current Business*. In each case our code names are shown next to the descriptions of the series. Sample pages are shown in Exhibits 3 to 6. The facsimile reproductions included in our directory are intended to facilitate the use of the data bank for people who are accustomed to working with these publications. A table of contents, by subject matter, and an alphabetical index are also contained in the dictionary.

The make-up of the alphabetical index, incidentally, is somewhat problematic. An alphabetic listing of the code names is obviously useful only for people who know the code names, and if they know the code names, they don't need an index. For finding code names what needs to be alphabetized is the series title. But a series title usually contains many "key words" and if you list each series under each of the key words you get a very voluminous index. To take a relatively harmless example, the series called "Manufacturers' unfilled orders, durable goods industries" would have to be listed under manufactures, under orders, under unfilled orders, and under durable goods. Still worse would be the listing of a series compounded from heterogeneous components, such as "Manufacturers' machinery and equipment sales and business construction expenditures (industrial and commercial construction put in place)." In addition, the selection of key words is hard to program if we want to avoid innumerable listings of series under "goods," under "industries," under "sales" and under "expenditures." One could, of course, let the computer do the alphabetizing and then take the nonsense items out, but in any case the resulting index would be quite voluminous. (N.B.: One well known data bank produced such a massive computerized compilation and its salesmen point with pride to the comparative richness of its collection and the comprehensiveness of its cross-classification system by reference to the weight of the printed index.) We are presently omitting an alphabetical index with multiple listings for each individual series. Our index is alphabetized by subject matter (orders, sales, construction, etc.) and refers the reader to a page in the printed dictionary.

On-line Documentation

Although hard-copy documentation is important, a certain amount of information must be available on line. One reason is that users, accustomed to the convenience of man-computer interaction afforded by time sharing, often do not bring their manual to the terminal when they are using the data bank. The second, perhaps more important, reason is that in a data bank such as ours, changes in documentation are needed quite frequently and printed copy would have to be kept up by some looseleaf arrangement or similar scheme. In cross-sectional or other single-time-period data banks, where the information usually does not change once it is in the bank, the documentation obviously need not change either. Our data bank, however, is a growing, constantly changing collection. Not only is the information contained in individual time series frequently revised and updated, but new series are added, old ones discontinued, samples, base periods, sources, and source descriptions are changed and so forth. The user must be informed of these changes as soon as they occur.

We are taking care of these needs in two ways. First, we keep an entire listing of all included time series by subject matter on-line in the data bank. Instead of looking up series titles in a printed book the user can let the computer list parts in which he is interested. Since most time sharing systems have editor programs which permit the listing of all lines containing specified combination of letters, it is usually quite easy for the user to find the series in which he is interested. (See pages 6–8 of the directory for an example of how this is done.) These on line files, called GINDEX for GNP series and INDEX for all others, are kept up-to-date: new series are added, old ones deleted, source notes revised and brought up-to-date, and so forth.

In addition to this kind of inventory of all series in the bank, we used to keep a record of "transactions." A file called "change," written by the update program whenever a series was revised or updated, contained changes made, by date and series code name. Ideally, a user could let the edit program list all the changes made to a particular series by just listing each line on which the code name of the series appeared. We thought that this would be a very useful thing to have. However, it turned out that nobody ever seemed to use it. Specifically, when a bug in the program resulted in the deletion of most of the file, no one ever brought this to our attention. Since there were also some technical difficulties caused by the file's becoming too large too fast and thus quite expensive, we decided to discontinue writing it. No one has ever missed it, or if they did, they spared our feelings. All the same, we still think that this type of information—or at least the date of the last change in a series—ought to be available to the user. If we find an inexpensive way to provide it we will certainly do so.

In the meantime, we have several other, perhaps minor, pieces of useful information on line. A file called "INFORM" contains such information as dropped series, revisions of whole batches of series, prospective revisions, etc.

Special Services

Users of our data bank vary widely with regard to experience, sophistication and expertise in economics, statistics and computer use. They need varying amounts of assistance in finding series, using series, writing and using programs, interpreting results and many other things. Some of the more technical computer and programming assistance is usually provided by the time sharing company, but many questions arise which we have to answer. Typically, somebody misreads a code name (we now try to avoid I's and 1's, as well as O's and zeros), confuses monthly and quarterly series or uses wrong starting dates. Occasionally users want to know when certain series will be updated and are very much upset if the dates cannot be predicted with accuracy since they vary somewhat from month to month. Other users enquire about the purpose and justification of particular revisions and changes in seasonal factors. Most of these questions are relatively easy to handle. But every once in a while somebody asks a really tricky question. Why do the turning points listed in the BCD differ from the ones given by us? What exactly is the difference between the insured unemployment rate and the total unemployment rate? How can he use the Durbin–Watson Statistics given in the Rapidata regression program? What variables should he use to forecast the sales of his company? Why do we not carry them in the data bank? We try to answer most reasonable questions to the best of our ability, particularly if they refer to data in the bank. Often questions are asked only because our documentation is not good enough to obviate them. This, we hope, will change in the near future. However, some questions will always need to be asked and, in principle, we welcome this fact, since it brings us in contact with the users of our data bank and provides a certain amount of feedback on how the data and the data bank are used.

5. THE ECONOMICS OF THE NBER DATA BANK

General Considerations

The National Bureau is a nonprofit publicly supported research organization. We do not intend to make any profit on the data bank operations, nor do we want to incur a loss. The entire venture is planned as a cooperative enterprise, with each member paying an equal share of the cost. However, breaking exactly even is an unusual managerial goal which is very difficult to attain. Originally, our price of $750.00 per user per year was set with the intention of breaking even, assuming a constant number of users. In principle we intended to add more series to the bank as more users joined the project and thus continue to break even. In practice, series were added much faster than users, i.e., the costs increased faster than the revenues. Furthermore, the original costs were somewhat underestimated, and thus we are losing money. The loss would be somewhat smaller if the imputed benefits derived by internal use were explicitly considered.

What can be done about the loss? There is the possibility of raising the unit price (before the price-wage freeze). But we do not know by how much since we are trying to reduce machine cost by shifting to the night shift, and we do not know yet how much we can shift. Furthermore, development expenditures on new time series and the directory will be reduced. On the other hand, we will have to spend more time on source documentation. Thus, it takes a lot of juggling and close watching to stay in the proximity of the break-even point.

User Characteristics

A large number of our users are members of the original "Project Economics." One reason for this may be that we have not advertised the availability of the bank, and many potential users do not know that it exists. There are now about 50 users who participate in the cost of maintaining the data bank. They consist of the economics departments of 15 banks, 13 large industrial corporations, 2 insurance companies, 3 public utilities, 3 economic consultants, 3 stock brokers and investment advisors, and several others.

We originally intended to make data bank tapes available to academic users at incremental costs, but to charge the full price (average estimated cost) if an academic user wanted fast updating and on-line services. However, if an academic user participates in a time-sharing system which contains our bank and happens to get fast updating and on-line services, our incremental costs are of course zero. We are therefore not charging anything to universities who want to use our data through one of our affiliated time sharing systems. Their only costs are computer costs, and whatever other costs they incur in their time-sharing system. However, some universities are interested in incorporating our series in their own system— time sharing or otherwise. For these users, we periodically dump the data base on tapes and they share in the cost for this service. At present 7 universities have a version of our bank.

Another, not unimportant, group of users is the National Bureau research staff. People whose work is in the field of business cycle analysis and current business conditions analysis are obviously heavy users, but model builders and others interested in time series make frequent use of our machine readable data.

Personnel

With the present configuration of about 2000 series in two time sharing systems, the permanent personnel consists of one senior analyst and three research assistants. However, the availability of a wide variety of specialized talent within the walls of the National Bureau is of great help in the running of the data bank. We can get the help and advice of specialists on many different subject matters with regard to the selection and definition of series to be included, particularly if they are derived and not directly taken from a published source; we can draw on the experience of business cycle analysts with regard to seasonal adjustments and other technical matters; we can get a programmer to do special purpose modifications of the general update program or to write a tape for use on another system; we can have the help of an experienced data librarian to trace discrepancies and write source descriptions; and, in emergencies, we can get the help of a typist to copy data from releases to paper tape. We could not, of course, support any of these talents on a full time basis.

Expenditures

Apart from the advance releases which we get by airmail from Washington, the data bank librarians are, of course, making use of the National Bureau's extensive library of current and historical publications. The availability of the library is important for checking historical data, for determining specific concepts and definitions of series, and for other tasks.

The time sharing systems in which our data bank resides are, like most time sharing systems, accessible through a variety of terminals. Since the Bureau research staff also uses a variety of terminals for access to different computers, it is possible for the data bank operation to use different terminals for different purposes. (Teletype for paper tape, 2741 for wide carriage, Novar for magnetic tape cassette and high speed transmission). At the present time we use about the equivalent of one-and-a-half terminals full time.

Telephone cost, particularly for long distance communication, is a potentially very expensive item. Fortunately Rapidata's computer is in New York, GE is accessible by a local telephone call from anywhere in the country, and ISC, the new system to be added, has a New York FX line. In addition, the Bureau has a Watts line to Massachusetts which we can use for data bank operations.

6. CONCLUDING REMARKS

I have tried to show you what kinds of problems we faced in setting up and running our data bank, and how we have attempted to solve them. We hope that some of our solutions can be regarded as sufficiently adequate to help those who face similar problems.

Our efforts are, of course, all conducted within the somewhat narrow framework of single private time-series-and-forecasting oriented retrieval systems. It has been suggested that an all-embracing central system, which includes all published macro-economic and related series and makes them widely available, would be greatly superior to the decentralized and often duplicative efforts of individual data banks. Such a central data bank would in all likelihood be government operated. Some countries do indeed have such government-run data banks,[9] or they plan to install them. We are confident that even such central data banks may profit from the experiences of past pioneering efforts—be they governmental or private.[10]

In the United States we are very far from the implementation of a central information system—farther than some smaller countries in which computers are almost exclusively in governmental hands. In the U.S. it is likely that private data banks such as ours will continue to exist and to fill an important function in the provision of data and programs, as well as in the improvement of information technology. On the other hand, several government departments—such as the Bureau of Labor Statistics and the Department of Commerce—installed data banks for their own data and analyses. These efforts vary widely in quality, depending on hardware and know-how available at the time of their installation. In time, these banks might well be consolidated into one system. However, even when a centralized government-run time-shared information system does become available, private banks may continue to play an important role as monitors, innovators, consultants, and providers of special services. I think it is unlikely, though, that the Bureau's bank will be among them. Typically, the Bureau has tended to turn over operational responsibilities for its systems to the government and to restrict its role to methodological and interpretative functions. This was true for the National Income Accounts, cyclical indicators, consumer credit statistics, and many other statistical systems. It is also likely to be true for data bank operations.

[9] The most advanced bank of this kind is probably the Canadian one, run by Statistics Canada, which, incidentally, is not available for time-sharing except through a commercial system.

[10] One of the earliest governmental efforts was made in 1962 by Rudolph C. Mendelsohn of the U.S. Department of Labor, Bureau of Labor Statistics.

APPENDIX

EXHIBIT 1
MAGNETIC TAPE FOR ACADEMIC USERS

Description of Data Base Distribution Tape

I. Physical Attributes (can be changed on request)
  1. 9-track
  2. EBCDIC
  3. No label
  4. 800 B.P.I.
  5. 132 characters per record
  6. 50 records per block (blocksize = 6600)

II. Format of data series

  Each series is preceded by two records with descriptive information.

  The first record contains:

  1. Line number from an index file (ignore)
  2. Series code (up to 6 alpha-numeric characters)
  3. Series name

  The second record contains:

  1. Columns 1–4   Number of observations
  2. Columns 6–9   First year
  3. Column 11   1—quarterly
                    2—monthly
                    3—annual

  4. Columns 13–18 Series name left adjusted.

  Following these two records come series data in one of the following formats:

  1. Quarterly (I2, 1X, 4F11.3), where columns 1–2 contain last two digits of year (e.g. 47 for 1947)
  2. Monthly (I3, 6F11.3), where columns 1–2 contain last two digits of year and column 3 is 1 for first six months and 2 for last six months of the year (e.g. 672 for July–December of 1967)
  3. Annual (I4, F11.3), where columns 1–4 contain last two digits of year plus two zeros (e.g. 6900 for 1969)

III. End of File ·

  The end of file is last record written on tape

EXHIBIT 2
SAMPLE PAGE OF DIRECTORY, TABLES

MANUFACTURING AND TRADE INVENTORIES AND SALES

(millions of $, seasonally adjusted)

	Sales		Inventories	
Manufacturing and Trade	MRWT	(48)*	IVMT	(48)*
Manufacturing	MFGS	(47)	IVM	(47)
Durable	MDS	(47)	IVMD	(47)
Nondurable	MNS	(47)	IVMN	(47)
Retail Stores	RT	(46)	IVR	(47)
Durable	RD	(46)	IVRD	(47)
Nondurable	RN	(46)	IVRN	(47)
Merchant Wholesalers	WT	(48)	IVW	(48)
Durable	WTD	(48)	IVWD	(48)
Nondurable	WTN	(48)	IVWN	(48)

See also:
Change in Book Value, Manufacturing and Trade Inventories IVCMT (48).
Change in Unfilled Orders, Mfg. Durable Goods Ind. IVCUD (47).
Ratio, Inventories:sales, Total Manufacturing and Trade IVSRMT (48).
Ratio, Unfilled Orders:Shipments, Mfg. Durable Goods Ind. MDUXS (53).

   * Billions of $.

   Source: U.S. Department of Commerce, Bureau of Economic Analysis, "Manufacturing and Trade Inventories and Sales." (M).

MANUFACTURERS' INVENTORIES AND SALES: ACTUAL AND EXPECTED

(Billions of dollars, seasonally adjusted, back data, starting in 1947, is actual)

	Sales Total for Quarter	Inventories* End of Quarter
All manufacturers	MFGSAN	IVMANT
Durables	MDSANT	IVMDAN
Nondurables	MNSANT	IVMNAN

   * Inventory expectations corrected for systematic biases.

   Source: U.S. Department of Commerce. Bureau of Economic Analysis. Manufacturers' Inventory and Sales Expectations (0).

EXHIBIT 3

SAMPLE PAGE OF DIRECTORY, SEQUENTIAL LISTING

09528–
09529–HOURS & EARNINGS:NBER & OTHER SPECIAL SERIES
09530–

09531	LHCH	AVG. WEEKLY HOURS WORKED, CLF:HOLIDAY ADJ.	HOURSA	47	#45(A–22, A–20):70 NBER 8, 354
09532	LHOURS	MANHOURS PER WEEK, EMPLOYED CLF	MWHOURSA	47	#45:70 NBER 8, 355
09533	LHLOST	POTENTIAL MANHOURS LOST PER WEEK, CLF	MWHOURSA	48	#45:70 NBER 8, 356
09534	LHPOT	POTENTIAL MANHOURS PER WEEK, CLF	MWHOURSA	48	#45:70 NBER 8, 357
09535	LPCNAG	HOURLY COMPENSATION, NONAG EMPLOYMENT	SSA	47	#70 NBER 8, 350
09536	LPCMFG	HOURLY COMPENSATION, MFG. EMPLOYMENT	SSA	47	#70 NBER 8, 332
09537	LEHGF6	FED. EXEC BRANCH, ALL EMPL. AHE	R7	65	#45 (C–3)
09538	LEMXO	MFG. AHE "STRAIGHT-TIME" PROD WORKERS	$	46	#45 (C–4)
09540	LEMXS6	MFG. AHE EXCL. OVERTIME & INTERINDUSTRY SHIFTS	R7	47	#65, BLS
09546–	LHSTOP	MAN-DAYS IDLE DUE TO LABOR-MANAGEMENT DISPUTES	THDAY	47	#93 (NBER 8, 257)

09550–REAL AND SPENDABLE EARNINGS (PRODUCTION WORKERS)

09552	LEW7	REAL AWE PRIVATE NONFARM, PROD WORKERS	$67SA	60	#45C or 50
09553	LPC3	REAL SPENDABLE AWE, PROD WORKER, 3 DEPENDENTS	$67SA	64	#45C or 50
09554	LPC2	REAL AHE, MFG. PROD WORKERS	$67SA	47	#45A and 50

09648–
09649–UNEMPLOYMENT INDICATORS:MANPOWER ADM., INSURANCE & OTHERS
09650–

09651	LUINC	AVG. WEEKLY INITIAL CLAIMS, UNEMPL. INSUR. (STATE PROGRAMS)	THSA	48	#52:70
09652	LNAGP	NONAGRICULTURAL PLACEMENTS, ALL INDUSTRIES	THSA	45–70	#37, 51:65
09653	LJOB	NONAG JOB OPENINGS, UNFILLED	THSA	47–70	#51:65
09654	LJOBXU	RATIO, UNFILLED NONAG JOB OPENINGS:NUMBER UNEMPLOYED	RSA	47–70	#51, 45:65:70
09655	LHEL	NICB INDEX OF HELP-WANTED ADVERTISING IN NEWSPAPERS	R7SA	48	#21:65
09657–	LAUREM	COVERED EMPLOYMENT, UNEMPL. INSURANCE ALL PROGRAMS	TH	46A	#51A(P. 93) OR 72
09659–	LURP	INSURED UNEMPLOYMENT, ALL PROGRAMS (WKLY. AVG.)	WAV	55	#37(P. 85) OR 72
09661–	LURPB	BENEFITS PAID, UNEMPL. INSURANCE, ALL PROGRAMS	M	58	#65, 51 OR 72
09663–	LURPS	INSURED UNEMPLOYMENT, STATE PROGRAMS	WAV:TH	56	#65,51 OR 72
09665–	LUNIC6	INITIAL CLAIMS, UNEMPLOYMENT INSURANCE, STATE PROGRAMS	WAV:TH	56	#65,45 OR 72
09667–	LUNEX	EXHAUSTIONS, UNEMPLOYMENT INSURANCE, STATE PROGRAMS	WAV:TH	56	#65, 45 OR 72
09669–	LURSP6	INSURED UNEMPLOYMENT AS % OF COVERED EMPLOYMENT	%	49	#65, 45 OR 72
09671–	LURSPB	BENEFITS PAID, UNEMPL. INSURANCE, STATE PROGRAMS, EXT. PROV.	$	46	#51A(P. 135), 35 OR 72
09672–	LURSPW	AVG. WEEKLY BENEFIT CHECK FOR TOTAL UNEMPL. STATE PROGRAMS	$	46	#51A(P. 136), 35 OR 72

09673–
09674–LABOR TURNOVER RATES

09675–			
09676 LPACCM ACCESSION RATE, MANUFACTURING	%SA	47	#37, 45B
09080 LPOFFM LAYOFF RATE, MANUFACTURING	%SA	47	#34, 45B
09685–			
09686–JOB VACANCIES IN MANUFACTURING			
09687–			
09688 LVM NUMBER OF JOB VACANCIES IN MANUFACTURING	TH	4/69	#45, 45B
09690–LVMR JOB VACANCY RATE, MANUFACTURING	%	4/69	#45, 45B
09692–LVLM NUMBER OF LONG-TERM JOB VACANCIES, MANUFACTURING	TH	4/69	#45, 45B
09694–LVLMR LONG-TERM JOB VACANCY RATE, MANUFACTURING	%	4/69	#45, 45B

EXHIBIT 4

SAMPLE PAGE OF DIRECTORY, ECONOMIC INDICATORS

ECONOMIC INDICATORS

New Housing Starts and Applications for Financing

	Housing starts (Thousands of units)		
Total private and public (including farm)	<H6SF	59	5406
Total private (including farm)	<H6SP	59	5405
	Housing starts (Thousands of units, s.a.a.r.)		
Private			
Total private (including farm)	HSF	59	5403
One unit	HSP1	64	5404
Two or more units	HSF–HSP1	64	Derive
Government home programs (nonfarm)			
FHA	<HSFHA	46	5431
VA	<HSVA	47	5432
New private housing units authorized[1]	HSBP × 0.0879569	46	Derive
Proposed home construction			
Applications for FHA commitments[2]	<HFFHA	45	5433
Requests for VA appraisals[2]	<HFVA	51	5434

[1] HSBP is a spliced index: the authorizations in 10,000 permit-issuing places prior to 1963 and in 12,000 permit-issuing places from 1963–66 have been raised to the level of 13,000 permit-issuing places. The factor converts the index to units.

[2] Units represented by mortgage applications for new home construction.

Business Sales and Inventories
  (millions of dollars, seasonally adjusted)

Total business (includes manufacturing)			
Sales[1]	MRWT	48	3251
Inventories[1]	IVMT	48	3261
Wholesale			
Sales	WT	48	3258
Inventories	IVW	48	3270
Retail Sales	RT	46	3255
Durable goods stores	RD	46	3256
Nondurable goods stores	RN	46	3257
Retail Inventories	IVR	47	3267
Durable goods stores	IVRD	47	3268
Nondurable goods stores	IVRN	47	3269

[1] Billions of dollars.

Series marked < are not on line but available if enough users request them.

EXHIBIT 5

SAMPLE PAGE OF DIRECTORY, BCD

SECTION III

BCD BUSINESS CONDITIONS DIGEST

NBER TIME SERIES DATA BANK

In the following pages, the series published in the Census Bureau's publication Business Conditions Digest (BCD), NBER's code name, and the starting year are shown in the order of their appearance in the BCD Index. Source references such as "1.1" or "1.14" indicate a table number of the National Income and Product Accounts as published in the Survey of Current Business, and indexed on-line on "GINDEX". Four digit references such as "1521" or "9907" refer to a line number in the on-line NBER INDEX and SOURCE.

The NBER data bank carries time series in units as published by the primary source. It is always advisable to consult the SOURCE listing for specific characteristics of a series.

All series except those marked * are updated in the data bank before they become available in the BCD.

BCD BUSINESS CONDITIONS DIGEST — NBER TIME SERIES DATA BANK

Code	Starting year	Number
HPCON	1948	5309
FCAPR	1953	99011
BUS	1948*	99012
INC	1947	99013
FAIL	1948	1064
PFTCM	1947	99015
GPAT	1946	1.10
PWKXLM	1947	99017
FSPCOM	1947	760
IVCHS	1947-1958	4364
IVCHP	1953	4365
LPMOSA	1956	9369
GKPATX	1946	1.14
PSMAT	1948	5200
MSOMA	1953	4347
IVCUD	1947	3278
IVPAG0	1950	99026
RSFR	1947	5401
RSBP	1947	5630
IVCMT	1948	3262
IVPAC	1948	99032
FHDC	1955	1060
IVMPA	1947	99037
CCI30	1948	1067

EXHIBIT 6
SAMPLE PAGE OF DIRECTORY, NATIONAL INCOME ACCOUNTS

SURVEY OF CURRENT BUSINESS

NATIONAL INCOME AND PRODUCT TABLES

Table 9.—Gross Corporate Product [1] (1.14)

Seasonally adjusted at annual rates	Billions of dollars (1946)
Gross corporate product..........	GK
Capital consumption allowances......	GCCCA
Indirect business taxes plus transfer payments less subsidies..............	GCTTS
Income originating in corporate business...................................	GKY
Compensation of employees..........	GCCOMP
Wages and salaries..................	GCW
Supplements........................	GCSUPP
Net interest........................	GKINT
Corporate profits and inventory valuation adjustment..........	GKIVA
Profits before tax................	GKPBT
Profits tax liability............	GPTAX
Profits after tax...............	GKPAT
Dividends...................	GKDIV
Undistributed profits........	GKUP
Inventory valuation adjustment..	GIVA
Cash flow, gross of dividends..........	GKFLOW
Cash flow, net of dividends..........	GKFLUP
Gross product originating in financial institutions..........	GKF
Gross product originating in nonfinancial corporations..........	GKJ
Capital consumption allowances......	GJCCA
Indirect business taxes plus transfer payments less subsidies..............	GJTTS
Income originating in nonfinancial corporations......................	GJY
Compensation of employees..........	GJCOMP
Wages and salaries..................	GJW
Supplements........................	GJSUPP
Net interest........................	GJINT
Corporate profits and inventory valuation adjustment..........	GJIVA
Profits before tax................	GJPBT
Profits tax liability............	GJTAX
Profits after tax...............	GJPAT
Dividends...................	GJDIV
Undistributed profits........	GJUP
Inventory valuation adjustment..	GIVA
Cash flow, gross of dividends..........	GJFLOW
Cash flow, net of dividends..........	GJFLUP
	Billions of 1958 dollars (1948)
Gross product originating in nonfinancial corporations......	GKJ58
	Dollars (1948)
Current dollar cost per unit of 1958 dollar gross product originating in nonfinancial corporations [2]	GDKJ
Capital consumption allowances......	GDJCCA
Indirect business taxes plus transfer payments less subsidies..............	GDJTTS
Compensation of employees..........	GDJCOM
Net interest........................	GDJINT
Corporate profits and inventory valuation adjustment............	GDJIVA
Profits tax liability............	GDJTAX
Profits after tax plus inventory valuation adjustment...	GDJPIV

1. Excludes gross product originating in the rest of the world.
2. This is equal to the deflator for gross product of nonfinancial corporations, with the decimal point shifted two places to the left.
3. Personal saving as a percentage of disposable personal income.

Table 10.—Personal Income and Its Disposition (2.1)

Seasonally adjusted at annual rates	Billions of dollars (1946)
Personal income....	GPY
Wage and salary disbursements......	GW
Commodity-producing industries...	GWCP
Manufacturing..........	GWCPM
Distributive industries...........	GWD
Service industries.................	GWS
Government........................	GWG
Other labor income.....................	GPOL
Proprietors' income....................	GPRO
Business and professional..........	GPROB
Farm.............................	GPROF
Rental income of persons.............	GPRENT
Dividends...........................	GDIV
Personal interest income..............	GPINT
Transfer payments.....................	GPT
Old-age, survivors, disability, and health insurance benefits.........	GPTOAS
State unemployment insurance benefits.........................	GPTINS
Veterans benefits..................	GPTVET
Other............................	GPTHO
Less: Personal contributions for social insurance..................	GPSIW
Less: Personal tax and nontax payments..............................	GPTX
Equals: Disposable personal income.......	GYD
Less: Personal outlays..............	GOUT
Personal consumption expenditures...	GC
Interest paid by consumers...........	GCINT
Personal transfer payments to foreigners...........................	GPTF
Equals: Personal saving.................	GPSAV
Addenda: Disposable personal income:	
Total, billions of 1958 dollars..........	GYD58
Per capita, current dollars.............	GYDPC
Per capita, 1958 dollars..............	GYDPC8
Personal saving rate,[3] percent....	GXSAV

Table 11.—Personal Consumption Expenditures by Major Type (2.3)

Personal consumption expenditures................................	GC
Durable goods........................	GCD
Automobiles and parts...............	GCDA
Furniture and household equipment.	GCDF
Other............................	GCDO
Nondurable goods........................	GCN
Food and beverages.................	GCNFO
Clothing and shoes.................	GCNC
Gasoline and oil...................	GCNG
Other............................	GCNO
Services.............................	GCS
Housing...........................	GCSH
Household operation................	GCSHO
Transportation.....................	GCST
Other............................	GCSO

Table 12.—Foreign Transactions in the National Income and Product Accounts (4.1)

Receipts from foreigners...	GEXF
Exports of goods and services	GEX
Capital grants received by the United States................................	GEXCG
Payments to foreigners.............	GEXF
Imports of goods and services........	GIM
Transfers to foreigners..............	GTF
Personal........................	GPTF
Government......................	GGFTF
Net foreign investment..............	GFINET

MICRO-ECONOMIC DATA BANKS: PROBLEMS
AND POTENTIAL

HAROLD W. WATTS*
University of Wisconsin

Recent and revolutionary advances in data processing and computing machinery, combined with expanding bodies of data and increasing numbers of analysts with basic quantitative skills, have led to the view that we are entering a new era of social analysis. There is also a new urgency to tackle the many tough social problems that can only be solved by analysis at the micro-unit level, which may well lead people to *need* such a new era in data collection whether or not it is actually round the corner.

There is not, in fact, very much evidence in the form of completed research that the vast potential created by these advances in computer technology is yet being exploited. From my own experience in this area, I have developed a view as to why this is so, and in this note indicate that there are very difficult and unsolved problems involved in harnessing these resources, and that these problems are peculiar to the collection, storage, and usage of micro-data.

Micro-data are collected from direct surveys of individual units rather than from the putting together of many subsets of secondary information into large-scale aggregates. And it is not at all unlikely that such direct data collection may be relatively more feasible in Latin America than in fully industrialized countries like the United States, because substitutes for such statistics are harder to come by and less reliable.

The remainder of this paper will be organized in the following way. After defining in more detail what I mean by "micro-data," I shall recount two specific episodes in which I have been involved because they illustrate the problems of such undertakings; then I shall draw a few conclusions and give my advice about what criteria should guide the setting up of generally usable systems to handle such data.

MICRO-DATA

Micro-economic data are here taken to be information pertaining to, and unique to, specific decision-making *units*. These may be individuals, families, firms, political units, and so on. The data may be cross-sectional—giving information on a unit's status at a point in time (or for one period of time), or they may provide information referring to (or collected at) several successive points in time. The full complexity of such data is reached when the information is collected for a series of points in time. A person is indivisible for these purposes; he is, however, born and he does die. And, the decision units of which he is a part can also change

* I would like to acknowledge here the editorial skills of Felicity Skidmore which made my disjointed thoughts into a paper. This paper was prepared while the author was Irving Fisher Research Professor at Yale University.

from one survey to another. This process—of birth, death, and mutation of multi-person units—is what makes it difficult to organize, store, and work with micro-data. Different analyses are likely to apply to different decision units or even different versions of what is nominally the same unit. Thus, choices of definition have to be made, and the questions of how units are to be matched, put together, followed from survey to survey, depend on these choices.

To be useful for analysis, collections of micro-data should provide input for research that is timely, and also responsive to important areas of uncertainty. There is now in operation computing and file-manipulating machinery that is enormously powerful and becoming steadily less costly. Operating systems and program libraries also reflect a high degree of development, and are still active areas for innovation. And there is a wide range of storage media—cards, tapes, disks, drums—and on the horizon are even more exotic and compact media. Finally, there is a growing inventory of data born of a recognition that many questions require detailed information on families or other decision-making units, including data on how variables for specific units have changed over time.

Why have these resources not been exploited more fully? Why have the theory and practice of social and economic systems been able to draw on them to such a limited extent? The answer may lie along the following lines. The organizational effort and the budget required to join all these components together into a working system are beyond the capacity of individual researchers. Such researchers are, therefore, led to ignore micro-data and devote their efforts to more traditional, heavily worked over, manageable sources of data.[1] At the other extreme, research groups with generous resources have been working toward generating the super-colossal type of micro-data bank that aims at building up to a level of generality which is almost if not completely impossible given the current state of the art.

The next two sections describe the problems encountered in two relatively modest micro-data gathering efforts, to lend some realism to the discussion of massive general-purpose data banks, and to give some idea of the magnitude of the problems which must be overcome before we can hope to operationalize such a concept.

The Survey of Economic Opportunity

When President Johnson's War on Poverty was declared, certain antipoverty government programs were initiated by the Office of Economic Opportunity (OEO). It did not take long for the research staff of the agency to realize that not very much was known about the characteristics of the poor in the United States, and even less about the impact that OEO's action programs might be having on those poor people. It was, therefore, decided to get new data on these questions by administering a survey to a large number of families (30,000). Low-income census tracts were sampled more than proportionally because of the central purpose of the survey. All the dwelling units were interviewed in early 1966 and a subset of them were interviewed again in early 1967, along with a new (independently drawn) subsample to make up the same total.

[1] F. Thomas Juster, "Microdata, Economic Research, and the Production of Economic Knowledge," *American Economic Review*, May 1970.

Since OEO did not have the machinery to undertake the survey themselves, they contracted with the Census Bureau to do it for them. However, in addition to providing up-to-date information on the ten-ongoing poverty programs, the SEO was also designed to provide a data base for more fundamental analytic studies of the social process that produces and perpetuates poverty. The instrument, therefore, included a broader set of household variables than had been traditional in Census surveys.

Although the interviews took place in 1966 and 1967, it is only within the past year that any volume of analytic work has been produced using these data, and the longitudinal subsample has not yet been exploited on a wide scale. Also, when the basic information on size and status of various parts of the poverty population were initially pulled together and made available they conflicted with other sources, producing inconsistencies that have yet to be satisfactorily and completely resolved. Why the three-year lag—which was totally unpredicted by the planners and was never recognized as inevitable even when the data were being processed?

The first data tapes were made available (from the initial, 1966 survey wave) by the Census Bureau in late Spring of 1967. This was much later than everyone had expected for the results of the first cross-section. Indeed there had been plans to use its results to guide the second wave administered in the first months of 1967.

The fielding and administering of the questionnaires caused no apparent problem; but reliable transcription of the data from the questionnaires into analyzable form proved intractable to a degree which was a complete surprise to the Census Bureau—hardly a novice at large-scale data collection.

The problem centered on the fact that the Census organization was geared to the ordinary operation of a multi-program, data-production system that was completely routinized. The adaptation of this system to a different task proved unexpectedly difficult even for experienced technicians. Most prominently, the variables which were unique to the Survey of Economic Opportunity required both new conceptual work and new computer-programming work before the data could be edited and checked, and before missing items could be accounted for and allocated.

In fact the Census Bureau divided the task—processing themselves the part which could use the existing routines for the Current Population Survey (C.P.S.), and subcontracting (to ARIES Corporation) the new or unique segments. Unfortunately the coded identifiers for individual families were not always unique so that it proved impossible to put the two segments back together for some of the households. This error was not discovered until the Fall of 1967 after a substantial amount of effort had been spent on further "data cleaning."

But there was a second major problem as well, connected with the problem of making data in unaggregated form available to researchers. Providing so-called "raw" data was not something the U.S. Census Bureau had done routinely or comfortably. They observe very high standards for all statistical products made available for general consumption. Their sense of responsibility may even be said to have developed to the point where, in their efforts to preclude all possibility of foolish or perverse interpretation of their statistics, they prevent interpretation of any kind. This instance proved no exception. They were extremely uneasy about releasing micro-data even to OEO (which commissioned them) for fear of the multifarious uses to which they might conceivably be put.

Their discomfiture was enhanced by another dimension to the problem. Many of the analyses anticipated for the SEO data involved multi-variable regression and multi-variate analysis. Such processes, of course, produce results that are much more sensitive to data editing and allocation practices than are the tabulations traditionally produced by the Census Bureau. In other words, cross tabulations usually have open-ended categories, and these can contain an occasional wild error without appreciable effect upon any interpretation that might be placed on the central or modal segment. Not so with more sophisticated statistical tools.

It is certainly the case that there is no reason to "clean" data beyond the point of diminishing returns for tabular analysis if that is all you need. But, at the same time, any census bureau must hesitate to provide ammunition for challenges to its authority; and the possibility that the data might not be absolutely clean when released must have been quite threatening. Since that time, however, the Bureau has relaxed its stance on release of micro-data, and it is now possible to get non-disclosing copies of the Current Population Survey tapes.

In any case, when the data were turned over to OEO in May of 1967 they were still well short of the micro-analytic standards the OEO sponsors required. Consequently, further data cleaning was contracted to the Brookings Institution, who, along with Assist Corp., also spent at least twice as much time on the job as they had anticipated. And, they also, no doubt, relinquished the data before being fully satisfied. The Brookings-Assist data, now including both annual Surveys were, however, clean enough in OEO's opinion to be made available to researchers on September 3, 1969 along with voluminous (and clear and complete) documentation, describing in detail the data on the actual magnetic tapes.

Now the cause for delay shifted to the potential users. In order to facilitate access to the data, OEO contracted with the Data and Computation Center at the University of Wisconsin to be the repository, distributor and service agency for the SEO files.[2] Consultation and guidance were also to be provided by the Institute for Research on Poverty. At the same time several other, mostly university-based, researchers obtained copies of the tapes. But despite the excellence of documentation, all users experienced unexpected delays of from two to six months in getting the data "running," i.e. in gaining enough familiarity with the files so that at least half the attempts to use it were successful.

After the required familiarity had been established, however, the data file appeared to be unnecessarily costly to use. It was clear that a specified restructuring would literally decimate the costs of any analysis at Wisconsin. We could not afford to ignore such a large cost factor, so the restructuring took place, with further frustrating delays for researchers who had by now been anticipating being able to use the data for three years. They were finally able to begin their analyses in the summer of 1970.

    [2] See the note by Max E. Ellis, "Social Science Computing at the University of Wisconsin: SIMS and SEOSYS," *Annals of Economic and Social Measurement*, Vol. 1, Number 2, April 1972.

Such work as has been done utilizes mainly the cross-sectional aspect of the SEO. So far very little work has been done with the continuous data records from both years. And there still remain further problems for users when the longitudinal aspects of the data begin to be exploited on a wider scale.

Two major problems exist. First, the longitudinal property of the data lies in the fact that the same "dwelling unit" was interviewed each time. Obviously this means that the same family may or may not have been there the second time. A certain number of records, therefore, are not going to be longitudinal in the micro-data sense. Before any analysis can be done, explicit account has to be taken of out-movers and in-movers so that they, and the truly continuous residents, can be treated appropriately.

The second problem is common to all micro-data sets, has to be solved by every analyst in a way that best fits his purposes, and is as follows. Even when it has been ascertained that the "same" family was indeed in the same dwelling unit both times, it may well be that the composition of that family has changed (slightly or drastically). A new child may be born or there may be a new family head, or a sub-family unit may have been created or destroyed. There are no obvious general rules about what changes require one to regard the changed unit as an essentially new one, but it is necessary to come up with some rule before the data can be properly used. The profession has not given much thought, hitherto, to the fact that a decision unit observed at time t may not exist at $t + 1$ or $t + 2$ (or may not have been there at $t - 1$). But when we attempt to use data generated by real units over a period of time such a problem is impossible to ignore. The solution, of course, depends on the conceptual foundations of one's specific analysis.

This, then, is the story of one relatively modest effort in the direction of a data bank. OEO aimed at producing a body of generally useful data (though focused on their concerns) and Census, Brookings, Assist, and the Poverty Institute have contributed in serial fashion to facilitating their use by researchers. It has taken a long while and we are still short of the goal.

Many of the problems appear to have been particular and specific to these data, but the order of magnitude of the problems, and the lack of any possibility of using previously-solved problems to expedite their solution, are common to all large micro-data bodies. And the person does not yet exist with the practical experience required to set up a data bank capable of handling such sets of data in their full generality. There are specialists who know about one specific applied concern, but their expertise is not yet transferable to other on-going data-collection efforts without a new learning process.

The Urban Graduated Work Incentive Experiment

The Graduated Work Incentive Experiment in New Jersey is a new departure in social experimentation which was funded in the summer of 1967 and fielded in August 1968. About 650 families (four sites in urban New Jersey and one in Pennsylvania) are receiving transfer payments of a negative income tax type, and roughly the same number are acting as a control group. The payments will continue over a three-year period. We collect income and family-size information for the experimental families every four weeks over the payment period, and during this period both experimental and control families are administered an hour-long interview every three months.

Although payments started in 1968, it was not until the summer of 1970 that we were able to use our automated data system to retrieve any data, and the lag between when the information was coming in from the field and when it was retrievable by researchers was on the order of eight months. Since that time the lag has been becoming shorter and shorter, and data are now retrievable that are only three or four months out of the field.

As this short description will indicate, the "data-banking" problems faced in New Jersey are quite distinct from those faced in connection with the SEO. There are relatively fewer units of observation, but the information on each is voluminous. First of all there is information from thirteen hour-long interviews over the three-year payment period. These interviews have the same fifteen-minute core section (on labor supply) each time, but the rest of the hour is taken up with questions that vary from interview to interview. Some of the variables are measured repeatedly and some only once. Some of the families get lost—cannot be found or refuse to be interviewed—and most of the families undergo a change in composition or residence or both during the period of observation. The questionnaire structure (skip patterns and questions asked of different family members) is complex, imposing stringent standards on interview administration and completeness and consistency checking. In addition, there are four-weekly records of income and experimental payments for the part of the sample receiving "treatments."

Our aim is to produce a data source which is readily usable by research personnel. We are, therefore, concerned that an analyst be able to draw freely on variables from different survey waves or from other sources in order to "compose" and analyze a simple rectangular array of data for any sample of decision units that he may want to examine. This sounds like a modest goal, particularly since the same organization is responsible both for collecting and "banking" the data in this case. But no matter how simple and ultimately feasible this task may be, we can only proceed with frustrating slowness. There is no fund of experience to draw on in designing and executing the kind of data system we need—partly because the nature of the sample and study design are both novel and partly also because the technology, soft and hard, has been changing so rapidly.

Choice of Technology

As far as technology is concerned, I regard it as important to make an early and resolute decision about the kind of equipment and systems to be used. The choice should be made only among those alternatives that are already in sufficiently wide use to ensure (1) that valid information can be obtained on their performances in comparable applications *and* (2) that they have evolved a relatively stable, bug-free, and optimal set of software systems.

It requires some determination to avoid the choice of the latest equipment on the frontier. Such machinery always offers an exciting challenge to the system- and program-development staff, and the promise is always held out that the system eventually evolved will be superior to the potential of the more proven hardware. But I would emphasize that the costs of unforeseen difficulties and delays are almost always very great. If the aim is to produce research in a reasonable period of time, the temptation to pioneer in computer systems must be resisted. Clearly one choice cannot be made for all time; but the strategy of *first* getting a working data facility and *then* catching up with the technology is the more prudent if delivering research products along the way is of any importance.

More needs to be said about how any micro-data system can, in the current stage of development, be ideally used by a researcher. The speed and cost of executing a given task of data manipulation is important in determining how much calculation will have to be done, and this may work in a somewhat perverse way: i.e., the slower and more costly it is to make one pass of the data file, the more likely it is that a researcher will try to anticipate all his potential needs on one pass. This strategy can be only partially successful in reducing future requests, but it does have a dramatic effect on the size of individual requests and on the amount of output accumulated: the more the analyst can replace an exhaustive set of possible choices with a sequence of choices conditioned upon previous outcomes, the more unnecessary calculation and superfluous output can be avoided. Hence the system should be designed to encourage a sharply-focused approach, and discourage the random shots.

The "Data Technician"

Ideally, a data system would be so automatic, self-describing, and well documented, that a research analyst could determine whether (and if so, how) the data could be used for his problem, and be able to carry out the job without assistance. It may well be possible to specify and design such a system, and it is certainly tempting to try and find one. But such an effort, again, will divert attention and resources away from getting research done in the near future. The more feasible approach for the next several years is to use a human intermediary who might be called a "data technician." The essential qualifications for such a person are: (1) the ability to communicate effectively with the researchers on the one hand, and with the computer technicians (operators, programmers, and system managers) on the other, and (2) a taste for detail that facilitates acquiring and retaining all of the "unwritten documentation," which seems to be an absolute requirement if one is to be able to use existing bodies of micro-data. To these might be added the third requirement—the capacity not to be easily discouraged.

There is now and for the foreseeable future a substantial fixed cost attached to the "first usage" of a new data set. Without the data specialist described above, who has become familiar with the data by struggling through that first use, much of that cost has to be incurred again by every subsequent user. Such a data technician can work directly with all users, determining first whether and generally how the data can be used to fill the researcher's need, and secondly whether to carry out the work him or herself or to train the user to do the job. This latter choice will depend on the size and complexity of the job and on the user's ability to learn enough to do it (or alternatively to pay for the service of having it done). But without such a person (who is either familiar with the data or has the responsibility for becoming so), users will be scared off a new data file by the complexity of "getting into" it. And those who are not put off immediately will become discouraged (or impoverished) to the point of abandoning the effort before they get any results. To repeat: Such a data-specialist could be dispensed with in an ideal "data bank," but for the foreseeable future I believe it to be an indispensable part of any organization that aims at facilitating the use of complex micro-data sources.

The Use of Still-Accumulating Data Files

Additional problems and opportunities are encountered when a body of data is being used while still in the process of collection—as is the case with the Negative Income Tax data being gathered in New Jersey. Such was (and is) the need for any information on this subject that the data system had to become operational before the eventual dimensions of the data base were fixed. Research production and the programming related to it, therefore, compete for time and budget with the development of the data system *per se*. Files extracted for analytic use will become obsolete as errors are corrected, coding is improved, data are added, and temporarily lost families recovered. Early results must, therefore, be expected to be inconsistent (usually in trivial ways) with those obtained later in the process.

Important offsetting advantages do, however, exist. The fact that data producers, data users, and system designers *have* to work together reduces the chance of serious mistakes—those requiring part of the basic job to be done over again. Interim or preliminary use of the data results in the discovery of problems and ambiguities in time for revisions, before the difficulty has been replicated throughout the data. In retrospect, for example, it is quite clear that the SEO would have been available in useful form much earlier (and would in fact have been a superior data set) if there had been serious and urgent analytic interest at the Census Bureau within the group responsible for producing the research-ready tape.

Summary and Advice

Despite the many recent technical developments in computer hardware and software systems I remain awed at the difficulty of building a usable data bank, and also awed at the readiness with which such a concept is often discussed as feasible. My own experience suggests that efforts in this direction err on the over-ambitious side, and consequently are so long in gestation that the interest of the research analyst is lost. I cannot overemphasize this: If the primary objective is to facilitate real research, start small and develop competence with one basic body of data. Once you have handled that task, proceed to others.

The very latest in technology is another pitfall to be avoided. Unless you have endless time, money, and patience, use equipment and software systems that have known and stable characteristics. The newest and fastest may eventually be the best, but getting it to work will *always* take longer than anyone expects.

At the present time, a person-plus-machine system, utilizing what I have called a data technician as a communicator and ambulating documentation file, is the best way to get started. Again, it may be that a more direct system can evolve from this, as the technician finds ways to reduce the number of simple and repeti-tive requests. But there is simply not enough experience in this area at this time for anyone to feel confident about starting out with an automated system alone.

Finally, I would urge that a data bank be focused from the start on the needs of specific analysts—people who exist, are alive, and on the premises. They must be persuaded to become involved in the process of system design from the start; and they must be impatient enough for results to try out and test pieces of the system and the data file as soon as they begin to take shape.

All this may sound like a counsel of despair. That is not my intent. But, however ambitious one wants to be in planning toward some ultimate general data bank, it is imperative to start somewhere and get some real work *done*. The beginning must be quite modest if we are to make any progress at all.

USES OF TAX FILES COMBINED WITH FIELD SURVEYS

BENJAMIN A. OKNER AND JOSEPH A. PECHMAN

The Brookings Institution*

For a long time, income-distribution analysts have been hampered in their research because the available data have not represented the entire income-receiving population or have failed to include all of the income known to have been received by that population. On the one hand, distributions of income based on tax returns omit persons who do not file; on the other, distributions based on field surveys, which provide demographic and other data not available on tax returns, omit a large fraction of total income because of underreporting by respondents. With the advent of the computer, it is now possible to combine the best information on tax files and field surveys so that the two sources can be used together for research purposes. The purpose of this paper is to describe the methods we at Brookings have used to merge the information in two such files for the calendar year 1966, to report briefly on the distribution of income that emerged, and to outline our plans for future research on the basis of the MERGE data file.

In creating the MERGE File, we combined information on 30,000 families and single persons included in the 1967 Survey of Economic Opportunity (SEO) conducted by the U.S. Census Bureau for the Office of Economic Opportunity, and a file containing information from 90,000 U.S. federal individual income-tax returns. Thus, the MERGE File contains data for low-income SEO families who are not in the tax-filing population, as well as the more complete—and, we believe, more accurate—income tax information for higher-income individuals. In addition, we corrected the income information in the MERGE File for non-reporting and underreporting, so that—with the appropriate weights applied to the sample units—the file accounts for the total income (on almost any desired definition of income) estimated to have been received in the United States in 1966.

The most important characteristic of the file is that calculations can be made on the basis of individual records at great speed and with a high degree of accuracy. Moreover, it is no longer necessary to make assumptions regarding the average characteristics of an entire income class or population cell in a cross-classification. The availability of information for individual families permits us to provide answers about a much wider variety of economic and social questions than has been possible heretofore.

---

* This study was financed under a research grant to the Brookings Institution from the U.S. Office of Economic Opportunity. The views presented in this paper are those of the authors and not necessarily those of the officers, trustees, or other staff members of the Brookings Institution, or of the Office of Economic Opportunity. All programming and computer operations described in the paper were performed at the Brookings' Social Science Computation Center. Stephen W. Kidd and Robert Wallace were responsible for the computer programming and we gratefully acknowledge their efforts on our behalf.

CREATING THE MERGE DATA FILE[1]

Since the SEO income reporting units are a sample of the entire U.S. population and the returns in the Tax File are a sample of only the tax-filing population, we based the final MERGE File on the demographic information for the families in the SEO File.[2] However, we substituted the income data in the Tax File for the corresponding information in the SEO File to take advantage of the superior income reporting on tax returns (including the information on capital gains that is excluded from the SEO-Census income concept). This was done by first estimating (on the basis of reported SEO information) the kind of tax return or returns that would have been filed by each family and, then, for tax-filers, by matching each "SEO tax unit" with a tax return selected from the Tax File.

The ideal method of matching the SEO data with the tax data would have been to obtain the tax information directly from the Internal Revenue Service. But this was not practical because neither the Census Bureau nor the Internal Revenue Service permits others to use their files, even for statistical purposes. In place of an exact one-to-one match, a less satisfactory—but feasible—means of simulating a match was developed. In effect, we randomly selected from the Tax File a return "similar" to the SEO return and then substituted the income data in the tax record for the information in the SEO record. Since close to 30,000 matches had to be made, the selection and linking of returns in the SEO and Tax Files was performed on a computer.[3]

For most families, the final MERGE File contains the demographic data and information on receipts of nontaxable income from the SEO File plus taxable income figures from the return or returns assigned to it from the Tax File. For SEO units deemed to be nonfilers, the MERGE File includes no tax return information. Since there are very few high-income units in the SEO File, the upper "tail" of the Tax File (returns with incomes above $30,000) was substituted in toto for the SEO tail. For this group, which represents less than 2 percent of the entire population, the MERGE File does not contain any SEO demographic data.

The basic definition of income in the MERGE File is adjusted family income (AFI),[4] a concept which was developed for the tax-burden study described below. The basic data for estimating AFI were obtained from the Office of Business Economics (OBE) personal income accounts, individual income-tax information

---

[1] For a detailed description of the methods described in this section, see Benjamin A. Okner, "Constructing a New Data Base From Existing Microdata Sets: The 1966 MERGE File," *Annals of Economic and Social Measurement*, Vol. 1 (July 1972).

[2] In this paper, the term "families" refers to both unrelated individuals (one-person families) and the conventional Census family consisting of two or more persons, related by blood, marriage, or adoption.

[3] The characteristics used to link the two files were (1) marital status, (2) age of head of the unit, (3) number of dependents, (4) pattern of income, and (5) major and minor sources of income. The basic rule was to match a SEO unit with a tax unit having the same characteristics and major source income within 2 percent of the major source income reported in the SEO survey.

[4] "Adjusted family income" as used in this paper corresponds to an augmented national income concept. Since this paper was completed the authors have decided that an income concept corresponding to augmented net national product is more appropriate for measuring effective tax burdens. In later work, therefore, the concept referred to here as "adjusted family income" is renamed "family income." "Adjusted family income" in subsequent work is equal to family income plus indirect business taxes.

from the Internal Revenue Service, and other government records, which were adjusted—where necessary—to take account of differences in income concept and of population covered. The AFI concept is intended to correspond as closely as practicable to an economic concept of income, i.e., it is equal to consumption plus tax payments plus (or minus) the net increase (or decrease) in the value of assets during the year. AFI includes only income which accrues *directly* to individuals and families; as a consequence, it does not include the income of fiduciaries and other recipients not represented in the SEO population.[5]

After substituting tax return data for the SEO income data, the total income accounted for by units in the MERGE File amounted to 93 percent of the AFI computed for 1966 (see Table 1). The next step in creating the MERGE File involved adjusting the SEO and Tax File income data to correspond with national aggregates. As Table 1 indicates, the aggregates for wages and salaries were very

TABLE 1

COMPARISON BETWEEN ADJUSTED FAMILY INCOME AND MERGE FILE INCOME BEFORE ADJUSTMENT,
BY SOURCE OF INCOME, 1966
[dollar figures in billions]

Source of Income	Adjusted Family Income (1)	MERGE File Income[1] (2)	Difference (3)=(1)-(2)	MERGE File Income as Percent of Adjusted Family Income (4)=(2)÷(1)
Wages, salaries, and other labor	$423	$415	$ 8	98%
Nonfarm proprietors	43	46	− 3	107
Farm proprietors	14	6	8	43
Rents and royalties	20	16	4	80
Personal interest	24	21	3	88
Corporate earnings	64[2]	60	4	94
Transfer payments	34	25	9	74
Accrued capital gains on inventories, farm assets, and nonfarm real estate	37	27	10	73
Total	$660	$616	$33	93%

Note: Details may not add to totals because of rounding.

[1] MERGE File income excludes adjustments for nonreporting and underreporting of income.

[2] Includes corporation income tax and undistributed profits.

close. On the other hand, reported farm proprietors' income was only 43 percent of the expected AFI amount, and there were less serious, but significant, discrepancies between the expected and reported amounts of interest, rent, and transfer payments. Some of the discrepancies were due to the partial coverage of the Census money-income concept, which was used in the field survey; the remainder was due to nonreporting and underreporting of income by respondents.

Although nonreporting and underreporting are conceptually separable, in practice it is difficult to distinguish these two types of response errors. On the

[5] For a detailed description of how the AFI figures were derived, see Benjamin A. Okner, "Adjusted Family Income: Concept and Derivation," Brookings Technical Working Paper II, for the Distribution of Federal, State, and Local Taxes Research Program, March 1971 (revised, mimeographed), which is available on request.

basis of data from other sources, we believe that most of the differences between
the reported and AFI aggregate factor-payment amounts resulted from underreporting, while transfer payments were understated primarily because of nonreporting.

For income components where we believed the discrepancies were due
to underreporting, the MERGE File data were adjusted to the AFI aggregates on
the assumption that the underreporting was not related to other characteristics
of the survey unit. A single ratio was therefore applied to the reported incomes
of all units to increase them to the aggregate adjusted family income amounts. In
the case of nonreporting, we imputed missing amounts stochastically to MERGE
File units, based on various other characteristics of the survey units.

In addition to the adjustments for underreporting and nonreporting, several
imputations were made to add information to the MERGE File which was not
available—because it was not collected—in either the SEO or the Tax Files. These
included imputed rent on owner-occupied homes, employer supplements to wage
and salary income, tax-exempt interest on state and local bonds, and accrued
capital gains on assets.[6]

The final MERGE File records each contain the original demographic,
income (corrected for underreporting), employment, education, and other data
derived from the SEO[7] plus one or more tax segments containing the income tax
data for these families. We have also prepared a 10 percent sample of the file for
use in rapidly checking out computer programs and estimation techniques. The
complete file and the sample are stored on disc packs for rapid calculations on the
Brookings' PDP-10 computer, but they are also available on magnetic tape. The
time required to obtain a simple tabulation of several characteristics of families
classified by, say, 30 income classes is roughly ten minutes on the sample and one
hour on the complete file. Using our "tax calculator program," calculations of
federal tax liabilities under the present tax law, or under several variants, can be
completed in less than two hours on the entire file. We have efficient cross-tabulation programs available for use on the file and a recently written output package
that provides us with a high degree of flexibility for printing tables in virtually
free-form format. In addition, we have a Calcomp 565 digital plotter and, with
the software developed for its use, we have the ability to produce graphic as well
as tabular displays of our results.

DISTRIBUTION OF INCOME

Before proceeding to income distributions derived from the current MERGE
File, we think it would be useful to describe more fully the relationship between
the SEO-Census and adjusted family-income concepts.

[6] Imputed rent was allocated on the basis of the equity in owner-occupied homes reported by
respondents. Wage supplements were based on the occupational, industrial, and wage characteristics
reported by the survey units. State-local bond interest was based on the distribution of state-local bond
ownership from the Federal Reserve Board's 1963 Survey of Financial Characteristics. Accrued gains
on assets were based largely on realized capital gains and property income reported on tax returns.
Details concerning these imputations are reported in Benjamin A. Okner, "The Imputation of Missing
Income Information," Brookings Technical Working Paper III, for the Distribution of Federal, State,
and Local Taxes Research Program, April 1971 (mimeographed), which is available on request.

[7] Even though they contain very limited data inferred from the tax return, the MERGE File does
contain a demographic record segment for each high-income "upper-tail" tax return.

SEO-Census money income is essentially a total money receipts concept (except that receipts from the sales of capital assets are excluded). AFI is an accrued income concept. Therefore, in order to go from SEO-Census to adjusted family income, it is necessary to: (1) subtract money receipts that do not represent current income; and (2) add income not counted as current receipts by the Census.

The derivation involves the following steps:

(figures in billions of dollars)

SEO-Census money receipts		524
Less:		
Federal government pensions	4	
State and local government pensions	2	
Veterans' life insurance	1	
Subtotal		−7
Plus:		
Employee wage supplements	40	
Net imputed rent	12	
Imputed interest	6	
Retained corporate profits	22	
Corporate income tax	26	
Accrued capital gains on inventories, farm assets, and nonfarm real estate	37	
Subtotal		143
Equals adjusted family income		660

In essence, adjusted family income is equal to national income (as defined in the national income accounts)[8] plus transfer payments plus accrued gains on farm assets and nonfarm real estate. In keeping with the national income concept, AFI includes corporation incomes before tax. The portion of corporate income distributed as dividends is included in money receipts and is not shown separately in the derivation above. However, undistributed profits and corporation tax liability must be added to income to derive AFI. This procedure has the advantage not only of consistency but also of providing a complete account of the accrued income claims of the household sector. Retained earnings of corporations, which are thus automatically included in adjusted family income, may be regarded as an approximation of accrued capital gains on corporate stock during the year.[9]

[8] The only departure from the official definition of income is the omission of interest imputed to individuals for the services rendered to them by the banking system.

[9] We used this approximation because the annual fluctuations in the value of corporate stock are high and even three-to-five-year averages may not give an adequate representation of accrued capital gains. Martin J. Bailey and Martin David have shown that over very long periods, capital gains on corporate securities are roughly equal to retained earnings. See Martin J. Bailey, "Capital Gains and Income Taxation" in Arnold C. Harberger and Martin J. Bailey, eds., *The Taxation of Income from Capital*, Brookings Institution, 1969, pp. 15–26; and Martin David, *Alternative Approaches to Capital Gains Taxation*, Brookings Institution, 1968, pp. 242–246.

Even after substituting tax return data for the income reported by the SEO respondents, total SEO-Census money income in the MERGE File totaled only $489 billion, or about $35 billion less than the amount expected.[10] The adjustments made to correct for underreporting and nonreporting of income raised the median money income from its initial level of $7,508 to $8,592 after correction.

TABLE 2
COMPARISON OF SHARES OF SEO-CENSUS MONEY INCOME RECEIVED BY EACH FIFTH OF FAMILIES BEFORE
AND AFTER ADJUSTMENT FOR NONREPORTING AND UNDERREPORTING OF INCOME

Families Ranked from Lowest to Highest	Before Adjustment		After Adjustment	
	Income Range (dollars)	Percent of Income Received	Income Range (dollars)	Percent of Income Received
Lowest fifth	Under 2,823	4.3	Under 3,261	3.4
Second fifth	2,823– 5,416	10.9	3,261– 6,057	10.7
Middle fifth	5,416– 7,878	17.4	6,057– 8,747	17.0
Fourth fifth	7,878–11,000	24.6	8,747–12,500	23.8
Highest fifth	11,000 and over	42.7	12,500 and over	45.1
Top 5 percent	16,922 and over	16.4	20,227 and over	19.1
Top 1 percent	28,333 and over	5.5	44,792 and over	6.8

In Table 2, we show the share of income received by each fifth of the families, when they are ranked from lowest to highest, before and after the income adjustments. Before correction, the lowest fifth of the families had incomes under $2,823 and received 4.3 percent of total income. The highest fifth of the families had incomes of $11,000 or more and received 42.7 percent of the total. After adjustment, the poorest fifth of the families had incomes under $3,261 and received 3.4 percent of the total; the highest fifth moved up to $12,500 and received 45.1 percent of total income.

Although the upward shift can be seen all along the income distribution, the effect is most pronounced among those at the very top. Before adjustment, the top 5 percent included families with incomes of $16,922 and over and they received 16.4 percent of total money income. After adjustment, the top 5 percent included families with incomes of $20,227 and over and this group received 19.1 percent of the total money income. The share of the total received by the top 1 percent of all families increased from 5.5 percent to 6.8 percent after adjustment.[11] This large change in the relative distribution of income mainly reflects the addition of high-income family units which were omitted from the original SEO population.

We now turn to the presentation of the MERGE data classified by still another income concept—money factor income (MFI). As shown in Table 3A, MFI is equal to the sum of wages, farm and nonfarm proprietors' income, rents

[10] This exceeds the $33 billion difference shown in Table 1 because of conceptual differences between items in the SEO-Census and adjusted family income concepts.

[11] It should be noted that we have chosen the SEO-Census money income concept for comparison purposes only because it is the most comprehensive one that is available on a before adjustment basis in the SEO. However, we have retained all the detailed income components in the MERGE File for maximum flexibility. Thus, the researcher is free to define income any way he wishes to suit his own particular needs.

TABLE 3A

DERIVATION OF 1966 TOTAL MONEY FACTOR INCOME IN THE FAMILY MERGE FILE, BY COMPONENT

[amounts in millions]

Money Factor Income (000's)	Wage & Salary Income	Nonfarm Proprietors' Income	Farm Proprietors' Income	Rent & Royalty Income	Dividend Income	Monetary Interest Income	Total Money Factor Income
Under 1	2,489.023	−1,135.015	−3,015.265	−1,679.803	330.265	957.598	−2,053.197
1–2	3,539.452	180.010	6.655	154.335	321.126	899.536	5,101.113
2–3	5,460.715	538.434	160.322	308.002	305.282	874.992	7,647.746
3–4	9,297.470	784.080	92.171	220.297	346.643	874.872	11,615.533
4–5	13,521.933	1,227.001	257.821	346.056	241.525	839.732	16,434.068
5–6	20,803.325	1,240.478	440.048	81.511	224.297	660.978	23,450.637
6–7	22,474.012	1,239.152	422.834	205.781	306.262	702.837	25,350.880
7–8	29,823.461	1,627.226	292.097	231.719	234.753	705.991	32,915.248
8–9	34,218.634	1,699.995	611.873	99.672	262.307	805.379	37,697.857
9–10	28,880.215	1,425.900	547.015	163.020	335.240	619.602	31,970.993
10–11	30,711.309	2,070.669	357.582	155.244	544.639	683.615	34,523.056
11–12	27,330.153	1,761.201	462.961	365.668	340.639	597.007	30,857.627
12–13	23,457.244	2,530.382	385.534	217.522	370.665	633.419	27,594.767
13–14	20,684.459	2,215.073	445.764	351.263	459.247	632.021	24,787.827
14–15	17,166.195	2,185.835	406.394	238.448	225.261	522.705	20,744.840
15–20	49,085.511	5,750.749	2,519.856	1,288.877	1,150.266	1,831.223	61,626.478
20–25	17,396.036	2,897.263	1,606.761	889.643	768.906	792.584	24,351.198
25–50	21,731.693	9,836.769	4,651.733	3,014.206	2,641.823	1,694.471	43,570.689
50–100	5,410.753	4,598.426	1,008.093	1,438.451	2,407.229	962.263	15,825.211
100–500	2,042.475	1,738.098	363.844	690.308	2,634.702	882.822	8,352.249
500–1,000	60.671	76.571	1.176	24.373	401.207	36.658	600.655
1,000+	20.916	42.582	−3.324	15.719	453.445	19.836	549.174
Total	385,605.660	44,530.879	12,021.945	8,820.311	15,305.729	17,230.140	483,514.650

TABLE 3B

NUMBER OF FAMILIES WITH 1966 TOTAL MONEY FACTOR INCOME IN THE FAMILY MERGE FILE, BY COMPONENT

[population in thousands]

Money Factor Income (000's)	Wage & Salary Income	Nonfarm Proprietors' Income	Farm Proprietors' Income	Rent & Royalty Income	Dividend Income	Monetary Interest Income	Total Money Factor Income
Under 1	2,457.957	511.323	430.889	616.838	678.343	3,435.113	9,357.429
1–2	2,382.836	330.967	214.146	544.397	586.357	1,701.577	3,447.173
2–3	2,379.826	354.548	307.496	393.006	468.173	1,409.837	3,074.655
3–4	2,851.253	435.630	164.838	363.616	461.004	1,411.806	3,316.938
4–5	3,178.775	549.791	186.630	336.985	387.038	1,592.963	3,645.549
5–6	3,990.247	493.874	174.154	266.499	502.543	1,929.612	4,253.833
6–7	3,668.725	411.803	150.254	258.433	505.253	2,050.490	3,886.884
7–8	4,174.483	496.773	158.357	330.647	652.752	2,395.625	4,386.948
8–9	4,273.991	479.613	170.591	345.919	753.630	2,610.897	4,442.586
9–10	3,241.476	335.722	127.362	271.748	604.806	2,113.139	3,364.848
10–11	3,136.919	428.016	226.588	283.802	788.207	2,192.650	3,285.386
11–12	2,590.504	333.780	284.356	305.400	665.965	1,932.792	2,685.208
12–13	2,059.316	346.676	219.937	224.526	607.219	1,524.591	2,206.159
13–14	1,717.743	331.400	211.707	177.300	645.901	1,360.911	1,837.235
14–15	1,352.595	311.139	192.464	187.700	489.588	1,120.242	1,432.035
15–20	3,344.962	700.826	509.311	565.174	1,419.797	2,843.125	3,607.209
20–25	991.349	264.326	187.384	288.932	615.657	933.868	1,108.326
25–50	1,043.833	538.435	303.546	350.025	826.737	1,136.851	1,330.302
50–100	157.164	133.689	48.593	97.118	196.791	227.472	238.876
100–500	35.190	31.548	11.684	25.146	49.659	53.785	54.633
500–1,000	0.529	0.598	0.223	0.502	0.878	0.893	0.900
1,000+	0.168	0.169	0.077	0.174	0.280	0.275	0.283
Total	49,029.842	7,820.648	4,280.586	6,233.886	11,906.578	33,978.514	60,963.395

TABLE 3C

AVERAGE AMOUNT OF 1966 TOTAL MONEY FACTOR INCOME PER RECIPIENT FAMILY IN THE FAMILY MERGE FILE, BY COMPONENT

Money Factor Income (000's)	Wage & Salary Income	Nonfarm Proprietors' Income	Farm Proprietors' Income	Rent & Royalty Income	Dividend Income	Monetary Interest Income	Total Money Factor Income
Under 1	1,013	-2,220	-6,998	-2,723	487	279	-219
1-2	1,485	544	31	283	548	529	1,480
2-3	2,295	1,519	521	784	652	621	2,487
3-4	3,261	1,800	559	606	752	620	3,502
4-5	4,254	2,232	1,381	1,027	624	527	4,508
5-6	5,214	2,512	2,527	306	446	343	5,513
6-7	6,126	3,009	2,814	796	606	343	6,522
7-8	7,144	3,276	1,845	701	360	295	7,503
8-9	8,006	3,545	3,587	288	348	308	8,486
9-10	8,910	4,247	4,295	600	554	293	9,501
10-11	9,790	4,838	1,578	547	691	312	10,508
11-12	10,550	5,277	1,628	1,197	511	309	11,492
12-13	11,391	7,299	1,753	969	610	415	12,508
13-14	12,042	6,684	2,106	1,981	711	464	13,492
14-15	12,691	7,025	2,112	1,270	460	467	14,486
15-20	14,674	8,206	4,948	2,280	810	644	17,084
20-25	17,548	10,961	8,575	3,079	1,249	849	21,971
25-50	20,819	18,269	15,325	8,611	3,195	1,490	32,752
50-100	34,427	34,397	20,746	14,811	12,232	4,230	66,249
100-500	58,042	55,094	31,140	27,452	53,056	16,414	152,879
500-1,000	114,690	128,044	5,272	48,552	456,955	41,050	667,394
1,000+	124,502	251,964	-43,172	90,337	1,619,446	72,130	1,940,543

and royalties, dividends, and monetary interest. About 80 percent of the $483.5 billion total is from wage and salary income; 11 percent is proprietors' income; and the remaining 9 percent of MFI is income from property.

The average amount of each component of MFI received by MERGE File families is shown in Table 3C. With but one exception, the average amount received of each component rises as income increases. The exception is farm proprietors' income where the average per recipient family rises with income over most of the income range, but then drops sharply at the very highest income levels. This is consistent with other findings and results from the large losses of very wealthy "hobby farmers."

The next group of tables illustrates the distribution of various employer supplements to wages and salaries. As shown in Table 4A, contributions for private pension and welfare funds and for social security account for $29.1 billion, or 73 percent of the $39.7 billion total. The average contributions for each wage supplement component are shown in Table 4C. The averages for social security are particularly interesting since the maximum employer (and employee) payment in 1966 was $377. Yet, the average for recipient families in all the income classes between $15,000 and $50,000 exceeds the $377 maximum. The reason for this is that in these classes, there are numerous families with more than one earner with wages subject to social security.

More than 63 percent of total transfer payment income is derived from social security benefits (Table 5A); these benefits are fairly evenly distributed among families all along the income scale. Although far smaller than social security in magnitude, the same fairly even distribution is found for veterans' disability payments and the work-related workmen's compensation and unemployment insurance benefits. While such payments do play a role in maintaining income for families for short periods of disability, their wide distribution over the entire income scale suggests that they do not play a major role in improving the lot of the very poor. On the other hand, we find that over 70 percent of all public assistance payments go to families with money factor income under $1,000. The average amount of public assistance received is about $1,000 at the very lowest income levels and falls to about $650 per recipient family at $9,000 to $10,000 of MFI (Table 5C).[12]

Finally, we show some of our preliminary tax-distribution results in Table 6. Federal personal income taxes were derived directly from the tax segments in the MERGE File; the federal payroll taxes are equal to the sum of employee and employer contributions for social security, unemployment insurance, and workmen's compensation. Summarizing very briefly, we find that: (1) transfers as a percent of total income before transfers start out greater than 100 percent (i.e., they exceed nontransfer income) and then drop sharply as a percent of income as income rises; (2) the effective income tax rate rises steadily with income (except at the very bottom and top of the income scale where the relationship is distorted

---

[12] Those who are familiar with the stringent requirements for receiving public assistance in the United States may wonder about the units in the $5,000 to $10,000 income range who are shown as benefit recipients. The number of such recipient families is quite small and misreporting could explain some of these cases. In addition, a large proportion of these anomalous cases result from conceptual differences between the SEO reporting unit and the public-assistance recipient unit.

TABLE 4A

DERIVATION OF 1966 TOTAL EMPLOYER WAGE SUPPLEMENT CONTRIBUTIONS IN THE FAMILY MERGE FILE, BY COMPONENT
[amounts in millions]

Money Factor Income (000's)	Private Pensions & Welfare Funds	Social Security	Workmen's Compensation	Unemployment Insurance	Civilian Govt. Retirement	Total Wage Supplements
Under 1	116.180	82.645	14.348	28.076	25.174	266.424
1–2	88.297	138.127	20.143	52.920	25.691	325.178
2–3	166.930	218.630	37.397	103.868	32.352	559.176
3–4	308.809	371.450	63.174	163.215	71.308	977.957
4–5	507.937	540.699	95.288	205.137	109.618	1,458.680
5–6	835.147	817.468	148.858	277.478	198.807	2,277.759
6–7	947.097	859.963	161.414	268.237	261.387	2,498.097
7–8	1,350.520	1,086.905	214.850	331.338	332.933	3,316.547
8–9	1,531.295	1,175.635	245.164	368.140	374.194	3,694.428
9–10	1,343.361	954.988	205.519	305.630	265.161	3,074.659
10–11	1,403.553	977.354	216.491	303.782	295.804	3,196.983
11–12	1,195.591	824.431	192.354	256.980	333.292	2,802.649
12–13	987.764	703.200	165.573	220.585	265.760	2,342.883
13–14	827.701	598.500	141.845	182.321	238.409	1,988.777
14–15	764.536	492.470	122.448	150.255	185.673	1,715.383
15–20	1,937.397	1,315.225	333.408	391.692	670.004	4,647.724
20–25	655.948	402.829	118.633	110.468	229.462	1,517.340
25–50	1,375.267	391.531	112.894	119.285	180.244	2,179.220
50–100	532.773	37.932	11.772	11.356	3.562	597.394
100–500	204.231	8.857	2.827	2.673	0.000	218.585
500–1,000	6.067	0.133	0.042	0.040	0.000	6.281
1,000+	2.092	0.039	0.012	0.012	0.000	2.155
Total	17,088.493	11,999.012	2,624.456	3,853.489	4,098.837	39,664.278

TABLE 4B

NUMBER OF FAMILIES WITH 1966 TOTAL EMPLOYER WAGE SUPPLEMENT CONTRIBUTIONS IN THE FAMILY MERGE FILE, BY COMPONENT

[population in thousands]

Money Factor Income (000's)	Private Pensions & Welfare Funds	Social Security	Workmen's Compensation	Unemployment Insurance	Civilian Govt. Retirement	Total Wage Supplements
Under 1	1,072.682	2,145.439	1,258.784	1,202.734	269.477	2,233.013
1–2	1,205.976	2,257.495	1,626.985	1,424.428	315.946	2,338.243
2–3	1,481.001	2,297.935	1,945.995	1,755.864	268.033	2,377.388
3–4	1,901.549	2,734.466	2,435.797	2,192.666	428.099	2,842.449
4–5	2,139.169	3,028.648	2,815.052	2,469.359	509.718	3,162.998
5–6	2,873.048	3,789.565	3,576.395	3,215.683	723.082	3,982.800
6–7	2,684.104	3,400.618	3,273.008	2,945.586	800.160	3,660.742
7–8	3,200.066	3,947.927	3,809.620	3,427.562	915.807	4,165.629
8–9	3,321.654	4,025.991	3,934.519	3,612.908	930.475	4,263.599
9–10	2,631.721	3,104.561	3,031.827	2,822.850	661.493	3,232.480
10–11	2,481.685	3,005.705	2,867.422	2,673.599	694.160	3,129.486
11–12	2,054.205	2,440.003	2,398.662	2,188.453	729.019	2,570.747
12–13	1,664.540	1,971.490	1,916.791	1,755.938	526.952	2,045.777
13–14	1,350.345	1,644.423	1,599.718	1,478.623	471.191	1,711.200
14–15	1,052.629	1,317.798	1,259.844	1,144.284	358.398	1,340.987
15–20	2,650.982	3,192.479	3,064.216	2,835.589	1,110.003	3,342.923
20–25	735.124	954.493	897.274	815.902	305.234	986.681
25–50	832.545	1,010.771	916.910	877.777	199.631	1,035.403
50–100	148.403	153.461	147.123	148.086	1.417	153.461
100–500	35.112	35.188	34.798	35.061	0.000	35.188
500–1,000	0.529	0.529	0.528	0.529	0.000	0.529
1,000+	0.168	0.168	0.168	0.168	0.000	0.168
Total	35,517.236	46,459.153	42,811.435	39,023.648	10,218.294	48,611.889

TABLE 4C

AVERAGE AMOUNT OF 1966 TOTAL EMPLOYER WAGE SUPPLEMENT CONTRIBUTIONS PER RECIPIENT FAMILY IN THE FAMILY MERGE FILE, BY COMPONENT
[dollars]

Money Factor Income (000's)	Private Pensions & Welfare Funds	Social Security	Workmen's Compensation	Unemployment Insurance	Civilian Govt. Retirement	Total Wage Supplements
Under 1	108	39	11	23	93	119
1–2	73	61	12	37	81	139
2–3	113	95	19	59	121	235
3–4	162	136	26	74	167	344
4–5	237	179	34	83	215	461
5–6	291	216	42	86	275	572
6–7	353	253	49	91	327	682
7–8	422	275	56	97	364	796
8–9	461	292	62	102	402	867
9–10	510	308	68	108	401	951
10–11	566	325	76	114	426	1,022
11–12	582	338	80	117	457	1,090
12–13	593	357	86	126	504	1,145
13–14	613	364	89	123	506	1,162
14–15	726	374	97	131	518	1,279
15–20	731	412	109	138	604	1,390
20–25	892	422	132	135	752	1,538
25–50	1,652	387	123	136	903	2,105
50–100	3,590	247	80	77	2,515	3,893
100–500	5,817	252	81	76	0	6,212
500–1,000	11,469	251	79	76	0	11,874
1,000+	12,450	234	74	72	0	12,829

TABLE 5A

DERIVATION OF 1966 TOTAL TRANSFER PAYMENTS INCOME IN THE FAMILY MERGE FILE, BY COMPONENT

[amounts in millions]

Money Factor Income (000's)	Social Security Income	Public Assistance Income	Veterans' Disability Compensation	Workmen's Compensation	Unemployment Insurance Income	Total Transfer Payments
Under 1	8,647.367	3,008.471	1,412.064	263.073	139.805	13,470.782
1–2	2,492.056	379.298	289.048	206.163	125.267	3,491.831
2–3	1,704.710	219.548	263.931	110.262	166.961	2,465.413
3–4	1,400.755	195.552	254.366	179.365	169.468	2,199.506
4–5	1,065.517	117.557	181.372	113.935	163.022	1,641.403
5–6	1,019.246	103.719	230.804	185.951	193.173	1,732.893
6–7	744.477	38.761	208.995	155.483	168.234	1,315.950
7–8	644.688	42.843	221.764	121.898	195.404	1,226.596
8–9	601.159	54.878	178.054	136.137	124.147	1,094.375
9–10	417.606	41.054	96.064	111.383	126.556	792.663
10–11	559.525	0.000	133.919	81.927	128.987	904.358
11–12	324.767	0.000	172.054	50.947	80.481	628.249
12–13	376.466	0.000	130.638	43.764	67.380	618.248
13–14	369.463	0.000	76.946	45.492	51.920	543.820
14–15	218.866	0.000	81.102	58.628	37.398	395.994
15–20	609.433	0.000	173.020	156.087	93.951	1,032.491
20–25	178.769	0.000	23.885	31.924	30.131	264.710
25–50	174.449	0.000	41.355	14.219	16.022	246.045
50–100	2.430	0.000	1.527	0.068	0.000	4.026
100–500	0.000	0.000	0.000	0.000	0.000	0.000
500–1,000	0.000	0.000	0.000	0.000	0.000	0.000
1,000 +	0.000	0.000	0.000	0.000	0.000	0.000
Total	21,551.747	4,201.683	4,170.911	2,066.707	2,078.305	34,069.354

TABLE 5B

NUMBER OF FAMILIES WITH TRANSFER PAYMENTS INCOME IN THE FAMILY MERGE FILE, BY COMPONENT

[population in thousands]

Money Factor Income (000's)	Social Security Income	Public Assistance Income	Veterans' Disability Compensation	Workmen's Compensation	Unemployment Insurance Income	Total Transfer Payments
Under 1	6,769.122	2,986.344	996.499	99.251	206.914	7,733.105
1–2	1,832.159	415.831	177.482	102.722	234.073	2,202.947
2–3	1,318.674	269.072	184.991	88.883	284.162	1,695.896
3–4	1,045.731	195.276	157.925	128.497	299.968	1,501.279
4–5	858.767	164.369	146.042	154.959	319.557	1,362.928
5–6	788.343	147.790	187.696	194.729	366.522	1,398.285
6–7	603.194	75.688	126.048	151.610	352.044	1,155.268
7–8	584.207	80.723	188.414	182.035	426.341	1,274.392
8–9	493.563	90.705	177.452	156.658	285.563	1,060.857
9–10	375.869	62.791	122.708	127.589	285.692	882.547
10–11	406.227	0.000	127.141	137.269	263.707	845.968
11–12	290.776	0.000	115.428	91.999	165.720	617.771
12–13	265.014	0.000	89.835	76.552	156.283	529.597
13–14	258.445	0.000	78.372	55.795	86.857	433.748
14–15	171.693	0.000	87.787	71.412	74.420	338.929
15–20	473.560	0.000	158.318	146.100	205.816	903.449
20–25	171.752	0.000	41.990	26.749	40.220	258.908
25–50	129.841	0.000	41.324	13.755	36.654	203.572
50–100	2.288	0.000	1.186	0.580	0.000	2.869
100–500	0.000	0.000	0.000	0.000	0.000	0.000
500–1,000	0.000	0.000	0.000	0.000	0.000	0.000
1,000+	0.000	0.000	0.000	0.000	0.000	0.000
Total	16,839.227	4,488.589	3,206.638	2,007.147	4,090.513	24,402.314

TABLE 5C

AVERAGE AMOUNT OF 1966 TOTAL TRANSFER PAYMENTS INCOME PER RECIPIENT FAMILY IN THE FAMILY MERGE FILE, BY COMPONENT
[dollars]

Money Factor Income (000's)	Social Security Income	Public Assistance Income	Veterans' Disability Compensation	Workmen's Compensation	Unemployment Insurance Income	Total Transfer Payments
Under 1	1,277	1,007	1,417	2,651	676	1,742
1-2	1,360	912	1,629	2,007	535	1,585
2-3	1,293	816	1,427	1,241	588	1,454
3-4	1,339	1,001	1,611	1,396	565	1,465
4-5	1,241	715	1,242	735	510	1,204
5-6	1,293	702	1,230	955	527	1,239
6-7	1,234	512	1,658	1,026	478	1,139
7-8	1,104	531	1,177	670	458	962
8-9	1,218	605	1,003	869	435	1,032
9-10	1,111	654	783	873	443	898
10-11	1,377	0	1,053	597	489	1,069
11-12	1,117	0	1,491	554	486	1,017
12-13	1,421	0	1,454	572	431	1,167
13-14	1,430	0	982	815	598	1,254
14-15	1,275	0	924	821	503	1,168
15-20	1,287	0	1,093	1,068	456	1,143
20-25	1,041	0	569	1,193	749	1,022
25-50	1,344	0	1,001	1,034	437	1,209
50-100	1,062	0	1,288	118	0	1,403
100-500	0	0	0	0	0	0
500-1,000	0	0			0	0
1,000+	0	0			0	0

TABLE 6

RELATION BETWEEN 1966 DIRECT FEDERAL TAX AND TRANSFER PAYMENTS AND TOTAL INCOME BEFORE TRANSFERS, BY INCOME CLASS

[amounts in millions]

Money Factor Income (000's)	Total Income Before Transfer Payments (1)	Total Transfer Payments (2)	Federal Income Tax (3)	Federal Payroll Taxes (4)	Transfers as Percent of Income (2)/(1)	Income Tax as Percent of Income (3)/(1)	Payroll Tax as Percent of Income (4)/(1)
Under 1	3,881.510	13,470.782	248.704	214.282	347.050	6.407	5.521
1-2	8,682.402	3,491.831	188.838	364.062	40.217	2.175	4.193
2-3	11,017.625	2,465.413	301.107	609.570	22.377	2.733	5.533
3-4	15,340.025	2,199.506	674.403	1,013.779	14.338	4.396	6.609
4-5	20,662.634	1,641.403	1,089.878	1,453.981	7.944	5.275	7.037
5-6	28,744.909	1,732.893	1,703.583	2,133.883	6.029	5.927	7.424
6-7	31,069.325	1,315.950	1,973.744	2,216.097	4.236	6.353	7.133
7-8	39,977.253	1,226.596	2,813.446	2,807.400	3.068	7.038	7.022
8-9	45,556.143	1,094.375	3,375.071	3,041.322	2.402	7.409	6.676
9-10	38,922.802	792.663	3,014.736	2,480.918	2.037	7.745	6.374
10-11	42,622.948	904.358	3,324.364	2,559.856	2.122	7.799	6.006
11-12	37,514.156	628.249	3,100.028	2,170.638	1.675	8.264	5.786
12-13	33,475.612	618.248	2,916.985	1,884.066	1.847	8.714	5.628
13-14	30,606.612	543.820	2,678.464	1,599.781	1.777	8.751	5.227
14-15	24,977.261	395.994	2,273.389	1,330.879	1.585	9.102	5.328
15-20	75,496.215	1,032.491	7,133.639	3,520.281	1.368	9.449	4.663
20-25	30,527.806	264.710	3,153.279	1,101.154	0.867	10.329	3.607
25-50	58,552.694	246.045	6,859.060	1,124.772	0.420	11.714	1.921
50-100	25,192.633	4.026	4,222.095	121.263	0.016	16.759	0.481
100-500	17,593.022	0.000	3,023.974	27.604	0.000	17.188	0.157
500-1,000	1,894.540	0.000	262.995	0.402	0.000	13.882	0.021
1,000+	1,991.324	0.000	264.264	0.114	0.000	13.271	0.006
Total	624,299.460	34,069.354	54,596.046	31,776.102	5.457	8.240	4.914

by negative incomes and the very large amount of capital gains and other income subject to preferential rates, respectively) but never reaches more than 17 percent of total income before transfers in any MFI class; and (3) the effective payroll-tax rate is roughly constant up to the $7,000 MFI level, where the taxable earnings maximum is reached, and then it declines as income rises. Thus, in terms of a comprehensive income concept, transfers and the individual income tax are progressive while the payroll taxes are regressive.

USES OF THE MERGE FILE

The initial purpose of the MERGE File was to provide the basis for estimating the distribution of federal, state, and local taxes by income levels. But the file has also been useful for a number of other purposes—mainly tax calculations—which require information not now available on individual income-tax returns. We have only just begun to exploit the many uses of the file; and in this section, we present a number of examples to illustrate the versatility of the file and the types of analyses that can be made with it.

Distribution of Tax Burdens

Approximately the same methodology has been used for the last thirty-five years in the United States and other countries to estimate the distribution of tax burdens by income classes. Essentially, the method is to allocate individual taxes to broad income classes on the basis of a large number of statistical series which are proxies for the tax distributions. Thus, for example, sales taxes are allocated on the basis of the distribution of consumption (adjusted when necessary, for items which are not taxable), payroll taxes are allocated on the basis of the distribution of payrolls, and so on.[13]

The major disadvantage of this methodology is that it distributes taxes on the basis of the average income and behavior of all households in a particular income class, rather than on the basis of the income and behavior of the individual micro-units in each class. This means that it is impossible to differentiate among households for the numerous differences (e.g., income, consumption patterns, marital status, living arrangements) that may lead to relatively large differences in tax payments among families with approximately the same amount of income.

Although we cannot make all the distinctions that are relevant to the estimation of tax liabilities, the MERGE File is the richest source of information developed thus far for this purpose. Among the characteristics that are particularly important for estimating tax payments are sources of income; marital status and family composition; home ownership and mortgage debt; and state and local tax payments. Unfortunately, the SEO survey did not obtain consumption data, but this gap was filled by simulation techniques, using a survey for an earlier year.[14]

[13] The classic study along these lines is by Richard A. Musgrave and others, "Distribution of Tax Payments by Income Groups: A Case Study for 1948," *National Tax Journal*, Vol. 4 (March 1951).
[14] The basic source was the 1960–61 Consumer Expenditure Survey, conducted by the U.S. Bureau of Labor Statistics in connection with its revision of the weights for the preparation of the official consumer price index.

In addition, whenever it is necessary to make assumptions about the economic behavior of households, we are not limited to a single assumption for all families in a given income class. The availability of the computer permits us to attribute characteristics to individual units in substantial detail through simulation techniques. For example, we have already prepared some twenty-odd multivariate regression equations for various consumption items in order to estimate sales and excise tax payments for each unit in the file. While these techniques will not insure absolute accuracy, they will, at least, permit us to depart from the assumption of uniformity which has been the hallmark of all previous tax-burden studies.

Aside from this major improvement in methodology, the MERGE File permits us to prepare distributions of tax burdens on the basis of numerous alternative assumptions of the incidence of various taxes. In the past, the number of incidence combinations has been limited by the sheer magnitude of the computational job. The computer gives us much greater flexibility and scope in this respect. Furthermore, it will be possible to classify the tax burden distributions not only by size of income, but also by family size; age, sex, and education of family head; housing status (homeowners versus renters); and many other characteristics. These classifications will provide new insights into the impact of the tax system on different socioeconomic groups in the population.

Reforming the Payroll Tax

In most countries, the social security system is financed by a payroll tax levied at a flat rate, without exemptions or deductions. There is often a limit on the earnings which are subject to tax, so that the payroll tax becomes regressive for those with earnings above the limit. The use of a regressive tax is justified primarily on the grounds that the social security system is a system of insurance, which requires separate financing on the basis of an earmarked tax, and which merits some contribution even by wage earners who are acknowledged to be poor.

The insurance rationale for social security has come under increasing attack as the burden of the payroll tax has increased. Many economists have pointed out that the insurance elements of social security are extremely tenuous, and that it is cruel to impose heavy tax burdens on persons with low incomes on this ground. According to this view, the social security system should be regarded as a tax-transfer system, which should be financed out of general revenues, just as other transfers are financed. The U.S. social security system distributes benefits to persons who experience a sharp decline in income at retirement or if they become disabled, but the amount of their tax contributions is not even approximately related to the eventual benefits they receive. It can be shown that in a country with rising per capita income and a growing population, each generation can afford to pay much higher benefits to the disabled and retired persons, without increasing tax rates.[15]

In the United States, there is great interest, inside and outside of Congress, in developing new methods of financing social security that will bear less heavily on low-income earners than does the present system. We have used the MERGE

---

[15] For further development of these ideas, see Joseph A. Pechman, Henry J. Aaron, and Michael K. Taussig. *Social Security: Perspectives for Reform*, The Brookings Institution, 1968.

File to illustrate the effect on the tax rate and on tax liabilities of introducing personal exemptions into the payroll-tax base. We have also made estimates of the rate required to replace the payroll tax on employees by a flat tax on total income less the personal exemptions. Since the Tax File does not include the earnings of nonfilers and only very limited occupational information, it was necessary to use the MERGE File for these calculations.

Our calculations show that the flat payroll tax paid by wage and salary earners can be replaced by a mildly progressive tax on total income or on earnings, at reasonably moderate rates. The progressive tax would relieve those who earn less than the officially defined "poverty lines" from making any contribution to social security out of their inadequate incomes; and it would reduce the taxes of the vast majority of income recipients, while raising taxes only for the top 10 or 15 percent of earners. The merits of these alternative methods of financing social security are just being recognized, and the public debate is already under-way.[16]

Developing a Comprehensive Income Tax

Much has been said in the United States about the "erosion" of the tax base resulting from the numerous exclusions, exemptions, and deductions permitted under various provisions of the Internal Revenue Code. The extent of the erosion has been estimated in aggregate terms, but reliable estimates of the differential impact of the special provisions at various income levels have never been available. The Tax File has been used to make some of the estimates, but, of necessity, they have been confined to the items that appear on tax returns. The MERGE File now permits us to make these estimates on the basis of the adjusted-family-income concept, which is a close approximation to the concept of "economic income."[17]

The computer program used to make these calculations provides us with estimates of the tax base and tax liability under the current law by income classes, and by marital status, and with similar data after the following successive tax-law revisions: (1) elimination of the rate advantages of income splitting; (2) treatment of capital gains as ordinary income; (3) constructive realization of capital gains at gift or death; (4) taxation of net imputed rent on owner-occupied houses and elimination of the deductions for mortgage interest and property taxes; (5) taxation of transfer payments as ordinary income; (6) elimination of most of the personal deductions; and (7) substitution of a flat standard deduction of $1,300 for the present standard deduction of 15 percent of income up to a maximum of $2,000.

After the tax basis and tax liabilities are calculated, it is relatively simple to estimate the lower tax rates that would yield the same revenue as is now collected from the income tax, after each of the changes is made. To make the estimates relevant to the current scene, we have also developed projection techniques to raise the incomes in the MERGE File to the expected 1972 levels.[18]

---

[16] Senators Mondale and Muskie introduced legislation, S. 2656, incorporating features similar to these, in the U.S. Senate on October 5, 1971.

[17] See pp. 68–69 above.

[18] The estimates for 1972 were based on projections of income from the 1966 base, assuming that the percentage change in individual income sources will be the same as the estimated change in the personal income components.

On the basis of MERGE File calculations we have estimated that the 1972 tax yield on such a comprehensive tax base would have been $77 billion higher than under existing law. Conversely, average tax rates could have been reduced by 43 percent without reducing the yield of the individual income tax.[19]

The MERGE File provides a mine of information for analytical work on the characteristics of income recipients at all income levels. In addition to tax analysis, the new file will be useful for making estimates of alternative income-maintenance programs. Other uses will doubtless be developed as we gain more experience with the use of the file and develop a more complete library of computer programs for its use. We hope that other analysts will be able to develop similar files on the basis of the tax and survey information in their own countries. Our experience indicates that the benefits will be well worth the costs.

[19] See Joseph A. Pechman and Benjamin A. Okner, "Individual Income Tax Erosion by Income Classes" in *The Economics of Federal Subsidy Programs*, A Compendium of Papers Prepared for the Use of the Joint Economic Committee, 92 Cong. 2nd session (1972) (Brookings Reprint No. 230).

COMPARATIVE SIMULATION ANALYSIS OF
SOCIAL SECURITY SYSTEMS*

JAMES H. SCHULZ

Brandeis University

INTRODUCTION

In a recent report by a "task force" studying the economic problems of growing old, the basic retirement preparation problem is succinctly stated:

> Every American—whether poor or rich, black or white, uneducated or college-trained—faces a common aging problem: How can he provide and plan for a retirement period of indeterminate length and uncertain needs? How can he allocate earnings during his working lifetime so that he not only meets current obligations . . . but has something left over for his own old age? (U.S. Senate Special Committee on Aging, 1969.)

This basic economic problem must be dealt with by all persons before the retirement period. Today, older persons in the United States are increasingly likely to find themselves "automatically" retired at a certain age from their regular job, without viable alternative work opportunities. At the same time, over the years that follow their departure from the labor force, they are faced with the prospect of expenditure needs which do *not* decrease very significantly. In the retirement period there usually are rising health expenditures, increased leisure activities, and increased need for supportive services. And there is a continuing desire or need for "regular" goods and services at levels not greatly diminished from preretirement consumption levels.

The aged must also deal with the general rising level of prices which is almost certain to occur throughout the retirement period. Moreover, the retired quickly become aware of the rising living standards of most non-retired families—as these younger families share in the general, long-run economic growth of the country. Such increases no doubt generate a desire among many, if not most, of the aged to "keep up."

All these factors when viewed together indicate that there are strong economic pressures on persons when they retire which make their perceived "needs" *in* retirement not much different from those just *prior* to retirement. Whether an individual's resources in retirement will be adequate to meet this situation depends on what sort of life style he wants in retirement, but, more importantly, it depends upon the economic preparations which have been made before retirement and which make the desired life style possible.

In recent decades, as many countries have reacted to the widespread poverty among the aged portion of the population, we have seen increased reliance placed upon institutional or collective means of providing economic resources for old

* The work reported on here is part of a larger project concerned with a comparative analysis of five social security systems. This project is supported by the Levinson Gerontological Policy Institute, Brandeis University. In addition, financial support for some of the simulation analysis was provided under contract with the Office of Research and Statistics, U.S. Social Security Administration.

age. Collective arrangements are not new, however; people since earliest times have attempted to mitigate or eliminate economic insecurity by banding together in groups—families, tribes, associations, guilds—to "share" income and goods. What is new is the increased importance of industrial and government action in this area. As Kenneth Boulding (1958) has observed:

> It is when the "sharing group" becomes too small to ensure that there will always be enough producers in it to support the unproductive that devices for . . . insurance . . . become necessary. When the "sharing group" is small there is always a danger that sheer accident will bring the proportion of earners to non-earners to a level at which the group cannot function.

For example, during the thirties and the postwar period, significant changes in retirement security provision took place in the United States. Social security eligibility has now been extended (along with higher benefits) to all but a very small minority of the regular work force. At the same time, the number of persons participating in private pension plans has mushroomed to a point where more than 28 million workers are now covered by private pension and deferred profit-sharing plans, about 50 percent of the industrial labor force.

The growth of public and private pension plans has had a significant effect on the incomes of older persons. In terms of the U.S. Social Security Administration's poverty index, the percentage of American aged couples living below the poverty line declined from 30 percent in 1959 to 17 percent in 1969. And the percentage of poor old persons living alone or with non-relatives declined from 66 percent to 49 percent during the same period.

The economic situation of the elderly has improved considerably. But, at the same time, the data clearly indicate that there is still a sizeable number of aged living under serious economic hardship. Moreover, there seem to be increased numbers of persons dissatisfied with the functioning and results of the existing pension mechanisms. And, as a consequence, discussion and analyses continue with a view to developing and perfecting more workable and equitable pension mechanisms.

There now seems to be a general acceptance in the United States that incomes should be raised as soon as possible to an agreed upon poverty level for Americans of all ages who do not adequately share in the Nation's economic abundance. Hopefully, it will not be too long before private and public pension systems—together with supplementary welfare programs where necessary—will insure all the aged a minimum level of income which will be adequate to provide for their most basic needs.

As the United States takes this giant step in providing *minimum* economic security to all Americans, a new look at our economic programs for the retired aged seems timely. In evaluating present pension systems, it is important to keep in mind the basic economic question of how much income is to be allocated by persons in their younger years, either individually or in groups, for retirement preparation purposes. For example, the United States has accepted in the design of its current social security system the concept that the current generation of workers provides the funds via payroll taxes to provide current retirees with pensions—in return for a promise of similar pension support from future workers.

At the same time, there is no political consensus as to what that level of support for various groups of the aged should be.

In addition to the aged who have *always* lived in poverty and the aged who find themselves for *the first time* in poverty because of inadequate pensions, there are many aged families *above* the poverty level whose earnings during worklife allowed them a comfortable living standard but whose retirement incomes have dropped far below their preretirement levels. Their income problem grows out of the cessation of earnings of one or more family members and the failure of their savings and/or private and public pensions to replace a sufficiently large proportion of these earnings.

In the United States, social security old-age benefits are related to prior earnings up to a specified earnings ceiling. Computation of these benefits, therefore, is affected not only by changes in the benefit formula but also by changes in "creditable earnings" ceiling and the period of years of average earnings upon which benefits are based. A recent estimate of the replacement rate or pension-earnings ratio provided by the system has been made by the U.S. Social Security Administration's Office of Research and Statistics (Horlich, 1970). The replacement of earnings in the year before retirement by a social security retirement pension *for a single male full-time industrial worker with average earnings in manufacturing* retiring at age 65 in 1968 was 29 percent. The replacement rate for a similar worker who had a wife who was at least aged 65 and receiving a spouse benefit was 44 percent.

The above rates are based upon preretirement earnings defined as earnings in the year before retirement. If the measure of preretirement earnings is defined to be average earnings during the 1950–1968 period and excluding the 5 years, 1950–1955, of lowest earnings, the replacement rate for a single male worker rises from 29 percent to 38 percent. Such replacement rates differ significantly from the 60 to 75 percent replacement rates necessary to maintain living standards if other financial resources are not available

It can be argued that both private and public pension systems in the U.S. have badly satisfied the relative adequacy standard (i.e., adequate earnings replacement) for the *non-poor* because of three major factors:

1. U.S. pension systems (especially the social security system) are purposely biased in favor of low wage earners.
2. Most U.S. public and private pension systems fail to explicitly take into account the increases in the general level of prices which occur before and after retirement. (Automatic price adjustment of OASI benefits was not enacted until 1972.)
3. U.S. pension systems do not provide any formal mechanism for taking account of economic growth and the resulting improved general living standards which result.

Regarding the first factor, the U.S. social security system has a minimum benefit, a benefit formula weighted in favor of low earners, and a creditable earnings ceiling which does not adjust automatically. These features operate with the objective of helping to provide "socially adequate" income to the low income aged. But they also operate, as a consequence, to keep the replacement levels for the non-poor low.

While one cannot generalize about private pension systems as easily because of the large number of independent systems and the wide diversity of provisions, it has been observed by Heidbreder, Kolodrubetz, and Skolnik (1966) that collectively bargained plans tend to provide uniform benefits that vary by length of service but not earnings—thus placing low-paid workers in an advantageous position. Minimum benefit provisions in private plans with earnings-related formulas also tend to favor the below-average wage earner.

Regarding the second factor, adjustment for price increases, U.S. social security benefits *paid in retirement* have been adjusted frequently by Congress to keep pace with price level increases—sometimes, however, after a considerable time lag between the price change and the benefit increase. At the time the *initial* social security benefit is calculated for a retiring employee, however, the benefit is based upon average earnings which include the worker's earlier earnings which were paid at a time when the price level was much lower. Thus, benefits are based upon earnings unadjusted for subsequent price increases.

In the case of private pensions, only a handful of plans currently have a provision for adjusting pensions *during* retirement for price level changes. Many plans in recent years have adjusted periodically the benefit formula used to calculate benefits *at the time of retirement*—raising benefits often more than necessary for compensating for price level changes. While no systematic analysis by government or private researchers has been made to quantify and generalize the extent to which such adjustments are occurring, one would not expect to find a very complete adjustment being made by private pension systems using various *ad hoc* procedures. And certainly we know that many plans, unfortunately, do little or no adjusting at and/or during retirement.

Finally, with regard to the third factor—productivity or economic growth adjustment—the practice of present pension systems is clear. Both the social security system and private pensions have done very little to adjust pension levels *in retirement* to reflect the general improvement in living standards over time.

Thus, the current lack of dynamic adjustment mechanisms in U.S. pension systems promises the continuation of a fundamental retirement problem. Even if aged poverty—as defined, for example, by the SSA poverty index—were to be eliminated, there would still remain the problem of *relative* income adequacy. Past public discussions regarding aged income adequacy (and the adequacy of private and public pension programs) have been dominated by a search for ways of improving the poverty or near poverty incomes of the aged. More attention needs to be given to the question of the desirability of creating pension systems which will not only provide adequate *minimum* old age incomes but which will also provide the elderly with pensions which permit them to maintain or more closely approach their preretirement living standard in retirement and, perhaps, even improve upon it.

Whether individuals wish to maintain or improve their standard of living in retirement is, of course, still an open question. It is possible that some people may prefer to reduce their living standard in old age if, as a result, they can live better before retirement. And even for those who do desire to maintain or improve living standards in retirement, there still remains the question as to whether this should be a matter of personal choice (and hence, personal savings) or whether the matter should be handled through the public and/or private pension systems.

In recent years the institutional pension mechanisms (both public and private) in the United States and many other countries have come under heavy criticism. Much of the criticism has centered around the adequacy of benefits realized and the extent to which the pension systems are fulfilling the needs of "social adequacy" at the expense of individual equity and public policy efficiency.

For example, in a well-reasoned critique of the American social security system—Pechman, Aaron, and Taussig (1968) have argued:

The basic dilemma in considering reform of the social security system is that the United States has attempted to solve two problems with one instrument—how to prevent destitution among the aged poor and how to assure to people, having adequate incomes before retirement, benefits that are related to their previous standard of living. The earnings replacement function calls for benefit payments without an income test. Basic income support, on the other hand, can be carried out most efficiently if payments are confined to households with low income.

Two separate systems are needed to accomplish the two functions at the lowest cost. The earnings replacement function should continue to be performed by a social security system. Social security would become strictly wage-related, with the replacement rate roughly the same at all earnings levels between subsistence and the median earnings level. The income support function should be transferred to a negative income tax system or to a comprehensively reformed system of public assistance. With a good negative income tax, dependents' allowances would be unnecessary under social security. The payroll tax might be retained, but it should be used only as a withholding mechanism for the individual income tax.

It is time that a broad review of the U.S. retirement income maintenance system was undertaken and serious thought given to the requirements of providing adequate retirement incomes for *the future aged*. Present trends indicate we must be prepared to deal with the economic implications of (a) ever increasing living standards in the working years, (b) retirement at earlier ages, (c) longer life, and (d) changing retirement life-style expectations.

COMPARATIVE ANALYSIS OF SOCIAL SECURITY SYSTEMS

In recent years there have been numerous calls for research to evaluate and build upon the social security experiences of various foreign countries in the old age income maintenance area. As early as 1963, Margaret Gordon wrote that "a promising method of inquiry that has been almost totally neglected is comparative analysis of the impact of various types of welfare programs, including old-age insurance programs, on the economy in various countries."

More recently, the 1967 U.S. Social Security Advisory Committee commented as follows:

A good deal of light could be shed on the issues involved through analysis of the rather wide variety of relationships among income-maintenance systems that have been developed in other industrial countries. There, income-conditioned pensions and payments not related to income, such as universal old-age pensions and family allowances, exist in varying combinations with social insurance and public assistance systems . . .

Concurrent with these calls for research, another important development has occurred. There have been developed and implemented in a number of industrialized countries a variety of highly innovative social security systems. These new systems have been in large part motivated by dissatisfaction with the existing programs of old age income maintenance in each country and have attempted to overcome many of the existing problems. Public pension developments in Austria, West Germany, Sweden, and Canada, for example, have been watched with increasing interest.

There have been a few articles and books which discuss the social security systems of various countries. In general these studies have concentrated on describing the laws guiding past and present social security systems and in highlighting the major historical developments and issues surrounding these evolving systems. There is little in the literature, however, to indicate how these new systems are working: the extent to which they are meeting objectives; the economic effects on income distribution and savings; their effects on private pension systems; and the general satisfaction or dissatisfaction with them.

Important exceptions to this lack of study of foreign systems are the works of Gordon (1963), Aaron (1967), Pryor (1968), Kreps (1968), and Rimlinger (1968). Gordon studied eighteen industrial countries and found a significant correlation between the date of establishment of an old-age pension program for a sizeable segment of the population and the level of average benefits measured as a percentage of national per capita income. Aaron also studied industrialized countries and found age of programs a major factor determining the size and adequacy of social security outlays, and similar findings are reported by Pryor. Kreps makes international comparisons of labor force activity and variations in leisure-time patterns. Finally, a comparative analysis of the *historical* development of the social security systems in Germany, Russia, France, Great Britain, and the United States has been recently published by Rimlinger.

In most countries with highly developed social security systems (including the United States), at least five broad concerns have dominated recent discussions with regard to developing satisfactory public systems of old-age income maintenance. First, there is the question of the appropriate public-private pension mix and the effect of developing public pension systems on personal and private institutional income provision for old age. Second, there is the problem of how to insure adequate incomes for the aged poor while maintaining the "integrity" of income maintenance programs for all income groups (i.e., maintaining a program which is equitable, financially viable, and without major economic disincentives). Third, there has been increasing interest in providing for middle-income groups public pension benefits which (with or without other income sources) would permit retired families to maintain a standard of living in old age which was very similar to that achieved during the later years of the workers' earnings period. Fourth, there is the question of the desirability of automatic public pension adjustments and the search for suitable adjustment mechanisms.

Finally, there is the question of what is the best way to finance a public income maintenance program for the aged.

With regard to the question of pension adequacy, there has been a shift in thinking away from accepting as the sole role of pensions the prevention of poverty through providing minimum levels of benefits—the so-called "floor of protection." Whether individuals can effectively and efficiently handle the major part of their retirement income planning is open to serious doubt, given historical experience and the nature of the problem. Even assuming a new individual awareness of the need for retirement preparation, a look at the uncertainties the individual has to deal with reveals the magnitude of the problem:

1. He does not know with certainty his time of death (or the time of death of his spouse). Hence, he must assume the worst and presumably save for age 100 (or more) or decide to go on public assistance (or perhaps seek help from relatives) at a certain age. Thus arises one reason for public and/or private retirement insurance. By pooling this risk, the cost of protection from uncertainty is decreased.

2. He does not know with certainty what his future income stream will be. He must protect himself from such hazards as ill health, cyclical economic fluctuations, and job obsolescence. Again, a case for public and/or private insurance arises (unemployment, disability, and medical insurance).

3. He does not know what his retirement needs will be. He cannot predict, for example, his state of health throughout the retirement period. Not only does his health have a direct influence on medical costs, but it also affects retirement mobility—influencing recreation and transportation expenditures.

4. He does not know when he will retire. Although the individual has some control over this, increasingly the decision is becoming institutionalized with (1) the growth of mandatory retirement rules, (2) the growth of early retirement options (often accompanied by management and/or union retirement pressures), and with (3) the continued existence of age discrimination practices in hiring.

5. He cannot easily predict the future rate of inflation which, if it occurs, will depreciate the value of his retirement assets and retirement income from sources which do not adjust fully for this happening. Furthermore, he cannot easily predict the rate of economic growth—which is likely to affect his economic position *relative* to the working population.

Thus, as a result of these problems and others, private and public institutions have been created to assist and in some cases to force changes (Musgrave, 1968) in the individual's consumption-saving pattern. And with the development of pension institutions and mechanisms has come the development of the concept of an "adequate pension." Many countries now have public pension systems which not only relate pension benefits to prior earnings but seek to guarantee through these benefits a relatively high level of earnings replacement at retirement. The trend seems to be toward developing public (and also private) pension systems which will be adequate enough to permit the retired population to at least maintain a level of living which approximates that which they enjoyed during their working years.

Social security benefits in the United States do not currently achieve this objective. Nor have past discussions and debates about future benefit increases explicitly dealt with the role of earnings replacement in determining the appropriate pension formulas. Thus, the 1971 Advisory Council on Social Security observed and recommended:

> While past and proposed legislative actions have approximately achieved the goal of maintenance of purchasing power, the replacement rates have shifted over time and between different levels of average wages. There have been insufficient analyses or public discussion of the role of replacement rate in prescribing the benefit formulas. If policy were formulated in relation to replacement rates, the method of calculating the rate should be stated precisely. A replacement rate derived from the relationship between the benefit and the average wage over the entire period of an individual's participation in the labor market will differ markedly from a ratio of the benefit to his average wage in the 5 year period immediately preceding retirement. Careful study and serious consideration should be given before establishing a specific policy about replacement rates. However, the policy should be explicit and not implicit as is inherent in the use of the level wage assumption.

THE SIMULATION METHODOLOGY

If we seek to change the social security system (or private pension system) of any country, an important policy question arises: How will various changes in the pension mechanisms affect not only the size of benefits but also the distribution of benefits? Policy discussions of such questions are usually based upon highly aggregate projections of pension benefits and the total cost of such reforms. Utilizing the computer and simulation techniques, however, the effects of pension mechanism changes can be estimated at a micro-level—permitting a much wider range of policy questions to be examined, including the distributional effects of such changes. In an earlier study (Schulz, 1968), for example, a model was developed to simulate U.S. public and private pensions as they existed and were developing in the late 60's. That study was able to look at whether the economic circumstances of the retired population in the United States would improve significantly in the near future as a result of the improvements in these pension systems during the post-World War II period. The effects of increased coverage, benefit formula changes, private pension vesting provisions, and other factors were investigated.

Using a simulation model, it is possible to take any proposed change in a pension system and subject it to extensive analysis. There are currently before the U.S. Congress literally dozens of bills which seek to change private and public pensions in some basic way. Using simulation techniques, the results of most of these changes can be examined and comparisons can be made. The Office of Research and Statistics of the U.S. Social Security Administration is currently developing a more detailed version of the model referred to above, to be used for just such purposes.

A related use for simulation analysis in the aged income maintenance area is analysis of a set of alternative pension mechanisms, such as they currently exist in a particular country. Valuable insights can be gained by studying the systems of other countries. A project is currently under way at Brandeis University to examine the economic implications for the United States of its adopting pension reforms similar to those in other countries. Currently simulation analysis is being utilized to analyze West German, Swedish, and Canadian-type social security systems.

The simulation model used for this purpose is a modification of the model developed by Schulz (1968) for simulating the U.S. pension system. The basic data for the simulations are from a sample of the U.S. population in 1960. This sample, called the "one-in-a-thousand sample," is on a set of tapes produced by the U.S. Bureau of the Census and contains separate records of characteristics of a 0.1 percent sample of the U.S. population as recorded in the 1960 census. Each record contains 40 coded characteristics about an individual—including certain demographic, work force, income, and family characteristic information.

From this sample are taken: (a) all married couples where the husband is between 45 and 60 years of age (inclusive), and (b) all unmarried individuals where the individual is between 45 and 60 (inclusive). These persons constitute the basic population which is "aged" into retirement.

In order to project pension income and assets of the retired aged, it is necessary to construct a "life process" model which will permit those activities of individuals to be simulated which have an important influence on pensions and assets. These activities can be divided into the following four categories: (a) demographic, (b) work force and earnings, (c) pension status, and (d) asset accumulation.

For example, not everyone in 1960 between 45 and 60 can be expected to live at least 20 years. Hence the first life process activity considered in the simulation model is death. A probability of death for each particular year is specified for individuals based on their sex, race, and age. A random drawing from the associated probability distribution is used to determine whether an individual will die or live that year. Similarly, probabilities are specified for other possible occurrences built into the model: labor force exit and entry, job change, pension coverage, vesting and unemployment.

Each possible "occurrence" specified in the model is treated in a manner similar to the live-die occurrence—each person being considered in turn. By sequential handling of the various occurrences, it is possible to make the consideration of any one occurrence dependent upon occurrences which were handled before it. For example, one possible occurrence for a person in the work force is a change of job. The consideration of this occurrence in the computer for a particular individual is made conditional on the outcome of the "leave work force" occurrence considered before it. If the individual "left" the work force, obviously there is no need to consider whether he has changed jobs.

Once one year's simulation is completed, the individual, if he survives, is aged another year and the process immediately repeated. This continues until the year 1980 is reached (that is, completion of 20 "passes" in the computer). Another individual is then considered, and the whole simulation process repeated. After all individuals are processed, the resulting sample population represents most of the future aged population, since the surviving individuals are now 65 to 85 years of age.

During the simulation, earnings histories are kept for each individual. Individuals in the simulation who work full-time during a particular year and do not change jobs are given an employment equal to their "wage level." Females who work part time receive earnings equal to 50 percent of their "wage level."

Individuals (full or part time) in the simulation who change jobs in any particular year are subject to a reduction of earning because of possible time lost between jobs. In the simulation, a random number is generated each time a worker changes jobs. The probabilities of losing (a) no time, (b) 1 to 4 weeks, (c) 5 to 10 weeks, (d) 11 to 26 weeks, or (e) more than 26 weeks are estimated using Bureau of Labor Statistics data. Using the earnings histories generated by the simulation process described above, pension benefits can then be calculated. Account is taken of trends in pension coverage, private pension vesting, and public and private pension levels.

Social security and private pension benefit levels are assumed to rise at various designated rates which can be varied to test the sensitivity of the pension income distributions to such assumptions. In the current simulations, social security benefits are assumed to increase in the future at an average annual rate of 4 percent. This assumption is quite liberal. It is a higher rate of increase than has been voted by the Congress in the past.

The type of analysis being undertaken in the project can be illustrated by describing the simulation of the set of mechanisms used in the West German social security system.

SIMULATING A WEST GERMAN TYPE SOCIAL SECURITY SYSTEM

The present system was introduced in West Germany in 1957 when the pension laws then operating underwent fundamental change. The changes which occurred in the "pension reform of 1957" were not small incremental adjustments to the old system; in effect the existing system was replaced by a radically different one.

The basic aim of the reform was "to avoid too great a decrease in the standard of living of insured persons at the end of their working lives." The amount of pension payable, therefore, is no longer dependent on the actual contributions paid during the insurance life, but on the earnings of the individual during his working life in relation to average earnings, as well as to the level of wages and salaries at the time the pension becomes "payable " (Zollner, 1970).

This dynamic principle which underlies the new system is probably the system's most interesting feature. The goal is to allow the retired individual to have a living standard roughly equivalent to that which is being enjoyed by a current worker of equivalent status. Equivalent status refers to a worker with current earnings which bear the same relationship to mean national earnings as do the retired worker's lifetime average earnings to average national mean earnings (over the same period). Thus, a worker who on average received earnings which were, say, one and a half times mean national earnings would receive a pension at retirement which was equal to the earnings of the "equivalent" current worker (reduced by the appropriate replacement percentage). Given that earnings over one's worklife tend to increase for many workers at a rate greater than national mean earnings—the resulting pension calculated by this mechanism would often be lower than a pension based on earnings just prior to retirement.

The second basic feature of the West German system is that the system is based upon the principle that pension benefits are deemed "adequate" to maintain prior living standards only if they replace a high proportion of preretirement earnings. Thus, the German system explicitly recognizes the need for adequate earnings replacement, not just that pension benefit levels should be related to earnings (or taxes paid). To this end, the pension formula is set up so that regular workers will receive between 60 and 75 percent of preretirement earnings adjusted for national price and productivity increases.

The third feature of the system is that benefit levels are further adjusted in relation to the number of years worked. Unlike the U.S. system and most other systems where the relationship between benefit amount and years worked is minimal once the worker meets the minimum coverage qualifications—the German system benefit size is directly related to the number of years worked, so that a worker with only half as many years of work coverage receives a pension which is one-half as large as another worker who is equal in all other respects.

The fourth feature of the German system worthy of note is the fact that no spouse benefits are paid. Wives who work get a pension based upon their earnings and number of years worked. But families without working wives, which were exclusively dependent before retirement on the earnings of one bread-winner, receive a pension for retirement based upon his earnings alone. This is consistent, of course, with the basic principles of the system and is possible without creating extreme hardship for couples because of the relatively high pension levels. Here, and in other ways, the Germans have attempted to clearly separate traditional welfare/redistributive objectives from pensions based on the "self-help principle."

The fifth feature of special interest is the dynamic adjustment of German pension levels during retirement. Initially, these adjustments were not adjusted automatically but instead by annual legislative review after the recommendations of an advisory council were announced. In reality, the pensions of retired persons have been adjusted by the legislature every year by the process specified in the social security law—a time lagged wage index. Therefore, it is generally agreed by pension experts in Germany today that the system is and will be adjusted (for all practical purposes) in an automatic fashion. Certainly the pension adjustment process in no way resembles the *ad hoc* process in use in the United States.

The effect of the German features described above are investigated by projecting the individual pensions, pension distributions, and pension-earnings ratios which would result in the U.S. if the West German system of social security were introduced in place of the current OASDI program. The pension system for Americans is simulated using the West German old age pension mechanisms.

The results of the German simulation (a census of all sample individuals) are stored on tape in a manner that will permit retrieval in a flexible manner. In this way, all basic output data are available on one tape for future tabulation and analysis purposes. In addition, a set of basic tables are tabulated and stored on another tape. In the German case, these tables represent the various possible combinations (2,016 tables) of the key variables listed below:

1. Three alternative measures of preretirement earnings.
2. "Social security pensions only" or "all pension income" (public and private).
3. Alternative German formula constants (0.015 or 0.0011).
4. Three alternative definitions of "work history."
5. Present U.S. versus German-type pensions.
6. The total U.S. population or only the nonagricultural population.
7. Couples, widowed women, single men, and women "never married."

A set of 53 of these tables were selected and have been printed for the initial analysis phase. As the project progresses and further questions or areas of inquiry arise, additional tables can easily be retrieved and printed.

SIMULATION FINDINGS

What would the distribution of social security old-age pension look like in the year 1980 if the West German system were used in the United States? Table 1 summarizes the simulation estimations for units age 65 or more who are *totally* retired from the work force.

Looking at Table 1, one is immediately struck by the very high pensions which would be paid by this type of system. In every category except that for women who never married, the pensions paid are two to four times higher than social security benefits currently paid. In the case of couples, 70 percent of the units are projected to have benefits of $5,000 or more; furthermore, 20 percent are projected to have social security benefits exceeding $10,000. The distribution for single men and widowed women indicates a lower proportion of relatively high pensions, but even among these units, there are about half with pensions equal to or greater than $5,000.

As was explained previously, the current German social security old-age pension system does not have a minimum benefit provision. Poverty problems are dealt with by a separate system administered primarily by state and local governmental units. Therefore, it is not surprising to find some very low pension recipients in Table 1. For example, 18 percent of the couples and 35, 32, and 84 percent of single men, widowed women, and women who never married (respectively) are projected to have social security benefits under $3,000. The large proportion of "never married" women without benefits or with very low benefits is explained by the fact that many have little or no work history which would qualify them for a large pension. One must remember that the West German system pays pensions whose amounts are directly related to the number of years worked.

Using the simulation projections, we can compare social security pensions for the U.S. population (based upon the West German system) with projected benefits of the U.S. system in 1971. The U.S. OASDI system as it existed in 1971 is used to make the comparative simulation projections, with the following exceptions and assumptions:

TABLE 1

PROJECTED SOCIAL SECURITY INCOME FROM A GERMAN-TYPE
SOCIAL SECURITY SYSTEM, 1980
[percentage distribution]

Income	Couples[1]	Single Men[2]	Widowed Women	Women Never Married
Total percent	100	100	100	100
Less than $2,000	13	29	26	74
$2,000–2,999	5	6	6	10
$3,000–3,999	6	6	7	6
$4,000–4,999	7	7	9	4
$5,000–5,999	9	8	11	3
$6,000–6,999	13	14	10	2
$7,000–7,999	10	8	9	1
$8,000–8,999	10	6	6	1
$9,000–9,999	8	6	5	[3]
$10,000–11,999	14	10	7	1
$12,000 or more	6	2	5	0

[1] If wife retired, pension is sum of husband and wife's pension; if wife not retired, husband pension only is used; if husband not retired, unit excluded from calculation.

[2] Never married or widowed men.

[3] Less than 0.5 percent.

1. In the simulation, it is assumed that all men qualify for OASDI pensions *in terms of time*; women, however, are tested for pension eligibility based upon their simulation and pre-simulation work histories.
2. "Creditable" earnings for pension calculation purposes was assumed to be similar to the West German system (two times the average national earnings of the three previous years) and were not assumed to be limited by the lower ceiling schedule of the 1971 U.S. law.
3. The earnings histories for the years before 1959 are based upon estimates described in Appendix A.
4. Social security benefits are assumed to rise at an average rate of 4 percent per year in the future as a result of various *ad hoc* increases authorized by the Congress and the President.
5. Widows' benefits are calculated as 100 percent of their husbands' earned benefits.

Table 2 presents a comparison of the projected 1980 U.S. and German-type social security pension distributions for couples, single men, and widowed women. The table gives a dramatic comparison of the generally static American social security system with low earnings replacement goals versus a system with higher replacement goals and adjustment features which take into account the dynamic factors of both price level changes and real economic growth in calculating benefits at retirement.

Of course, the difference in the cost of the two systems is equally dramatic. To estimate the relative costs, the individual pensions amounts making up the pension distribution were aggregated. It was found that the West German system costs would be 2.2 times greater than the costs of the U.S. system. However, if the replacement level goal of the present West German system were lowered (by

TABLE 2

PROJECTED SOCIAL SECURITY INCOME FOR U.S. PENSION RECIPIENTS
BASED UPON THE U.S. AND WEST GERMAN SYSTEMS, 1980
[percentage distribution]

Income	Couples[1] U.S.[3]	German	Single Men[1] U.S.	German	Widowed Women U.S.	German
Total percent	100	100	100	100	100	100
Less than $2,000	23	13	52	29	47	26
$2,000–2,999	28	5	39	6	46	6
$3,000–3,999	27	6	9	6	6	7
$4,000–4,999	17	7	0	7	0	9
$5,000–5,999	6	9	0	8	0	11
$6,000–6,999	2	13	0	14	0	10
$7,000–7,999	0	10	0	8	0	9
$8,000–8,999	0	10	0	6	0	6
$9,000–9,999	0	8	0	6	0	5
$10,000–11,999	0	14	0	10	0	7
$12,000 or more	0	6	0	2	0	5

[1] See footnotes 1 and 2 of Table 1.
[2] Less than 0.5 percent.
[3] U.S. benefits increased in 1973 as a result of legislation; the projections shown here were completed before this increase took place.

reducing the constant used in the benefit calculation formula), the costs would drop accordingly.

REPLACEMENT RATES

If we assume that earnings prior to retirement is a good proxy for a family's level or standard of living *before* retirement—then the ratio of a family's pension income to preretirement earnings is one useful indicator of retirement income adequacy. Using this measure, one can get a good indication of the extent to which pensions, in this case social security pensions, replace earnings lost by retirement and, therefore, of the amount of supplemental effort required by the individual in order to maintain a standard of living similar to the one experienced before retirement.

In another paper, I have discussed extensively various measures of the "preretirement standard of living" (Schulz, 1971). The amount of financial resources required varies considerably, depending upon the *measure* of the preretirement standard used. Three basic types of measures are embodied in various different social security programs today: (a) the average of lifetime earnings, (b) the average of a certain number of the *best* years of earning, and (c) an average of a certain number of the *last* years worked. In this study, the latter method, which uses the final work years as the measure of the standard of living, is used. Three different sets of projections are made—using the *last* year, the last *five* years, and the last *ten* years before retirement, respectively. Only the projections using the "last ten years" measure are discussed in this paper.

Table 3 presents the pension-earnings ratio distributions for the various demographic groups. It is important to note that in addition to the fact that the ratios were calculated using an average of the last ten years of earnings in the

TABLE 3

Projected Ratio at Retirement of Social Security Pension Income
to Preretirement Earnings[1], based upon a German-type System
[percentage distribution]

Ratio	Couples[3]	Single Men[3]	Widowed Women[4]	Women Never Married
Total percent	100	100	100	100
Less than 0.20[2]	2	0	19	19
0.20 to 0.29	2	1	5	17
0.30 to 0.39	4	1	7	19
0.40 to 0.49	6	2	12	12
0.50 to 0.59	12	4	15	7
0.60 to 0.69	21	12	16	5
0.70 to 0.79	29	32	14	3
0.80 to 0.89	17	31	9	2
0.90 to 0.99	4	12	3	2
1.0 or more	3	6	1	14

[1] Average of ten years prior to retirement.
[2] Includes persons receiving no pension but with some earnings in the relevant years.
[3] See footnotes 1 and 2 of Table 1.
[4] Ratio based upon dead husbands earnings (if appropriate) and own earnings (if any).

denominator, the pension used in the numerator is the simulated pension received by each individual in the first year of retirement (between 1960 and 1979) and not the 1980 pension (which is higher because of the 4 percent annual benefit increase assumed in the study). As in the previous tables showing the projected distribution of income, only social security old-age pensions are included. Estimates which include projected private pensions were also made but are not discussed.

In evaluating the results presented in' Table 3, we can use two benchmark measures: (a) the proportion of units with a pension-earnings ratio below 0.50 and (b) the proportion of units with a ratio above 0.60. These benchmarks are used because "in the United States, some social planners currently speak of an assured flow of income of probably 50 percent of the earnings of recent years—not the lifetime earnings—for a single worker and 66⅔–70 percent for a couple" (Horlich, 1970). In the case of couples, nearly three-quarters (74 percent) are projected as having a ratio of 0.60 or higher. Only 14 percent receive pensions amounting to less than 50 percent of their earnings and, as we will show below, most of these couples have very high earnings (probably above the social security earnings ceiling). The proportion of single units with a ratio of 0.60 or more varies from a high of 93 percent for single men to a low of 26 percent for women who never married—with female widows being in-between with 43 percent.

Of course, any pension system can provide very high benefits with the appropriate formula specification. What is unusual and, I would argue, desirable about the German system (and certain other European systems) is that its formula explicitly embodies a *relative* concept or definition of income adequacy by guaranteeing long term workers a relatively high earnings replacement rate consistent with historical price level changes and rising real earnings levels—*irregardless of what those changes might be in the unforeseen future.*

Contrast the pension-earnings ratio resulting from a German-type system with those resulting from the current U.S. system. Whereas the German-type system results in very few couples with a pension-earnings ratio below 0.50—the 1971 U.S. social security system results in almost all of the same couples receiving a social security pension at retirement which will be less than 50 percent of their prior average earnings.

CONCLUDING OBSERVATIONS

To a large extent, pension benefit levels in the past and the increases in these levels have been stimulated not so much with the purposeful intent of tapping a greater part of the nation's rising national product for old people but rather as a secondary result of attempts to deal with the severe and potentially explosive hardship problems facing many older people. In consequence, these past efforts have been aimed primarily at raising the economic status of the aged to some minimum standard or subsistence level in the face of rising prices.

What has been proposed by some, however, is to develop mechanisms which allow the retired aged to share in the growing productivity and output of the nation—to share in some of the "harvested fruits." What this no doubt requires is the development of means to permit an orderly, equitable *but substantial* transfer of income from the working to the retired population in order to improve the latter's relative economic status. The national dialogue and debate over such a change of focus with regard to developing better retirement income programs is just beginning.

Simulation analysis provides a flexible tool for evaluating various important economic implications of alternative social security reform proposals. Its usefulness in American policy discussions is reflected in the widespread interest which the results of the Orcutt, Pechman, and Schulz simulations have generated among American politicans, government analysts, and academics working in the income maintenance field. It is no accident that the Office of Economic Opportunity, the U.S. Treasury, and the Social Security Administration have cooperated with and encouraged these projects.

Simulation as a tool of policy analysis is appropriate even in countries where existing data are scarce. Simulation makes it possible to remain at the microeconomic level and bring to bear on the questions under consideration a wide variety of data from many different sources—data available at different levels of aggregation. As Orcutt (1964) has observed, "selection of a probabilistic approach to predicting the behavior of micro components does not reflect any particular philosophical position about the nature of causation or about the meaning or existence of free will." Such an approach is chosen in order that the limited data that exists can be utilized in investigating problems for which non-stochastic models do not seem feasible. The whole area of social welfare economics presents many such problems.

APPENDIX A

1. Age of Entering the Labor Force (AGENT) in the German System

In previous simulations, AGENT was assumed to be 20 years of age. In this simulation, the age was kept variable with the years of schooling received. The relationship between the years of schooling and the age is as follows:

AGENT	Type of schooling received and completed
15	High school, grade 10, or less schooling
16	High school, grade 11
17	High school, grade 12
19	College, three years, or less college
21	College, four years, completed
25 + N	College, five years, or more.

In the case of five or more years of college, a normally distributed random variate was generated and added to the value 25 of AGENT. The variate N had a mean of zero and a standard deviation of one. Consequently, the average age generated was 25 years, and approximately all cases generated (99.7 percent) fell within the interval of 22 years to 28 years. The "type of schooling" used for estimating was based upon the 1960 census information.

2. Wage History of Individuals (WAGE)

In the absence of a detailed knowledge of wage histories of individuals in different trades and occupations, a method was developed to generate these wages for the years 1940 to 1959—based on the individuals' recorded wages for 1960.

Using national wage averages, a linear regression line was fitted according to the least squares criterion. The slope of the regression was found to be $144.5 per year. In the simulation an individual's recorded wage for 1960 was successively reduced by this amount to give his deflated wages for the years 1959 to 1940.

In order to introduce variation, a normally distributed random variate N with mean zero and standard deviation of 5.8 was added to the deflated value; consequently, almost all variations (99.7 percent) ranged between −17.4 and 17.4. In other words, the 1960 recorded wage of an individual was successively reduced by an amount normally distributed within the limits of $127.1 and $161.9 per year.

In the above scheme, the minimum wage permissible was $500 per year, and the maximum was not allowed to exceed a value twice the average of the last three years of the national wage averages. In addition to the 1960 recorded wage, the status of employment and the last year of work were known. Accordingly, the annual wage was set to zero when an individual had not worked.

3. German Pensions (GP)

The calculation of German pensions can be readily understood by following these steps:

(a) At the year of retirement, the general earnings base (GB) is defined as the average of the prior three years of average national wages.

(b) Departing from the practice in Germany, three factors to adjust the general earnings base were calculated. These factors are defined as the average of the prior ten, twenty, or lifetime ratios of an individual's annual earnings to the national wage averages. In Germany, the average of all (i.e., lifetime) ratios of wages to national wage averages are calculated.

(c) Given these three factors, the general earnings base is multiplied to form three (as opposed to one) personal earnings bases (PB10, PB20, and PBLIFE).

(d) Given the personal earnings base—the number of years worked and the age at retirement minus the age of entering the workforce were determined.

(e) In this simulation two legal constants (LCON) were used to give weight to the number of years worked. Presently in Germany this constant is 0.015 for every year worked. In the simulation the constant 0.0111 was also used.

(f) Given three personal earnings bases and two legal constants, six different pensions were calculated. These pensions were obtained by multiplying the personal earnings base with the number of years worked and with the legal constant.

BIBLIOGRAPHY

Aaron, Henry. "Social Security: International Comparisons," in Otto Eckstein (ed.) *Studies in the Economics of Income Maintenance* (Washington: Brookings Institution, 1967).

Advisory Council on Social Security. *The Reports of the 1971 Advisory Council on Social Security*, Communication from Secretary of Health, Education and Welfare, House Document No. 92-80, 92nd Congress, 1st Session (Washington, D.C.: U.S. Government Printing Office, 1971).

Boulding, Kenneth. *Principles of Economic Policy* (Englewood Cliffs, N.J.: Prentice-Hall, 1958).

Gordon, Margaret. *The Economics of Welfare Policies* (New York: Columbia University Press, 1963).

———. "Income Security Programs and the Propensity to Retire," in Richard H. Williams, *et al.*, eds., *Processes of Aging*, Vol. 2 (New York: Atherton Press, 1963).

Heidbreder, Elizabeth, Kolodrubetz, W. W., and Skolnik, Alfred. "Old Age Programs," in U.S. Joint Economic Committee, *Old Age Income Assurance*, Pt. II (Washington, D.C.: U.S. Government Printing Office, 1966).

Horlich, Max. "The Earnings Replacement Rate of Old-Age Benefits: An International Comparison," *Social Security Bulletin*, Vol. 33 (1970).

Kreps, Juanita, *Lifetime Allocation of Work and Leisure*, U.S. Social Security Administration, Research Report No. 22 (Washington: Government Printing Office, 1968).

Musgrave, Richard. "The Role of Social Insurance in an Overall Program for Social Welfare," in Bowen, *et. al.*, *The American System of Social Insurance* (New York: McGraw-Hill, 1968).

Orcutt, G. H. *Views on Simulation and Models of Social Systems*, Social Systems Research Institute Reprint No. 61 (Madison: University of Wisconsin Press, 1964).

Pechman, Joseph A., Aaron, Henry J., and Taussig, Michael. *Social Security: Perspectives for Reform* (Washington, D.C.: The Brookings Institution, 1968).

Pryor, Frederick. *Public Expenditures in Communist and Capitalist Nations* (Homewood, Illinois: Irwin, 1968).

Rimlinger, Gaston. "Social Change and Social Security in Germany," *The Journal of Human Resources*, III (Winter, 1968).

Schulz, James. "Aged Retirement Income Adequacy—Simulation Projections of Pension-Earnings Ratios," in U.S. Joint Economic Committee, *Old Age Income Assurance*, Pt. 2 (Washington, D.C.: U.S. Government Printing Office, 1967).

———. *The Economic Status of the Retired Aged in 1980: Simulation Projections*, Research Report No. 24, Office of Research and Statistics, Social Security Administration (Washington, D.C.: U.S. Government Printing Office, 1968).

————. "The Role of Savings and Pension Systems in Maintaining Living Standards in Retirement," *Journal of Human Resources*, VII (Summer, 1972).

U.S. Senate Special Committee on Aging. *Economics of Aging: Toward a Full Share in Abundance* (Washington, D.C.: U.S. Government Printing Office, March 1969).

U.S. Social Security Advisory Committee. *The Research Program of the Social Security Administration*, Report of the 1967 SSA Advisory Committee on Research Development (Washington, D.C.: Government Printing Office, 1968).

Zoellner, Detlev, *Social Legislation in The Federal Republic of Germany*, 2nd revised ed. (Bonn: Asgard-Verlag GMBH, 1970).

MICROANALYTIC SIMULATION OF HOUSEHOLD BEHAVIOR*

1. INTRODUCTION TO THE MICROANALYTIC SIMULATION MODEL

HAROLD W. GUTHRIE

Surely the most vexing condition that plagues social science research is the great heterogeneity of the human population. There is great variation between persons with respect to their capabilities for working, their tastes as consumers, and their responses to income changes. Also, a given person, as he proceeds through his life cycle will display many different kinds of behavior over time. Social scientists have faced the tasks of formulating a meaningful description and developing an analytic structure for understanding human behavior by resorting to both extreme abstraction and minute but incomplete details of reality. Given that one function of social science should be to furnish guidance for public policy, the results of social science research have been disappointing. We have offered a mixture of deductive theory too highly simplified to be very relevant to real world issues and inductive empirical findings too remote from a systematic view of a socioeconomic structure.

On its part, government, especially the Federal government, has implemented both macro and micro policy measures on the basis of very scanty information about the expected effects of those policies. For example, we still know very little about the dynamics of an inflationary process and about the dynamics of a deteriorating labor market. With respect to micro policy, Congress has legislated and adminstrators must operate a vast array of special programs aimed at specific subgroups of a heterogeneous population.

One example of a totally chaotic approach to public policy making has been called "American Roulette" and refers to the legislative and administrative processes concerning health care in the United States.[1] Lacking a well-designed plan for provision of health care, a very large number of "health publics," each with its own highly specific self interest, is served by as many as 24 different Federal offices. The resulting combination of a primarily private medical sector and a jumble of public programs oriented to special needs produces extreme inequality in the opportunity to live a healthy life. The social and economic consequences of this inequality are issues seldom raised and never systematically analyzed.

What is needed is a dynamic and comprehensive model of our socioeconomic system to guide formulation of public policy. An ideal model would be rich in heterogeneous detail; it would include all of the dominant relationships and variables that describe human behavior; it would allow assessment of a wide variety of social needs; it would be a tool for evaluating the prospective costs and benefits of alternative proposals for changing public policy.

---

* Senior author Guy H. Orcutt and his coauthors are with the Urban Institute.

[1] Christa Altenstetter, "American Roulette: National Health Policy-Making and Health Programs Implementation," The Urban Institute, Washington, D.C. Working Paper 107-20.

This paper describes a model and a methodology that the authors believe is a first step toward the construction of an ideal model. They are reporting here the results of efforts to build and test a model that encompasses the demography of the U.S. population, as it has changed and as it might be expected to change over time under alternative assumptions about public policy. These efforts are the beginning of a continuing process of expanding the model to be more comprehensive and therefore more useful. The expanded model will include the first stage demographic component reported here, but will also focus, in a second stage, on some important economic issues.

A. MODEL-BUILDING FOR ECONOMIC POLICY

Deductive micro-economic theory has provided an elegantly logical picture of a heterogeneous world by assuming exact and simple relationships, usually unspecified. This degree of abstraction of the complex real world has led to a model superior to all others yet developed in its comprehensiveness and its ability to reflect an economic system of interdependent activities. Only rarely, however, have data been available to allow specification of the relationships to the degree required for many public policy questions. Even with specification this simplified approach can lead only to single value estimates for large and heterogeneous groups.

The advent of aggregative national accounts data and electronic computers brought a new kind of capability to produce simultaneous equation econometric models. These models focused on fluctuations of the national product in highly specific terms; they have provided useful guidance in the formulation of macroeconomic policy. But the econometric models, even when they are broken down into many sectors and subsectors do not give many insights into the distributional effects of macro policy.

While the importance of macro policy is not to be minimized, the policy needs of our present world are becoming increasingly oriented to micro policy issues. We need to know more than we are now capable of knowing about the distributional dynamics of population change, tax systems, and transfer payment systems. The decade of the 60's brought new awareness of social and economic inequities and proposals of micro policies to reduce the inequities. Given our present methodology in the social sciences, we can only speculate about the long-run effects of these policies. The need, then, is for a method of looking at economic and social processes in a dynamic time dimension but also in as great detail as possible.

As Orcutt has explained elsewhere, changes in state over time for any given variety of elements can easily be conceptualized in terms of a matrix of transitional probabilities.[2] Given specification of the transitional probabilities, this approach would allow extension of the model through time and would allow microanalysis of distributional effects. The number and the complexity of the matrices required to achieve a comprehensive socioeconomic model not only boggles the mind but would choke even the most advanced electronic computer.

---

[2] Guy H. Orcutt, "Microanalytic Models and Their Solution" in *Mathematical Model Building in Economics and Industry*, London: Charles Griffin & Company Ltd., 1970.

B. PURPOSE AND DESIGN OF A MICROANALYTIC SIMULATION MODEL

In 1961 Orcutt and his former colleagues at Harvard University, Martin Greenberger, John Korbel, and Alice Rivlin, published the results of their pioneering attempt, started some five years earlier, to build a new kind of model.[3] This model, involving sample representation of decision making units as well as Monte Carlo simulation methods for its solution, laid the foundation for further efforts to provide a basis for policy decisions that would capture the heterogeneity of human behavior.

Three underlying themes form part of the rationale for this kind of simulation model:

(1) The main goal of such efforts is to provide information as input to a decision process leading to the formulation of public policy. While there is methodological ground-breaking to be done, the guiding spirit of the earlier, present, and continuing efforts has as its main focus the fact that wise public policy choices must be made from a wide range of options. The methodology of the model is specifically designed to evaluate alternative social policies by simulation prior to selection of a single policy for implementation.

(2) The output from the model may well have implications for aggregative measures of social well-being, but its principal usefulness lies in its value as a descriptor of the distribution of the population with respect to given characteristics. Thus the model takes as given that the world of social behavior is extremely complex, that the persons and families who make individual decisions vary widely in their states or conditions, and that proper evaluation of social policy must include an examination of its effect on small subgroups of the population. The microanalytic focus of the model attempts to reflect the heterogeneity of the real world.

(3) The model reflects another aspect of reality in that it recognizes that economic behavior and certain elements of social behavior are so closely linked that they should not be separated by traditional disciplinary lines. For example, the welfare position of poor families is determined at least partly by the size of families. Understanding poverty as a social phenomenon therefore requires understanding reproduction as a social process.

The design of the model requires an initial population base at a point in time. The initial population could be arbitrarily designated or it could be a sample representation of the real world. In the demographic model reported here two initial populations were used—the 1/1,000 sample of the 1960 Census of Population and the 1967 Survey of Economic Opportunity.[4] The initial population is then moved forward through time in annual intervals by imputing changes in the characteristics of the persons or imputing certain events. These imputations are based on relationships that have been discovered through various research efforts

[3] Guy H. Orcutt, Martin Greenberger, John Korbel, and Alice M. Rivlin, *Microanalysis of Socioeconomic Systems: A Simulation Study*, Harper & Row, 1961.

[4] The 1967 Survey of Economic Opportunity, conducted by the U.S. Bureau of the Census for the Office of Economic Opportunity, is a large sample survey which was stratified and weighted to yield a large number of poor persons. For purposes of the simulation model a self-weighting subsample was selected.

in the social sciences. The relationships are referred to as operating characteristics. The imputation proceeds by matching a random number generated within the computer against a calculated probability of occurrence for a given event for a given person; this is the Monte Carlo simulation process. For example, suppose the mortality rate for 85 year old white males is 20 percent. A uniformly distributed random number will be generated for the event, death, for each person of that description in the sample. Any person for whom the random number falls in the bottom 20 percent of the random numbers range will be assumed to have died.

Selection of the operating characteristics is obviously a crucial element in the design of the simulation model. Ideally, the operating characteristics will consist of causal relationships or representations of beliefs and attitudes that motivate human behavior. In the model presented here, the imputation of births best approximates this ideal because the operating characteristics form a sub-model believed to represent the decision processes and other circumstances affecting the occurrence of births. Descriptions of the operating characteristics for births and changes in marital status will be presented here. Operating characteristics for deaths and education have also been developed and they will be described in forthcoming publications. We attempt to validate each operating characteristic as it is developed in order to be assured that we are at least portraying accurately the real world of the past. Currently we are using the 1/1,000 sample of the 1960 Census as an initial population and comparing our annual simulation results with vital statistics for the decade of the 1960's. For the purpose of projecting the future behavior of households we have to rely on our own best judgment, as well as the insights of other social scientists, about changes in our operating characteristics over time.

Research efforts are under way to expand the microanalytic demographic model to a comprehensive representation of the economic behavior of households. Building upon the demographic base we are well advanced toward specifying operating characteristics concerning labor force participation, weeks worked, annual earnings, receipts of transfer payments, the yield on earning assets held by families, income tax liabilities, disposable income, and saving out of income. We are preparing to be able to project the effects of various manpower programs that are of special interest to the U.S. Office of Economic Opportunity, our current source of funding. We also expect to be able to consider public policy questions relating to transfer payments programs.

Another significant sub-model developed as part of the total simulation modeling effort is an auxiliary model of output and price movements. This model, developed by Orcutt, will complement the micro model by providing an economic environment within which the micro simulation can proceed, and by serving as a calibration device for some of the economic variables in the micro model. The auxiliary model is described in the next section of this paper.

Clearly the development of sub-models and specification of the operating characteristics requires a substantial input of the best products of social science that we can find. But the model would be of little use if we could not implement it with simulation runs on a computer. The design of a simulation system has been a second crucial element in our modeling effort, and George Sadowsky describes the system that he has developed in the concluding section of this paper.

2. THE AUXILIARY MODEL

GUY H. ORCUTT

The microanalytic operating characteristics provide the core for our simulation model because the desired output from the model is the assessment of the effects of alternative public policies on the distribution of income and assets. The usefulness of the core model of household behavior can be greatly enhanced, however, by an auxiliary aggregative model that provides closure.

The value of providing closure is two-fold. In the first place the microanalytic models under development need an environment in which to operate. The household sector, after all, does not operate in a vacuum; it is affected by the general condition of the economic system as it is reflected in aggregate unemployment rates, changes in price level, and growth rates. In the second place economists think they know something about the control of some macrovariables such as unemployment rates and changes in price level. It would be useful to trace out the impact of fiscal, monetary, and other policies operated at the macrolevel on the behavior and well being of individuals and families. The macromodel under development represents a first step in providing both an environment for the microanalytic models and a useful link to variables which can be controlled or at least influenced by available monetary and fiscal tools.

The simplest expedient for providing a needed environment for the Urban Institute model of the populations of individuals and families would be to treat unemployment, real GNP, price level changes, and fractions of GNP going to earned income and wealth holders as direct exogenous inputs. The disadvantage of this approach is that no explicit account is taken of the extensive interrelatedness of these variables or of the impact on these variables of what is going on in the microanalytic model. By leaving such variables entirely unconnected the user of the microanalytic model would be given a very unrealistic view of the extent to which outcomes could be independently manipulated by use of policy tools at the macrolevel. The primary objective behind the auxiliary macromodel is to take a useful step towards capturing the close interconnectedness of household inputs from the macrolevel and still leave points at which policy assumptions could be entered either by alteration of target unemployment or by alteration of parameter values. A secondary objective is to provide a macromodel designed to receive inputs from microanalytic models and so extend the range of application of such models.

In developing an auxiliary macroanalytic model extensive simplification has been achieved by assuming that the federal government can and will cause aggregate demand to vary so as to control approximately the percentage of the labor force which is unemployed. The advantage of this assumption is that if total aggregate demand actually is controlled by the federal government it becomes less critical and possibly unnecessary for present purposes to account for the role of non-household sectors in generating aggregate demand. The behavior of the private sector in this area is simply regarded as being supplemented or offset as necessary to achieve a desired unemployment rate given past price movements.

Of course this would not do for a model intended to be useful in guiding short-run stabilization efforts. It is hoped and expected that the model described here will be useful in tracing out the main longer run consequences of monetary and fiscal policy for household behavior and welfare.

In its current stage of development the following relationships form the infra-structure of the macro-model:[5]

1. Target unemployment rates as specified by the user or as a user selected function of change in price level.
2. Unemployment rate as a function of the target rate and a lagged unemployment rate.
3. Labor force exogenously given or as an input from the microanalytic model.
4. Employment as an identity relating to unemployment rate and labor force.
5. Real GNP as a function of lagged GNP, capital, and employment.
6. Real gross private domestic investment as a function of lagged investment, GNP, change in GNP, and change in population given exogenously or as an input from the microanalytic model.
7. Real capital consumption as a function of lagged capital stock.
8. Real capital stock as an identity relating to lagged capital stock, capital consumption, and investment.
9. Implicit price deflator for GNP as a function of lagged price level, unemployment rate and change in unemployment rate.
10. GNP at current prices as an identity relating to price level and real GNP.
11. Capital consumption allowances at current prices as a function of lagged capital consumption allowances and GNP.
12. Net national product as an identity relating to GNP and capital consumption allowances.
13. Indirect business taxes as a function of lagged indirect business taxes and net national product.
14. National income as a function of lagged national income, net national product and indirect business taxes.

At this stage of its development the auxiliary macromodel should be regarded as a start toward establishing useful links between monetary and fiscal policies and a microanalytic model of the population of individuals and families. It also is of interest in that it provides for and makes important uses of the output of a microanalytic model as input into a macroanalytic model; for example, the labor force and population are estimated from the micro-model.

This model has several deficiencies which hopefully can be reduced with additional effort. Perhaps the most serious of these is that the gap between what policy makers might do at the macrolevel and appropriate alteration of parameter values in this auxiliary model is still uncomfortably large. Also it is unfortunate but true that, while relationships used in this auxiliary model do fit past data very well, important causal relations may not have been successfully captured. In

[5] A complete description of the initial version of the macromodel which has been computerized is available in Urban Institute Working Paper 504-1, "An Auxiliary Model for Generating Employment, Income and Price Movements," by Guy H. Orcutt and Sara D. Kelly.

addition, while it may be possible to use fiscal policy and monetary policy to control the level of aggregate demand while also influencing the share of GNP going as a return to wealth holders, this possibility is not explicitly provided for in this auxiliary model as it now stands.

This model has been used to generate a wide variety of outputs including: outputs based on use of observed values as equation inputs; outputs obtained using generated values of endogenous variables as equation inputs; outputs involving a replay of history since 1929 with assumed alterations of policy; conditional predictions for the 1970's assuming alternative unemployment rates and population growth rates; and outputs obtained from sensitivity experiments. Outputs have been generated both with and without suppression of error terms.

The macromodel already developed is considered to be one potential component of a more ambitious and gradually evolving macromodel with several components which interact with each other and with the micromodel. A time series data bank plays a key role in the articulation of macromodel components with each other and with the micromodel. Each model or model component is operated in sequence and when it is being operated can make use of whatever is in the time series data bank as well as add to what is in the bank. Series being generated are distinguished from observed or assumed time series so as to facilitate comparison of generated series with historical observations for purposes of testing, alignment and guidance in seeking improvements. All series in the time series data bank are available for statistical analysis and output is generated in tabular or graphical form.

3. BIRTHS

GERALD E. PEABODY

Individual family decisions about the number of children to have are the most important factors affecting fertility in the United States. A couple's desires about the number of children they wish to have is the best predictor of the number of children they will have. Extensive use of contraception has made it possible for a majority of families to control their fertility to the level they desire. In the Growth of American Families Study, a national survey of fertility conducted in 1955[6] and 1960,[7] it was found in 1960 that 98 percent of the women in the United States intended to use contraception at some point in their life to limit their fertility. Thirty percent of the couples in that study had completely planned their fertility in the sense that all births were planned; each woman conceived only after contraception use was stopped so that she could become pregnant, and she had no unwanted births.

[6] R. Freedman, P. K. Whelpton, and A. A. Campbell, *Family Planning, Sterility and Population Growth* (New York, 1959).
[7] P. K. Whelpton, A. A. Campbell, and J. E. Patterson, *Fertility and Family Planning in the United States* (Princeton, 1966).

A model that is to explain adequately past fertility or anticipate the probable course of fertility in the future must therefore incorporate considerable detail about family planning. The factors that influence the couple's decision about the number of children they wish to have must also be included along with their attitudes about spacing of children. Their propensity to use contraception when a birth is not desired and the efficacy with which it is used should be analyzed. In addition to these volitional factors, it is necessary to incorporate the physiological capacity of the couple to bear children, and the variation of this capacity over time.

The complete model of the household is being developed as a tool to analyze the potential impact of public policy on the individual and family. Fertility is likely to be affected by changes in attitudes about desired family size, either in response to changes in public policy or other factors affecting attitudes, by changes in the availability of information about existing contraception devices (again, possibly, from new public programs), by changes in the technology of contraception, and so on. By incorporating these features into the fertility model we are well equipped to attempt to anticipate how fertility might respond to such changes effected by public policy or other influences.

A. THEORETICAL MODEL

The conventional economic approach to decisions at the family level is to assume a utility function for the family, add a budget and possibly other constraints, and then maximize the utility function subject to these constraints. This approach was initially applied to fertility by Becker[8] some years ago. Becker was led to apply the economic theory of household behavior to fertility since he felt that attempts by psychologists and sociologists had been unsuccessful in accounting for fertility behavior, while economic factors appeared to account for a significant, if small, fraction of fertility behavior. By assuming that children are analogous to consumer durables Becker concluded that couples with high incomes would want larger families than those with low incomes.

While the empirical testing of the economic theory has been scanty, the available evidence indicates that there is very little relation between income and desired number of children. Other economic factors, though, do have a significant effect upon fertility; labor force participation of the wife is one such example. However, much of the work on fertility by economists is flawed by the failure to incorporate significant social and physiological factors which are crucial to a complete understanding of fertility.[9] For example, attitudes toward desired fertility are a complex interaction of social, psychological, economic and other causes. Completed fertility is determined not only by these desires, but also by the

[8] Gary S. Becker, "An Economic Analysis of Fertility," in *Demographic and Economic Change in Developed Countries*, NBER (Princeton, 1960).

[9] See Richard A. Easterlin, "Towards a Socioeconomic Theory of Fertility: Survey of Recent Research of Economic Factors in American Fertility," in S. J. Behrman, L. Corsa, Jr., and R. Freedman (Eds.), *Fertility and Family Planning: A World View*, (Ann Arbor, 1969) for a review of much of the economic literature on fertility (including a survey of the empirical basis of the Becker model) and an examination of some of the shortcomings in the economic theory of fertility as developed at that time. A survey of analytic models constructed by demographers that emphasize physiological factors is contained in M. C. Sheps, J. A. Menken, and A. P. Radick, "Probability Models for Family Building: An Analytic Review," *Demography*, vol. 6 (May, 1969) pp. 161–183.

couple's motivation to meet their desires by controlling excess fertility, and by fecundity factors which are in part outside the control of the couple. Finally, the fertility process occurs over a reasonably long time span during which many of these determining factors may change.

In order to capture this complexity in as much detail as possible, we analyze several components of fertility separately in a recursive framework.[10] No attempt is made to achieve a closed analytic model in which completed fertility is the immediate outcome of the model. Rather, the "solution" of the model is obtained through the cumulative interactions of the equations over the course of the simulation. We first assume that each couple determines the number of children that they wish to have and that they make some decision about the spacing of their children. Not using contraception after marriage or a birth is considered a decision in this framework. It will be further assumed that couples who do not wish to have a child in a given time period will use contraception. Couples will not wish to conceive either because they have already had their desired number of children or because they want to delay the date of their next birth. An effectiveness of contraception use is assigned to those couples who use it. The final factor incorporated into this model is fecundity, the physiological capacity of the couple to conceive and bear a child to full term.

These four aspects of fertility have been incorporated into the following recursive model.

(1) $$N^* = N^* \text{ (Dem, SES, Att, N)}$$

(2) $$S^* = S^* \text{ (Dem, SES, Att, } N^*, N, S)$$

(3) $$\text{Eff} = \text{Eff (Dem, SES, Att, N, } N^*, S, S^*)$$

(4) $$\text{Fec} = \text{Fec (Dem, SES, N, } N^*, S).$$

Here N^* is the number of children the couple wishes to have. It is a function of the couple's demographic attributes, Dem, including their ages, their ages at marriage and their race, and of their socioeconomic status, SES, which includes their education, income, labor force status of the wife, and occupation. It may also be a function of the attitudes and values, Att, of the couple and of the number of children, N, the couple now has. Given their desired number of children, we determine the couple's desired minimum interval between children which is a function of the same set of independent variables and in addition may depend upon the desired number of children and some measure, S, of the spacing of their previous children. The effectiveness of contraception use, Eff, is a function of all of these preceding variables. The fecundity of the couple, Fec, is primarily a function of the woman's age, but may also be a function of N and N^* (to allow, for example, for the possibility of voluntarily sterilization if $N \geq N^*$) and the other variables indicated.

The number of children that the couple have is then determined by applying this model within the simulation framework. In each year the couple's desired

---

[10] Further description of this model and the theoretical model underlying it are contained in Gerald E. Peabody, "A Simulation Model of Fertility in the United States," The Urban Institute, Working Paper 709-5, April 30, 1971.

number of children and desired spacing are determined so we know whether or not they desire a birth. Contraception is used or not depending upon whether a birth is not or is desired. The birth probability is a function of the efficacy of contraception, if used, and the couple's fecundity. The Monte Carlo technique is used to determine if the occurrence of a birth is to be imputed. This cycle is repeated for each year of the simulation over the fertile period of the woman, and the total number of children the couple have is determined by the successive outcomes of the Monte Carlo drawings over the total period of the simulation.

By drawing upon a variety of sources it is possible to make reasonable estimates of the equations in the model. Further details of the estimations will be given below, but a brief survey is in order here. The Growth of American Families studies and the National Fertility Surveys[11] provide a twenty year record of families' attitudes toward family planning and their success or lack thereof in carrying out their plans. From these studies, data are available on the desired number of children and the efficacy of contraception use. Additional economic and sociological research and surveys provide other information on the desired number of children. Data on the fecundity of couples, both the distribution among couples of a given age and the decline of fecundity with advancing age, are available from the demographic and biological literature, although it is sometimes sparse. The biggest data gaps are in attitudes about spacing of children. The Princeton Study[12] did ask about spacing desires, but the published results do not link these attitudes to the socioeconomic characteristics of the family.

B. Simulation Model

The term fecundability has been applied by demographers to the monthly probability that a fecund woman will conceive in one month. It is a function of the woman's age and length of the time from her last birth and may be expressed as

$$(5) \qquad \text{FEC}(i, t) = F \cdot f_{it} \cdot F_1(\text{age}) \cdot F_2(\text{interval}).$$

Here F is the mean value of fecundability, f_{it} is a parameter that reflects the distribution of fecundity among women, F_1 gives the age dependence of fecundity, F_2 incorporates the infertile period during a pregnancy and a few months following a birth or miscarriage.

F_1 is zero until a woman reaches puberty, quickly rises to a constant value for the late teens and twenties, and then declines roughly linearly to zero at menopause. F_2 is zero during a pregnancy and for several months after a pregnancy has terminated. For the first two or three months after a birth or miscarriage a woman is sterile, and for several additional months her menstrual cycles are anovulatory. Thus, the period for which a woman is infecund following a pregnancy may be three to five months for a woman who does not nurse and up to a year for one who does.

[11] Norman B. Ryder and Charles F. Westoff, *Reproduction in the United States: 1965* (Princeton, 1971).
[12] C. F. Westoff, R. G. Potter, Jr., P. C. Sagi, and E. G. Mishler, *Family Growth in Metropolitan America* (Princeton, 1961).

When a couple is not using contraception, their birth probability, by definition, is their fecundability. Thus for women i in period t

(6) $$\text{PBIRTH}(i, t) = \text{FEC}(i, t).$$

For any couple that does not want to give birth we assume they use contraception. In this model it is assumed that couples for whom $N \geq N^*$ or $S < S^*$ do not want to give birth. For these women the birth probability is given by

(7) $$\text{PBIRTH}(i, t) = \text{FEC}(i, t)[1 - \text{EFF}(i, t)]$$

where EFF is the efficacy of contraception use as given by equation (3).

C. Model Implementation

The first step in the simulation procedure is to assign the variables not originally in the file to women in the initial population. For simulations currently being carried out to align the model, the 1960 Census 1/1000 sample is being used. In this sample no information is available on the desired number of children, desired spacing, or fecundability, so that each of these variables must be imputed. In the initial population, values for these variables are assigned to all married women, and during the course of the simulation they are imputed to women when they marry. Fecundability and effectiveness must be calculated in each year since they depend, respectively, upon the woman's age and whether contraception is used to delay or terminate fertility.

As currently implemented, the desired number of children is expressed as a set of probability functions; i.e., the discrete distribution of N^* is given explicitly. The probability that a couple will desire n children is taken to be given by

(8) $$\text{Prob}(N^* = n) = N_n^*(\text{race, age-at-marriage})$$

$$= a_n + b_n(\text{race}) + c_n(A_m) + d_n(\text{race})(A_m).$$

Here race and A_m (age-at-marriage) are dummy variables; for example

$$\text{race} = 1, \quad \text{if race} = \text{Negro}$$

$$= 0, \quad \text{otherwise.}$$

A similar relation holds for A_m except that it is a vector of variables corresponding to the different ages-at-marriage that are distinguished. The reasons for this choice of independent variables has been given elsewhere.[13] The Monte Carlo procedure is used to assign a desired number of children to each woman on the basis of this set of probability functions.

One important variable that has been omitted is the labor force status of the woman. Women who want to work and do so have a much lower desired fertility than those who do not work. This variable will be included when the income segments of the model are implemented. Another important variable that has been omitted is the religion of the family. In the U.S. Catholics on average desire almost a full child more than do Protestant families, while Jews desire slightly

---

[13] Gerald E. Peabody, *op. cit.*

less children than Protestant families. However, religion is a difficult variable to incorporate into the simulation framework. In the first place it is not available on the census surveys that are being used for the initial populations and so would have to be imputed. More importantly, religion by itself is not the only important factor. The degree of religious commitment also has an important influence on fertility, so that we would also have to determine how religious a couple is. The difficulties of making these imputations are so large that this variable is being omitted.

Other variables that are important in determining completed fertility have not been included in equation (8) since they are not very significant for *desired* fertility. Included in this category are education and income. While fertility does vary considerably with education and income, it appears that this variation is a result of the relative effectiveness of contraception practice of different education classes rather than their attitudes about the number of children desired. A final factor that has been omitted for now is the higher fertility that is characteristic of rural farm areas, particularly in the south, relative to urban areas.

The desired minimum interval is also expressed as a series of probability functions:

(9) $\text{Prob}(S^* = n) = S_n^*(\text{race, education})$.

These equations have also been estimated in the dummy variable form indicated in equation (8) with two dummy variables for education to distinguish between education of less than high school graduate, high school graduate, and at least some college. Spacing desires are also known to be a function of the desired number of children, but this dependence has not yet been incorporated. We know of no body of survey data available that would enable us to estimate equation (9) directly, so these equations are being estimated by constraining the simulation to replicate the available census data on completed intervals.

Efficacy of contraception use is a function of the variables indicated in equation (10).

(10) $\text{EFF} = \text{EFF}(\text{race, education, intention})$.

Intention is the reason for using contraception: either to delay the arrival of the next birth, or to terminate fertility and have no more children. The values of efficacy have been estimated from failure rates for contraception users given in the 1965 National Fertility Survey.[14] They range from a low of 0.44 for Negro women who had not completed high school and who wished to delay the next birth to a high of 0.88 for white women with some college education who wished to terminate child bearing. In the absence of empirical data, divorced and widowed women are arbitrarily given efficacy values of 1.0; never-married women are given values of efficacy that will reproduce the rates of births to non-married women.

Fecundability is calculated for each year from equation (5). Since we simulate in intervals of a year rather than a month, the constant F is the probability that a fecund couple will have a live birth in a year rather than the monthly probability of conception. f_{it} is currently solely a sterility index; it is 0 for sterile women

---

[14] N. B. Ryder and C. F. Westoff, *op. cit.*

and 1 for fecund women. This index is part of each woman's permanent record, although the probability of her being sterile increases with her age. The age dependence in F_1 has been given a simple form that roughly fits the available empirical data. It is taken to be 0 until the age of 17 and then assumes a constant value of 1 until age 28; it then declines linearly to 0 at age 48. F_2 accounts for the fact that a couple that has a birth in one year has a reduced probability of having a birth in the next year due to the reduced exposure time resulting from the infecund period following a birth.

In assigning values to the initial population, more independent variables are required than indicated in equations (8) and (9). Since the married women in the initial population have already had some fertility experience, it is necessary to make the assignment of additional desired number of children conditional upon the current fertility status of the woman. Thus N^* is a function of race and the woman's current age, parity and length of marriage. A similar procedure should be followed for the desired interval. However, we are not familiar with any data that would enable us to do so.

Simulations with this model have been conducted with an initial population drawn from the 1960 Census 1/1000 sample consisting of 16,321 individuals who comprise 5,256 households. Simulation runs have been made for a period of ten years, and the resulting simulated birth rates and other fertility measures have been compared with statistics of the actual experience in the 1960s. These initial simulation results are encouraging, and indicate that this model can capture the fertility experience of the decade of the 1960s. Further simulations are currently underway to further improve the model alignment, and detailed simulation results will be made available in forthcoming publications.

4. CHANGES IN MARITAL STATUS

Steven Caldwell

Marital status is an important defining characteristic of American adults which assumes an immediate importance for the Urban Institute microanalytic modeling effort because of its close relationship to other personal and family attributes, such as female labor force participation, number and spacing of children, mortality, and family income. To incorporate marital status into the model, transition probabilities must be generated to move persons between the several marital states. One set of generating functions has already been implemented and simulations made; that set will be described below and some simulation results presented. In addition, recent work has improved the conceptualization and estimation of the functions generating these probabilities. Although they have not yet been implemented in an operating model, these newer versions will be described.

A. The Operating Model

Marriage probabilities for never-married persons are generally substantially lower than those for widowed or divorced persons. Thus, for purposes of estima-

TABLE 1

HISTORICAL COMPARED TO SIMULATED MARRIAGE RATES IN THE U.S., 1960–69

Year	Total Number of Marriages in 1,000's			Marriage Rate per 1,000 Unmarried Women over 14			Marriage Rate per 1,000 Unmarried Women, 15–44		
	Historical (H)	Simulated (S)	Percent Deviations[1]	Historical (H)	Simulated (S)	Percent Deviations[1]	Historical (H)	Simulated (S)	Percent Deviations[1]
1960	1523	1490	-2%	73.5	68.9	-6%	148.0	128.3	-13%
1961	1548	1545	0	72.2	71.8	-1	145.4	135.7	-7
1962	1577	1545	-2	71.2	77.8	9	138.4	143.3	4
1963	1654	1755	6	73.4	81.2	11	143.3	148.2	3
1964	1725	1847	7	74.6	81.1	9	146.2	142.1	-3
1965	1800	1831	2	75.0	79.6	6	144.3	139.7	-3
1966	1857	1886	2	75.6	80.0	6	145.1	142.6	-2
1967	1927	2026	5	76.4	82.7	8	145.2	145.6	0
1968	2069	1939	-6	79.1	77.7	-2	147.2	140.5	-5
1969	2145	2038	-5	80.0	82.8	-3	149.1	147.7	-1

[1] $\dfrac{S-H}{H} \cdot 100$.

tion the population of all single persons is broken into "never-married" and "all others". For the operating model first-marriage probabilities have been made a function of sex, race, and single years of age from 15 through 50. Females have generally higher first marriage probabilities up to age 25 (for whites) and 34 (for non-whites); thereafter males have higher probabilities. In effect, the age profile of transition probabilities both rises and declines more steeply for females. The racial difference in age profiles is also distinct, though perhaps on the decline. Non-white males exhibit a rather flat age profile, which rises fairly rapidly to a peak at a younger age but at a considerably lower level than that of white males and then falls only very slowly for the following 15 years. Roughly the same differences exist between white and non-white females, with the non-white peak being earlier but lower, and the decline considerably slower. Put another way, age seems less useful as a predictor of first marriage decisions for non-whites. Moreover, for both sexes and for almost all ages recent experience reveals non-white nuptiality rates to be substantially lower than white rates.

In the United States, about one-quarter of all marriages in a year are re-marriages. Re-marriage probabilities for those with at least one marriage terminated by death or divorce have been taken from registration data in which the probabilities are tabulated by previous marital status (widowed vs. divorced), age (in three or four broad categories), and sex. Mean values of age-sex specific rates for 1960–1966 were used; no time trend on age-sex-marital status specific parameters was included.

Marriage dissolutions occur in the model through death or divorce. The mortality function, of course, creates widows and widowers. Data on divorce rates reveal that the probability of divorce generally rises to a peak in the third year of marriage and declines thereafter. For the third year and beyond, an exponential function was estimated relating divorce rates to the duration of marriage and used for predicting divorce probabilities for marriages of up to 25 years duration.

TABLE 2

HISTORICAL COMPARED TO SIMULATED DIVORCE RATES IN THE U.S., 1960–69

Year	Total Number of Divorces in 1,000's			Divorce Rate per 1,000 Married Women		
	Historical	Simulated	Percent Deviations	Historical	Simulated	Percent Deviations
1960	393	442	12%	9.2	9.9	8%
1961	414	436	5	9.6	9.8	2
1962	413	435	5	9.4	9.6	2
1963	428	425	−1	9.6	9.3	−3
1964	450	436	−3	10.0	9.2	−8
1965	479	448	−6	10.6	9.4	−11
1966	499	452	−9	10.9	9.3	−15
1967	523	465	−11	11.2	9.4	−16
1968	584	485	−17	12.4	9.6	−23
1969	639	510	−20	13.4	9.8	−27

Using the above operating characteristics for generating transition probabilities for marriage and divorce, simulation runs have been made on an initial population drawn from the 1960 Census 1/1000 tape. This population was "grown" for 10 annual periods and the observed and expected marriage and divorce rates calculated for various population groups. The results can be seen in Table 1 for marriage and Table 2 for divorce in which the simulated rates are compared to historical data. Given the small sample size utilized (1,554 persons in the initial sample) it is difficult to draw meaningful conclusions about the discrepancies; however, it does appear likely that the recent rapid increase in divorces beginning in 1967 was not accounted for satisfactorily by the increase in the number of marriages. That is, the rise in the number of low-duration marriages may not be sufficient to account for the increase in divorce; it seems likely that the duration specific rates also changed over time.

B. THE NEWER VERSION

As the model is developed further a richer set of functions to generate probabilities of change in marital status will be incorporated. These newer versions are being developed to help remedy some of the major deficiencies in the operating characteristics described above. These deficiencies are:

(1) lack of time variation in the transition probabilities;

(2) insufficient policy relevance of the independent variables;

(3) important socioeconomic differentials omitted.

All three deficiencies are really aspects of the extent to which the existing functions fall short of a true structural model of the marriage and divorce process. With further development and refinement of the operating characteristics for changes in marital status, we hope to capture basic attitudes and behavior that will bring us closer to a structural model and will make it more possible to explore social policy issues concerning marital status.

The distribution of the states of being single (never married), married, separated, divorced and widowed in the national population has long been a matter of public concern, with Americans seeming generally to have considered marriage to be the desirable condition and to have treated other states as, to some degree, "social problems". Thus rising divorce rates have been taken as cause for alarm (although the rising proportion of marriage age persons who are actually married has received less attention). The value placed on being married is at least partly rooted in evidence showing that, for the U.S., married persons have lower death rates, lower suicide rates, lower usage of facilities for the mentally ill, and probably also lower rates of alcoholism than those widowed, divorced, or never married. It is not clear to what extent, if any, these relationships are causal. But it does seem likely that the possibilities of inter- and intragenerational mobility, both for parents and children, are in general influenced by the distribution and timing of marital transitions. For example, it has been argued that certain of a child's opportunities depend upon whether or not he grows up in a home with both parents.

The new version of the model for first marriage will include a parameter which incorporates education differentials determined from analyses of data in the Survey of Economic Opportunity. Age-sex-race-education specific rates are divided by age-sex-race specific rates, yielding a ratio which is then used to distribute these rates among education classes. This education-specific parameter, however, is not allowed to affect the overall levels of age-race-sex specific rates; a tracking routine scales the education specific ratio up or down to match the predicted age-race-sex rates. Thus, education is, in effect, used as a selective, rather than a causative, factor.

In general, education in moderate amounts seems to increase the marriage rates. Those with a high school education marry at higher rates than the average for nearly all ages. The least attractive partners (strictly from the point of view of marriage probabilities), especially at middle age or above, seem to be those with the least education followed by those with the most. It has been hypothesized that women "marry up" in socioeconomic status; consequently, high status women and low status men should have the hardest time finding partners and thus have relatively low marriage probabilities. Though such an effect is not easy to locate in available data, college educated women have tended to have lower marriage rates than other women and than college educated males.

Using retrospective data on age at first marriage from the 1960 census, we are now trying to decompose first marriage rates by race and sex into three separate effects:

(1) an age effect—the hypothesis being that there is a constant tendency to marry as a function of age;
(2) a cohort effect—the hypothesis being that all persons born the same year and sharing the same national social atmosphere over their lifetimes have a specific bias about marriage, a greater or lesser enthusiasm for it, which manifests itself in a specific probability at which members of the cohort tend to marry which is more or less than the rate of an average cohort;
(3) a year effect—the hypothesis being that a given year, for economic or other reasons, has a certain depressing or stimulating effect on first marriage rates.

First results from this approach, using parameters estimated from an analysis of variance technique, are promising. The age parameters are all significant and fit a smooth curve with the expected shape. The cohort parameters exhibit an increasing tendency to marry for recent cohorts. And the year parameters seem to be sensitive to wars and economic trends. We will attempt to use the year effect parameters as a dependent variable with economic outputs from the macro model as independent variables. If successful, this would provide an interesting additional link between the macro and micro models.

The importance of such a decomposition of the independent variables is that it moves us toward a more meaningful policy simulation context by putting more realistic constraints on the ways in which we can vary first marriage probabilities. Furthermore, this does allow time variation in rates, which means we might better capture past experience.

Analyses of data in the Survey of Economic Opportunity allow us to incorporate additional differentials into the re-marriage functions: race, education, and length of time since marriage ended. Again, education is treated as a distributive factor in this function. We also have data for four time periods (1960–1966, 1950–1959, 1940–1949, 1930–1939) so this opens up some possibility of capturing a time trend in these parameters. However, only quite clear trends will be incorporated. The possibility of putting in a time trend simply for simulation purposes is always open.

Given that a set of males and females have "decided to marry," they will be ranked according to their race, education, age and perhaps other variables. The two lists will then be merged to create a marriage in which the partners match as well as possible. Left over males or females will be placed in the lists for the following year. If one sex is consistently in excess, this will in effect replicate the phenomenon of the "marriage squeeze."

Divorce probabilities are increased in sophistication by adding differentials by (1) race, (2) education, and (3) number of children. Number of children could be allowed a causal impact, which might account for some portion of the sharp rise in divorce rates in 1967–1970, since the number of children is inversely related to divorce probability and family size declined over that period.

Finally, we will create a fifth marital status category—separation. We do this for purposes of family income calculation. Separated persons are presently treated as married in our model, but in general we know they must support separate residences, automobiles, etc. Further, the incidence of separation is especially high among non-whites. Thus, to avoid giving an artificially optimistic picture of the non-white population we will create a function which separates marriage partners. Its purpose will simply be to reproduce approximately the incidence of separation in the population.

In the case of divorce or separation, both assets and children must be allocated. We will arbitrarily assign all children to the female. In the case of asset division, we have yet to find any data to guide us.

Some of the most interesting simulation experiments, when the larger model is completed and running, will have to do with the following:

(1) most important, examining the effects of early marriage on fertility, labor force participation, completed education and wealth accumulation;

(2) examining the effects of divorce on subsequent life histories, including the histories of children involved;

(3) and, if it proves fruitful to include in the marriage function year-specific parameters related to the dynamics of the macro economy, examining the interactions of macroeconomic policy and marriage decisions through such intervening variables as labor force participation and fertility.

5. COMPUTER IMPLEMENTATION

GEORGE SADOWSKY

Our microanalytic simulation model of the U.S. household sector is currently being implemented on a PDP-10 computer manufactured by the Digital Equipment Corporation. The PDP-10 computer is a high speed electronic stored program digital computer which operates in a "time sharing" mode. The PDP-10 used for our work is physically located at The Brookings Institution in Washington, D.C., which is approximately one-half mile away from our offices. Its configuration includes 98,304 36-bit words of immediate access memory (of which a maximum of about 70,000 words are available to any one user), 3 demountable disk drives each having a capacity of approximately 5,000,000 words of random access storage, 3 IBM-compatible magnetic tape drives, a punch card reader, a line printer, 5 DECtape drives (a low speed, specialized tape drive), and communications equipment controlling teletypewriter terminals. The computer is accessed by members of the research staffs of several social science research organizations in the Washington area. Access to the computer is obtained through teletypewriters which are connected at the user's end through acoustic couplers to standard voice communication public telephone lines emanating from the computer.

The PDP-10 computer is a "time-sharing" system in the sense that it allows many users concurrent access to its computing resources and that its software is designed primarily for interactive use. Users of such a system typically engage in a "dialogue" with the computer system: a user will type a command to the computer system using a typewriter-like device and will receive a reply typed on the same device indicating the outcome of his request. The computing system may prompt the user to ask for more information during the process of fulfilling the request.

A major difference between this method of using computing machinery, often called interactive or on-line computing, and its historical alternative, batch computing, is that an interactive user can make decisions concerning his research or programming strategy in a sequential manner with assistance from the feedback supplied by the computer, whereas the user of a batch computing system must either prespecify a longer sequence of operations or use more system resources and more of his own time to obtain such flexibility. Interactive computing systems are feasible because of the great disparity between the speeds at which computers and people function and because of the disparate requirements placed upon a computer system by members of its user population. The PDP-10 interactive computing system is analogous to a chess master who can play "simultaneous" games of chess with many human opponents because he can remember more and think more quickly than his opponents. In the same manner, an interactive computer circulates among its users and allocates its resources to their requirements according to a predetermined system of priorities.

An integrated system of computer programs named MASH (an acronym representing "*MicroAnalytic Simulation of Households*") is being written for the PDP-10 to help develop, implement and use the family of microanalytic models that will result from the microanalytic research efforts of our staff and of others. The basic unit of simulation within this family of models is the interview unit. As defined by the U.S. Bureau of the Census, it consists of all individuals in a household or other housing unit who are related to each other by blood, marriage or adoption. An interview unit may contain one or more families, and each family may contain one or more persons. Thus, each unit of simulation has a three-level hierarchic structure or tree structure.

Within the MASH system, each interview unit, family and person are assigned names (which are positive integers for programming convenience). For every initial simulation population, the initial set of data describing each interview unit, family, and person is assigned to and is stored in a specific logical address occupied by that interview unit, family, or person. In addition, cross reference information is generated that defines the structure of that initial simulation population. Membership lists generated contain the "names" of all families initially contained within each interview unit and the "names" of all persons initially contained within each family. Address lists generated contain the current logical "address" within computer storage of each interview unit, family, and person in the population. The data for each person include the "name" of the family containing him, and the data for each family include the "name" of the interview unit in which the family is contained. These membership lists, address lists and containment pointers define the structural relationships between entities within the simulation population.

As demographic processes are applied to the simulation population, the initial population structure will change. New names will be assigned to new births, and the data describing the newly born child, including inherited characteristics, will be stored in a new logical person address assigned to the child. Marriages and divorces will generally cause a new family and perhaps also a new interview unit to be created. Deaths will annihilate a person and possibly a family and an interview unit also. For each structural change, the cross reference information is adjusted to reflect the change. In addition, whenever a person changes his family affiliation or creates a new family, the data for the person are moved to a new "address" and the person's address list entry is altered. The person's new family name and a code denoting his reason for leaving his old family are added to the person data at the old address, and the person's old family name and a code denoting his reason for joining his new family are included in the person's data at his new address. After the person has been moved, the data in his old address are preserved indefinitely by the system. Thus, every simulation generates a genealogical record of population structure changes. This information is useful both for programming purposes while building the model and for implementing operating characteristics that require transfers of information among related persons and family units. One use of this genealogical structure is to provide a mechanism for the inheritance of assets when a family is dissolved due to the deaths of all its members.

An important component of the MASH system is the use of machine readable codebooks for all population data definition and documentation. A MASH codebook is a file of documentation that exists physically as a deck of punch cards or its machine-readable equivalent on magnetic tape or magnetic disk storage. Each sample survey population file that is read by MASH must be defined by such a codebook, and a codebook is automatically generated for every new population file that MASH creates. Each codebook contains: (1) a precise definition of all record types contained in the file; (2) the physical specifications and format layout for each type of record in the file; (3) the unique name, mode, position and label of each attribute (field) in each record; (4) for each attribute, an exhaustive list of values that it can take on and associated labels defining the meaning of each of these values; and (5) sufficient free form text to provide additional file, record and attribute documentation in human readable form. Such a codebook not only provides a unified and complete source of data documentation, but it also allows users of the MASH system to reference any population attributes by specifying the name of the attribute alone.

In addition to providing interactive computing services, the PDP-10 computer system allows its users to maintain on-line random access program and data files of moderately large size. MASH utilizes this feature of the PDP-10 by maintaining its entire current microsimulation population, its address and membership lists, the machine readable codebook describing the population, the user's dictionary of attribute, code and sample definitions, and the time series data bank in on-line random access storage. This form of data organization provides a number of significant advantages for microsimulation modelling. First, the mechanisms for making structural changes within the simulation populations are considerably simpler than they would be within a sequential file processing environment. Second, data browsing functions become quite easy to provide. The MASH user can examine and change any attribute of any entity of the simulation population quickly and at very low cost. Finally, on-line documentation allows the MASH user to refer to attributes solely by name and can provide him with properly labelled output on an interactive basis. The availability of on-line storage devices having substantial capacity is as essential to the viability of the MASH system as it now exists as is the interactive computing environment.

The Fortran IV programming language was chosen as the major implementation language for the MASH system for a number of reasons. Among them were: (1) widespread knowledge and readability of Fortran IV among programmers; (2) efficiency of programming process using a high-level language; (3) ease of interfacing Fortran IV programs with assembly language subroutines; (4) relative ease of exporting and importing programs to and from other computer centers; and (5) existence of an acceptable Fortran IV translator on the PDP-10. Some PDP-10 assembly language subprograms have been added for reasons of efficiency.

The MASH system is designed to be used at different levels for different purposes. For the research user there exists a free form, high level, interactive control language that allows him to create initial simulation populations, control a simulation process based on any one model, examine his population data in any sequence of his choosing, take censuses of his population and perform a variety of statistical analyses. The existence of this language reflects a belief that productive research is encouraged in an environment that provides a researcher with computing tools sufficiently powerful for him to be in direct contact with and exercise control over his computing activities.

Unfortunately it would be prohibitively expensive to expand such a control language to contain the complexity required for a general microsimulation language, and primarily for this reason the programming implementation of the model's operating characteristics is done in Fortran IV, with some assistance inherent in the MASH system structure. Once the MASH system is complete, we expect that a custodial programmer will be associated with the system to perform the programming required by the inevitable extension, alteration, and maintenance of the model and the education functions associated with an ongoing computer-intensive research project.

The present repertoire of MASH commands may be categorized in the following functional areas: (1) entering and modifying definitions, displaying user defined entities, and other "housekeeping" chores; (2) creating initial simulation populations; (3) data browsing; (4) microsimulation control and execution; (5) taking censuses and obtaining statistical outputs; and (6) adding to, modifying and displaying sections of time series data bank and performing aggregate statistical analysis. The MASH system is organized internally as a modular interpreter, and this form of organization allows us to add to the command repertoire as our experience with the system grows and as we evolve new computing tasks for it. We also intend to modify the syntax of existing commands so that it parallels as closely as possible the language and concepts of social science research.

The scope and character of this high level, interactive command language and some functions are best displayed for the purposes of this paper by a hypothetical computer run using MASH. The example below is indicative of the command language, but does not encompass the entire set of commands.

Let us suppose that a researcher named Gomez wishes to perform a microsimulation of the household sector using a model which contains a known set of operating characteristics. In general, most of these operating characteristics will be embedded within the MASH program, although for the purposes of policy experimentation one or two new ones may have been specified by the researcher and added to the system by the custodial programmer. Further suppose that his population data source is a sample survey file named SEO67 for which there is a machine readable codebook named COD67, and that the attributes in the codebook include those in the following table as well as others:

Level	Attribute Name	Description
Interview unit	REGION	Region of residence
	NUMFAM	Number of families in interview unit
	URBAN	An urban/rural code
Family	TOTINCOME	Total family income
	NUMPERSONS	Number of persons in family
	ASSETS	Amount of family assets
	DEBTS	Amount of family debt
	FARMVALUE	Value of farm, if any exists
	TAXESPAID	Federal taxes paid by the family
	PENSIONS	Value of private pensions received by family
	SOCSEC	Value of public pensions received by family
	NETWORTH	Net worth of family
Person	AGE	Age of person
	RACE	Code for race of person
	SEX	Code for sex of person
	WAGES	Yearly wages received by person
	WEEKS	No. of weeks person worked

MARRY	Code for marital status of person
JOB	Occupation code for person
HIGHGRADE	Highest grade of school completed

To initiate his simulation activity, the researcher sits at his computer console, dials the computer and makes the connection between the two. He obtains access to the system by entering his account number and his confidential "password." He then enters MASH by typing:

RUN MASH

Each user of the MASH system has his own dictionary which may be used to store variable definitions, recodes, commonly used commands and other system entities. A user would often initially instruct the system to use his dictionary in the event he might want to retrieve from or store into it. To do this, he types:

USE DICTIONARY BELONGING TO GOMEZ;

In order to perform a microsimulation, an initial population must be constructed. The user may include in this population only those attributes and those simulation units that he specifies. Simulation populations are identified by number, and the user declares his intention to describe one by typing:

DESCRIBE POPULATION NUMBER 71;

Information about where to obtain the data for this initial population and how to interpret it are transmitted to MASH in the statement:

EXTRACT FROM SURVEY FILE SEO67 ON UNIT 20
DESCRIBED BY CODEBOOK COD67 ON UNIT 21;

The attributes to be included in the initial population are then specified in one or more statements of the following type:

INCLUDE SURVEY ATTRIBUTES REGION, NUMFAM;

INCLUDE SURVEY ATTRIBUTES TOTINCOME, ASSETS,
DEBTS, NETWORTH, SOCSEC, PENSIONS,
NUMPERSONS, FARMVALUE, TAXESPAID;

Since typing lists of names repeatedly is time consuming, the user is given the option of defining a list of names and then referencing the attributes indirectly through the name of the list. The list will be stored in the user's dictionary as he has defined it, and can be referenced by name by him during subsequent runs. For example the following statements include all the person attributes listed above in the initial simulation population.

DEFINE LIST LABORDATA AS WEEKS, JOB, WAGES;

DEFINE LIST DEMOGRAPHY AS MARRY, AGE, RACE, SEX;

INCLUDE SURVEY ATTRIBUTE LIST DEMOGRAPHY;

INCLUDE SURVEY ATTRIBUTE LIST LABORDATA;

INCLUDE SURVEY ATTRIBUTE HIGHGRADE;

Some attributes are not defined within the original sample survey data and must be imputed to simulation units as the initial simulation population is created. The computer instructions to perform the imputation are similar to those that define an operating characteristic, and they have already been added to the system by the custodial programmer. The documentation that describes this attribute has previously been entered in another machine readable file, the attribute library. This library contains attribute definitions for newly created attributes in much the same way that the codebook describing a file contains attribute definitions for attributes whose values are recorded within that file. An example of such an attribute is the number of children desired by a family; it is an important variable for determining the probability of occurrence of a birth. Such attributes are included in the collection of attributes for the initial population by executing a statement of the form:

INCLUDE LIBRARY ATTRIBUTE KIDSWANTED;

MASH includes a facility for generating a time series of values for an attribute at an individual unit level. For example, suppose it is desired to observe peak net worth achieved and taxes paid by families during the course of the simulation, and in addition the most recent values of public and private pensions received for the last five years. The following commands achieve this:

GENERATE HIGHEST 3 YEAR SERIES FOR
NETWORTH, TAXESPAID;

GENERATE LAST 5 YEAR SERIES FOR PENSIONS, SOCSEC;

For each series to be generated, a sequence of new attributes is generated, e.g. NETWORTH01, NETWORTH02, NETWORTH03, for each entity in the population having NETWORTH as an attribute, i.e. all families. These new attributes are initially undefined. As the simulation progresses, sequential values of the attribute in time are considered for retention as values of the generated attributes according to the criterion specified in the GENERATE command. Thus, for example, if this population were used as the basis for a simulation of three years or more, then after the simulation was finished *each* family would have values of the attributes NETWORTH01, NETWORTH02, and NETWORTH03 corresponding to the highest values of the attribute NETWORTH generated by the simulation for that family. Using this command, time series may be generated on an individual basis for any set of attributes at all levels of the hierarchical simulation unit.

After all desired attributes have been specified for inclusion in the population and all time series have been described, the initial population can be drawn. The command to initiate this action is:

CREATE POPULATION;

Each interview unit in the self-weighting sample survey file SEO67 will appear in the initial simulation population identified by the number 71; i.e., no sub-selection of interview units will have taken place. If subselection were desired, it could easily be accomplished by defining a *sample* of interview units and extracting only those interview units that satisfied the sample definition. For example, suppose that only single family interview units living in urban areas (URBAN code of 2) were desired. The following command defines a sample of interview units named URBAN1 and stores the definition in the user's dictionary:

DEFINE SAMPLE URBAN1 OF INTUNIT AS NUMFAM = 1
.AND. URBAN = 2;

Then the command:

CREATE POPULATION USING SAMPLE URBAN1;

will restrict the initial simulation population to only those interview units that satisfy the definition of URBAN1.

Data browsing commands allow a MASH user to examine the contents of a newly created population or the results of a partial or total simulation. For example, suppose it is desired to search for an old person and examine his pension status and family structure. The following dialogue might take place (MASH responses are underlined):

FIND FIRST PERSON WITH AGE > = 65;

PERSON 23 FOUND

EXHIBIT STRUCTURE OF PERSON 23;

INTUNIT 6 CONTAINS 1 FAMILY
        FAMILY 7 LIVES AT ADDRESS 8 AND CONTAINS 3 PERSONS
                PERSON 23 LIVES AT ADDRESS 23
                PERSON 24 LIVES AT ADDRESS 24
                PERSON 25 LIVES AT ADDRESS 25

WHAT IS AGE OF PERSON 23?;
74 . . . AGE IN YEARS

WHAT IS AGE OF PERSON 24?;
68 . . . AGE IN YEARS

WHAT IS AGE OF PERSON 25?;
44 . . . AGE IN YEARS

LOOK AT FAMILY 7;

WHAT ARE PENSIONS?;
1760 . . . VALUE IN DOLLARS

WHAT IS SOCSEC?;
825 . . . VALUE IN DOLLARS

WHAT ARE WAGES OF PERSON 23?;
0 . . . VALUE IN DOLLARS

WHAT ARE WAGES OF PERSON 24?;
520 . . . VALUE IN DOLLARS

WHAT IS MARRY?;
2 . . . MARRIED, SPOUSE PRESENT

WHAT ARE WAGES OF PERSON 25?;
2350 . . . VALUE IN DOLLARS

FIND NEXT PERSON AFTER PERSON 24 WITH AGE $> = 65$;
PERSON 48 FOUND

. . . .

Simulation control commands allow the MASH user to proceed with his simulation run in an incremental manner. For example, to advance the simulation population forward one year in time, executing the following command will suffice:

SIMULATE FOR 1 YEAR USING POPULATION 71;

Suppose that it is desired to observe the effect of the simulation on people who are at least 65 years old. The results of the previous browsing commands can be combined with the incremental simulation commands to halt the simulation for further browsing. For example:

PAUSE AT INTUNIT 6;
SIMULATE FOR 1 YEAR USING POPULATION 71;
AT INTUNIT 6

WHAT ARE PENSIONS OF FAMILY 7?;
1760 . . . VALUE IN DOLLARS

WHAT IS NETWORTH?;
11750 . . . VALUE IN DOLLARS

CONTINUE;
AFTER INTUNIT 6

WHAT ARE PENSIONS?;
1842 . . . VALUE IN DOLLARS

WHAT IS NETWORTH?;
10900 . . . VALUE IN DOLLARS

PAUSE AT INTUNIT 11;
CONTINUE;

. . . .

The browsing and simulation control commands may be interspersed to provide on-line control of any simulation. If it is desired, original or calculated values of any attribute may be changed by using the CHANGE command:

> CHANGE PENSIONS OF FAMILY 7 TO 1800;
> ...VALUE IN DOLLARS
>
> CHANGE NETWORTH TO 11708;
> ...VALUE IN DOLLARS
>
> CONTINUE;
>
> ....

Output is obtained by the user in two forms: (1) sample surveys of the simulated population; and (2) tabular and statistical outputs. Sample surveys allow the MASH user to extract from a simulation population a new data file, defined by an accompanying system generated codebook, containing only those attributes and those observations the user wants. For example, suppose it is desired to obtain from a simulated population asset, income, and tax data for all families that paid some Federal tax. The following MASH commands:

> DEFINE SAMPLE TAXPAYERS OF FAMILY AS TAXESPAID > 0;
>
> CONDUCT SURVEY TAXED OF FAMILIES OBTAINING
> NUMPERSONS, ASSETS, TOTINCOME, NETWORTH, TAXESPAID
> GENERATING CODEBOOK TAXCB ON SAMPLE TAXPAYERS;

will produce a rectangular data file named TAXED containing one observation for each simulated family that paid some Federal tax in the last year of the simulation. Each observation will contain five data values corresponding to the five attributes listed in the CONDUCT command. A machine readable codebook file named TAXCB will also be produced; TAXCB will describe the sample survey file TAXED. These files may be used with other, independent computer programs on either the PDP-10 computer or another computer to perform any analysis for which programs exist.

Statistical and tabular outputs can also be generated directly within the MASH system. To compute a regression equation of personal wages as a function of age, race, sex and education for all persons working at least 47 weeks per year, it is only necessary to execute the following MASH statements:

> DEFINE SAMPLE FULLYEAR OF PERSON AS WEEKS $\geq$ 47;
>
> COMPUTE REGRESSION OF WAGES ON AGE, RACE, SEX,
> HIGHGRADE ON SAMPLE FULLYEAR;

Suppose it is desired to tabulate the distribution of income by taxes paid for each family in the sample. Each attribute must first be coded, or classified into intervals. The intervals are defined in the form of a code:

> DEFINE CODE MONEY AS (*−0=1/ 1−2000=2/ 2001-4000=3/
> 4001−6000=4/ 6001−10000=5/ 10000−25000=6/ 25000−*=7);

Each term of the code statement specifies a mapping, or functional transformation, of a range of money values into an integer value. For example, all values between 2001 and 4000 are to be mapped into the value 3. The symbol "*" represents either the lowest value possible or the highest value possible within the computer depending upon which side of the hyphen it appears. Codes are applied by defining new attributes as in the following examples:

DEFINE ATTRIBUTE CODEDY OF FAMILY AS TOTINCOME CODED.BY MONEY;

DEFINE ATTRIBUTE CODEDTAX OF FAMILY AS TAXESPAID CODED.BY MONEY;

In practice, a code having somewhat different intervals would be defined and applied to the tax variable. Generating cross-tabulation output is then performed by executing the command:

COMPUTE CROSSTAB   OF CODEDY, CODEDTAX;

If the cross-tabulation were desired for only those families which were "not in poverty" according to a standard definition, and if percentage distributions were desired, the following commands would obtain the output:

DEFINE SAMPLE NOTPOOR OF FAMILY AS TOTINCOME > =
1000 + 800*NUMPERSONS;

COMPUTE CROSSTAB OF CODEDY, CODEDTAX WITH
ROWPCTS, COLPCTS, CELLPCTS ON SAMPLE NOTPOOR;

For purposes of efficiency and automatic scheduling of output generation, output procedures can be grouped into censuses which can be scheduled to occur automatically. For example, suppose that the above regression and cross-tabulation are to be computed every two years during the course of a simulation. The MASH user would enter the following commands:

DEFINE PROCEDURE REG AS COMPUTE REGRESSION
OF WAGES ON AGE, RACE, SEX, HIGHGRADE ON
SAMPLE FULLYEAR;

DEFINE PROCEDURE XTAB AS COMPUTE CROSSTAB
OF CODEDY, CODEDTAX WITH ROWPCTS, COLPCTS,
CELLPCTS ON SAMPLE NOTPOOR;

DEFINE CENSUS BIENNIAL AS REG, XTAB;

TAKE CENSUS BIENNIAL EVERY 2 YEARS;

The MASH system is currently being extended to include an aggregate time series data bank which will form the data base for the macroeconomic portion of the model. Commands planned to access and manipulate the data bank include statements of the form:

USE DATABANK BELONGING TO ORCUTT;

ENTER SERIES GNP FROM 1929 TO 1937 AS 94.3, 91.7,
72.6, 78.5, 86.9, 88.2, 89.7, 96.1, 98.6;

CHANGE SERIES GNP IN 1931 TO 70.6;

RELABEL SERIES GNP TO GNPCONP;

TYPE TABLE FROM 1946 TO 1957 OF SERIES GNP, INVEST, CONSUMP, EXPORTS, MONEYSUPLY;

TYPE INDEX FOR MY DATABANK;

LAG GNP BY 1, CREATING GNP.LAGGED;

CLOSE DATABANK;

Little has been said about the integration of the operating characteristics of a microanalytic model into the MASH system. This step is accomplished in MASH without much difficulty by relying upon a traditional programming language, Fortran IV, and a custodial programmer to function as the interface between non-programming model builders and the computer programs containing the model. The derivation of operating characteristics for this class of models is sufficiently challenging and difficult that the model builder should not be restricted in his effort by being concerned with (and often restricted by) the details of the process of implementation.

Work is currently proceeding in several areas: (1) the refinement and extension of the set of operating characteristics basic to the structure of our model; (2) the integration of the auxiliary macro model with the microanalytic simulation model; and (3) programming and testing the MASH system which implements them. We expect to have an initial model implemented shortly. Following this first implementation will be a continuing process of extension, revision and modification as new useful knowledge becomes available and as new demands are placed upon the model by researchers and policy makers. It is our hope that those demands can be met successfully as a result of our present efforts.

MODELS OF THE BRAZILIAN ECONOMY

JANES ANGELO DE SOUZA

Brazilian Institute of Economics of the Getúlio Vargas Foundation

AND

JORGE VIANNA MONTEIRO

Economics Department of the Catholic University of Rio de Janeiro

This paper is intended as a survey of quantitative model building concerned with the Brazilian economy. Part 1 gives an overall picture of the attempts so far carried on, while Part 2 points out more specific characteristics of some of these models. Part 3 is a summary-conclusion section, which one hopes will discourage further attempts along lines so far explored that have not proved very useful.

1. THE MODELS OF THE ECONOMY

Macromodeling of the Brazilian economy is a recent activity with which there has not yet been much experience. In general, the initiatives for macro-modeling came either in connection with development plans or from some international agency. Putting aside the simple exercises with the Domar equation, we may list the following attempts:

(a) the Ten-Year-Plan Model (1966–1976), developed in 1966 by the Ministry of Planning;
(b) the Baer-Kerstenetzky (1966) framework for long-run forecasting;
(c) the Three-Year Plan (PED) Model (1968–1970), also by the Ministry of Planning;
(d) the Behrman-Klein model, by the Economic Services Research Unit of the University of Pennsylvania (1968);
(e) the ECLA/Fukuchi model for long-run forecasting (1969);
(f) the Naylor et al. model, developed at the Brazilian Institute of Economics of the Vargas Foundation (1970); and
(g) the Tintner et al. econometric model (1970).

Application of a single performance format to all of these models is not easy; first, because of their different purposes; and second, due to the different volume of information available for each. Only (a), (d), and (f) underwent some kind of operational simulation, and hence presented some validation tests of their results. Both (a) and (c)—which are supposedly planning models—were used mainly as forecasting devices, although in (a) some interesting tests of alternative sets of policy parameters were performed. After sketching the main features of these various models, we shall comment, in the next section, on the different techniques and different relationships among some macrovariables introduced in the models.

The Ten-Year-Plan Model [4] consists of a block recursive system of 7 behavioral equations and 16 control and accounting relations, which makes it possible to trace out the repercussions of a priori specifications of policy targets on some macroeconomic variables. These targets relate to: (i) the overall growth

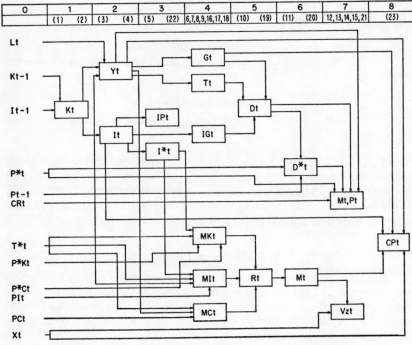

FIGURE 1   CAUSAL ORDERING OF VARIABLES IN THE TEN–YEAR–PLAN MODEL[1]

[1] The symbols used here correspond to the original source.

rate of the economy; (ii) the government share of global expenditure and inflation; (iii) the growth rate of exports; (iv) the deficit on current foreign transactions; and (v) credit expansion. The structure of the model consists of 5 blocks: Technological Restrictions, Government, Money and Banking, Foreign Trade, and Private Sector (Consumption and Investment).

The 23 basic equations, together with one auxiliary equation, trace out a chain of events from output to final consumption. A flow diagram of that structure is presented in Figure 1. The exogenous and lagged endogenous variables of zero order are shown in the first column. The variables of order two, for instance, depend on the variables of order zero, or one, or both. In general, variables of order greater than one depend only on variables of smaller order; hence Figure 1 shows that it is necessary to have the values of 12 variables to obtain the values of all subsequent series of variables in a given year. In the simulation process, the outputs at t become inputs at $t + 1$, with the equation:

$$K(t) = I(t - 1) + (1 - \delta)K(t - 1),$$

where δ, for depreciation rate, is the dynamic linkage.

The Baer-Kerstenetzky Model [1] is a hybrid of the three-limit-type model and the Domar equation. Starting with the well-known Domar formula, the level

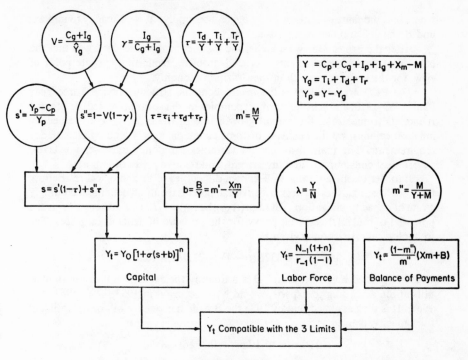

FIGURE 2   THE BAER–KERSTENETZKY MODEL[1]

[1] The symbols used here correspond to the original source.

of the National Product (Y), in terms of the domestic and external savings rate and the marginal output/capital ratio are obtained in three stages (see Figure 2). First, the sole limitation to growth is taken to be the labor-force absorption through the identity:

$$Y(t) = \frac{N_{-1}(1 + n)}{r_{-1}(1 - l)},$$

in which N is the labor force; n, its annual growth rate; r, the labor/output ratio; and l, the annual growth rate of labor productivity.[1]

Next, taking the previous constrained rate of growth, we determine levels of domestic and external savings rates compatible with those of $Y(t)$. Finally, having determined the foreign savings rate, we proceed to forecast $Y(t)$ through the identity:

$$Y(t) = \frac{(1 - m)}{m}[X(t) + B(t)],$$

[1] In Baer-Kerstenetzky [1], the magnitudes were: $n = 3$ percent, $l = 2.9$ percent (average in 1940–1960) and 3.2 percent (recent trend). Taking ($t - 1$) as 1957–1960, the alternatives for overall growth by 1975 would be 6.08 and 6.41 percent.

where m is the share of imports in the aggregate supply; X, the capacity to import; and B, the deficit on current transactions.[2]

After the projections were made, the main conclusion reached was that the balance of payments represents a crucial problem, from an aggregate point of view, for the long-run growth of the Brazilian economy.

The PED Model [5] gives the macroeconomic structure of the Three-Year Plan (1968–1970) and is by far the most complex model so far presented for Brazil.[3] It intends to maximize the overall growth rate of the economy constrained by inflation ceilings, by the behavior of some economic agents, and by consistency requirements. The main instrumental variables for policy purposes are taxes, government consumption and investment, and relative prices of imports.

In order to obviate some well-known difficulties of technological restriction, the model distinguishes between effective and potential output, defining accordingly a rate of capacity utilization. Taking $z(t)$ as the ratio $Y(t)/Y^p(t)$, where $Y^p(t)$ is the potential output, $z(t)$ acts as a proxy for the pressure of demand on prices. The technological restriction is given by

$$\Delta Y(t) = 0.332 I_f(t - 1) - 23.0D + 10.67,$$

where I_f is fixed investment, and D is a dummy for capacity utilization (underutilization, according to experts, would have occurred in 1953, 1956, 1963, and 1964). It is then assumed that by 1975 the Brazilian economy will be operating at full capacity, defined as

$$Y(t) = 0.95[10.67 + 0.322 I_f(t - 1)],$$

implying an annual rate of investment of 17.8 percent in 1975, if the economy were to grow at 6.2 percent.

The Behrman-Klein Model [2] is a 44-equation model, where boldness goes along with sophistication. The equations encompass variables such as price averages of Egyptian and United States cotton, in New York, in current United States cents per pound, "average price of synthetic fabrics in New York," "government military consumption expenditures," "marginal real tax rate on agricultural added value," and so on. Especially in the foreign sector, the model offers a unique treatment of exports—so far treated as an exogenous variable in all other models presented for the Brazilian economy.

Again the scant information available to the writers precludes a more specific comment on the performance of the model, and makes one wonder where some of the data series came from, and how helpful it can be to have variables such as the ones cited in a model of the Brazilian economy, even when they are treated as exogenous. However, the innovations introduced by Behrman-Klein should not be overlooked.

The ECLA/Fukuchi Model [3] is basically a recursive framework for long-term forecasts (up to 1980). It consists of some 66 equations, disaggregated by regions

[2] In Baer-Kerstenetzky [1], it is supposed $m = 8.53$ percent, and in some cases, $m = 6.13$ and 5.86 percent.

[3] Unfortunately the formal sophistication of this model is not accompanied by methodological rigor. Also the scarce information available precludes any serious appraisal of it as a programming tool.

(five) and sectors (three). Although limited in its "universalism" to Latin America, it contains a number of relevant points: (i) population, interregional migration, and labor force are taken endogenously; (ii) regionalization is introduced—though quite primitively; (iii) an attempt is made to achieve consistency of ad hoc data with the National Accounts estimates (especially the series on capital stock).

Given the fact that the basic structure of the model is very simple, Fukuchi's forecasts are surprisingly in accord with projections made by other macromodelists. The GDP growth rate in the seventies is set at 6.7 percent (quite the same as that recently announced by the Vargas Foundation).

The Naylor et al. Simulation Model [7] is a more recent attempt, covering the period 1947–1968. Its structure is quite simple and similar to an earlier model by Liu-DeVries.[4] Basically, this model reflects the first attempt of a model-building research unit established on a permanent basis (at the Brazilian Institute of Economics of the Vargas Foundation), and as such, it is a pedagogical device and should not be viewed as a definitive result. However, simulation tests show a remarkably good performance of the model, especially when compared with the Liu-DeVries model.

The Tintner et al. Econometric Model [8] is just a modest exercise on time series. This model describes the Brazilian economy through the use of five equations, only two of which are behavioral, and is merely a pedagogical device. The practical result arrived at, for the period 1953–1964, was simulated values overestimating the observed results by an average margin of over 100 percent.

2. SECTORS AND SPECIFICATIONS

Technological restrictions. Data problems rather than theoretical reasons have limited the use of overall production functions in models of the Brazilian economy. The simplest forms have to make allowance for the unreliable capital-stock and factor-shares data. The direct estimation of the parameters of a Cobb-Douglas function, for instance, implies negative values for capital productivity —which is an unacceptable result. Some preliminary results of the use of different estimation procedures (nonlinear techniques) performed by one of the authors seem encouraging, given the unreliability of the input data.

RECENT ESTIMATES OF COBB-DOUGLAS-TYPE FUNCTIONS FOR THE BRAZILIAN ECONOMY

$$Y(t) = e^{\lambda t} L^{\alpha(t)} K^{\beta(t)}$$

Author	Base period	λ	α	β
(1) Ten-Year Plan	1947–1965	1.14%	0.60	0.40
(2) Maneschi-Nunes	1947–1960	1.63	0.73	0.27
(3) Naylor et al.	1947–1968	2.20	0.73	0.27

Note: In (3) the estimates are based on the results obtained in (2), except for the estimates of λ.

[4] "An Econometric Analysis of Inflation and Growth in Brazil " (mimeographed), presented at the New York meeting of the Econometric Society, December 1969.

A popular variant to avoid the shortcomings of using a production function in econometric models of Brazil is the introduction of demand equations. That was done in the Liu-DeVries and Behrman-Klein models and, in general, in models where the output is disaggregated.

DEMAND EQUATIONS IN SOME MODELS OF THE BRAZILIAN ECONOMY

Liu-DeVries	$Y_1(t) = 0.022A(t) - 141.4$	$R^2 = 0.89$
(1953–1964)	$A(t) = 5.79P_1(t - 1) + 9.28C(t) + 9148$	$R^2 = 0.89$
	$Y_2(t) = 0.247C(t) - 25.2$	$R^2 = 0.68$
	$Y_3(t) = 1.31G(t) + 234.7$	$R^2 = 0.76$
Behrman-Klein	$Y_1(t) = 3.08POP(t) - 71.12$	$\bar{R}^2 = 0.93$
(1948–1964)	$Y_2(t) = 0.2586I(t) + 0.2412C(t) - 13.39$	$\bar{R}^2 = 0.96$
	$Y_3(t) = 1.538Ig(t) + 1.343Cg(t) + 77.76$	$\bar{R}^2 = 0.94$

Note: Y_1, Y_2, Y_3, respectively, output of primary, secondary, and tertiary sectors; P_1, agricultural prices; A, harvested land; C, total consumption; G, government expenditure; I, total investment; Ig, government investment; Cg, government consumption; POP, population.

Depending upon which specification is chosen, there are questions that can, or cannot, be treated analytically in the model. A production function reflects the technological restriction of the economy and, hence, traces the effects of changes in the utilization of inputs and technological change—an essential concern in a long-term model and an important question in a short-run model. But in the field of macroeconomic data there is, perhaps, no basis for favoring the aggregate consumption or investment time series, for example, over labor or capital data; and hence, the choice between the production function and demand functions should be based on theoretical reasons.

Investment. Capital formation is usually broken down into private fixed investment, government fixed investment, changes in inventories, and depreciation. The results obtained in the models so far presented relative to private fixed investment are quite acceptable. The investment functions $I_p(t)$ dismiss the rate of interest as an explanatory variable. It is not clear if this is due to the narrow influence of the capital market upon investment, or due to the difficulty in getting reliable data on interest. On the other hand, a connection with the monetary sector is obtained through an inflation coefficient—usually significant and of positive sign.[5] Naylor et al. got for 1948–1968:

$$I_p(t) = 0.638\Delta GDP + 0.581 \frac{\Delta P}{P_{-1}} + 33.269 \qquad R^2 = 0.635$$

Other possible specifications involve credit availability to the private sector, the inflow of foreign capital, and import capacity. Liu-DeVries, however, report that they did not get significant results when they correlated credit availability and inflow of foreign capital with the inflation rate and the growth of GDP.[6] Also, in recent years, the capacity to import has been shown to give meager results. Perhaps due to all of this, Behrman-Klein introduce a specification in terms of

[5] For an interpretation of this result, see, for instance: W. Baer, *Industrialization and Economic Development in Brazil*, Homewood, Ill.: Richard D. Irwin, 1965.

[6] Liu and DeVries, *op. cit.*, p. 13, footnote 9.

"nonwage factor payments" and lagged inventory changes. The fact that the first variable is significant in 1948–1964 could mean that private investment was fundamentally dependent on internal funds. However, an $\bar{R}^2$ of 0.79 does not reinforce that conclusion very much.

As to the change in inventories, attempts to associate it with changes in prices, national income, and similar factors, have invariably led to poor results. But this is not surprising when we check on the composition of this figure in the Brazilian National Accounts. It consists of variations in (i) livestock; (ii) coffee stocks; (iii) stock of import-export farm products; and (iv) stocks held by government firms. Some components, such as (ii), are related to autonomous export policies and to undesirable accumulations. Hence, the variable is introduced through a definition (Liu-DeVries, Behrman-Klein) or added to private investment (Naylor et al.).

INVESTMENT SECTOR IN SOME MODELS OF THE BRAZILIAN ECONOMY

Naylor et al. (1947–1968)	$I_p(t) = 0.635 \Delta PIB(t) + 0.581 \dfrac{\Delta P}{P_{-1}} + 33.269$	$R^2 = 0.63$
	$K(t) = K(t-1) + I(t)$	
	$I(t) = I_p(t) + I_g(t)$	
Liu-DeVries (1953–1964)	$I_p(t) = 0.663 \Delta PNB(t) + 1.58 \dfrac{\Delta P}{P_{-1}} + 76.8$	$R^2 = 0.64$
	$I_g(t) = 0.252T(t) - 12.8$	$R^2 = 0.88$
	$\Delta INV(t) = PNB(t) - C(t) - I(t) + B(t)$	
	$I(t) = I_p(t) + I_g(t)$	
Behrman-Klein (1948–1964)	$I_p(t) = 0.2729 \dfrac{(L + Y_1 - TD)}{P} - 0.1740 \Delta INV(t-1) - 17.06$	$\bar{R}^2 = 0.79$
	$\Delta INV(t) = \dfrac{PNB(t)}{P(t)} - C(t) - B(t) - DPR(t) - RS(t) - F(t)$	
	$DPR(t) = 0.02532K + 1.498$	$\bar{R}^2 = 0.97$
	$DPR_p(t) = \dfrac{\displaystyle\sum_{1948}^{64} I_{pi(t)}}{\displaystyle\sum_{1948}^{64} I_{i(t)}} DPR(t)$	
	$DPR_g(t) = DPR(t) - DPR_p(t)$	
	$K(t) = K(t-1) + I(t)$	
	$I_g(t) = 0.1418 \dfrac{T(t)}{P(t)} + 0.1036TK(t) + 0.044$	$\bar{R}^2 = 0.86$

Note: In addition to the self-explanatory symbols, INV is change in inventories; B, deficit on current transactions; RS, net factor payments to abroad; TK, capital transfers to Brazil.

Public Sector. As to government equations, the models usually explore a narrow band of government activities—a serious shortcoming if the models intend to depict the possible effects of policy measures. The Ten-Year-Plan Model only explores limited questions on fiscal policy, to the extent that it tests alternative values of the size of government investment, fiscal burden, and public debt.

GOVERNMENT SECTOR IN SOME MODELS OF THE BRAZILIAN ECONOMY

Liu-DeVries (1953–1964)	$T(t) = 0.295PNB - 149.8$	$R^2 = 0.97$
	$TR(t) = 3.58POP - 145.1$	$R^2 = 0.93$
	$SUB(t) = 67.53P_3/P_2 + 82.5$	$R^2 = 0.63$
	$Ig(t) = 0.252T(t) - 12.8$	$R^2 = 0.88$
	$D(t) = G(t) + Ig(t) + TR(t) + SUB(t) - T(t) - O(t)$	
	$E(t) = G(t) + Ig(t)$	
Behrman-Klein (1948–1964)	$Ti(t) = 0.729OT(t) - 6.255$	$\bar{R}^2 = 0.99$
	$Td(t) = 0.1323L(t) + 0.1557Y_1P + 2.405$	$\bar{R}^2 = 0.99$
	$Ig(t) = 0.1418\dfrac{T(t)}{P(t)} + 0.1036TRK(t) + 0.044$	$\bar{R}^2 = 0.86$
	$DEPg(t) = DEP(t) - DEP_p(t)$	
	$T(t) = Ti(t) + Td(t)$	
	$E(t) = G(t) + Ig(t) + DEPg(t)$	
	$D(t) = E(t) + TR(t) + SUB(t) - T(t)$	

Note: T, total taxes; TR, current transfers; SUB, subsidies; P_3/P_2, ratio of price indexes of transportation and communication to general wholesale index; D, deficit; G, government consumption; Ig, government investment; O, other government receipts; L, other nonagricultural factor payments; Y_1, value added in the primary sector; P, implicit deflator of GDP.

IMPORT FUNCTION IN SOME MODELS OF THE BRAZILIAN ECONOMY

PED Model (1948–1964)	(1)	$M_1(t) = 1.03941I_f(t) - 0.3139\dfrac{PM(t)}{P(t)} - 0.0310t + 3.719$	$\bar{R}^2 = 0.86$
	(2)	$MTR(t) = $ exogenous	
	(3)	$MSER(t) = $ exogenous	
	(4)	$M(t) = M_1(t) + \overline{MTR} + \overline{MSER}$	
	(5)	$RLE(t) = $ exogenous	
Naylor et al. (1947–1968)	(6)	$M(t) = 1.1091(t) - 0.097TXC(t) - 0.805$	$R^2 = 0.887$
Liu-DeVries (1953–1964)	(7)	$MF(t) = 0.056I(t) + 9.65$	$R^2 = 0.56$
	(8)	$MI(t) = 0.361(t) - 4.01t - 18.9$	$R^2 = 0.66$
	(9)	$MK(t) = 0.201(t) - 0.27TXCK(t) - 1.67$	$R^2 = 0.73$
	(10)	$RES(t) = 0.151 + 1.04$	$R^2 = 0.67$
	(11)	$M(t) = MF(t) + MI(t) + MK(t) + RES(t)$	
Behrman-Klein (1948–1964)	(12)	$MF(t) = 0.00265(Y_2 + Y_3) + 0.154Xm(t) + 0.2856MF(t-1)$ $\quad - 1.550$	$\bar{R}^2 = 0.89$
	(13)	$.MK(t) = 0.1479\dfrac{TXC(t)}{P(t)} + 0.1511I(t) + 13.853$	$\bar{R}^2 = 0.47$
	(14)	$MC(t) = 0.03568\dfrac{TXC(t)}{P(t)} - 0.00403C(t-1) + 5.514DUM$ $\quad + 14.19$	$\bar{R}^2 = 0.66$
	(15)	$RES(t) = 0.1940Xm(t) - 0.1461\dfrac{TXC(t)}{P(t)} + 0.4299TRK(t)$ $\quad + 12.01$	$\bar{R}^2 = 0.43$
	(16)	$M(t) = [MF(t) + MK(t) + MC(t) + RES(t)]\dfrac{PM(t)}{P(t)}$	

Note: (i) The original form of (1) is logarithmic; (ii) in (1), (6), (12) to (16), the magnitudes are 1953 Cr$, while in (7) to (11), 1959 Cr$; (iii) symbols adopted are self-explanatory except for RLE, net income to abroad; MF, imports of fuels; MI, imports of raw materials; MR, imports of capital goods; RES, residual imports; Y_2 and Y_3, respectively, value added in the secondary and tertiary sectors; TRK, capital transfers to Brazil.

Foreign Trade. The equations of the foreign sector of an econometric model may be expressed in terms of the export-import of goods and services, and of the export-import of capital.

As to exports, this variable is usually taken as exogenous, being determined by autonomous policy decisions. The endogenous treatment presents great difficulties, and the attempts that have been made to estimate the behavior of Brazilian exports have led to considerable forecasting errors. However, Behrman-Klein offer valuable suggestions in explaining the level of exports through the model.

On the other hand, imports (as shown in the comparison in the table below) present countless possibilities for inclusion in a model of the Brazilian economy. In most of the cited attempts, it is the most complete sector. Because of their critical nature, fuels are usually shown separately from other raw materials (Behrman-Klein, Liu-DeVries). The ratio of the exchange rate to a domestic price index enters significantly in most of the specifications (except fuels). The import capacity (Behrman-Klein) and the exchange rate (Behrman-Klein, Liu-DeVries, Ten-Year Plan) are the only variables which introduce the effects of commercial policies. Little attention has been paid to the movements of short-run and long-run capital.[7]

Consumption. This is no doubt the weakest part of any model of the Brazilian economy, due to the lack of data, or to the extreme unreliability of available estimates. When coupled with the well-known difficulties of econometric estimation, it becomes quite difficult to obtain any good results through a consumption function. For this reason, the Ten-Year Plan takes $C(t)$ as residual, exactly as in the National Accounts estimates.

Among some results available, we have Rizzieri's result for 1948–1964:[8]

$$C_p(t) = 0.631\,Y_d(t) - 52.64\,\frac{\Delta P}{P_{-1}} + 0.224C_p(t-1) + 16.866, \quad R^2 = 0.995$$

where C_p is personal consumption; Y_d, disposable income deflated by the implicit personal consumption deflator; and P, general price index.

The inclusion of the lagged variable, $C_p(t-1)$, is usually not significant, and certainly this hypothesis of "habit persistency" on an annual basis is weaker than on a quarterly basis, as in most models of the U.S. economy. In regard to the Brazilian economy, the test of the "forced savings" hypothesis, shown by a significant negative sign of the inflation term in the consumption function, is always interesting.

As to the inclusion of a distribution aspect, available statistical data permit only crude approximations, using some National Accounts estimates on factor

---

[7] In general, the need for foreign capital is projected through ad hoc mechanisms such as three-limit models. For a recent example of this, see Centro Latinoamericano de Proyecciones Economicas, *Proyecciones Economicas para los paises Latinoamericanos en el segun decenio de las Naciones Unidas para el desarollo. Introduction General,* Santiago, Chile, July 1970.

[8] J. Rizzieri, "Função Consumo no Brasil," Instituto de Pesquisa Econômica [Institute of Economic Research], Universidade de Sao Paulo, 1968.

payments in the urban sector. For instance, as in Rizzieri,

$$\frac{C_p(t)}{Y_d(t)} = 0.9554 \frac{L}{W} + 1.25, \qquad\qquad R^2 = 0.634$$

where L/W stands for "nonlabor"/"labor" factor payments.
A recent estimate comes from Naylor et al. for 1947–1968:

$$C_p(t) = 0.8949 Y_d(t) - 131.1489 \frac{\Delta P}{P_{-1}} + 1.9894. \qquad R^2 = 0.996$$

3. Critical Appraisal

The various models mentioned above have been sporadic attempts. As we have said before, the major experiments came from an occasional necessity to give form to the strategy of a development plan. Even now there is little activity on model building on a more permanent basis in Brazil. We may list in this respect the activities of the research units at the Catholic University of Rio de Janeiro and at the Brazilian Institute of Economics of the Vargas Foundation.

This lack of continuity has negative implications in terms of methodological improvement and technical knowledge. For instance, the advantages or disadvantages of the Ten-Year-Plan Model were not taken into consideration when the Three-Year-Plan Model was built. The experience and methodological rigor of the first attempt were forgotten in the second. In fact, only recently has an attempt at surveying the models of the Brazilian economy been made.[9]

The sketches of the analytical treatment in various models surveyed suggest a specific group of comments. The growing complexity of policy questions makes it necessary to include a greater number of policy variables in the models, especially as regards expansion and improved accuracy of the government equations; for example, more detail in government expenditures, in terms of broad categories such as education, health, and housing. On the other hand, to the extent that the share of state and local budgets assumes growing relevance, we should not insist on having a single aggregate variable for government. That aggregation overlooks the possibility of singling out an important instrument of regional development, such as the fund transfers from federal to state and local levels (which, in 1969, amounted to some 1.2 billion Cr$).

The sensitivity of the GDP to changes in government global expenditures is easy to assess, as in the models we surveyed; however, it seems that nowadays the relevant policy questions require more detail: what is the possible impact on labor-force absorption of an increase of investment by the Housing Bank, or which are the implications of a fiscal-federalism type of policy vis-à-vis the global structure of the Brazilian economy in the next decade.

In order to face such questions we need a different model from those already described. There exist large amounts of data which could be included in such a macroeconometric model. As to the government sector, there are great possibilities

[9] Jorge Vianna Monteiro, "Uma Análise de Macromodelos da Economia Brasileira—Relatório de Pesquisa," PUC-RJ, Depto. de Economia, Jan. 1971.

in current research being done by the Ministry of Planning and the Vargas Foundation. The regional breakdown could be approached, even if on an elementary basis, following Fukuchi's attempt.

In terms of more specific themes, we would stress the necessity of analyzing the price level as an endogenous variable. Both in the Liu-DeVries and Naylor et al. models, the forecasts of the price level involve substantial error margins. In both models we could, for instance, test different hypotheses as to the Brazilian inflation, or consider an alternative treatment stating the price level through a definition, as in Behrman-Klein. Some preliminary results of the research work done by Vianna show that prices are one of the main causes of trouble in the behavior of simultaneous systems, even when introduced via a definition, rather than through a behavioral equation.

REFERENCES

[1] Baer, W. and Kerstenetzky, I., "Patterns of Brazilian Economic Growth," preliminary version, presented at the conference "The Next Decade of Latin American Development," Cornell University, April, 1966.

[2] Behrman, J. and Klein, L. R., "A Tentative Model of Brazil" (mimeographed), University of Pennsylvania, 1968.

[3] Economic Commission for Latin America/Fukuchi, "Regional and Sectoral Projection of the Brazilian Economy," Santiago, Chile, July 1970.

[4] Escritório de Pesquisa Economica Aplicada [Bureau for Applied Economic Research]/Ministério do Planejamento, "Bases Macro-econômica do Plano Decenal" (mimeographed), 1966.

[5] Ministério do Planejamento, "Programa Estratégico de Desenvolvimento," 1968, 2 vols.

[6] Monteiro, J. V., Uma Análise de Macromodelos da Economia Brasileira, PUC-RJ, Depto. de Economia [Department of Economics of the Pontifical Catholic University in Rio de Janeiro], Jan. 1971.

[7] Naylor, T., Fioravante, M., and Monteiro, J. V., "A Comment on Tintner's Econometric Model of Brazil," Revista Brasileira de Economia, Jan.-March 1971.

[8] Tintner. C., Consigliere. I., and Carneiro. J., "An Econometric Model Applied to the Brazilian Economy," Revista Brasileira de Economia, Jan.-March 1970.

A SIMULATION MODEL OF THE ECONOMY OF BRAZIL*

Thomas H. Naylor
Duke University

AND

Martin Shubik
Yale University

AND

Moacyr Fioravante
Getulio Vargas Foundation

AND

Ibrahim A. S. Ibrahim
Duke University

Introduction

In the summer of 1970, the Fundaçao Getulio Vargas embarked on a project to develop a series of socioeconomic models of Brazil. This paper describes a small-scale computer simulation model of the economy of Brazil, which was constructed by economists from the Fundaçao Getulio Vargas (FGV) in collaboration with economists from the Catholic University of Rio de Janeiro (PUC), the Brazilian Census Bureau (IBGE), and the Ministry of Planning (IPEA). An earlier version of this model estimated with ordinary least squares appeared in [7]. The version described in this paper has been estimated using two-stage least squares.

The objectives of this research were: (1) to formulate a model of the Brazilian economy which could be used to perform policy simulation experiments to test the effects of alternative economic policies on the behavior of the economy of Brazil, (2) to develop a tool which could be used to check the consistency of existing sources of time-series data, (3) to suggest new data series which might possibly be collected by IBGE or FGV in the future, and (4) to provide students of economics with a meaningful way of obtaining a better understanding of the operations of the Brazilian economy.

The model consists of 16 equations, of which 5 are behavioral equations and the remaining 11 are identities. There are 4 exogenous variables and 9 policy variables. All data which are in monetary units have been deflated and expressed in 1953 cruzeiros. The variables and equations of the model are given below.

* This research was partially supported by the Fundaçao Getulio Vargas, Centro Internacional de Servicos Executivos, and the National Science Foundation, Grant GS-2981. We are indebted to the following people for their assistance in the construction of this model: Jorge Vianna Monteiro, Isaac Kerstenetzky, Ralph Zerkowski, Sergio Pereira Leite, Graciano de Sa, Luiz Aranha Correia do Lago, and Jayme Porto Carreiro Filho. Eugenio Decourt and Ascendino Rodrigues Araujo wrote the computer programs for the IBM 1130 Computer.

VARIABLES

Endogenous Variables

B Deficit in balance of trade in billion 1953 Cr$

C Private and public consumption in billion 1953 Cr$

Cp Private consumption in billion 1953 Cr$

D Government deficit in billion 1953 Cr$

G Government expenditure in billion 1953 Cr$

GDP Gross domestic product in billion 1953 Cr$

ΔGDP Change in gross domestic product in billion 1953 Cr$

I Total gross fixed-capital formation in billion 1953 Cr$

I_p Private gross investment in billion 1953 Cr$

K Value of capital stock in billion 1953 Cr$

M Total imports of goods and services plus net factor payments abroad in billion 1953 Cr$

$\Delta P/P$ Percentage change in implicit GDP deflator (P = 100 in 1953)

S Gross domestic savings in billion 1953 Cr$

T Total direct and indirect taxes in billion 1953 Cr$

Y Net domestic product at factor cost in billion 1953 Cr$

Y_d Disposable domestic income in billion 1953 Cr$

Policy Variables

C_g Public consumption expenditure in billion 1953 Cr$

I_g Gross public investment in billion 1953 Cr$

O Other government receipts in billion 1953 Cr$

Q Money supply in billion 1953 Cr$

R Implicit exchange rate Cr. per U.S.$ (1953)

T_d Direct tax in billion 1953 Cr$

T_i Indirect tax in billion 1953 Cr$

U Government subsidies in billion 1953 Cr$

V Government transfer payments in billion 1953 Cr$

Exogenous Variables

L Size of labor force in millions

t 47, 48, 49, . . . corresponding to 1947, 1948, 1949, . . .

W Depreciation in billion 1953 Cr$

X Import capacity of goods and services in billion 1953 Cr$

THE MODEL

Production function

(1)
$$\log Y = 0.803 + 0.022t + 0.728 \log L + 0.272 \log K$$
$$(0.015)$$

Consumption function

(2)
$$C_p = 1.9894 + 0.8949 \, Y_d - 131.1489 \, \Delta P/P$$
$$(7.706) \quad (0.0192) \quad (38.0788)$$
$$\bar{R}^2 = 0.996 \quad S.E. = 10.9652 \quad DW = 2.6527$$

Investment function

(3)
$$I_p = 25.9421 + 118.3066 \, \Delta P/P + 0.6367 \, \Delta GDP$$
$$(8.0057) \quad (25.1985) \quad (0.1283)$$
$$\bar{R}^2 = 0.7028 \quad S.E. = 11.6130 \quad DW = 0.9692$$

Import function

(4)
$$\log M = -0.7459 - 0.0894 \log R + 1.0872 \log I$$
$$(0.7750) \quad (0.0353) \quad (0.2046)$$
$$\bar{R}^2 = 0.8484 \quad S.E. = 0.0831 \quad DW = 1.8067$$

Price determination

(5)
$$\Delta P/P = 0.0035 + 0.4705 \, \Delta Q/Q - 0.0005 \, \Delta GDP + 0.5372 \, (\Delta P/P)_{-1}$$
$$(0.0357) \quad (0.1521) \quad (0.0006) \quad (0.1373)$$
$$\bar{R}^2 = 0.8030 \quad S.E. = 0.0503 \quad DW = 2.3184$$

THE MODEL (continued)

Identities

(6)	$C \equiv C_p + C_g$
(7)	$I \equiv I_p + I_g$
(8)	$D \equiv C_g + I_g + V + U - T - O$
(9)	$G \equiv C_g + I_g$
(10)	$B \equiv M - X$
(11)	$S \equiv GDP - C$
(12)	$GDP \equiv Y + T_i - U + W$
(13)	$\Delta GDP \equiv GDP - GDP_{-1}$
(14)	$K \equiv K_{-1} + I$
(15)	$T \equiv T_i + T_d$
(16)	$Y_d \equiv GDP - T - O + V + U$

SPECIFICATION OF THE MODEL

There are five behavioral equations in the model: production function, consumption function, investment function, import function, and price determination equation. For each equation, we examined the specifications of all of the previous econometric models of Brazil and attempted to incorporate into our model those features of previous models which: (1) seemed plausible from a theoretical standpoint, and (2) gave empirical results which were statistically significant.

The production function (1) is based on a modified version of a production function estimated by Maneschi and Nunes [3]. The general form is given by:

$$(17) \qquad Y_t = me^{\lambda t}L^{\alpha}K^{\beta}, \qquad \alpha + \beta = 1$$

where α and β were estimated indirectly by a method attributed to Wolfson [9], and m and λ were estimated by a method developed by Tinbergen.

The specification and estimation of the equation explaining private consumption were somewhat more straightforward. We simply employed a modified version of the consumption function contained in the World Bank Model [1]. Private consumption is expressed as a function of disposable domestic income and the percentage change in the price index over the last period. Private consumption varies directly with disposable domestic income, a basic relationship in most consumption theories, and inversely with the percentage change in the price index. This inverse relationship seems to reflect the expectations that price level changes will not continue to be of the same magnitude, in percentage terms, or that savings are increased to compensate for the drop in future income from savings as the price level continues to increase. Also, since price increases are associated with a shift in income distribution against wage earners[1] and fixed-income recipients, the tendency is for a drop in the consumption of both groups. Such a drop in consumption is greater than the increase in the consumption of the profit recipients due to taxes, retained earnings, and, possibly, their lower propensity to consume. In addition, the drop in consumption can also be traced to the decrease in credit availability as the price level rises, with a consequent increase in the transaction demand; it is assumed that the level of real income does not drop.

[1] The shift in income distribution against wage earners rests on the assumption that price-level increases would not be associated with sufficient increases in employment to offset the drop in the real income of the currently employed.

TABLE 1
VALUES OF EIGHT ENDOGENOUS VARIABLES, 1949–1968

	ΔP/P			GDP		
Year	Simulated	Actual	% Error	Simulated	Actual	% Error
1949	.120	.100	−20.371	358.809	373.800	4.010
1950	.178	.100	−78.104	379.823	397.800	4.519
1951	.152	.110	−38.183	408.738	421.300	2.982
1952	.128	.120	−7.042	439.773	458.200	4.022
1953	.138	.130	−6.149	460.292	469.500	1.961
1954	.139	.180	22.783	506.009	516.800	2.088
1955	.136	.140	2.505	532.388	552.500	3.640
1956	.149	.190	21.796	558.239	570.100	2.081
1957	.181	.120	−50.559	602.554	616.100	2.199
1958	.158	.100	−57.606	654.071	663.400	1.406
1959	.202	.230	12.243	704.316	700.700	−0.516
1960	.220	.210	−4.591	748.607	768.400	2.576
1961	.261	.250	−4.411	785.711	847.500	7.291
1962	.305	.350	12.865	828.321	892.200	7.160
1963	.330	.440	24.890	869.003	905.900	4.073
1964	.368	.470	21.696	929.760	932.400	0.283
1965	.374	.360	−3.784	992.382	957.900	−3.600
1966	.223	.280	20.198	1,072.473	1,006.800	−6.523
1967	.240	.210	−14.326	1,120.735	1,054.900	−6.241
1968	.220	.220	0.019	1,229.006	1,143.500	−7.478
Mean absolute % error			21.206			3.732

The standard errors of the coefficients are shown within the parentheses below the coefficient estimates. $\bar{R}^2$ denotes the coefficient of multiple determination; DW denotes the Durbin-Watson statistic; and $S.E.$ denotes the standard error of the estimate.

The private investment equation (3) was adapted from the World Bank Model [1]. Private investment is found to vary directly with the changes in gross domestic product and with the percentage change in the price index. This relationship makes use of the accelerator principle and suggests an outward shift in the marginal efficiency of capital schedule as the price level rises. This shift in the schedule implies expectations of a continuation of price-level increases, in absolute terms.

The import equation (4) is based on the specifications proposed in the Three-Year-Plan Model and the Ten-Year-Plan Model [4]. Imports are directly related to investment, since a rise in investment is associated with an increase in capital goods importation and the secondary effect of a rise in income. Imports are inversely related to the exchange rate since that rate is an ability-to-pay constraint. The data for the implicit exchange rate R are not considered to be very reliable and, therefore, the entire equation should be viewed with some skepticism.

The price equation (5) represents the only linkage with the monetary sector in our model. The percentage change in the price index is a distributed lag on the changes in output and the quantity of money. The supply of money is treated as a policy variable. This is a rather serious limitation of the model because, in fact,

TABLE 1 (*continued*)

Y			C		
Simulated	Actual	% Error	Simulated	Actual	% Error
303.409	318.400	4.708	298.880	317.000	5.716
322.223	340.200	5.284	314.235	330.100	4.806
341.138	353.700	3.552	335.696	353.600	5.063
370.573	389.000	4.737	369.753	385.300	4.035
389.593	398.800	2.309	397.448	396.000	−0.366
420.310	431.100	2.503	426.190	435.700	2.183
449.088	469.200	4.286	457.109	465.900	1.887
468.739	480.600	2.468	484.361	487.500	0.644
505.454	518.700	2.554	515.789	515.500	−0.056
536.671	546.000	1.709	548.350	562.600	2.533
572.717	569.100	−0.636	586.391	578.600	−1.346
606.507	626.300	3.160	621.467	656.100	5.279
645.111	706.900	8.741	672.510	717.100	6.218
683.922	747.800	8.542	717.091	757.300	5.309
723.803	760.700	4.850	746.518	779.100	4.182
769.160	771.800	0.342	799.697	787.300	−1.575
818.882	784.400	−4.396	845.294	792.600	−6.648
869.774	804.100	−8.167	918.269	857.200	−7.124
921.335	855.500	−7.695	981.594	902.700	−8.740
980.606	895.100	−9.553	1,054.057	965.700	−9.149
		4.510			4.143

the money supply depends on a number of policy variables administered by the Central Bank.

The remaining set of identities are fairly conventional and require no additional explanation.

VALIDATION OF THE MODEL

Although our primary objective in building this model was not forecasting, if one is going to use such a model for policy-simulation experiments, or as a pedagogical tool for students of economics, one would like to know to what extent it is capable of emulating the actual behavior of the Brazilian economy. For this reason, we did subject our model to the following validity test.

Starting in 1949 (since the price equation has a two-period lag), we solved our sixteen-equation model each year for the sixteen endogenous variables of the system in terms of the given values of the exogenous variables and the policy variables, as well as of the lagged values of the endogenous variables generated in previous time periods. Since the model is nonlinear in variables, we used the Gauss-Seidel Method [5] to solve the simultaneous nonlinear equations. In this manner, we simulated the behavior of the Brazilian economy over the data base period 1949 through 1968.

The simulation results were indeed encouraging, for although our simulation ran for a total of twenty years, it gave better predictive results than any previous

TABLE 1 (continued)

Year	S			I		
	Simulated	Actual	% Error	Simulated	Actual	% Error
1949	59.929	53.900	−11.185	61.591	59.600	−3.341
1950	65.588	65.100	−0.749	78.693	64.400	−22.194
1951	73.042	65.600	−11.345	78.335	78.900	0.716
1952	70.021	72.100	2.884	77.099	84.800	9.082
1953	62.845	69.900	10.093	70.432	71.600	1.631
1954	79.819	77.300	−3.259	86.894	77.900	−11.545
1955	75.279	82.500	8.753	74.285	73.400	−1.206
1956	73.878	78.600	6.008	74.980	79.100	5.208
1957	86.765	97.200	10.736	100.132	89.700	−11.630
1958	105.721	96.300	−9.783	104.889	95.000	−10.409
1959	117.926	116.900	−0.877	106.712	107.300	0.548
1960	127.140	106.200	−19.717	111.427	111.700	0.245
1961	113.201	125.500	9.800	109.548	117.400	6.689
1962	111.230	126.500	12.071	119.652	121.000	1.114
1963	122.486	121.400	−0.894	118.343	117.600	−0.632
1964	130.062	139.000	6.430	138.666	120.500	−15.075
1965	147.088	155.100	5.166	145.115	117.400	−23.608
1966	154.205	140.100	−10.068	140.172	141.000	0.587
1967	139.140	140.600	1.038	129.474	143.700	9.900
1968	174.949	167.400	−4.510	164.301	174.700	5.953
Mean absolute % error			7.268			7.066

simulations with econometric models of Brazil, all of which were of a shorter duration than twenty years. Table 1 contains the simulated values, actual values, and percentage error for the eight most important endogenous variables of our model over the period 1949 through 1968. These variables correspond to the eight variables of the World Bank Model [1] for which the simulation results were reported in [6].

Using the mean absolute value of the percentage error as a criterion of validity, we find that our model gives better predictive results than the World Bank Model for five of the eight variables in Table 2. It should be noted that since we have made use of gross domestic product (GDP) in our model rather than gross national product (GNP), which was used in the World Bank Model, two of the variables are not strictly comparable in Table 2. GNP and S in the World Bank Model were defined respectively as:

$$(18) \qquad GNP = Y + T_i - U + W + F;$$

$$(19) \qquad S = GNP - C;$$

where F denotes net factor payments abroad. Our definitions of GDP and S are given in equations (12) and (11) respectively.

Examining Tables 1 and 2, we observe that our model outperforms the World Bank Model in predicting $\Delta P/P$, S, I, G, and M. Although our ability to predict

TABLE 1 *(concluded)*

G			M		
Simulated	Actual	% Error	Simulated	Actual	% Error
60.000	60.000	.000	31.192	28.600	−9.063
65.100	65.100	.000	41.547	33.800	−22.921
65.700	65.700	.000	40.957	50.600	19.057
68.200	68.200	.000	39.639	44.400	10.722
80.100	80.100	.000	34.966	32.400	−7.921
77.400	77.400	.000	43.793	42.400	−3.286
81.700	81.700	.000	35.758	35.500	−0.726
89.600	89.600	.000	35.634	37.900	5.979
101.800	101.800	.000	50.037	43.100	−16.095
109.700	109.700	.000	52.318	40.900	−27.918
112.600	112.600	.000	51.631	49.000	−5.369
133.600	133.600	.000	52.827	56.000	5.665
141.600	141.600	.000	49.910	51.900	3.833
143.400	143.400	.000	53.001	50.700	−4.538
148.300	148.300	.000	49.260	47.300	−4.144
148.600	148.600	.000	55.575	43.100	−28.943
145.100	145.100	.000	56.240	43.700	−28.695
154.000	154.000	.000	52.282	52.400	0.226
169.600	169.600	.000	46.396	58.500	20.691
175.000	175.000	.000	60.534	68.000	10.980
		.000			11.839

Note: For definition of variables see p. 152.

price changes is not particularly good, it is substantially better than that of the World Bank Model. We also achieved considerable improvement over the World Bank Model in forecasting investment and imports. It is not surprising that there was no predictive error with regard to government expenditures in our model, for G is determined exogenously in our model, whereas it was endogenously determined in the World Bank Model. Although we did not do as well as the World Bank Model in predicting GDP, Y, and C, our results do not differ substantially from the World Bank Model results with respect to these variables.

It should be mentioned, however, that even though our predictions of Y, as well as of GDP and C (both of which are closely linked to Y), are not quite as good as those of the World Bank Model, our production function (1) certainly rests on a more solid theoretical foundation than does the production function of the World Bank Model. The World Bank Model contains an extremely naive production function which explains production in the agricultural, industrial, and tertiary sectors, respectively, as three separate functions of acreage, consumption, and government spending, respectively. Both labor and capital are excluded from the production function of the World Bank Model. By selecting the production function which we have used, we may have traded predictive power for explanatory power.

To be sure, we do not feel that the results displayed in Tables 1 and 2 constitute proof of the validity of our model, but they are sufficiently encouraging to cause

TABLE 2
COMPARISON OF PREDICTIVE PERFORMANCE OF THE WORLD BANK MODEL AND OUR MODEL USING
MEAN ABSOLUTE PERCENTAGE ERROR AS THE CRITERION

World Bank Model		Our Model	
$\Delta P/P$	45.3%	$\Delta P/P$	21.2%
GNP	3.6	GDP	3.7
Y	3.4	Y	4.5
C	4.0	C	4.1
S	11.2	S	7.3
I	15.7	I	7.1
G	4.9	G	0.0
M	18.1	M	11.8

Note: For definition of variables see p. 152.

us to continue the development of the model. In the meantime, we shall feel reasonably confident in using the model as a training tool and as a vehicle for running simple policy simulation experiments to test the effects of various monetary and fiscal policies on the behavior of the Brazilian economy.

FUTURE DEVELOPMENTS

Obviously there is room for considerable improvement in the model which we have described here. We shall outline some of the steps which we plan to take to improve it.

1. Andrea Maneschi of IPE [Institute of Economic Research], in Sao Paulo, has proposed and, indeed, estimated a number of alternative formulations of consumption, production, and investment functions. It is quite likely that one or more of these alternative specifications may lead to significant improvements in the predictive performance of our model. We plan to run simulation experiments to test the effects of some of these alternative formulations of consumption, production, and investment functions.

2. Our import equation rests on rather shaky ground, and we shall, therefore, try several other specifications developed by IPEA.

3. The absence of a monetary sector is a serious omission which must be corrected. Drawing heavily on the work of Pastore at IPE, in Sao Paulo, we hope to develop a complete model of the monetary sector of Brazil. This model will then be appended to the present model.

4. In a country whose economy is characterized by a high rate of population growth and a high rate of inflation, it makes little sense to construct a model which excludes such variables as wages, employment, population, migration, fertility, mortality, and so on. We expect to devote considerable attention to the inclusion of variables of this type in our model.

5. As important as the agricultural sector is (particularly coffee) to the economy of Brazil, we hope to be able to develop an agricultural model which can be integrated into the total model. We already have a model of the coffee industry developed by Mary Lee Epps, at Duke University, which may be of some use in this regard.

6. Following the work of Fukuchi [2] we may eventually attempt to disaggregate our model by regions.

REFERENCES

[1] DeVries, B. A. and Liu, J. C., "An Econometric Analysis of Inflation and Growth in Brazil." Presented at the Econometric Society Meetings in New York, December 1969.

[2] Fukuchi, Takao, "Regional and Sectoral Projection of the Brazilian Economy," ECLA Latin American Projection Center, Santiago, Chile, July 13, 1970.

[3] Maneschi, Andrea and Nunes, Egas Moniz, "Função de Produçao Agregada e Progresso Technologico na Economia Brasileira," *Revista de Teoria e Pesquisa Economica*, I (April 1970).

[4] Ministeiro do Planejamento, "Bases Macroeconomicas do Plano Decenal" (mimeographed), 1966.

[5] Naylor, Thomas H., *Computer Simulation Experiments with Models of Economic Systems* (New York: John Wiley and Sons, 1970).

[6] Naylor, Thomas H., Shubik, Martin, and Zerkowski, Ralph, "Econometric Models of Brazil: A Critical Appraisal," *Revista Brasileira de Economia*, XXV (March 1971).

[7] Naylor, Thomas H., Fioravante, Moacyr, Monteiro, Jorge V., and Shubik, Martin, "A Simulation Model of the Economy of Brazil," *Revista Brasileira de Economia*, XXV (March 1971).

[8] Shubik, Martin, Kerstenetzky, Isaac, and Naylor, Thomas H., "Development: Models, Simulation and Games," *Revista Brasileira de Economia*, XXV (March 1971).

[9] Wolfson, R. J., "An Econometric Investigation of Regional Differentials in American Agricultural Wages," *Econometrica*, XXVI (April 1958).

MACROECONOMETRIC MODEL BUILDING IN LATIN AMERICA: THE MEXICAN CASE

ABEL BELTRAN DEL RIO AND LAWRENCE R. KLEIN
Wharton Econometric Forecasting Associates, Inc.*

1. INTRODUCTION

Walras' great vision of describing mathematically the functioning of a complete economy has been realized in our time.[1] With the advent of social accounting, the Keynesian macroeconomic shortcut, and the computer, the construction of big mathematico-statistical representations of national economies has been made possible. The first macroeconomic models appeared during the 1930s and 1940s as descriptions of the advanced economies. The models of the developing economies began appearing during the 1950s, but it was not until the second half of the 1960s that macromodels were constructed for the Latin American economies. Since then, they have proliferated rapidly.

At the beginning, some of the macroeconometric models for developing economies did not differ much from those of the mature, industrialized economies. Their general structure and the specification of the individual equations was similar, if not identical, to the pioneer models. This is perfectly understandable. However, the usefulness of these models for alternative policy simulations or forecasting was limited. They were not faithful representations of their economies and could not be expected to follow their movements very closely.

More recently, however, stimulated by the post-Keynesian theorizing on economic growth and development, and by the efforts of econometricians to tailor their models better to the features of each country, the LDC models have begun to differ from those of the advanced economies. The differences intend to represent variety in economic development, behavior, technology, and institutions that characterize the developing economies, as well as the economic peculiarities of the country in question. This does not mean that the structure and specification of the LDC models are (or are expected to be) totally different from those of the advanced nations. After all, the anatomy and physiology of all economies are essentially the same. The difference seems to be in size, complexity, refinement of market mechanism, and speed with which the macroeconomic organs function, using as the standard of comparison those of the advanced economies. Macro

* The research of the Mexican Department (DIEMEX) of Wharton EFA is sponsored by the following institutions: Banco Interamericano de Desarrollo; Banco Nacional de Comercio Exterior, S.A.; Banco Nacional de Mexico, S.A.; Celanese Mexicana, S.A.; Cerveceria Cuauhtemoc, S.A.; Conductores Monterrey, S.A.; Credito Mexicano, S.A.; Du Pont, S.A. de C.V.; Financiera Acepta-ciones, S.A.; Financiera del Norte, S.A.; Grupo Cydsa, S.A.; Hojalata y Lamina, S.A.; I.B.M. de Mexico, S.A.; Instituto Nacional de Planificacion de la Republica Peruana; Interamericana de Arrendamientos, S.A.; Manufacturera Corpomex, S.A.; Nacional Financiera, S.A.; Procesos y Sistemas, S.A.; Representaciones Generales, S.A.; Tecnica Industrial, S.A.; Tesoreria del Estado de Chihuahua; Troqueles y Esmaltes, S.A.; Valores Industriales, S.A.

[1] Walras had a micro vision; modern econometric models have been aggregative. The basic principle, however, is the same in both cases, and modern models are now moving strongly in a micro-economic direction.

bottlenecks, which are most useful for econometric specifications, appear in different parts of the system—agriculture being a typical example. Latin American models, being the last to appear so far, have received the benefits of these efforts for more faithful econometric portrayal.

The purpose of this paper is to present the Mexican econometric model that we have developed at the Department of Econometric Research on Mexico of Wharton EFA[2] and to make some general comments on econometric model building for the developing economies. Applications of the Mexican model will also be included.

2. Some Preliminary Considerations of Model Building for the Developing Economies

The best procedure for model specification of developing economies is to try to translate into econometrics their characteristic features. These have been elaborated extensively by the development theorists in their efforts to distinguish conceptually the LDC from the MDC.[3] A brief listing and discussion of these distinctive traits seem a natural way to start. This list can be considered as a kind of descriptive model, or standard, which should help in the specification of the Mexican model, and in evaluating the specifications of other macroeconometric models of developing economies in which we may be interested. For this reason, the list will be supplemented with some features peculiar to the Latin American economies and, particularly, to the Mexican economy.

Since the differences between the LDC and the MDC arise from their relative position in the development race, all of the traits listed are also present, in some degree, in the advanced countries. That is why there is a fundamental similarity in the models of both kinds of economies. Moreover, social accounting systems, whose entries are to be explained by macromodels, are essentially the same in layout for all market economies. This is a recognition not only of the basic underlying similarity between the LDC and the MDC, but also of the accounting source of similarity between their models. Accordingly, both types of macromodels attempt, with their equations, to explain consumption, investment, exports, imports, production, prices, and so on. Consequently, the differences which we are listing below should be seen as traits that are only more apparent and pronounced in the LDC but not totally absent in the MDC. However, they do call for differences in the models, through endogenization of some variables, or through new, special equations, or through different specifications for the common ones.

In the list that follows, two related features of the developing economies, one external, the other internal, seem to be dominant: (1) their comparative overall productive backwardness vis-à-vis the MDC, and (2) the relative unevenness of their productive sectors, when compared internally. In the literature, (1)

---

[2] One of the main purposes of this department (DIEMEX) has been to determine the extent to which econometric tools can be applied to developing countries. The cases of Mexico and Peru have been explored so far.

[3] We take these common abbreviations, less developed (LDC) and more developed country (MDC), from the development literature. See, for example, E. E. Hagen, *The Economics of Development* (Homewood, Ill.: Irwin, 1968), p. 6. By an LDC, we understand here an economy in transition, active in the process of growth, not a stationary one.

has also been called supply deficiency, output constraint, technological backwardness, and so forth, (2) has been called "dualism," sectoral gaps, traditional versus modern sectors, agricultural versus industrial sectors, regional or structural imbalance, and so on. Most of the other features and problems of the developing economies seem to arise from these two. The external problems of capital and technological imports, exports of primary goods, balance-of-payments problems, as well as the internal problems of maldistribution of income, rural-urban labor migration, the big economic role of the government, existence of overcapacity in the modern productive sectors, and in some cases, even inflation, can be traced to them.

Supply Deficiency

If we take the Keynesian view that the main characteristic of industrialized nations is their possession of a developed and efficient productive sector, and that their short-run problem is the recurrent deficiency in aggregate demand, we can say, by contrast, that the main trait of developing countries is their comparative deficiency in aggregate supply.[4] Agricultural supply, still bound to old-fashioned productive methods, is very much the result of the whims of the weather. Industry is relatively underdeveloped, concentrated on a few products (automobiles and steel are the favorites in Latin America), subject to bottlenecks in physical (raw materials or machinery) or technological (operative know-how, organizational knowledge) inputs, and likely to be affected by political events. Services are comparatively small, hampered, too, by lack of skilled technicians and adequate capital equipment.

This does not mean that the developing countries have no short-run problem of aggregate demand. They do, and they need the Keynesian tools to keep their existing productive capacity as fully utilized as possible, without undue inflationary pressure. However, their crucial problem is to enlarge that productive capacity in order to make employment, income, and demand possible. They have before them the example of the MDC and of recent productive successes, like Russia and Japan. Internal social demands arising from growing expectations also contribute to making supply enlargement their basic economic concern.

The process of economic growth, then, is central in the developing economies, and it should be captured in their economic descriptions. Other characteristics and processes are, one way or another, connected with growth. Those connections should be given special importance in model building. Growth of inputs, especially capital, which is the bottleneck in developing economies, should be given special attention. Labor migration from the rural to the urban productive sector should also be considered. By the same token, the determinants or major constraints of these capacity-enlarging inputs, normally frozen into the assumptions of the short run, should be examined and made to play their part, if possible, in the main process of development.

[4] The Keynesian problem was why factories and machines shut down in a rich country or the paradox of poverty in the midst of plenty. The developing nations' problem is how to bring machines and factories to the country or how to break the ancestral condition of poverty by importing superior productive methods.

Besides, the actual duration of the "long-run" process of growth of the LDC has been reduced substantially when compared with that of the MDC. The former are essentially importing from the latter the scientific industrial revolution. This takes less time to accomplish. A statistical sample of a decade from an LDC probably compresses growth processes that took from thirty to forty years in the economic history of the MDC.

Capital Accumulation and Its Financing

The first binding constraint of development is capital, the nonhuman input. The task of circumventing this bottleneck has become the responsibility of both private and public sectors. Governments of some developing economies have tried not only to provide the capital for infrastructure, but to contribute to the addition of productive capacity as manufacturers and entrepreneurs. The Mexican economy is a clear example, with its three-hundred "empresas descentralizadas y organismos de participacion estatal." The Japanese government at the start of the big capacity-creating efforts of the Meiji restoration provides another one.[5]

With the exception of the socialist developing economies, capacity creation, however, has been the responsibility of the private entrepreneur. Private investment has been the larger flow in the accumulation of capital in plant and equipment. Public investment, in the form of roads, irrigation projects, communication, and other infrastructure, has supported these direct productive efforts. Private and public savings (surplus in current account) have been the sources of financing funds for the investment flows. The first source, in the LDC especially, has been explained as arising from the unequal distribution of income, as we will see below. The second is constrained by the low taxing ability of most of the developing countries.

Nevertheless, internal savings are not necessarily the first stumbling block met by the LDC in accumulating capital. The lack of enough foreign reserves can be their binding constraint.[6] Since they cannot produce the plant and equipment necessary for new industries, capital imports from the MDC become the only way to grow industrially. Thus, exports and external finances arise as crucial means of payment for capital accumulation and capacity enlargement.

Exports of Primary Goods

Since agricultural and extractive production are predominant, and manufactures and services are being developed, the LDC is an exporter of primary products. Its main exports are limited in number and frequently consist of one or two agricultural or mineral exports. Coffee represents 40 percent and 60 percent of the total merchandise exports of Brazil and Colombia, respectively; sugar accounts for more than 70 percent of Cuban exports; and copper accounted for 76 percent of Chilean goods exports in 1969. Agricultural exports, due to defi-

---

[5] M. Baba and M. Tatemoto, "Foreign Trade and Economic Growth in Japan: 1858–1937," in *Economic Growth, the Japanese Experience Since the Meiji Era*, L. R. Klein and K. Ohkawa, eds. (Homewood, Ill.: Irwin, 1968), p. 169.

[6] H. B. Chenery and A. M. Strout, "Foreign Assistance and Economic Development," *American Economic Review*, Vol. LVI, No. 4, Part 1 (September, 1966), pp. 680–733; or Hagen, *op. cit.*, pp. 366–71.

ciencies in irrigation infrastructure, ineffective pestilence controls, inadequate fertilizers, and acts of God, are subject to wide fluctuations. In the long run, prices of primary goods are believed to be deteriorating in relationship to the prices of the capacity-creating imports (capital goods and technical services) that the LDC need from the MDC.[7]

The capacity to import, then, of the developing country is constrained to a large extent by the value of its exports. The analysis and quantification of this bottleneck is indispensable for the econometric understanding of the developmental process. Equally important here is the transmission of cycles of the MDC to the LDC. To the instability of supply of the primary exports, demand instability should be added. Primary exports depend on the demand-oriented imports of the industrial countries. Instability in effective demand, the Keynesian problem, is felt in the export position of the developing countries and is carried through to capital imports and the expansion of the LDC supply.

External Debt and Foreign Investment

As a corollary of the constraint posed by its export earnings, the developing country tends to rely on its capital-account imports to finance its efforts to grow. Normally, this is accomplished by incurring external debt. Debt service increases as a proportion of export earnings but eventually the added capacity should repay for itself by increasing exports and/or reducing imports by at least the amount of debt and interest incurred.[8]

Foreign direct investment is the other item of capital account sought by the LDC to finance their capital imports. In spite of its economic advantage in solving simultaneously the savings and foreign-currency gaps, foreign investment has political and historical drawbacks (excessive profits, low wages) that limit its use. Some Latin American countries are trying, however, to enlarge it, while legislating ways of reducing its harmful aspects. Recently, in the case of Brazil, large inflows of foreign investment seem to be one of the main causes of a spectacular increase in the rate of growth. This achievement has been associated with a shift in the composition of exports—moving away from traditional goods to manufactures —and has also been associated with a reduction of the rates of inflation.[9]

Foreign aid, the third element in capital accounts, does not now make a substantial contribution toward the deficit balance of LDC's current account. Its importance, however, is clear, being a way in which the MDC, or the international organizations supported by them, can perform the function of spreading their technology (or share their productive surpluses) at minimum cost to the developing nations.

---

[7] R. Prebisch. "The Economic Development of Latin America and Its Principal Problems." *Economic Bulletin for Latin America* (February, 1962), pp. 1–22.

[8] Hagen, *op. cit.*, p. 365.

[9] Some writers believe that inflation per se is not the main hindrance to growth. They claim that the fluctuations in the rate of inflation are the problem. See R. A. Krieger, "Inflation and Growth: the Case of Latin America," *Columbia Journal of World Business*, Vol. V, No. 6 (Nov.–Dec. 1970).

Income Distribution

The characteristic unevenness of the developing economies shows in income distribution. The contrast between the "haves" and "have-nots" is more notable in the LDC. It also plays a role in development. Savings and investment are essentially done by the recipients of nonwage income. On the other hand, the size of the internal market for consumption goods is determined by wage earners. Income distribution, then, plays a crucial role in investment and consumption by influencing the flow of internal savings available, while at the same time tending to limit the size of the internal market for consumption demand. It is also useful in understanding import substitution in light durable consumer goods, as a common strategy of supply enlargement in the LDC.

Population

Rapid population growth can be interpreted as another characteristic of the LDC, resulting from their uneven adoption of modern technique and outlook. Their adoption of modern medicine has substantially reduced the death rate—especially among infants. Birthrates, however, continue at traditionally high levels. Abatement of this condition must await the eventual adoption of values and views of the MDC on family size, education of children, and the process of urbanization. Migration, in principle, should also be considered. In most of the Latin American countries, however, its role is not significant.

Internal Labor Migration

Internal labor migration is another consequence of the unevenness in the agricultural and industrial sectors in the LDC. Rural labor migration to the cities is mainly caused by the difference in productivities and wages between these sectors. In the Mexican case, for example, the ratio of urban-rural labor productivity is approximately 5:1. Uneven capital accumulation stands at the bottom of the process. A Mexican urban worker has eight times more real capital to work with than does his rural counterpart. This problem calls for exploration of its demographic aspects in order to gain a better understanding of what is involved for econometric purposes.

Labor Force and Population

Since models for developing countries should be cast in a long-term framework, the growth of human input requires consideration. Enlargement of the labor force depends on economic and demographic factors. Production functions, converted into labor-requirement functions, and capital-labor ratios have been used for short-run, demand-oriented determination of employed labor. Population growth, with sex and age composition, are, on the other hand, the long-run supply determinants of the working force. In the LDC, the rapid growth of population makes the supply approach indispensable. "Development with unlimited supplies of labor" (and especially when the supply of labor is clearly outmatching the periodic supply of capital) calls for particular attention on the part of the econometrician.

Growth of the skilled and technical part of the labor force is the second important constraint on capacity creation of the LDC in addition to capital. Essentially, this growth is related to education and, particularly, to technological education. This aspect, so evident and so important, is difficult to introduce explicitly in statistical models.

Prices, Wages, and Money Supply

Inflation is an unsolved, worldwide problem, but in the developing countries, it appears in its extreme form. Brazil and Chile, with annual price increases of 30 percent or more, are two well-known examples. The severity of the problem in the LDC, and especially in Latin America, has had two main explanations in the literature: (1) structural imbalance in the productive sector (agricultural versus industrial), and (2) government monetary excesses.[10]

However, production bottlenecks, as well as rises in import or export prices, can explain the start, but not the persistence and high rates, of Latin American hyperinflations.[11] The prolongation and aggravation of the process requires the addition of other reinforcing factors, namely excessive growth of the money supply, the appearance of the price-wage spiral, and recurrent devaluation. In other words, structural imbalance can explain inflation; hyperinflation requires a monetary explanation.

Since, generally speaking, organized labor has not been politically independent or strong in Latin America, the price-wage vicious cycle has not been the basic pressuring force. This does not mean that the LDC's unions have not learned from hyperinflation. They have, but their reactions have, in general, been patient and modest. In Mexico, for example, they endured substantial real-wage reductions during the 1940s and early 1950s. The main fuel, thus, has come from the activity of the government printing presses. This governmental tendency arises from growing deficits caused by lack of taxing power (rooted, in turn, in political weakness) and the growing public expenditures required by growth and welfare programs. The third self-preserving mechanism, periodic devaluation, enters both as a result and a further cause of the inflationary process. Internal inflation erodes the capacity to import development goods, the pace of growth is retarded, and a devaluation is in order to move the economy again. This gives a new impetus to inflation and the mechanism of periodic devaluation is incorporated into the process.

Overcapacity

A paradox common to the LDC is the existence of particular pockets of overcapacity in the midst of general supply limitation. It appears essentially in the modern productive sectors, and it can be larger than that of the MDC's corresponding sectors. Some examples are the automobile industries in Argentina, Chile, and Mexico; other cases are the Mexican poultry industry and its hotel

---

[10] These two opposite schools, the structuralists and the monetarists, are very well represented in *Inflation and Growth in Latin America*, W. Baer and I. Kerstenetzky, eds. (Homewood, Ill.: Irwin, 1964).

[11] See W. A. Lewis, "Closing Remarks," in Baer and Kerstenetzky, *op. cit*, p. 24.

industry.[12] There are several reasons for this: (1) inaccurate demand estimates, due to lack of statistical information or the cost of gathering it; (2) the mirage of protectionism and the entrepreneurial desire to control the new market; and (3) the oversized plant and equipment available in the MDC.

Length of Lags

Based on observation of the behavior in the LDC, it seems that the time delays, or lags, between economic impulse and economic reaction differ from those of the MDC. With regard to private consumption, impulsiveness or lack of careful consumer planning may very well produce shorter income-consumption lags. In investment, the reverse may be true, because of the much larger construction and installation periods. The decision lag is perhaps shorter here, due to lack of long investigations and planning, but the implementation lag is certainly longer, even when the smaller size of investment goods in the developing economy is considered. Demographic processes are probably longer, due to poorness of communications, illiteracy, and traditional inertia.

Government and Political Change

The role of the government in the economy is usually bigger in the developing country. In most cases, the degree of economic intervention and direct participation in economic life is larger than in the MDC. It is not unusual, then, to find the government of the LDC with more economic instruments at its disposal than its MDC counterpart has. Also, it is common to find these governments as one of the larger (if not the largest) of the industrialists or merchants. When this is the case, a cyclical element is introduced in the economy which coincides with the political cycle: this arises not only from the stop-and-go nature of government investment at each administrative change, but also from the impact on private investment, which normally takes a waiting position during political changes.

3. THE MEXICAN MODEL

The Mexican macroeconometric model presented here is the latest one in a succession of versions developed in an ongoing project of research on Mexico at Wharton EFA. This version, V, has been produced by enlargements and modifications of the earlier attempts. The purpose of these additions and changes has been to incorporate successively, as we were able to secure more and better data, additional aspects of the economy, and to respecify equations as we tried to approximate more closely the actual workings of the economy.

Each successive version was an attempt to make the model closer to what we consider to be the defining characteristics of the Mexican economy. Owing to limitations of space, we will not give here a full explanation of the theoretical

[12] "Weeding Out Auto Plants," *Business Week*, May 22, 1971, p. 36, and "Crecimiento Desordenado en la Industria Avicola," *Excelsior*, May 9, 1971. A recent general statement of overcapacity in the Mexican economy can be found in A. J. Yarza, "El Futuro del Proceso de Industrializacion en Mexico," *El Trimestre Economico*, No. 151 (July–Sept., 1971), pp. 87–88.

and institutional justification of the behavioral equations. For that, the interested reader is referred to the full document presented at the Cuernavaca conference. We will, however, list briefly the main features that we have tried to incorporate, which are those of section 2, plus those peculiar to the Mexican economy:

1. Internal and external sources of instability: the impact of the political climate on the economy and the dependence on foreign trade; the internal and external sources of inflation.

2. The dominant role played by the federal government as infrastructure builder and entrepreneur; public finances.

3. The general unevenness in economic life as exemplified in functional income distribution, in rural versus urban production, in federal versus non-federal taxation.

4. The rapid demographic processes resulting in high population growth, urbanization, or rural-urban labor-force migration.

5. The proximity to the U.S. markets with its effects on international labor migration, tourism and border transactions, and trade in general.

6. The development process of creating capacity, through capital and technological imports, in the context of general capital limitations and abundance of unskilled and semiskilled labor.

7. The comparatively shorter decision-making horizon in all economic processes, resulting in shorter lags vis-à-vis the MDC.

8. The simplicity of economic organisms and behavior when compared with those of the MDC.

The rest of this section consists of the nomenclature and the full listing of the equations of the model. The list contains 143 equations, 40 of which are behavioral; the rest are accounting and other identities. The behavioral equations have been estimated by the ordinary least squares method; the 10 containing distributed lags were estimated by fitting a polynomial of third degree with two end-point restrictions.

We list now alphabetically the symbols used and their meanings. The symbols are of two kinds: simple (consisting of only one letter) and compound (consisting of two or more letters and numbers). In the case of the compound symbols, the final letters and numbers have the following meaning:

Ending in C	Current billion pesos
Ending in R	Real billion pesos of 1950
Ending in DC	Current billion dollars
Ending in L	Per worker of the productive sector in question
Ending in N	Per capita
Ending in $\%$	Annual rate of change
Ending in 1, 2, or 3	Lags of one, two, or three previous years

All predetermined variables (exogenous or lagged endogenous) are underlined. The only exceptions to these rules are two compound symbols: $L1$ and $L23$, rural and urban labor force. The number endings here do not mean lags, but primary and secondary plus tertiary productive sectors, respectively. They are not, thus, underlined. The abbreviations NIA and BOP mean National Income Accounts and Balance of Payment Account.

A condensed flow chart of this model and, in fact, a very condensed version of this whole paper, can be found in Abel Beltran del Rio, "Mexico: an Economy at the Crossroads," *Wharton Quarterly*, University of Pennsylvania, Fall 1971.

LIST OF VARIABLES

B

BFR	Balance of productive factors in NIA
BFR*	Balance of productive factors in BOP
BGR	Balance of goods in BOP
BGSFR	Balance of goods, services and factors or net foreign demand in NIA
BGSFR*	Balance of goods, services and factors or net foreign demand in BOP
BGSR	Balance of goods, tourism and border transactions in NIA
BGSR*	Balance of goods, tourism and border transactions in BOP
BOTR	Balance of other items in current account in BOP
BTBR	Balance of tourism and border transactions in BOP

C

CGR	Public consumption
CITR	Domestic or internal aggregate demand
CMC	Capacity to import or current earnings deflated by import price-index
COCDU	*COCOP* multiplied by *DUMRS*
COCOP	Domestic, physical consumption of copper (millions of tons)
COCOT	Domestic, physical consumption of cotton (millions of bales)
COLEA	Domestic, physical consumption of lead (millions of tons)
COMET	Domestic, physical consumption of nonferrous metals: lead, copper and zinc (millions of tons)
CPR	Private consumption
CPRN	Private consumption per capita (thousands of 1950 pesos per person)
CR	Consumption

D

DBGEDC	Public external debt
DBGER	Public external debt
DC	Depreciation
DDBGR	Change in public external debt
DGDPR	Change in gross domestic product
DGR	Public depreciation
DIPRN	Disposable personal income per capita (thousands of 1950 pesos per person)
DIUDC	Disposable personal income in the U.S.
DIUR	Disposable personal income in the U.S.
DPEUEJ	Change in export price index, *PEUEJ*, of main exporting countries to Mexico
DPGNP	Change in GNP price deflator
DPR	Private depreciation
DR	Depreciation
DUMBR	Dummy for government restrictions to the bracero program, 1.0 for 1965–1968; 0.0 elsewhere
DUMCU	Dummy for U.S.' suspension of sugar buying from Cuba; 1.0 for 1960–1968; 0.0 elsewhere
DUMDV	Dummy for aftereffects of devaluation of 1954; 1.0 for 1956–1961; 0.0 elsewhere
DUMPO	Dummy for political change in Mexico: presidential transitions and other major political events; 1.0 for 1952–1953, 1958–1959, 1964–1965, and 1961–1963; 0.0 elsewhere
DUMRE	Dummy for census revisions of labor data; 1.0 for 1960–1968; 0.0 elsewhere.
DUMRS	Dummy for U.S.' trade protection to its nonferrous metal producers; 1.0 for 1958–1968; 0.0 elsewhere
DUMTFE	Dummy for exceptional federal exports tax collection; 1.0 for 1955–1956, 1961, and 1967; 0.0 elsewhere

$DUMTPC$ Dummy for exceptional federal nontax collection; 1.0 for 1965; 0.0 elsewhere
$DUX23P$ Change in idle urban productive capacity
$DX1PRU$ Change in rural potential population productivity
$DX231P$ Gaps between urban and rural potential population productivity

E

$EAADC$ Net production of gold and silver
$EAAR$ Net production of gold and silver
$EAGR$ Main agricultural goods exports: cotton, coffee and sugar
$EBRR$ Labor exports or bracero earnings
$EBRRL$ Labor exports or bracero earnings per Mexican worker (thousands of 1950 pesos per worker)
$ECOFR$ Exports of coffee
$ECOPR$ Exports of copper
$ECOTR$ Exports of cotton
EGC Goods or merchandise exports
$EGDC$ Goods or merchandise exports
$EGER$ Goods exports, explained by equations in the model
$EGMFR$ Manufactured goods exports
EGR*   Goods or merchandise exports
$EGSFR$*   Exports of goods, services and factors or total trade exports
$ELEAR$ Lead exports
$EMETR$ Nonferrous metals exports: lead, copper and zinc
$EOGR$ Other goods exports
$EOTDC$ Exports of other items in current account
$EOTR$ Exports of other items in current account
$ESUGR$ Sugar exports
$ETBR$ Tourism and border exports
$EZINR$ Zinc exports

F

$FBGFC$ Domestic banking credit to the federal government
$FBGFR$ Domestic banking credit to the federal government
$FRDC$ Foreign reserves
FRR Foreign reserves

G

GC Public expenditure
$GDPC$ Gross domestic product
$GDPR$ Gross domestic product
$GNPC$ Gross national product
$GNPR$ Gross national product
$GNPUDC$ U.S. gross national product
$GNPUR$ U.S. gross national product
GR Public expenditure
GSC Government surplus or deficit

I

$ICHR$ Inventory investment
$IGGR.$ Government fixed, gross investment
$IGOER.$ Federal organizations and enterprises fixed, gross investment
IGR Public gross, fixed investment
IPR Private gross, fixed investment
$IPUSF$ U.S. index of industrial production of food and beverages (1957–1959 = 1.0)
IR Gross fixed investment
ITR Investment

K

$KGF1R$ Federal government capital stock in the rural sector
KGR Government capital stock
KPR Private capital stock
KR Capital stock
$K23R$ Private and federal government capital stock in urban sector

L

L	Labor force (millions of workers)
*L*1	Labor force in rural or primary sector (millions of workers)
*L*1*NRU*	Rural labor participation rate: ratio of labor force over population in rural sector
*L*23	Labor force in urban or secondary and tertiary sectors (millions of workers)
*L*23*NB*	Urban labor participation rate: ratio of labor force over population in urban sector

M

MCAPR	Capital goods imports
MCONR	Consumption goods imports
MFR	Factor imports
MGC	Goods or merchandise imports
MGR	Goods or merchandise imports
*MGSR**	Imports of goods, services and factors or total trade imports
MIGR	Government payments of interest to foreign bond holders
MOTDC	Imports of other items in current account
$\overline{MOTR}$	Imports of other items in current account
MPGR	Imports of production goods
MPPR	Private payments of profits to foreign stockholders
MRDC	Imports of raw materials and fuels
$\overline{MRR}$	Imports of raw materials and fuels
MTBR	Imports of tourism and border transactions

N

N	Population (millions of persons)
NG	Population rate of growth
$\overline{NIC}$	National income in NIA
NIC:	National income generated by the model
NIR	National income
NNPC	Net national product
NRUL	Rural population (millions of persons)
NURB	Urban population (millions of persons)
NURBN	Ratio of urban to total population
NWIC	Nonwage income

P

PCFMB	Ratio of Mexican over Brazilian price of coffee
$\overline{PCOFB}$	Brazilian price of coffee (dollars per hundred lbs.)
$\overline{PCOFM}$	Mexican price of coffee (dollars per hundred lbs.)
$\overline{PEEU}$	European (EEC plus EFTA) export price index (1953 = 1.0)
$\overline{PEJP}$	Japanese export price index (1960–1962 = 1.0)
PEUEJ	Weighted export price index of main exporting countries to Mexico (U.S., Europe and Japan), weights of 1968
PEUS	U.S. export price index (1958 = 1.0)
$\overline{PGNP}$	GNP price deflator (1950 = 1.0)
PGNP%	GNP price deflator rate of change
PM	Imports price index (1950 = 1.0)
PM%	Imports price index rate of change
PRCDU	*PRCOP* multiplied by *DUMRS*
PRCOP	Domestic, physical copper production (thousands of tons)
$\overline{PRCOT}$	Domestic, physical cotton production (thousands of tons)
$\overline{PRLEA}$	Domestic, physical lead production (thousands of tons)
$\overline{PRMET}$	Domestic, physical nonferrous metals production: lead, copper and zinc (thousands of tons)
PSGMP	Ratio of Mexican over Philippines price of sugar
PSUGM	Price of Mexican sugar (dollars per hundred lbs.)
$\overline{PSUGPH}$	Price of Philippines sugar (dollars per hundred lbs.)

R

$\overline{RDPAV}$	Paved roads (thousands of kilometers)
$\overline{REX}$	Rate of exchange (dollars per peso)

S

SBGSFR	Discrepancy between NIA and BOP data on balance in current account
SDBFR	Discrepancy between NIA and BOP data on balance of factors
SDBGSR	Discrepancy between NIA and BOP data on balance of goods and services
SDNIC:	Discrepancy between NIA data and the model's identity of national income
SDTFNC	Discrepancy between two data sources used on federal indirect or nonincome taxes

T

T	Time (1948 = 1.0)
TC	Total taxes and nontaxes
TFC	Federal government taxes
TFEC.	Federal export taxes
TFIC.	Federal income taxes
TFMC.	Federal import taxes
TFMGC	Rate of taxation on imported merchandise
TFNIC	Federal indirect or nonincome taxes
TFNIC.	Federal indirect or nonincome taxes
TFOC:	Other federal taxes
TFPAC.	Federal nontax income: "productos, derechos y aprovechamientos"
TFSC.	Federal sales taxes: "ingresos mercantiles"
TNFC	Nonfederal taxes: D.F., state and local
TNIC	Total indirect or nonincome taxes
TNIC%	Total indirect taxes rate of growth
TR	Total taxes and nontaxes
TRDGR	Total taxes plus public depreciation

U

UXRP	Idle capacity
UX1RP	Rural idle capacity
UX23RD	*UX23RP* multiplied by *DUMRE*
UX23RP	Urban idle capacity
WIC	Wage income
WMAC	Daily, average minimum wage rate (current pesos per worker)
WMRC	Daily, minimum rural wage rate (current pesos per worker)
WMUC	Daily, minimum urban wage rate (current pesos per worker)
WRC	Yearly, average wage rate (thousand current pesos per worker)
WRC%	Yearly, average wage-rate rate of growth
WRCA	Unit labor cost or ratio of average wage rate to labor productivity
WRCA%	Unit labor cost rate of change
WRFUDC	U.S. hourly manufacturing wage rate (dollars per worker)
WRMMUC	Ratio of daily, minimum urban wage to U.S. hourly manufacturing rate converted into current pesos

X

X1R	Rural production
X1RL	Rural labor productivity (thousands of 1950 pesos per worker)
X1RP	Potential rural production or rural capacity
X2R	Secondary production
X3R	Tertiary production
X23R	Urban production
X23PBD	*X23PNB* multiplied by *DUMRE*
X23PNB	Potential urban population productivity (thousands of 1950 pesos per urban person)
X23RL	Urban labor productivity (thousands of 1950 pesos per worker)
X23RP	Potential urban production or urban capacity
XRP	Potential production or capacity

I. Generation of Aggregate Demand

IA. Generation of Domestic Demand

Private consumption per capita

(1) $CPRN = 0.10488 + 0.39560\,DIPRN + 0.34350\,\underline{DIPRN1} + 0.11960\,\underline{DIPRN2}$
              (2.337)   (3.6918)   (32.0987)   (1.0605)

$$\sum_{i=0}^{2} w(i) = 0.8587 \quad = \text{sum of distributed lag coefficients}$$

$$R^2 = 0.9877 \quad S.E. = 0.0215 \quad DW = 2.0793 \quad F(2, 13) = 603.3416$$

Public consumption

(2) $CGR = -0.68719 + 0.60410\,TR$
                         (−4.817)   (32.961)

$$R^2 = 0.9837 \quad S.E. = 0.2247 \quad DW = 1.2862 \quad F(1, 17) = 1086.4641$$

Private gross, fixed investment

(3) $IPR = 1.37563 - 0.76030\,\underline{DUMPO} + 0.05611\,\underline{KPR1} + 0.18120\,DGDPR$
              (3.111)   (−2.702)   (2.521)   (2.3973)
             $+ 0.34350\,\underline{DGDPR1} + 0.33410\,\underline{DGDPR2}$
              (5.2569)   (4.6544)

$$\sum_{i=0}^{2} w(i) = 0.8588$$

$$R^2 = 0.9552 \quad S.E. = 0.4816 \quad DW = 2.0697 \quad F(4, 11) = 80.9639$$

Public gross, fixed investment

(4) $IGR = -0.16872 + 0.83383\,DDBGR + 0.40620\,TRDGR + 0.20362\,FBGFR$
              (−0.405)   (3.310)   (4.907)   (2.636)

$$R^2 = 0.9765 \quad S.E. = 0.3603 \quad DW = 2.1081 \quad F(3, 15) = 250.3858$$

Investment of federal government organizations and enterprises

(5) $IGOER = 0.62296 + 0.32234\,\underline{FBGR1} + 1.35670\,DDBGR + 0.5008\,\underline{DDBGR1}$
              (3.004)   (10.581)   (5.6944)   (2.1109)

$$\sum_{i=0}^{1} w(i) = 1.8575$$

$$R^2 = 0.9185 \quad S.E. = 0.3766 \quad DW = 1.2617 \quad F(3, 12) = 57.3715$$

Inventory changes

(6) $ICHR = 0.31206 + 2.5922\,DPGNP + 0.05210\,DGDPR + 0.07080\,\underline{DGDPR1}$
              (1.889)   (2.061)   (2.5810)   (6.1489)
           $+ 0.06330\,\underline{DGDPR2} + 0.03730\,\underline{DGDPR3}$
             (4.3152)   (1.6367)

$$\sum_{i=0}^{3} w(i) = 0.2235$$

$$R^2 = 0.8515 \quad S.E. = 0.1610 \quad DW = 2.0251 \quad F(3, 12) = 29.6755$$

Private consumption

(7) $CPR = CPRN \times N$

Consumption

(8) $CR = CPR + CGR$

Gross, fixed investment

(9) $IR = IPR + IGR$

Investment: gross fixed plus inventory changes

(10) $ITR = IR + ICHR$

Public investment net of federal organizations and enterprises investment

(11) $IGGR. = IGR - IGOER.$

Domestic aggregate demand

(12)
$$CITR = CR + ITR$$

IB. Generation of Foreign Demand
IB(i). Exports
Exports of cotton

(13)
$$ECOTR = 1.74205 - 3.41745 \underline{COCOT2} + 0.52469 \underline{PRCOT1}$$
$$ (8.999) \quad (-5.489) \quad\quad\quad (3.683)$$
$$R^2 = 0.6156 \quad S.E. = 0.1944 \quad DW = 1.7479 \quad F(2, 16) = 15.4124$$

Relative price of Mexican to Brazilian coffee

(14)
$$PCFMB = \underline{PCOFM/PCOFB}$$

Exports of coffee

(15)
$$ECOFR = 0.64692 + 0.77732 \underline{ECOFR1} - 0.44755 \underline{PCFMB}$$
$$ (1.883) \quad (5.044) \quad\quad\quad (-1.566)$$
$$R^2 = 0.5741 \quad S.E. = 0.1076 \quad DW = 2.3463 \quad F(2, 16) = 13.1329$$

Relative price of Mexican to Philippines sugar

(16)
$$PSGMP = \underline{PSUGM/PSUGPH}$$

Exports of sugar

(17)
$$ESUGR = -0.13087 + 0.44480 \underline{IPUSF} + 0.20956 \underline{DUMCU} - 0.27291 \underline{PSGMP}$$
$$ (-1.087) \quad (2.831) \quad\quad\quad (4.814) \quad\quad\quad (-1.872)$$
$$R^2 = 0.9311 \quad S.E. = 0.0441 \quad DW = 2.6200 \quad F(3, 15) = 82.1127$$

Exports of nonferrous metals: lead, copper and zinc

(18)
$$EMETR = 0.27415 - 0.56093 \underline{DUMRS} + 1.57891 \underline{PRMET} - 0.20054 \underline{COMET}$$
$$ (0.351) \quad (-8.258) \quad\quad\quad (1.083) \quad\quad\quad (-0.221)$$
$$R^2 = 0.8974 \quad S.E. = 0.1062 \quad DW = 2.4087 \quad F(3, 15) = 53.4719$$

Exports of lead

(19)
$$ELEAR = -0.19166 - 0.16455 \underline{DUMRS} + 3.03442 \underline{PRLEA} - 0.61904 \underline{COLEA}$$
$$ (-0.888) \quad (-4.113) \quad\quad\quad (3.241) \quad\quad\quad (-1.000)$$
$$R^2 = 0.9228 \quad S.E. = 0.04596 \quad DW = 1.6541 \quad F(3, 15) = 72.7337$$

Consumption of copper in the period of U.S. restrictions

(20)
$$COCDU = \underline{COCOP} \times \underline{DUMRS}$$

Production of copper in the period of U.S. restrictions

(21)
$$PRCDU = \underline{PRCOP} \times \underline{DUMRS}$$

Exports of copper

(22)
$$ECOPR = 1.13451 - 1.09724 \underline{DUMRS} - 16.04651 \underline{PRCOP} + 19.88620 \underline{PRCDU}$$
$$ (2.297) \quad (-2.106) \quad\quad\quad (-2.306) \quad\quad\quad (2.627)$$
$$ + 7.69851 \underline{COCOP} - 11.75707 \underline{COCDU}$$
$$ (1.717) \quad\quad\quad (-2.552)$$
$$R^2 = 0.9088 \quad S.E. = 0.04806 \quad DW = 2.1233 \quad F(5, 13) = 36.8633$$

Exports of manufactured goods

(23)
$$EGMFR = -1.17954 + 0.00052 \underline{GNPUR}$$
$$ (-6.711) \quad (9.114)$$
$$R^2 = 0.8201 \quad S.E. = 0.10685 \quad DW = 0.6438 \quad F(1, 17) = 83.0712$$

Tourism and border exports

(24)
$$ETBR = -2.39964 + 0.02245 \underline{RDPAV} + 0.75075 \underline{DUMDV} + 0.00238 \underline{DIUR}$$
$$ (-5.071) \quad (1.947) \quad\quad\quad (7.854) \quad\quad\quad (7.039)$$
$$R^2 = 0.9594 \quad S.E. = 0.1888 \quad DW = 2.5961 \quad F(3, 15) = 142.8593$$

Exports of labor per worker

(25)
$$EBRRL = 0.09415 - 0.01248 \underline{DUMBR} - 0.07318 \underline{WRMMUC} - 0.01846 \underline{X1RL}$$
$$ (8.407) \quad (-3.551) \quad\quad\quad (-2.947) \quad\quad\quad (-3.322)$$
$$R^2 = 0.9152 \quad S.E. = 0.0038 \quad DW = 1.8624 \quad F(3, 15) = 65.7711$$

Production of gold and silver

(26)
$$EAAR = (\underline{EAADC} \times \underline{REX})/PGNP$$

Exports of zinc
(27) $$EZINR = EMETR - ELEAR - ECOPR$$

Exports of agricultural goods
(28) $$EAGR = ECOTR + ESUGR + ECOFR$$

Exports of goods explained by the model
(29) $$EGER = EAGR + EMETR + EGMFR$$

Exports of other goods
(30) $$EOGR = [(\underline{EGDC} \times \underline{REX})/PGNP] - EGER$$

Exports of goods
(31) $$EGR = EGER + EOGR$$
(32) $$EGC = EGR \times PGNP$$

Exports of labor: bracero earnings
(33) $$EBRR = EBRRL \times L1$$

Other exports in trade account
(34) $$EOTR = (\underline{EOTDC} \times \underline{REX})/PGNP$$

U.S. gross national product
(35) $$GNPUR = (\underline{GNPUDC} \times \underline{REX})/PGNP$$

U.S. disposable personal income
(36) $$DIUR = (\underline{DIUDC} \times \underline{REX})/PGNP$$

Total trade exports: goods, services and factors
(37) $$EGSFR^* = EGR + EBRR + EAAR + EOTR + ETBR$$

IB(ii). Imports
Imports of consumer goods
(38) $MCONR = 0.23921 + 0.00426\ CR + 0.11120\ FRR + 0.1233\ \underline{FRR1} + 0.07370\ \underline{FRR2}$
        (1.295)   (2.222)   (2.4134)   (3.9358)   (1.6357)

$\sum_{i=0}^{2} w(i) = 0.3082$

                 $R^2 = 0.6926$ $S.E. = 0.1209$ $DW = 2.1126$ $F(3, 12) = 12.2677$

Imports of capital goods
(39) $MCAPR = 1.78374 - 0.13774\ X2R + 0.23077\ FRR + 0.33850\ IR + 0.0430\ \underline{IR1}$
        (7.625)   (−5.197)   (2.656)   (4.9568)   (0.7785)

$\sum_{i=0}^{1} w(i) = 0.3815$

                 $R^2 = 0.9218$ $S.E. = 0.1449$ $DW = 2.7021$ $F(4, 11) = 45.1882$

Imports of raw materials and fuels
(40) $$MRR = (\underline{MRDC} \times \underline{REX})/PGNP$$

Tourism and border imports
(41) $MTBR = -1.05262 + 0.26925\ CMC$
          (−6.497)   (16.955)
     $R^2 = 0.9409$ $S.E. = 0.1446$ $DW = 1.1732$ $F(1, 17) = 287.4587$

Private payments of interest and dividends abroad
(42) $MPPR = 0.16413 + 0.01082\ X23R$
           (1.938)   (8.120)
     $R^2 = 0.7830$ $S.E. = 0.12409$ $DW = 0.8460$ $F(1, 17) = 65.9364$

Public payments of interest abroad
(43) $MIGR = -0.06879 + 0.05542\ DBGER$
         (−1.996)   (9.854)
     $R^2 = 0.8422$ $S.E. = 0.07264$ $DW = 0.6560$ $F(1, 17) = 97.0940$

Imports of production goods

(44) $$MPGR = MCAPR + MRR$$

Imports of goods
(45) $$MGR = MPGR + MCONR$$
(46) $$MGC = MGR \times PGNP$$

Imports of factors of production
(47) $$MFR = MPPR + MIGR$$

Other imports in trade account
(48) $$MOTR = (\underline{MOTDC} \times \underline{REX})/PGNP$$

Total trade imports: goods, services and factors
(49) $$MGSFR^* = MGR + MTBR + MFR + MOTR$$

Weighted price index of main exporting countries to Mexico
(50) $$PEUEJ = 0.63\,\underline{PEUS} + 0.25\,\underline{PEEU} + 0.04\,\underline{PEJP}$$

Annual change in price index of main exporting countries to Mexico
(51) $$DPEUEJ = PEUEJ - \underline{PEUEJ1}$$

Price index of imports
(52) $$PM = 1.32176 + 3.92619\,TFMGC + 5.03750\,DPEUEJ + 2.15990\,\underline{DPEUE1}$$
$$(12.371) \quad (4.696) \quad\quad (2.6029) \quad\quad\quad (1.1100)$$

$$\sum_{i=0}^{1} w(i) = 7.1973$$

$$R^2 = 0.7684 \quad S.E. = 0.1331 \quad DW = 0.9219 \quad F(3, 12) = 17.5894$$

Rate of change of import price index
(53) $$PM\% = (PM - \underline{PM1})/\underline{PM1}$$

Capacity to import: export earnings deflated by import price index
(54) $$CMC = [(EGSFR^*) \times PGNP]/PM$$

IB(iii). Balance of Trade or Net Foreign Demand
Balance of goods
(55) $$BGR = EGR - MGR$$

Balance of tourism and border transaction
(56) $$BTBR = ETBR - MTBR$$

Balance of goods and services
(57) $$BGSR^* = BGR + BTBR$$

Balance of factors
(58) $$BFR^* = EBRR - MFR$$

Balance of other items in trade account
(59) $$BOTR = EOTR - MOTR$$

Balance of trade: goods, services and factors
(60) $$BGSFR^* = BGR + BTBR + BFR^* + BOTR + EAAR$$

Balance of goods and services in NIA (conciliation)
(61) $$BGSR = BGSR^* + \underline{SDBGSR}$$

Balance of factors in NIA (conciliation)
(62) $$BFR = BFR^* + \underline{SDBFR}$$

Balance of trade: goods, services and factors in NIA
(63) $$BGSFR = BGSR + BFR$$

IC. Total Aggregate Demand
Gross national product
(64) $$GNPR = CITR + BGSFR$$
(65) $$GNPC = GNPR \times PGNP$$

II. Generation of Value-Added Output

Output originating in primary sector

(66)
$$X1R = 1.54792 + 0.17425\,CPR + 1.15516\,EAGR$$
$$(2.167) \quad (30.559) \quad\quad (4.070)$$
$$R^2 = 0.9816 \quad S.E. = 0.4133 \quad DW = 1.2108 \quad F(2,16) = 489.6113$$

Output originating in secondary sector

(67)
$$X2R = -4.16634 + 0.63336\,IR + 0.35448\,CR$$
$$(-6.160) \quad (4.113) \quad\quad (9.552)$$
$$R^2 = 0.9965 \quad S.E. = 0.5996 \quad DW = 1.0393 \quad F(2,16) = 2534.3875$$

Output originating in tertiary sector

(68)
$$X3R = -2.06446 + 0.59023\,ETBR + 0.57309\,CR$$
$$(-4.317) \quad (2.557) \quad\quad\quad (52.772)$$
$$R^2 = 0.9980 \quad S.E. = 0.5303 \quad DW = 1.2959 \quad F(2,16) = 4510.9609$$

Gross domestic product

(69) $\quad\quad\quad\quad\quad\quad\quad\quad GDPR = X1R + X2R + X3R$

(70) $\quad\quad\quad\quad\quad\quad\quad\quad GDPC = GDPR \times PGNP$

Annual change in gross domestic product

(71) $\quad\quad\quad\quad\quad\quad\quad\quad DGDPR = GDPR - \underline{GDPR1}$

Gross domestic urban product

(72) $\quad\quad\quad\quad\quad\quad\quad\quad X23R = X2R + X3R$

III. Capital Formation

Capital stock in the urban sector

(73)
$$K23R = -4.43803 + 0.97649\,KR$$
$$(-47.108) \quad (899.786)$$
$$R^2 = 1.000 \quad S.E. = 0.1444 \quad DW = 0.3752 \quad F(1,17) > 999$$

Private capital stock

(74) $\quad\quad\quad\quad\quad\quad\quad\quad KPR = IPR + 0.90\,\underline{KPR1}$

Public capital stock

(75) $\quad\quad\quad\quad\quad\quad\quad\quad KGR = IGR + 0.95\,\underline{KGR1}$

Capital stock

(76) $\quad\quad\quad\quad\quad\quad\quad\quad KR = KPR + KGR$

Capital stock of federal government in rural sector

(77) $\quad\quad\quad\quad\quad\quad\quad\quad KGF1R = KR - K23R$

Private depreciation

(78) $\quad\quad\quad\quad\quad\quad\quad\quad DPR = 0.10\,\underline{KPR1}$

Public depreciation

(79) $\quad\quad\quad\quad\quad\quad\quad\quad DGR = 0.05\,\underline{KGR1}$

Depreciation

(80) $\quad\quad\quad\quad\quad\quad\quad\quad DR = DPR + DGR$

(81) $\quad\quad\quad\quad\quad\quad\quad\quad DC = DR \times PGNP$

IV. Creation of Capacity: Potential Value-Added Production

Rural capacity

(82)
$$X1RP = -12.49223 + 4.41883\,\underline{KGF1R2}$$
$$(-8.144) \quad (17.487)$$
$$R^2 = 0.9442 \quad S.E. = 0.6933 \quad DW = 0.3739 \quad F(1,17) = 305.7893$$

Urban capacity

(83)
$$X23RP = 6.83255 + 0.81752\,\underline{K23R1}$$
$$(5.044) \quad (45.072)$$
$$R^2 = 0.9912 \quad S.E. = 2.1628 \quad DW = 0.4497 \quad F(1,17) = 2031.5142$$

Capacity

(84) $\quad\quad\quad\quad\quad\quad\quad\quad XRP = X1RP + X23RP$

Unused rural capacity
(85)
$$UX1RP = X1RP - X1R$$

Unused urban capacity
(86)
$$UX23RP = X23RP - X23R$$

Unused capacity
(87)
$$UXRP = XRP - GDPR$$

Annual change in used urban capacity
(88)
$$DUX23P = UX23RP - UX23RP1$$

V. Demography Processes and Labor Supply

Population
(89)
$$N = NG \times N1$$

Urban-rural potential productivity gaps
(90)
$$DX231P = (X23RP/NURB) - (X1RP/NRUL)$$

Ratio of urban to total population: urbanization

(91)
$$\begin{aligned}
NURBN = \quad &0.36908 + \quad 0.00849 \; T + 0.00280 \, DX231P + \quad 0.00360 \, DX231P1 \\
&(208.854) \quad (251.877) \qquad (7.6985) \qquad\qquad (12.4946) \\
&+ \; 0.00290 \, DX231P2 + 0.00150 \, DX231P3 \\
&\quad (8.8262) \qquad\qquad (3.5369)
\end{aligned}$$

$$\sum_{i=0}^{3} w(i) = 0.0107$$

$$R^2 = 1.000 \qquad S.E. = 0.0001 \qquad DW = 5.5279 \qquad F(3, 12) = > 999$$

Urban population
(92)
$$NURB = N \times NURBN$$

Rural population
(93)
$$NRUL = N - NURB$$

Annual change in rural potential productivity
(94)
$$DX1PRU = (X1RP/NRUL) - (X1RP1/NRUL1)$$

Rural labor participation rate

(95)
$$\begin{aligned}
L1NRU = \quad &0.38528 - \quad 0.00196 \, DUMRE - \quad 0.32790 \, DX1PRU - \quad 0.51720 \, DX1PRU1 \\
&(87.379) \quad (-0.974) \qquad\qquad (-1.6638) \qquad\qquad (-3.8388) \\
&- \; 0.54270 \, DX1PRU2 - \quad 0.37870 \, DX1PRU3 - \quad 0.00070 \, DUX23P \\
&\quad (-9.3369) \qquad\qquad (-2.7378) \qquad\qquad (-5.6660) \\
&- \quad 0.00110 \, DUX23P1 - \quad 0.00110 \, DUX23P2 - \quad 0.00070 \, DUX23P3 \\
&\quad (-9.6770) \qquad\qquad (-5.6311) \qquad\qquad (-3.1876)
\end{aligned}$$

$$\sum_{i=0}^{3} w_1(i) = -1.7665$$

$$\sum_{i=0}^{3} w_2(i) = -0.0036$$

$$R^2 = 0.9867 \qquad S.E. = 0.0013 \qquad DW = 2.2905 \qquad F(5, 10) = 223.1250$$

Rural labor force
(96)
$$L1 = L1NRU \times NRUL$$

Urban potential productivity
(97)
$$X23PNB = X23RP/NURB$$

Urban potential productivity in the revised data period
(98)
$$X23PBD = X23PNB \times DUMRE$$

Unused urban productive capacity in the revised data period
(99)
$$UX23RD = UX23RP \times DUMRE$$

Urban labor participation rate

(100) $L23NB =$ $0.68591 -$ $0.12852\ X23PNB +\ 0.10019\ X23PBD -$ $0.30454\ \underline{DUMRE}$
           (36.351) (-20.934) (8.301) (-6.967)
             $+\ 0.00301\ UX23RP -$ $0.00242\ UX23RD$
              (4.700) (-3.419)

$$R^2 = 0.9674 \quad S.E. = 0.00241 \quad DW = 1.9357 \quad F(5, 13) = 107.9482$$

Urban labor force

(101) $$L23 = L23NB \times NURB$$

Labor force

(102) $$L = L1 + L23$$

Rural labor productivity

(103) $$X1RL = X1R/L$$

Urban labor productivity

(104) $$X23RL = X23R/L23$$

VI. Income Distribution

VIA. National Income Breakdown: Wage and Nonwage Income

Average minimum daily wage rate (current pesos per worker)

(105) $$WMAC = (\underline{WMRC} \times L1 + \underline{WMUC} \times L23)/L$$

Ratio of minimum rural wage rate to U.S. manufacturing wage rate

(106) $$WRMMUC = \underline{WMRC}/(\underline{WRFUDC} \times \underline{REX})$$

Rate of change of wage rate

(107) $WRC\% =\ 0.01307 -$ $0.00356\ UX23RP +$ $1.68756\ PGNP\%$
           (1.305) (-2.530) (18.430)

$$R^2 = 0.9659 \quad S.E. = 0.0156 \quad DW = 1.3768 \quad F(2, 16) = 256.1040$$

Average annual wage rate

(108) $$WRC = (1.0 + WRC\%) \times \underline{WRC1}$$

Wage income

(109) $$WIC = WRC \times L$$

Labor unit cost

(110) $$WRCA = WRC/(GDPR/L)$$

Rate of change of labor unit cost

(111) $$WRCA\% = (WRCA - \underline{WRCA1})/\underline{WRCA1}$$

Net national product

(112) $$NNPC = GNPC - DC$$

Model's national income

(113) $$NIC: = NNPC - TNIC$$

National income

(114) $$NIC = NIC: + \underline{SDNIC:}$$
(115) $$NIR = NIC/PGNP$$

Nonwage income

(116) $$NWIC = NIC - WIC$$

Disposable income per capita

(117) $$DIPRN = [(NIC - TFIC.)/PGNP]/N$$

VIB. Public Income and Finance

Federal income taxes

(118) $TFIC. =\ -1.27427 +\ 0.04001\ NIC$
                 (-4.201) (20.957)

$$R^2 = 0.9605 \quad S.E. = 0.6501 \quad DW = 1.0844 \quad F(1, 17) = 439.2012$$

Federal export taxes
(119)
$$TFEC. = 0.35076 + 1.02380 \underline{DUMTFE} + 0.06586 \, EGC$$
$$(5.975) \quad (7.625) \qquad\qquad (11.527)$$
$$R^2 = 0.9038 \quad S.E. = 0.0811 \quad DW = 1.4300 \qquad F(2, 16) = 85.5648$$

Federal import taxes
(120)
$$TFMC = -1.45476 + 0.23801 \, MGC$$
$$(-4.206) \quad (10.235)$$
$$R^2 = 0.8522 \quad S.E. = 0.5258 \quad DW = 0.8140 \qquad F(1, 17) = 104.7648$$

Federal sales taxes
(121)
$$TFSC. = -0.23470 + 0.00962 \, GDPC$$
$$(-4.317) \quad (31.564)$$
$$R^2 = 0.9822 \quad S.E. = 0.1167 \quad DW = 0.7020 \qquad F(1, 17) = 996.2786$$

Federal nontax income
(122)
$$TFPAC. = 0.24270 + 0.00750 \, GDPC + 2.67050 \underline{DUMTPC}$$
$$(2.865) \quad (15.392) \qquad (13.926)$$
$$R^2 = 0.9692 \quad S.E. = 0.1810 \quad DW = 2.6903 \qquad F(2, 16) = 284.6804$$

Other federal taxes
(123)
$$TFOC: = 0.7211 + 0.11610 \, TFC$$
$$(5.696) \quad (12.821)$$
$$R^2 = 0.9008 \quad S.E. = 0.2797 \quad DW = 2.2890 \qquad F(1, 17) = 164.3864$$

Nonfederal taxes: D.F., state and local
(124)
$$TNFC = -0.84372 + 0.37313 \, TFC$$
$$(-6.827) \quad (42.213)$$
$$R^2 = 0.9900 \quad S.E. = 0.2730 \quad DW = 2.1512 \qquad F(1, 17) = 1781.9036$$

Federal indirect or nonincome taxes
(125) $\quad TFNIC. = TFMC. + TFEC. + TFSC. + TFOC: + TFPAC.$
(126) $\quad TFNIC = TFNIC. + \underline{SDTFNC}$

Indirect or nonincome taxes
(127) $\qquad\qquad\qquad TNIC = TFNIC + TNFC$

Rate of change of indirect taxes
(128) $\qquad\qquad TNIC\% = (TNIC - \underline{TNIC1})/\underline{TNIC1}$

Federal taxes
(129) $\qquad\qquad\qquad TFC = TFIC. + TFNIC$

Taxes
(130) $\qquad\qquad\qquad TC = TFC + TNFC$
(131) $\qquad\qquad\qquad TR = TC/PGNP$

Average tariff on imports of goods
(132) $\qquad\qquad\qquad TFMGC = TFMC./MGC$

Public expenditure
(133) $\qquad\qquad\qquad GR = CGR + IGR$
(134) $\qquad\qquad\qquad GC = GR \times PGNP$

Public surplus or deficit
(135) $\qquad\qquad\qquad GSC = TC - GC$

Taxes plus public depreciation
(136) $\qquad\qquad\qquad TRDGR = TR + DGR$

Public foreign debt
(137) $\qquad\qquad DBGER = (\underline{DBGEDC} \times \underline{REX})/PGNP$

Annual change in public foreign debt
(138) $\qquad\qquad DDBGR = DBGER - \underline{DBGER1}$

Banking system credit to the federal government
(139) $\qquad\qquad\qquad FBGFR = \underline{FBGFC}/PGNP$

Foreign reserves
(140) $$FRR = (\underline{FRDC} \times \underline{REX})/\underline{PGNP}$$

VII. Price Formation
Rate of change of the general price index: GNP deflator
(141) $PGNP\% = 0.01667 + 0.38848 \ WRCA\% + 0.32394 \ PM\% + 0.00746 \ TNIC\%$
             (4.007)   (4.103)   (2.680)   (0.236)
                   $R^2 = 0.9520$ $S.E. = 0.0100$ $DW = 2.3499$ $F(3, 15) = 119.8805$

General price index: GNP deflator
(142) $$PGNP = (1.0 + PGNP\%) \times \underline{PGNP1}$$

Annual change in the general price index
(143) $$DPGNP = PGNP - \underline{PGNP1}$$

---

4. SIMULATIONS

This final section is devoted to econometric results. We will present two long-term simulations of the Mexican economy obtained from model solutions. They cover the full six-year term, 1971–1976, of the new administration of President Echeverria. We provide actual figures for 1968–1970, to give a basis of comparison. It should be noted, however, that some of the figures for this previous period are preliminary or even our own estimates, given the unusual delay in the publication of data. We think, however, that they are good enough to be included.

Given the uncertainties that go with long-term simulations, we have followed two procedures to give empirical meaning to our results. First, we have used the available information at mid-1971 on the exogenous variables and adjustments of the behavioral equations to try to produce a realistic forecast for 1971. Secondly, for the rest of the period, 1972–1976, we have used two contrasting assumptions about the behavior of the federal government: one deflationary, the other expansionary. In this way, we expect to set up lower and upper bounds within which the real economy will probably move.

With regard to the contrasting assumptions from 1972 to 1976, we can summarize them in the following table. They represent divergent hypothetical policy packages that the administration could take in a single-minded pursuit of stability or high employment.

Essentially, the two policies boil down to different spending patterns by the federal government. Being the dominant economic agent, the federal impact is

AVERAGE ANNUAL GROWTH OF THE POLICY VARIABLES: 1972–1976

	Deflationary Hypothesis	Expansionary Hypothesis
Fiscal Measures		
Government investment	7.5%	9.9%
Federal enterprise investment	6.8	9.9
Public works: highways	5.0	7.0
Government consumption	7.0	8.7
Monetary Measures		
Banking credit to federal government	7.0	15.0
External debt	7.0	10.0

critical in the system, and, as can be seen in the two tables which follow, it can turn the economy into different paths. In each table, there are two sections, I and II, in real and current billions of pesos respectively, for each simulation, containing a selection of the original computer print-outs. Reference to concepts in the tables will be made by section and line. Thus, for example, real gross national product and current inventory change are (I-2) and (II-14) in both tables.

Analysis of the Simulations

Since 1971 is the same in both projections, and since 1972 exhibits the same tendencies in both cases (more pronounced in one than in the other), we will analyze 1971–1972 first. Then, we will make a comparison of the divergent long-run patterns, 1973–1976. In the short run, the most striking facts are the following:

1. A sharp deceleration of economic activity in 1971 and a revival in 1972. This can be seen in the rates of growth of *GDPR* (I-1) and *GNPR* (I-2), the first one being the measure commonly used by Mexican economists.

2. A slowing down of the rate of inflation in 1971 and a tendency to grow again in 1972. See GNP deflator (I-21) and its rate of growth (I-22).

3. A consecutive improvement in the balance on current account in 1971 and in 1972. See (I-18).

These three basic facts are, of course, closely interrelated. The 1970–1971 recession is, in part, the normal result of Mexican political change and, in part, the effect of conscious effort on the part of the new administration to fight inflation and deterioration of the external position in 1970 by means of an austerity program. Another contributing external deflationary element is the 1969–1970 U.S. recession, whose lagged effects have been clearly felt in the sluggishness of exports. The U.S. inflation, on the other hand, has also contributed to Mexican inflation by filtering through imports, 65 percent of which come from there.

The two simulation patterns diverge after 1973. They can be summarized in four points:

1. The deflationary policy induces economic growth of 6–6.5 percent, as measured by gross domestic product (I-1); the expansionary policy produces 7–7.5 percent growth.

2. Deflation stabilizes and reduces the external deficit; expansion destabilizes and increases it, as measured by the real balance on current account (I-18). In fact, by the end of the period, the expansionary calculation projects a deficit of the magnitude of last year's − 3.6 to − 3.7 billion.

3. Deflation succeeds in breaking the inflationary growth; expansion keeps it going at approximately the 1970–1971 rates, according to the GNP deflator (I-21) and (I-22).

4. Deflation increases the rate of idle productive capacity; expansion tends to keep it constant, as shown by the ratio of unused capacity to gross domestic product, i.e., (I-23) divided by (I-1).

These facts give support to the contention of some Mexican economists that rapid rates of growth of 7–7.5 percent tend to "overheat" the economy and to produce rising prices and growing external deficits. Slower rates of 6–6.5 percent, on the other hand, appear to be too sluggish, given past Mexican experience. If

TABLE 1
EXPANSIONARY SIMULATION, WHARTON-DIEMEX MACROMODEL, SELECTED VARIABLES
[full Echeverria term: 1971–1976]

			1968	1969	1970	1971	1972	1973	1974	1975	1976
			Section I: In Billions of 1950 Pesos								
1	Gross domestic product	GDPR	122.68	132.30	142.55	150.79	160.99	172.11	185.04	199.16	213.90
2	Gross national product	GNPR	120.42	130.21	141.14	150.86	162.22	174.49	188.65	204.00	219.76
3	Internal aggregate demand	CITR	123.70	133.83	145.99	155.13	166.42	178.82	193.07	208.77	224.73
4	Consumption	CR	99.98	108.11	118.71	127.23	136.35	146.56	157.74	170.22	183.30
5	Private per capita[1]	CPRN	1.96	2.05	2.18	2.26	2.33	2.42	2.51	2.61	2.72
6	Private	CPR	92.67	100.09	110.28	118.49	126.81	136.21	146.44	157.92	170.01
7	Public	CGR	7.31	8.02	8.43	8.75	9.54	10.35	11.30	12.29	13.28
8	Investment	ITR	23.72	25.73	27.29	27.90	30.07	32.27	25.32	38.55	41.43
9	Gross fixed investment	IR	21.70	23.50	25.21	25.66	27.84	29.90	32.85	35.72	38.32
10	Private	IPR	11.94	12.89	13.84	14.19	15.16	16.04	17.45	18.91	19.98
11	Public	IGR	9.76	10.62	11.37	11.48	12.69	13.87	15.39	16.81	18.35
12	Government	IGGR.	4.53	4.56	4.78	4.69	5.44	5.80	6.30	6.84	7.47
13	Fed. gov. enterprises	IGOER.	5.24	6.06	6.59	6.79	7.25	8.07	9.09	9.97	10.88
14	Inventory change	ICHR	2.02	2.22	2.08	2.24	2.22	2.36	2.48	2.83	3.11
15	Balance of trade (concil. NIA)	BGSFR	−3.28	−3.62	−4.85	−4.27	−4.20	−4.33	−4.42	−4.76	−4.98
16	Balance of factors	BFR	−2.27	−1.84	−1.44	−1.54	−1.63	−1.74	−1.90	−2.08	−2.28
17	Bal. goods and services	BGSR	−1.01	−1.79	−3.42	−2.72	−2.58	−2.59	−2.52	−2.68	−2.69
18	Balance of trade	BGSFR*	−2.84	−2.32	−3.63	−3.04	−2.95	−3.11	−3.22	−3.57	−3.71
19	Total exports	EGSFR*	11.27	13.18	13.41	13.56	14.75	15.59	16.76	17.50	18.37
20	Total imports	MGSFR*	14.11	15.50	17.04	16.60	17.70	18.70	19.99	21.07	22.08
21	Price index: GNP deflator[2]	PGNP	2.78	2.82	2.95	3.06	3.21	3.37	3.50	3.64	3.78
22	Rate of change[3]	PGNP%	3.60	1.60	4.80	3.90	4.90	5.00	3.90	4.00	3.80
23	Unused capacity	UXRP	−0.02	3.70	3.51	6.40	7.10	7.71	7.47	7.60	8.64
24	Labor force[4]	L	14.86	15.38	15.78	16.31	17.01	17.87	18.39	18.87	19.26
			Section II: In Billions of Current Pesos								
1	Gross domestic product	GDPC	340.70	372.99	420.63	462.03	516.13	579.99	647.25	724.40	809.13
2	Gross national product	GNPC	334.41	367.10	416.47	462.24	520.06	588.02	659.89	742.03	831.30
3	Internal aggregate demand	CITC	343.51	377.31	430.80	475.31	533.53	602.60	675.35	759.36	850.13
4	Consumption	CC	277.64	304.78	350.28	389.84	437.13	493.87	551.78	619.13	693.39
5	Private per capita[5]	CPRNC	5.44	5.77	6.42	6.92	7.48	8.15	8.78	9.51	10.27
6	Private	CPC	257.34	282.19	325.41	363.04	406.55	459.01	512.25	574.42	643.14

7	Public	CGC	20.31	22.60	24.87	26.80	30.59	34.86	39.53	44.72	50.25
8	Investment	ITC	65.87	72.53	80.52	85.47	96.40	108.73	123.57	140.23	156.74
9	Gross fixed investment	IC	60.25	66.25	74.38	78.62	89.27	100.76	114.90	129.93	144.97
10	Private	IPC	33.15	36.34	40.84	43.47	48.60	54.04	61.05	68.79	75.58
11	Public	IGC	27.11	29.94	33.54	35.16	40.68	46.73	53.84	61.16	69.40
12	Government	IGGC.	12.57	12.86	14.10	14.35	17.44	19.53	22.05	24.88	28.25
13	Fed. gov. enterprises	IGOEC.	14.54	17.09	19.44	20.81	23.23	27.20	31.79	36.28	41.15
14	Inventory change	ICHC	5.61	6.27	6.14	6.85	7.13	7.96	8.67	10.29	11.77
15	Balance of trade (concil. NIA)	BGSFC	-9.10	-10.22	-14.33	-13.07	-13.47	-14.58	-15.46	-17.33	-18.83
16	Balance of factors	BFC	-6.30	-5.18	-4.24	-4.73	-5.21	-5.86	-6.65	-7.58	-8.64
17	Bal. goods and services	BGSC	-2.80	-5.03	-10.08	-8.34	-8.26	-8.72	-8.81	-9.75	-10.19
18	Balance of trade	BGSFC*	-7.90	-6.53	-10.71	-9.31	-9.47	-10.48	-11.28	-12.99	-14.03
19	Total exports	EGSFC*	31.30	37.17	39.57	41.56	47.28	52.54	58.64	63.64	69.50
20	Total imports	MGSFC*	39.20	43.70	50.29	50.87	56.75	63.02	69.92	76.63	85.53

1 Thousands of 1950 pesos.
2 1950 = 1.0.
3 GNP price deflator rate of change in percent.
4 Millions of persons.
5 Thousands of current pesos.

TABLE 2

DEFLATIONARY SIMULATION, WHARTON-DIEMEX MACROMODEL, SELECTED VARIABLES

[full Echeverria term: 1971–1976]

		1968	1969	1970	1971	1972	1973	1974	1975	1976
				Section I: In Billions of 1950 Pesos						
1 Gross domestic product	GDPR	122.68	132.30	142.55	150.79	160.00	169.50	180.40	192.15	204.46
2 Gross national product	GNPR	120.42	130.21	141.14	150.86	161.02	171.60	183.67	196.69	210.10
3 Internal aggregate demand	CITR	123.70	133.83	145.99	155.13	165.12	175.49	187.22	200.21	213.48
4 Consumption	CR	99.98	108.11	118.71	127.23	135.76	144.87	154.60	165.37	176.66
5 Private per capita[1]	CPRN	1.96	2.05	2.18	2.26	2.33	2.40	2.47	2.55	2.63
6 Private	CPR	92.67	100.09	110.28	118.49	126.41	134.92	143.89	153.90	164.42
7 Public	CGR	7.31	8.02	8.43	8.75	9.35	9.96	10.71	11.47	12.24
8 Investment	ITR	23.72	25.73	27.29	27.90	29.37	30.62	32.62	34.83	36.82
9 Gross fixed invest.	IR	21.70	23.50	25.21	25.66	27.26	28.53	30.61	32.54	34.30
10 Private	IPR	11.94	12.89	13.84	14.19	14.98	15.39	16.15	17.13	17.85
11 Public	IGR	9.76	10.62	11.37	11.48	12.28	13.15	14.45	15.41	16.46
12 Government	IGGR.	4.53	4.56	4.78	4.69	5.31	5.72	6.14	6.51	7.09
13 Fed. gov. enterprise	IGOER.	5.24	6.06	6.59	6.79	6.97	7.43	8.31	8.90	9.36
14 Inventory change	ICHR	2.02	2.22	2.08	2.24	2.11	2.09	2.01	2.30	2.53
15 Balance of trade (concil. NIA)	BGSFR	−3.28	−3.62	−4.85	−4.27	−4.10	−3.89	−3.55	−3.52	−3.38
16 Balance of factors	BFR	−2.27	−1.84	−1.44	−1.54	−1.61	−1.69	−1.83	−1.97	−2.12
17 Bal. goods and services	BGSR	−1.01	−1.79	−3.42	−2.72	−2.49	−2.20	−1.72	−1.54	−1.27
18 Balance of trade	BGSFR*	−2.84	−2.32	−3.63	−3.04	−2.85	−2.65	−2.30	−2.26	−2.04
19 Total exports	EGSFR*	11.27	13.18	13.41	13.56	14.62	15.68	17.21	18.21	19.29
20 Total imports	MGSFR*	14.11	15.50	17.04	16.60	17.47	18.33	19.51	20.47	21.33
21 Price index: GNP deflator[2]	PGNP	2.78	2.82	2.95	3.06	3.18	3.30	3.35	3.44	3.55
22 Rate of change[3]	PGNP%	3.60	1.60	4.80	3.90	3.90	3.80	1.70	2.70	3.20
23 Unused capacity	UXRP	−0.02	3.70	3.51	6.40	8.09	9.85	10.51	11.21	12.15
24 Labor force[4]	L	14.86	15.38	15.78	16.31	16.84	17.51	17.85	18.41	18.96
				Section II: In Billions of Current Pesos						
1 Gross domestic product	GDPC	340.70	372.99	420.63	462.03	509.03	559.02	605.06	661.92	726.07
2 Gross national product	GNPC	334.41	367.10	416.47	462.24	512.28	565.94	616.02	677.55	746.08
3 Internal aggregate demand	CITC	343.51	377.31	430.80	475.31	525.33	578.77	627.02	689.67	758.09
4 Consumption	CC	277.64	304.78	350.28	389.84	431.90	477.78	518.52	569.68	627.33
5 Private per capita[5]	CPRNC	5.44	5.77	6.42	6.92	7.40	7.91	8.28	8.78	9.34
6 Private	CPC	257.34	282.19	325.41	363.04	402.15	444.95	482.61	530.16	583.87

7	Public	CGC	20.31	22.60	24.87	26.80	29.75	32.83	35.91	39.52	43.46
8	Investment	ITC	65.87	72.53	80.52	85.47	93.43	100.99	109.40	120.00	130.77
9	Gross fixed investment	IC	60.25	66.25	74.38	78.62	86.72	94.10	102.66	112.09	121.80
10	Private	IPC	33.15	36.34	40.84	43.47	47.66	50.76	54.18	59.01	63.37
11	Public	IGC	27.11	29.94	33.54	35.16	39.07	43.35	48.47	53.08	58.44
12	Government	IGGC.	12.57	12.86	14.10	14.35	16.88	18.85	20.60	22.42	25.19
13	Fed. gov. enterprise	IGOEC.	14.54	17.09	19.44	20.81	22.19	24.50	27.87	30.66	33.24
14	Inventory change	ICHC	5.61	6.27	6.14	6.85	6.71	6.88	6.74	7.91	8.97
15	Balance of trade (concil. NIA)	BGSFC	-9.10	-10.22	-14.33	-13.07	-13.04	-12.83	-11.91	-12.12	-12.02
16	Balance of factors	BFC	-6.30	-5.18	-4.24	-4.73	-5.11	-5.58	-6.15	-6.80	-7.51
17	Bal. goods and services	BGSC	-2.80	-5.03	-10.08	-8.34	-7.93	-7.25	-5.75	-5.32	-4.51
18	Balance of trade	BGSFC*	-7.90	-6.53	-10.71	-9.31	-9.07	-8.74	-7.71	-7.78	-7.25
19	Total exports	EGSFC*	31.30	37.17	39.57	41.56	46.52	51.71	57.74	62.73	68.51
20	Total imports	MGSFC*	39.20	43.70	50.29	50.87	55.59	60.45	65.45	70.51	75.76

[1] Thousands of 1950 pesos.
[2] 1950 = 1.0.
[3] GNP price deflator rate of change in percent.
[4] Millions of persons.
[5] Thousands of current pesos.

this is the case, the 6.5–7 percent range seems to be the golden mean. It is clear, however, that the unemployment problem, the most serious of the Mexican problems, will not be solved with this rate. If the labor force keeps growing at 3.5 percent (the rate of population growth), it is necessary to create approximately 552,000 jobs in 1971 to accommodate new workers alone, given the 1970 total labor force of 15.78 million. If we extend this calculation, Mexico will have 19.39 million people looking for work in 1976. Our high simulation estimates a figure of 19.26 million in I-24, and we can take this, for practical purposes, as a full-employment projection. Any calculation below this will result in unemployment. Our low projection, for instance, indicates an excess of labor supply of 300,000 workers in 1976, in spite of its being a 6.3 percent average-growth simulation. It should be noted that this number is probably an underestimate of unemployment. In his excellent econometric study, David Ibarra,[13] for example, compares a full-employment projection and a 6.2 percent projection and comes up with an estimate of 2.5 million workers in excess labor supply for 1976. His high figure (or full employment) is 18.76 million workers; his low (6.2 percent growth) is 16.29. In spite of these differences, there is here a basic agreement on the fundamental issue: a full-employment path is not compatible with internal and external stability, unless structural changes (in capital-labor ratios and import content of investment, to start with) are introduced into the system.

This is precisely what the new administration seems to have in mind in its plan of introducing labor-intensive investment programs in the rural sector, instead of traditional, large-scale capital-intensive projects. When implemented, these new projects may help to alleviate rural unemployment and reduce the migratory flow to the cities. The numerical solution, however, cannot be estimated yet because of the absence of information on the magnitude and nature of the projects.

The basic dilemma of the Mexican economy raises the broader question of stability versus employment for some of the Latin American economies. Argentina, Brazil, Colombia, Chile, and Peru, up to the end of the 1960s, have also been unable to combine growth with stability. The apparent inability of Mexico to achieve this joint objective, in spite of its favorable political, economic, and trade positions, makes it doubtful that the other countries will, at least in the next half decade, considering their demographic and political circumstances.[14]

The long-run comparison also yields some aspects, which although similar in direction, are different in magnitude. Private consumption and investment, exports and imports, and government finance are some cases in point. The fast-growth simulation produces a substantially higher private consumption per capita

[13] David Ibarra, "Mercados, Desarrollo y Politica Economica: Perspectivas de la Economia de Mexico," *El Perfil Economico de Mexico en 1980, Vol. I* (Mexico: Siglo Veintiuno Editores, 1970), Cuadro 24, p. 144.

[14] This doubt of reconciling high growth (5 percent or more) with external and price stability (5 percent or less) seems to be supported by the data. With the possible exception of Brazil, which has managed simultaneously to speed up its growth, reduce its inflation, and substantially increase its foreign reserves during the late sixties (very favorable international coffee prices, due to a large extent to the Brazilian coffee frost of 1969, has been one of the contributing factors to this happy state of affairs), high growth and stability, especially external stability, seem unattainable for the major developing Latin American economies at their present capacity-creation stage.

(I-5) than the slow case: 7.5 percent average rate of growth versus 6.8 percent for 1971–1976. This means that the size of the internal market—commonly blamed for the high industrial average fixed costs and for being the bottleneck of industrial development—can be enlarged by aggressive public investment. Apparently, the argument should be reversed in the long run: it is not the lack of consumption power that keeps Mexican industry small, with high fixed average costs. It is the lack of industrial growth, and especially efficient public industrial growth, that is mainly responsible for insufficient employment, income, and consumption. This is the case when the government assumes a leading industrial role, as in Mexico. Its initiative becomes the basic driving force of the system.

Private investment (I-10), a more passive element in capital formation, responds favorably to the better rate of economic growth stimulated by the government. In the fast calculation, it grows at an average rate of 7.1 percent compared with 4.7 percent in the slow case. In real terms, exports (I-19) and imports (I-20) differ slightly in the two simulations. In current prices, however, they differ substantially, as can be seen in (II-19) and (II-20). The net result is a much larger deficit in current account in the fast simulation (II-18). This shows that at the present stage of industrialization, Mexico's growth is partially financed by deficits in current account, of which productive imports take the largest share. The public deficit (not included in tables) grows at a much faster pace in the expansionary simulation. In 1976, it grows to −31.88 billion, in comparison with −22.73 billion in the slow case. In both cases, however, a fiscal impasse seems to be reached—especially in the fast simulation, where external and internal public debt are already growing at their limits. This clearly points toward the need for a fiscal reform that will permit sustained growth (somewhere between our two alternatives), while minimizing the impact on consumption and private investment. More progressivity in the higher levels of the income-tax scales seems to be a reasonable way of solving the fiscal impasse of Mexican growth.

We close the comparison by pointing out some facts that seem to remain basically unaltered in both simulations, during 1972–1976. The traditional Mexican structural imbalances in income distribution, in government finance, and in regional development stay almost unaffected.

1. The relative shares of labor and capital remain nearly constant, with labor getting one-third and capital two-thirds of national income. A slight gain for labor, however, appears in the expansionary economy. (Not shown in tables.)

2. The ratios of total and federal taxes to gross domestic product also remain essentially unaffected, 11 percent and 8.2 percent respectively. The nonfederal tax ratio stays at 2.7 percent in both simulations.

3. The urban-rural gap will result in almost constant productive shares, with the urban sector accounting for 89 percent, and the rural for 11 percent, of GDPR in both projections. The basic source and the consequences of this regional productive imbalance can be found in the capital formation and demographic tables, respectively (not included in this condensation). The disproportion in urban-rural capital-labor ratios will remain unaffected. On the average, the urban worker will have at least 7.5–8 times more real capital to work with than his rural

counterpart in both cases.[15] The effects of the continuation of the productive gap will be to maintain a steady migratory flow to the urban centers (Mexico City, Guadalajara, Monterrey and towns bordering on the United States), with the consequent pressures on city facilities, enlargement of the "belts of poverty" around metropolitan areas, and growth of urban unemployment and underemployment.[16]

A Final Word

In closing, we would like to formulate briefly our stand on some important questions commonly asked with regard to econometric models as empirical tools for the analysis of growth in the LDC's.

Specification of developing-country models poses a challenge in building a new macro theory, but why go to the next step and create formal statistical models? Since we are in the economic-model business, we have thought often about this question and have formulated answers to the frequent charges that LDC data are poor in quality and sparsely available, and that economic behavior is erratic or irrational.

Economists are masters at working with poor and inadequate data. The issue for econometricians is to make as much systematic sense as possible out of sparse, "noisy" data. The basic statistical materials for the developing countries are, in many respects, like those we had to work with twenty or thirty years ago in the industrial countries. Our MDC models now stand on firmer footing as a result of all the spadework of the intervening years.

Economic and social problems are so intractable that we should do everything possible to make gains in knowledge, no matter how modest. It is for modest, systematic gains that we are working with macromodels of LDC's. The most sophisticated methods must be applied to eke out precious gains. Much of the sophistication concerns the attempt to obtain estimates of parameters that are consistent in the statistical sense of the term. This is extremely important because the most useful application of macromodels of the LDC economies is in simulations of long-term growth patterns. In such studies, biases (lack of consistency) build up over time and can throw decade growth results far off track.

Methods of dealing in modern econometrics with "undersized" samples have been developed, and it is with these methods in mind that we have tackled the empirical task of implementing this measurement of the econometric structure of Mexico. We hope that it can set a pattern for future econometric research in the rest of Latin America.

[15] The actual capital-labor ratios result in 15 to 16 times more capital per worker in the urban than in the rural sector for 1972–76. We have halved them in order to account for the lack of data on private rural capital.

[16] It should be remembered that even the fast calculation does not reduce the present unemployment and underemployment rates—whatever they are in 1971. The only thing it does is to keep them constant over the period.

DEVELOPMENT ALTERNATIVES UNDER CONDITIONS OF REDUCED EXTERNAL DEPENDENCY

ALEJANDRO FOXLEY

Center for National Planning Studies, Catholic University of Chile

1. INTRODUCTION

The purpose of this paper is to make a quantitative analysis of development alternatives faced by the Chilean Economy in the period 1970–1975, when objectives of full employment and reduced external dependency are considered as first-priority targets in the economic program.[1] The analysis will put special emphasis on the reformulation of the role that the foreign sector should play within that strategy. In particular, the implications of a strategy based on export promotion (as an alternative to the more traditional import-substitution policies) will be studied by using a multisectoral programming model. A description of the model used in the study is given in section 2.

In section 3, four growth alternatives for the Chilean Economy are presented: alternative (1) represents the historical growth pattern; alternative (2) is called "Full Employment through Internal Savings and Import Substitution"; alternative (3) is "Full Employment through External Aid"; and, alternative (4) is "Full Employment through Export Promotion and Reduction in the External Dependency in the Economy."

In section 4, the sectoral implications of alternative (4) are discussed, giving special emphasis to the relative priorities of different export-promotion, import-substitution, and investment programs in the economy. The results are compared with existing qualitative analysis.[2]

Section 5 deals with a determination of the "optimal" diversification in Chilean exports. The alternatives discussed here are the concentration of the export drive in the sector of highest productivity (copper) versus the alternative of diversifying the export structure, mainly by increasing nontraditional exports in the manufacturing sector. Under what conditions one is preferable to the other, and what are the main macroeconomic effects attached to each one, are two basic questions that we attempt to answer in this section.

2. THE MODEL

The quantification of the development strategies for the Chilean economy is done using a 15-sector optimizing model.[3] The model has 116 variables and 104

---

[1] The other objective of high priority is income redistribution. Because of methodological problems, it was introduced only in a "passive" way in our study. That is, we assume a redistributive tendency in favor of wage and salary earners similar to the one observed between 1960 and 1969, a period in which the participation of these groups in national income increased from 46.7 to 51.1 percent.

[2] See, for example, CORFO [Industrial Development Corporation], División de Planificación Industrial, *Bases de Discusión de una Estrategia de Desarrollo Industrial para la Década del 70*, Santiago, 1970.

[3] The basic model was developed jointly with Peter B. Clark, when we both worked in ODEPLAN (Oficina de Planificación Nacional de Chile), with the collaboration of Mario Gómez, Ricardo Infante, and Ana María Jul. The present application is solely the responsibility of the author, however. The computational aspects were carried out by Adriana Francos and Eugenio Mardones.

constraints. It is solved for one terminal year, 1975. It is basically a static model, although some dynamic characteristics are included in the investment function. The equations of the model are given in the Appendix.

The external sector is specified in the model by distinguishing between competitive and noncompetitive imports by origin and destination. There exists the possibility of choice in the way foreign exchange is allocated among competitive imports.

Exports are determined by the model within exogenously determined minimum and maximum bounds specified by sector. In one sector (copper), a price-elasticity of demand for copper in the world markets is introduced. A linearly approximated relationship between net foreign-exchange revenues from copper and the quantum of copper exports is deduced from the elasticity function. Given that copper exports constitute between 70 and 80 percent of total export revenues in Chile, a high proportion of exports is determined by considering not only supply but also demand factors.[4] Both the tariff structure that affects imports and subsidies for exports are explicitly taken into account, differentiated by sector.

Intermediate demand is calculated by means of a RAS-adjusted input-output matrix. Among the components of final demand, both sectoral consumption and investment are determined endogenously. Sectoral consumption is calculated by means of expenditure elasticities of demand. Investment is a function of capital-output ratios per sector, increases in sectoral production, investment lags per sector, and interplan and postterminal growth rates in capacity.

Employment is specified as a function of average labor productivities per sector and the levels of sectoral output. Three scarce resources are considered: capital, labor, and foreign exchange. These act as constraints on the maximization of consumption in the terminal year. The model is solved by means of the linear programming technique, using an IBM 360/50 computer.

The statistical information used to estimate the parameters in the model corresponds to the period 1960–1968, although exogenous projections are also included. Parametric variation is used whenever there is high uncertainty as to the future value of some key parameters, due to expected structural changes. The data is available in other documents.[5]

3. THE SOLUTION OF THE MODEL

The model is solved taking 1970 as the base year and 1975 as the terminal year. Four development patterns are examined with the model. In three of them, the objective of reduced external dependency is given high priority (alternatives (1), (2), and (4)). An additional objective of full employment is introduced in alternatives (2), (3), and (4). In what follows, we will briefly describe the results for these alternative patterns.

A. Alternative (1): Traditional Growth Pattern

This first alternative represents the introduction of a target of reduced external dependency within a framework of traditional behavior of the economy, as far as

---

[4] Most programming models consider only supply factors in the specification of exports, due to either methodological or data problems.

[5] See Alejandro Foxley, "Structural Disequilibria and Alternative Growth Patterns for the Chilean Economy, 1970–1980," Ph.D. dissertation, University of Wisconsin, 1970.

generation of internal savings and employment is concerned. There is no employment target here.

The maximum savings rate that the economy could generate under these conditions is the historical one (0.15), and the employment level is the one that the economy would spontaneously generate. The goal of decreasing external dependency is introduced by allowing a maximum net foreign indebtedness per year of 80 million dollars (298 million 1965 escudos).[6]

The results, appearing in the first column of Table 1, show an unsatisfactory growth rate in GDP (4.2 percent), a more than proportional expansion of consumption with respect to GDP (4.4 percent), a high unemployment rate (7.6 percent), and a net import desubstitution (the proportion of domestic production in total supply decreases by 1.4 percent).

TABLE 1
FOUR DEVELOPMENT STRATEGIES: MACROECONOMIC RESULTS, 1970–1975
[monetary values in millions of 1965 escudos]

	Alternative (1)[1] (1)	Alternative (2)[1] (2)	Alternative (3)[1] (3)	Alternative (4)[2] (4)
Balance of payments gap	298	290	1,187	298
Marginal savings rate	0.15	0.30	0.15	0.26
Gross domestic product	27,766	30,595	30,560	30,744
(annual growth rate)	0.042	0.061	0.061	0.061
Private consumption	19,992	21,176	22,366	21,551
(annual growth rate)	0.044	0.055	0.066	0.059
Gross domestic investment	4,492	6,137	5,699	5,911
(annual growth rate)	0.051	0.114	0.098	0.106
Imports	4,586	4,589	5,376	4,866
(annual growth rate)	0.064	0.064	0.096	0.076
Exports	4,935	4,935	4,935	5,212
(annual growth rate)	0.065	0.065	0.065	0.076
Internal savings	4,194	5,039	4,614	5,613
(average rate over GDP)	0.151	0.191	0.151	0.183
Unemployment rate	0.076	0.000	0.000	0.000
Supply balance $[X/(X + M)]$	0.858	0.876	0.847	0.857
Change in supply balance $[X/(X + M)]$	−0.014	0.03	−0.025	−0.012
Average investment rate over GDP	0.162	0.201	0.186	0.192
Net incremental capital-output ratio	2.122	2.084	1.900	1.945
Gross incremental capital-output ratio	3.875	3.293	3.075	3.106

[1] Exports specification fixed.
[2] Exports specification variable.

B. Alternative (2): Full Employment Through Internal Savings and Forced Import Substitution

From the results given above, it becomes clear that the reduction in external indebtedness is not a viable objective, as long as consumption tendencies in the economy are such that the marginal savings rate does not increase with respect to the historical pattern. Low internal savings and reduced external savings cannot but result in slow growth and high unemployment.

[6] Net indebtedness per year in the period 1960–1968 was 150 million dollars.

We will now explicitly introduce a full-employment target in the model. Exports are fixed exogenously, and there is no savings constraint. The model then increases consumption and GDP up to the point at which it reaches full employment, using whatever internal savings are required and the available (exogenously predetermined) external savings. Results are shown in column (2), Table 1. We can see that full employment and reduced external dependency are compatible only if the marginal savings rate increases to 0.30. If this rate were achievable, the economy could sustain a growth rate of 6.1 percent a year, which would allow the absorption of the unemployed by 1975.[7] This type of growth pattern is characterized by a rapid increase in investment (11.4 percent a year) and a moderate increase in consumption as compared to the expansion in GDP.

Another characteristic of the development process would be its reliance on import substitution as the basic mechanism for growth in the economy; 87.6 percent of total supply would be generated by internal production, whereas in alternative (1), this proportion reached only 85.8 percent.

There are two critical questions concerning this alternative. One refers to the efficiency of a forced import-substitution process (and, thus, the convenience of pursuing such a course); while the second refers to the feasibility of a marginal savings rate as high as implied here (0.30).

With respect to the import-substitution process, there is increasing evidence in the literature showing that there are a number of negative effects associated with the forced import-substitution policies pursued by most Latin American economies in the past.[8] They refer mainly to an increased degree of both economic and technological inefficiency associated with indiscriminate import substitution, as well as to consumption liberalization, which prevents the economy from achieving the higher savings rates required for accelerating growth.[9]

As far as the feasibility of maintaining marginal savings rates on the order of 0.30 is concerned, several studies show that for a great number of countries, such rates have not been obtained in the past.[10] The analysis of both aspects tends to cast some doubts on the feasibility and convenience of pursuing a development strategy like the one implied in alternative (2).

If the marginal savings rate cannot be increased to 0.30, the other alternatives open for the attainment of full employment would be: (a) to finance the growth rate required for full employment through external resources, which implies eliminating the reduction in external dependency as an objective in the economic program; (b) to accept this objective and to achieve full employment through a combination of internal effort (savings up to a "feasible" level) and foreign-exchange generation through export-promotion policies. These two constitute alternatives (3) and (4), which we now discuss.

[7] We are not considering the disguised unemployed here.

[8] See papers by A. Bianchi, M. C. Tavares, and O. Sunkel in A. Bianchi, ed., *Ensayos de Interpretación Económica* (Santiago de Chile: Editorial Universitaria, 1969). See also J. Power, "Import Substitution as an Industrialization Strategy," *Philippine Economic Journal*, Spring 1967; K. Griffin and J. Enos, *Planning Development* (Reading, Mass.: Addison-Wesley, 1970), Chapter 5; D. Felix, *Beyond Import Substitution, A Latin American Dilemma*, Harvard Economic Development Report No. 30, 1966.

[9] See J. Power, *op. cit.*

[10] See H. Chenery and A. Strout, "Foreign Assistance and Economic Development," *American Economic Review*, Sept. 1966.

C. *Alternative (3): Full Employment by Increasing External Dependency*

In this alternative, we assume a marginal savings rate not different from the historical one. Full employment would be achieved through a massive inflow of foreign aid.

The model's results (appearing in Table 1, column (3)) show that a net inflow of foreign resources equivalent to 300 million dollars per year would be required to reach full employment by 1975. This would imply almost doubling the total external debt accumulated up to 1970.

By looking at the model's results, it can be seen that this kind of strategy results in a fast growth in imports (at a rate of 9.6 percent a year). This facilitates consumption liberalization, which could achieve a growth rate of 6.6 percent per year. Let us recall that the growth in consumption for the same expansion in GDP under alternative (2) was only 5.5 percent a year, the residual being used to increase the savings rate up to 0.30.

Summing up, alternative (3) implies an acceleration in the process of increased external dependency in the Chilean economy, and a fast rate of expansion in consumption, which could presumably prevent the economy from increasing savings in the future.

D. *Alternative (4): Full Employment Through an Opening Up of the Economy and Internal Effort*

So far, we have specified the model with fixed exports. Export potential was determined by considering both historical trends and some new projects.[11] These figures were introduced exogenously into the model.

In this fourth alternative, we assume a flexibility in the structure of production such that exports could be expanded over the predetermined level given by ODEPLAN's estimates. This additional expansion would take place only if it represents the best alternative use for existing resources. Formally, this is measured in the model through the dual solution, where resources are allocated according to their scarcity values (shadow prices).

The practical way of measuring the optimal expansion in exports is by relaxing the assumption of fixed exports and allowing the model to choose the level of sectoral exports between predetermined minimum and maximum bounds (± 5 percent from the ODEPLAN estimates). Results are shown in column (4), Table 1. They indicate that it is possible to achieve full employment if the marginal savings rate is increased to 0.26, and if, at the same time, exports grow at 7.6 percent per year, instead of the 6.5 percent growth rate assumed in ODEPLAN's figures.

Given that, in this alternative, the model is free to choose both exports and competitive imports levels, the results indicate a preference (in the aggregate) for export expansion vis-à-vis import substitution, which is negative in the solution. On the other hand, the marginal savings rate is within what has been observed for other countries.[12] In the next section, we will analyze in detail the sectoral implications of the strategy implicit in alternative (4).

---

[11] Figures given by the External Sector Unit, ODEPLAN.
[12] See Chenery and Strout, *op. cit.*

TABLE 2
EXPORT SELECTION THROUGH PARAMETRIC VARIATION OF INTERNAL SAVINGS
$[F = 0$; subsidies for exports included in costs and price elasticity for copper]

MSR (1)	P_f (2)	P_{GDP} (3)	P_s (4)	$P_f + P_{GDP} - P_s$ (5)	$P_{Agriculture}$ (6)	P_{Copper} (7)
0	2.649	.0	1.533	1.116	↓2.048	↓1.358
.00124	2.585	.002	1.463	1.124	↓1.977	↓1.326
.03312	2.617	.048	1.461	1.204	↓1.978	↓1.343
.04762	2.441	.057	1.207	1.291	↓1.782	↓1.256
.05367	2.433	.064	1.187	1.310	↓1.768	↓1.252
.05673	2.390	.064	1.127	1.327	↓1.730	↕1.225
.09531	2.403	.105	1.099	1.409	↓1.729	↑1.221
.15423	2.599	.196	1.270	1.525	↓1.869	↑1.322
.16213	2.606	.205	1.267	1.546	↓1.862	↑1.325
.20572	2.725	.275	1.335	1.665	↓1.966	↑1.387
.21585	2.765	.295	1.367	1.693	↓1.996	↑1.408
.22771	2.790	.310	1.361	1.739	↓1.993	↑1.422
.25178	2.759	.309	1.225	1.843	↓1.882	↑1.414
.29158	2.008	.186	0.638	1.556	↓2.006	↑1.093
.29466	1.307	.026	0.087	1.246	↓1.995	↑0.781
.29538	1.205	.0	0.0	1.205	↓1.986	↑0.734

4. EXPORT PRIORITIES

The previous section has shown that the objectives of maximum growth, full employment, and reduced external dependency are only compatible if the Chilean economy is able to substantially increase savings in the next five years while, at the same time, undertaking a significant export effort. In this section, we shall consider the sectors in which the export efforts should be concentrated.

We shall examine this problem assuming a net flow of foreign financing equal to zero by 1975. Parametric variation of the marginal savings rate from 0.0 to full employment will allow us to determine export priorities. Thus, it is possible that whenever savings are very scarce, the marginal effort in terms of export expansion will take place: (a) in those sectors where there is idle capacity; (b) in sectors where the cost of generating an additional unit of foreign exchange is the lowest. As savings and the growth rate of the economy increase, some sectors utilize all existing capacity to meet internal demand and the expense of expanding production for exports is not worth undertaking. Alternatively, in other sectors, even with no idle capacity, the benefits associated with export expansion are higher than the costs of production and of using scarce resources, and consequently, exports should be increased to the maximum level. This kind of evaluation is done within the general equilibrium framework provided by our multisectoral optimizing model.

Export priorities according to the availability of savings can be deduced from the results shown in Table 2. These results are complemented by Tables 3, 4, and

TABLE 2 (concluded)

$P_{Other\ Mining}$ (8)	$P_{Food,\ Textiles}$ (9)	$P_{Wood,\ Paper}$ (10)	$P_{Nonmet.\ Min.}$ (11)	$P_{Basic\ Metals}$ (12)	$P_{Chemicals}$ (13)	$P_{Metallurgical}$ (14)
↑0.737	↓1.618	↓1.593	0.681	↑1.106	↕1.116	↑0.862
↑0.722	↓1.568	↓1.541	0.667	↑1.089	↓1.311	↑0.842
↑0.825	↓1.578	↓1.561	0.758	↑1.124	↓1.345	↑0.959
↑0.994	↓1.445	↓1.463	0.905	↑1.222	↕1.291	↑1.147
↑1.019	↓1.436	↓1.459	0.926	↑1.253	↑1.292	↑1.174
↑1.010	↓1.408	↓1.440	0.918	↑1.242	↑1.280	↑1.164
↑1.034	↓1.411	↓1.463	0.938	↑1.271	↑1.309	↑1.190
↑1.119	↕1.525	↓1.581	1.015	↑1.375	↑1.416	↑1.290
↑1.120	↑1.524	↓1.583	1.016	↑1.377	↑1.418	↑1.329
↑1.184	↑1.605	↕1.665	1.776	↑1.454	↑1.497	↑1.405
↑1.202	↑1.631	↑1.689	1.870	↑1.477	↑1.520	↑1.427
↑1.209	↑1.633	↑1.706	1.879	↕1.739	↑1.530	↑1.474
↑1.183	↑1.565	↑1.693	1.827	↓2.733	↑1.494	↑1.595
↑1.019	↕1.556	↑1.487	1.469	↓2.151	↑1.281	↑1.386
↑0.834	↓1.464	↕1.246	1.107	↓1.578	↑1.044	↑1.145
↑0.862	↓1.445	↓1.206	1.057	↓1.496	↑1.012	↑1.106

5, which show the optimal investment, imports, and import-substitution programs per sector.

The first column in Table 2 gives the marginal savings rate (MSR), which varies from 0.0 up to the point when full employment is reached. Points where the solution of the model is accompanied by a change in base are indicated in that column. The next three columns indicate the shadow prices of scarce resources (P_f = shadow price of foreign exchange; P_{GDP} = shadow price of GDP; P_s = shadow price of savings). Column (5) is obtained by adding columns (2) and (3) and subtracting column (4). It measures the net benefits associated with an increase of one unit in foreign-exchange availability, produced by the export expansion.

These benefits are composed of a direct factor, which is the increase in consumption (the objective function) produced by one additional unit of foreign exchange (P_p), and an indirect benefit through the expansion in GDP. Given that a higher GDP implies higher savings, and that this is a scarce resource, expanding exports allows an increase not only in the supply of foreign exchange but also in that of savings. This effect is measured through the shadow price of GDP (P_{GDP}).

From the point of view of costs, these include the social cost of production for each productive sector including all inputs but capital (P_i = shadow prices given in columns (6) to (14) in Table 2) and the opportunity cost of capital measured through the shadow price of savings (P_s).

The equation that relates costs and benefits is:

$$P_F + P_{GDP} \ge P_i + P_s, \quad \text{or}$$
$$P_F + P_{GDP} - P_s \ge P_i.$$

TABLE 3
SECTORAL INVESTMENT PROGRAMS
[cumulative 1970–1975 in millions of 1965 escudos]

MSR	Agriculture	Copper	Other Mining	Food, Textiles	Wood, Paper	Nonmetallic Minerals	Basic Metals	Chemicals	Metallurgical
.0	492	1,071	—	321	438	—	—	—	—
.001	497	1,072	—	322	439	—	—	—	—
.033	589	1,077	—	353	467	—	—	43	—
.047	635	1,088	—	367	479	—	—	66	—
.053	619	1,089	—	365	482	—	—	121	—
.056	629	1,089	—	368	485	—	—	141	—
.095	563	1,593	—	362	500	—	—	187	—
.154	779	1,594	—	428	565	—	—	569	—
.162	830	1,594	—	468	572	—	—	576	—
.205	1,031	1,596	—	531	637	—	—	772	225
.215	1,000	1,600	—	522	843	—	—	769	206
.227	1,065	1,601	—	543	864	25	—	825	280
.251	1,234	1,602	—	593	912	86	—	912	464
.291	1,488	1,614	—	672	995	191	213	1,069	767
.294	1,483	1,617	—	646	1,033	206	260	1,089	822
.295	1,510	1,616	—	655	947	214	279	1,099	849

TABLE 4
COMPETITIVE IMPORTS BY SECTOR
[millions of 1965 escudos]

MSR	Agriculture	Copper	Other Mining	Food, Textiles	Wood, Paper	Nonmetallic Minerals	Basic Metals	Chemicals	Metallurgical
.0	407 ↑	—	116 ↕	767 ↑	115 ↑	31 ↕	203 ↑	410 ↑	940 ↕
.001	407 ↑	—	117 ↕	766 ↑	115 ↑	31 ↕	203 ↑	410 ↑	939 ↕
.033	403 ↑	—	125 ↕	759 ↑	114 ↑	37 ↕	201 ↑	406 ↑	887 ↕
.047	400 ↑	—	134 ↕	754 ↑	113 ↑	40 ↕	144 ↕	404 ↑	908 ↕
.054	405 ↑	—	137 ↕	764 ↑	114 ↑	41 ↕	144 ↕	409 ↑	917 ↕
.057	405 ↑	—	139 ↕	763 ↑	114 ↑	42 ↕	144 ↕	396 ↕	922 ↕
.095	429 ↑	—	147 ↕	808 ↑	121 ↑	47 ↕	153 ↕	398 ↕	996 ↕
.154	415 ↑	—	179 ↕	783 ↑	117 ↑	63 ↕	161 ↕	176 ↕	1,109 ↑
.162	422 ↑	—	181 ↕	795 ↑	119 ↑	65 ↕	162 ↕	179 ↕	1,126 ↑
.206	411 ↑	—	203 ↕	774 ↑	116 ↑	82 ↑	196 ↕	92 ↕	1,097 ↑
.216	428 ↑	—	205 ↕	806 ↑	121 ↑	85 ↑	201 ↕	105 ↕	1,141 ↑
.228	424 ↑	—	212 ↕	799 ↑	120 ↑	85 ↑	212 ↑	82 ↕	1,131 ↑
.252	411 ↑	—	227 ↕	775 ↑	116 ↑	82 ↑	205 ↑	58 ↕	1,098 ↑
.292	396 ↑	—	259 ↕	746 ↑	112 ↑	79 ↑	198 ↑	16 ↕	1,056 ↑
.294	387 ↑	—	263 ↕	729 ↑	109 ↑	77 ↑	193 ↑	5 ↕	1,032 ↑
.295	381 ↑	—	264 ↕	717 ↑	107 ↑	76 ↑	190 ↑	—	1,016 ↑

NOTE: The arrows indicate whether imports are at the upper (↑) or lower (↓) bound; or at intermediate levels (↕).

TABLE 5
IMPORT SUBSTITUTION, DOMESTIC SHARE IN TOTAL SUPPLY

MSR	Agriculture	Copper	Other Mining	Food, Textiles	Wood, Paper	Nonmetallic Minerals	Basic Metals	Chemicals	Metallurgical
0	.834	1.0	.811	.874	.854	.874	.591	.628	.474
.001	.834	1.0	.811	.874	.854	.874	.592	.628	.475
.033	.836	1.0	.800	.876	.855	.856	.608	.635	.501
.047	.837	1.0	.788	.877	.856	.848	.699	.638	.496
.054	.836	1.0	.784	.876	.855	.845	.697	.643	.493
.057	.836	1.0	.782	.876	.855	.844	.697	.650	.492
.095	.829	1.0	.774	.870	.850	.830	.685	.654	.474
.154	.835	1.0	.740	.875	.853	.793	.670	.763	.451
.162	.834	1.0	.738	.874	.852	.787	.669	.761	.447
.206	.838	1.0	.717	.879	.855	.751	.634	.802	.470
.216	.834	1.0	.715	.874	.862	.744	.630	.797	.460
.228	.836	1.0	.708	.875	.863	.750	.620	.807	.467
.252	.841	1.0	.695	.880	.865	.764	.623	.818	.485
.292	.847	1.0	.667	.887	.868	.784	.652	.836	.508
.294	.849	1.0	.664	.887	.870	.789	.661	.840	.515
.295	.850	1.0	.662	.889	.869	.793	.665	.843	.519

Exports are profitable if benefits are equal to, or higher than, costs.[13] By comparing column (5) in Table 2 with columns (6) to (14), one can learn in which sector there is a net benefit over costs associated with export expansion. In the sector where the net benefit is positive, the model chooses to expand the export activity to the maximum level. This is indicated in Table 2 by means of an upward-oriented arrow. The reverse occurs if costs are higher than benefits. When the arrow points in both directions, it denotes that costs equal benefits at the margin, so that export activity is at an intermediate level between the upper and lower bounds. Priorities for export selection are determined by examining Tables 2, 3, 4, and 5 jointly.

The behavior of the main sectors is as follows:

1. Noncopper mining exports always have a high priority (they are at the maximum level irrespective of the availability of savings). This is due to the existence of unutilized capacity in the sector. The latter fact is verified by observing in Table 3 that net investment is always zero in this sector. Exports constitute an adequate mechanism to dispose of excess production. (This sector includes mainly nitrates, coal, and iron ore.)

2. Basic metals also show the existence of an exportable surplus up to a marginal savings rate of 0.22. At this level, the growth of the economy is such that production with existing capacity is totally used to supply the expanding internal demand. At this point, exports go to the lower bound and it is more efficient to expand imports to the maximum level (see Table 4) as a cheaper way of meeting internal demand. When the MSR goes up to 0.29, the relative abundance of savings makes new additions to capacity in the sector profitable (as can be seen in Table 3).

3. In the metallurgical sector, there seems to be enough productive capacity available to permit meeting internal demand, while at the same time expanding exports to the maximum. This occurs whenever the savings rate is not significantly higher than the historical rate (0.15). When MSR reaches 0.20, the higher growth in the economy generates additional internal demand that could be supplied either by reducing exports or by investing to increase the productive capacity in the sector (notice that imports are already at the maximum, see Table 4). The model shows that export activity is profitable enough to make the cost of new investment worthwhile, instead of reducing the supply of foreign exchange by decreasing exports. The cost-benefit calculation for export activity is shown in detail in Table 2.

4. Export activity in the copper sector is always profitable. We can observe in Table 3 that even when savings are very scarce ($MSR = 0.0$), big investments in the copper sector are indicated in the model's solution (see Table 3, the column for copper under $MSR = 0.0$). This investment should be undertaken in order to increase exports to the maximum. However, due to limits in productive capacity, the maximum bound for exports can only be reached when MSR is higher than

---

[13] It should be noticed that the specific form of the cost-benefit equation depends on the substitutions done in the model (that is to say on the form of the tableau in the LP problem). It is possible that by means of additional substitutions in the system of equations, one would get a simpler expression where all benefits (direct and indirect) were measured through only one shadow price (the foreign-exchange shadow price). The same could be done with the cost equations.

0.053. Given that this is way below the historical MSR (0.15), it is clear that exports should be expanded to the maximum in the range for MSR that is relevant.

5. The chemical industry sector is another where programs of export expansion seem efficient, regardless of the value for MSR (see Tables 2 and 3).

6. In the agricultural sector, exports stay at the minimum level and imports at the maximum (see Tables 2 and 4). This behavior is explained by insufficient productive capacity even to satisfy internal demand. The model's results suggest the convenience of high investments in the sector in order to reduce the deficit with respect to internal demand. At any rate, the remaining deficit is met by importing food products.[14]

7. As far as the traditional consumption industries (food, textiles, leather products, and so on) are concerned, new additions to capacity are very significant, as can be seen in Table 3. However, as long as the MSR is below 0.154, the new investment is good enough to meet internal demand, but not to expand exports (see Tables 2 and 4). When savings increase over $MSR = 0.154$, it is possible to undertake additional investment so as both to satisfy internal demand and to push exports to the upper boundary.

When the economy approaches full employment ($MSR = 0.25$), exports in this sector go to the lower bound (see Table 2). This is due to the fact that this is a relatively labor-intensive activity. When labor becomes a scarce resource, it is more convenient to expand capital-intensive activities, like the metallurgical sector. If we look at Table 3, we can see that for high MSR, investment in the metallurgical sector goes up very rapidly. At the same time, exports in the food and textiles sector go to the lower bound. Thus, when full employment is reached, there is a reallocation of resources away from labor-intensive sectors and into capital-intensive activities.

Sectoral Priorities: Exports, Investment, Import Substitution

The preceding analysis makes possible some general conclusions as to the sectoral priorities of export, import-substitution, and investment activities. These are summarized in Table 6. By looking at this table, it can be concluded that:

1. There are sectors where investment programs have a low priority, since idle capacity exists in them. Exports are a good way of disposing of excess supply. These are noncopper mining and basic metals. The metallurgical sector shows the same behavior up to $MSR = 0.20$, where new investment for exports becomes profitable.

2. There are sectors where new additions to capacity have the highest priority. They are agriculture, food and textiles, wood and paper products, and copper. Even when savings are very scarce, investment seems to be desirable in these sectors, although for different reasons, according to each particular case: in the

---

[14] This result might be surprising, particularly with respect to exports. Two comments might be relevant: (a) this sector does not include food products with some degree of processing, since they appear in sector 4 (Food, Textiles); these are the products that should generate more foreign exchange per unit of resources utilized; (b) the high degree of aggregation hides the fact that within the agricultural sector some exports should be expanded to the maximum level; in others, it might be more efficient not to expand. In this sense, our analysis is not particularly useful when it deals with all the agricultural sector as one aggregate.

TABLE 6
SECTORAL PRIORITIES

Investment	Exports	Import Substitution
Agriculture, copper, food and textiles, wood and paper	Copper	Chemicals
Chemicals	Chemicals	Metallurgical
Metallurgical	Food and textiles	Basic metals
Nonmetallic minerals	Wood and paper, metallurgical	
Basic metals	Basic metals, other mining [1]	
Other mining	Agriculture	

[1] Maximum exports due to excess capacity.

agricultural sector, in order to meet internal demand; in food and textiles, and wood and paper, for the same reason but also to increase exports. Investment in the copper sector, on the other hand, seems profitable whatever the availability of savings.[15]

3. In the chemical and metallurgical sectors, both export-promotion and import substitution programs seem to be justified, with a higher priority for the chemical industry, since it does not start with excess capacity, as is the case with the metallurgical industry.

4. New net investment and import substitution seems justified in basic metals only when the economy approaches full employment.

The preceding results are, in general, coincident with qualitative studies done by the Industrial Development Corporation (CORFO) in Chile.[16]

5. CONCENTRATING OR DIVERSIFYING EXPORTS

By looking at the results of the previous section and comparing the resultant composition of exports in the final year with the composition in the initial year, it can be seen (in Table 7) that export diversification tends to increase.

We have come to this result, however, by putting an upper boundary on export expansion, including copper. We cannot, then, conclude from the previous results that a strategy of export diversification is in any sense "better" than one in which the export effort is concentrated mainly in copper. From the theoretical point of view, there are good arguments in favor and against one or the other strategy.[17]

The case for copper could be made along the following lines: it is a high-productivity sector, facing favorable conditions in the world markets; it could, thus, generate a surplus big enough to be used to finance export diversification in a second stage.

[15] We have introduced a fixed price for copper in the world markets, 55 cents per pound. If the price is lower, the conclusions might be different, as will be shown in the next section.

[16] See CORFO, op. cit.

[17] See A. M. Jul, Diversificación de Exportaciones, el Caso Chileno, Memoria de Prueba, Escuela de Economía, U. de Chile, 1969; Daniel Schydlowsky, Latin American Trade Policies in the 1970's: A Perspective Appraisal, Harvard Economic Development Report No. 150, 1970; O. Sunkel, op. cit.

TABLE 7
EXPORT STRUCTURE
[monetary values in millions of 1965 escudos]

	1970		1975	
	Level	Percent	Level	Percent
Agriculture	116	3.3	128	2.6
Copper	2,211	62.2	3,102	61.0
Other mining	402	11.3	444	8.7
Food and textiles	159	4.5	224	4.5
Wood, paper	127	3.6	386	7.6
Nonmetallic minerals	6	0.2	2	–
Basic metals	50	1.4	80	1.6
Chemicals	31	0.9	116	2.3
Metallurgical	59	1.7	120	2.4
Construction	0	–	0	–
Energy	2	–	2	–
Housing	7	0.2	9	0.2
Transportation	172	4.8	172	3.4
Education and health	2	–	2	–
Commerce, service, etc.	208	5.9	266	5.3
Total	3,552	100	5,053	100

Arguments against export concentration relate to the degree of vulnerability in the economy when it relies basically on one product to supply its need for foreign exchange. This vulnerability is due to price fluctuations in the world markets (short run) and to the limit imposed on the investment rate (long run). This limit appears when the domestic economy does not have a significant capital-goods sector and must rely on imports to increase the investment rate in the economy. If the strategic export sector (in this case copper) is not able to grow fast enough, this puts a limit on the rate of expansion in the supply of foreign exchange and consequently on the investment rate.[18]

Export diversification usually implies increasing exports of manufactures. These are justified, from the social cost-benefit analysis: (a) if there is idle capacity or unemployed labor: here the social cost of exporting would be zero;[19] (b) if economies of scale, knowledge of markets, and technology can be developed fairly rapidly so that a competitive position can be gained in the world markets.

From what has been said in the previous paragraph, it is quite clear that export diversification is a process which is not to be pushed as far as possible, irrespective of the importance of the variables mentioned above.

Under what conditions would it be better for Chile to concentrate the export effort on expansions in copper production? Alternatively, what factors would make a diversification strategy more favorable?

Let us again use the multisectoral model to attempt an answer to some of these questions. We will eliminate now the exogenous limit on copper exports

[18] See O. Sunkel, op. cit.
[19] The Argentine case is one where export of manufactures seem to be closely related to the degree of capacity utilization in the industrial sector. See David Félix, Subsidies, Recession and Non-traditional Industrial Exporting in Argentina, Harvard Economic Development Report No. 107, 1968.

and will allow the model to choose the optimal equilibrium point for copper exports. This equilibrium point depends on: (a) the world market price for copper before Chile's expansion in copper exports; (b) the amount by which that price is affected by the decision of Chilean producers (this is measured through the introduction of a price elasticity of demand for copper in the world markets and a linearly approximated function that relates net foreign-exchange revenues from copper to quantities of copper exported); (c) the opportunity cost of resources in terms of alternative uses in other sectors.

The optimal expansion point for copper determines not only the quantity to be exported, but also the equilibrium price in the world market after the Chilean expansion.[20] It also implies a structure of sectoral exports compatible with the copper expansion, and "optimal" from the point of view of efficiency in the use of scarce resources in the economy (capital, labor, foreign exchange).

Five experiments were undertaken to determine export diversification, given five different initial prices for copper in the world market.[21] Presumably, if the initial price is very high, a greater degree of concentration on exports would be justified. The reverse should occur when the price goes down.

The experiments maintain the objective of reduced external dependency. We assume that net external savings are zero in 1975. The assumption is made also that the marginal savings rate is 0.15 (historical).

Results for copper prices going from 65 cents per pound to 45 cents are summarized in Table 8. There we show the optimal export structure for each initial price, and also the equilibrium price after expansion.[22]

For initial prices equal to 65 and 60 cents, profitable expansions in copper would be of the order of 33 percent and 27 percent respectively, with respect to the "normal" levels for 1975 if the expansion does not occur.

The export composition corresponding to the initial prices of 65 and 60 cents is such that the only sectors other than copper whose exports would be at the maximum level would be noncopper mining, basic metals, and the metallurgical industry. These are precisely the sectors characterized by the existence of idle capacity, as we have seen in the previous section of this paper. In other words, for copper prices over 60 cents, the optimal degree of diversification in exports would be that which allows for maximum utilization of existing capacity, but in which new investment effort for exports is concentrated basically in one sector, that is, copper. A "concentrated structure" for exports seems to be the best under these conditions.

If the initial price is 55 cents, the profitable copper expansion would be in the order of 20 percent, which would be accompanied by a higher degree of export diversification. Under these conditions, it would be profitable to start new investment projects for exports in the chemical sector. Exports would be at the maximum level, according to the model's results, in this sector.

[20] A detailed description of the methodology may be found in Alejandro Foxley and P. B. Clark, "Rentabilidad Social de Nuevas Expansiones en el Cobre Chileno," *Estudios de Planificación*, CEPLAN [Center of Studies on National Planning], Santiago, 1972.

[21] This initial price reflects the medium-term equilibrium price if there are no additional expansions on the part of Chile or the other producers, except that which maintains their share of the market.

[22] Under the assumption that other producers do not retaliate when Chile expands—that is, that they expand only at the rate given by the increase in demand. See Foxley and Clark, *op. cit.*

TABLE 8
EXPORT STRUCTURE FOR DIFFERENT COPPER PRICES, 1970–1975
[millions of 1965 escudos; $F = 0$; $MSR = 0.15$]

Sector	65¢ (52¢[1])		60¢ (49¢[1])		55¢ (46¢[1])		50¢ (46.5¢[1])		45¢ (42¢[1])	
	LIM. E.	Exports	LIM. E.	Exports	LIM. E.	Exports	LIM. E.	Exports	LIM. E.	Exports
Agriculture	MIN	128	MIN	128	MIN	128	MIN	128	MIN	128
Copper	MIN-MAX	3,980	MIN-MAX	3,803	MIN-MAX	3,641	MIN	2,821	MIN	2,821
Other mining	MAX	444	MAX	444	MAX	444	MAX	444	MAX	444
Food, textiles	MIN	160	MIN	160	MIN	160	MAX	224	MAX	224
Wood, paper	MIN	227	MIN	227	MIN	227	MIN	227	MIN	227
Nonmetallic minerals		2		2		2		2		2
Basic metals	MAX	124	MAX	124	MAX	124	MAX	124	MAX	124
Chemicals	MIN	63	MIN	63	MAX	116	MAX	116	MAX	116
Metallurgical	MAX	120	MAX	120	MAX	120	MAX	120	MAX	120

NOTE: LIM. E. indicates whether exports are at the maximum (MAX), minimum (MIN), or intermediate level (MIN-MAX).
[1] Equilibrium price after expansion.

Finally, for prices below 55 cents, a strategy of further diversification would be preferred, as can be seen in Table 8, under the columns corresponding to 50 cents and 45 cents for the price of copper.

There are other effects connected with the process of concentrating exports in one sector that are worth mentioning. They refer to the structure of production and the level of employment obtained.

In Table 9, we give macroeconomic results for two runs of the model where the same growth rate in GDP is obtained: in one case, by diversifying exports; in the other, by concentrating them in the copper sector. When the diversified scheme is pursued, a greater balance between the GDP and consumption growth is achieved (4.2 percent and 4.4 percent respectively). Also, sectoral production seems to be more balanced, and perhaps the most important effect, a lower level of unemployment is reached. This last result would indicate that, given the existence of unemployed labor in the economy and the full-employment objective, a policy of export diversification could very well be justified even for high copper prices if one considers the employment effects attached to it.

TABLE 9
CONCENTRATION VERSUS DIVERSIFICATION IN EXPORTS, 1970–1975

	Diversification	Concentration
MSR	0.15	0.15
F	298	0
Copper price (cents)	42	60
GDP growth rate	0.042	0.043
Sectoral growth rates:		
Agriculture	0.029	0.007
Copper	0.059	0.107
Food, textiles	0.034	0.020
Basic metals	0.025	0.0
Metallurgical	0.029	0.0
Import growth rates	0.064	0.116
Consumption growth rates	0.044	0.054
Unemployment rate	0.076	0.092

APPENDIX

Equations of the Multisector Linear Programming Model

(1.0)
$$X_i + d_i \cdot \tilde{M}_i + d_i \hat{M}_i \geq \sum_j a_{ij} \cdot X_j + C_i + G_i + I_i + S_i + E_i + \sum_j d_{15,j}^M \cdot M_j$$

(2.0)
$$C_i = -\bar{c}_i + y_i C$$

(2.1)
$$\sum_i C_i + \bar{c}_d + y_d C = C$$

(3.0)
$$G_i = g_i \cdot \bar{G}$$

(4.0)
$$I_i = N_i + R_i$$

(4.1)
$$N_j \geq b_j [X_j \cdot (1 + P_j)^{\theta_j} - \bar{X}_j(0) \cdot (1 + i_j)^{\theta_j}]$$

(4.2)
$$N_i = \sum_j K_j^i \cdot b_{ij} \cdot N_j$$

(4.3)
$$K_j^i = P_j (1 + P_j)^{\theta_j - 1} / (1 + P_j)^{\theta_j} - (1 + i_j)^{\theta_j - t}$$

(4.4) $$R_j = r_j \cdot X_j$$

(4.5) $$R_i = \sum_j b_{ij} \cdot R_j$$

(4.6) $$\Delta S_i = K_i^s \left[\sum_j (s_j + s_j^T) \Delta X_j + s_j^T \Delta M_j \right]$$

(5.0) $$\tilde{M}_i = \sum_j \tilde{m}_{ij}^A \cdot x_j + \tilde{m}_i^C \cdot C_i + \tilde{m}_i^B \cdot I_i + \tilde{m}_i^G \cdot \bar{G}$$

(5.1) $$V = F + \sum f_j E_j - \bar{Y}E - \sum_j \tilde{M}_j - \sum_j \bar{e}_j$$

(5.2) $$\hat{M}_i \le \hat{m}_i \cdot V$$

(5.3) $$M_i = \tilde{M}_i + \hat{M}_i$$

(6.0) $$E_{iMIN} \le \dot{E}_i - E_{iMAX}$$

(6.1) $$Y_{N2} = e_2 + f_2 E_2$$

(7.0) $$\sum_j M_j - F - \sum_j f_j E_j \le -\bar{Y}E + ET - \sum_j \bar{e}_j$$

(7.1) $$F \le \bar{F}$$

(8.0) $$A^N = \sum_j K_j^I \cdot N_j + \sum_j R_j + \sum_j k_j^s (s_j + s_j^T) \Delta X_j + \sum_j k_j^s \cdot s_j^T \cdot \Delta M_j - F + \bar{ET}$$

(8.1) $$A^N - t^N \cdot Y \le A^{-N}(0) - t^N \cdot \bar{Y}(0)$$

(9.0) $$L_j = l_j \cdot X_j$$

(9.1) $$\sum_j L_j \ge (1 - u)\bar{L}$$

(10.0) $$Y = C + \bar{G} + \sum_j K_j^I \cdot N_j + \sum_j R_j + \sum_j K_j^s (s_j + s_j^T) \Delta X_j + \sum_j K_j^s s_j^T \Delta M_j - \sum_j M_j$$
$$+ \sum_j f_j E_j + \bar{ET} + \sum_j \bar{e}_j$$

(0.0) $$Max : C$$

Variables and Parameters of the Model

a_{ij} Input-output coefficients for domestic plus imported intermediate goods

b_j Average capital-output coefficient in sector j; b_{ij} = distribution matrix

$\bar{c}_i$ The constant term of the consumption function for expenditure on good i

$\bar{c}_d$ Constant term for the nonworker's expenditure for domestic servants

d_i Coefficient of distribution (one plus the tariff plus the commercialization cost) of imports of type i

$d_{15.j}^M$ Aggregate commercialization coefficient for all imports estimated as a fixed proportion of the total CIF value of imports

$\bar{e}_i$ Constant term of the linear function approximating the price-elastic foreign-exchange revenue function for exports of sector i

f_2, f_1 Marginal coefficient of the foreign-exchange revenue function, used especially to reflect the effect of a change in the price of copper ($i = 2$) and other goods (i) exported to new markets (e.g., f_p is used for the cellulose project)

g_i Fixed proportion government expenditure for goods from sector i (where government expenditures for factor payments—value added—is denoted by $g_g \cdot v_g$)

i_j Vector of intraplan rates of growth of production (i.e., in the first years)

K_j^I Stock-flow conversion factor, as defined by equation (4.3)

K_i^s Stock-flow conversion coefficient for the inventory level of national goods in sector i

l_j Inverse of the productivity of labor employed in sector j

$\hat{m}_i$ Distribution coefficient of foreign exchange, among different sectors of origin for competitive imports measured in CIF

$$\sum_i m_i = 1.0$$

(This allows a certain amount of positive substitution of imports in some sectors, negative in others)

$\tilde{m}_{ij}^A$ Technical coefficient of noncompetitive intermediate imports, measured on CIF prices

$\tilde{m}_i^B, \tilde{m}_i^C,$ Coefficient for noncompetitive imports of capital goods, consumption goods, and government

$\tilde{m}_i^G$ expenditure for goods from sector i, measured in CIF prices

θ_j Average gestation period (lag) for capital information by sector j

P_j Vector of postterminal rates of growth of production in sector j

q_i Expenditure elasticity per capita (or per family) for goods from sector i

r_j Replacement coefficient estimated as a proportion of the gross value of production in each sector j

r_j' Reciprocal of the average useful life of the stock of capital in sector j

s_i Stock to output coefficient of goods in process or finished products from sector i

s_i^I Stock to output coefficient of transactions stock held by retailers and wholesalers

t Number of years in the plan

t^N Maximum marginal-savings rate for aggregate national savings

u Maximum unemployment rate

y_d Marginal propensity to consume domestic services

$$y_i = q_i \frac{\bar{C}_i^0}{\bar{C}^0}$$

A^N Gross national savings

C_i Private consumption of goods from sector i

C Total consumption expenditure in the terminal year

E_i Total exports of goods from sector i constrained between the minimum and maximum values

F Foreign capital inflow, equal to the deficit on current account of the balance of payments at constant prices

G_i Total government consumption expenditure for goods from sector i. Payments to factors (wages, salaries, rent, and interest payments) are included in a special sector as G_v

I_i Gross investment demand for capital goods of sector i

L_j Employment in sector j

M_i Total imports, at CIF prices, of goods from sector i

$\tilde{M}_i$ Noncompetitive imports of goods from sector i, at CIF prices $(i = j)$

$\hat{M}_i$ Competitive imports at CIF prices

N_j Net investment by destination accumulated during the planning period (5 years)

R_j Replacement investment destined for sector j

ΔS_i Change of stocks of national origin for goods of sector i

V Balance of foreign exchange remaining after financing the noncompetitive imports, at CIF value

X_i Gross value of production in sector i

ΔX_i Change in the gross value of production in sector i during the period of the plan

Y Gross domestic product in the terminal year in variable prices, i.e., including the effect of variable prices in the foreign sector

$\bar{A}^N(0)$ Gross national (internal) savings in the initial year

$\bar{C}^0$ Total consumption expenditure in the initial year

$\bar{C}_i^0$ Consumption of goods from sector i in the initial year

$\bar{F}$ Maximum external financing at constant prices (exogenously determined)

$\bar{G}$ Total government spending in the terminal year

    $\bar{G} = g_i G_i$ (i = number of sectors plus payment to factors used by the government)

$\bar{L}$ Available labor force in terminal year

$\bar{P}$ Population in the terminal year

$\bar{P}^0$ Population in the initial year

$\bar{X}_j(0)$ Value of production in the base year of sector j

$\bar{Y}^0(0)$ Gross domestic product in the initial year

$\bar{Y}E$ Net remittances (interest, profits) paid abroad

ECONOMIC ALTERNATIVES FOR MEXICO:
A QUANTITATIVE ANALYSIS*

ALAN S. MANNE†

Stanford University

1. INTRODUCTION

This work is intended as a step toward multilevel planning—identifying the information flows necessary for consistency between project, sectoral, and macroeconomic decisions. (Parallel process-analysis models of Mexico's agricultural and energy sectors have been constructed.) To build a macroeconomic model that will yield shadow prices relevant to specific project decisions, it appears essential to allow for labor inputs. Otherwise, it is implied that the marginal productivity of labor is zero. With a constant-returns technology, this, in turn, implies that the marginal productivity of capital will coincide with the economy-wide average output-capital ratio. As noted by Harberger (1967, p. 142), a zero shadow price for labor (hence a high shadow price for capital) is "virtually a kiss of death for projects with long gestation periods or long economic lives."

For a macroeconomic model to generate meaningful criteria for project decisions, it is not sufficient that "labor" have a positive shadow price. Since the skill-mix differs substantially among alternative investment projects, and since wage differentials between skill groups appear quite wide in Mexico, it is essential to separate labor by skill categories. Skill disaggregation is easier said than done.

In our initial experiments, we adopted a manpower requirements formulation —hoping to avoid the data difficulties inherent in a human-capital-formation approach. The manpower availability in each skill category was projected exogenously—as though the supply of labor skills were completely inelastic. Employing this formulation, plus an activity-analysis technology that turned out to be virtually as rigid as a Leontief system, we ran into major difficulties with respect to the shadow price of labor. The efficiency price differentials between skills were either zero—or with a minor perturbation in labor availability, these differentials became unbelievably large.[1] Under the influence of Marshall's dictum ("*natura non facit saltum*"), we have therefore searched for additional elements of substitution and

* A revised version of this paper will form a chapter in a forthcoming book titled *Multi-Level Planning: Case Studies in Mexico*, North-Holland Publishing Co. Data-gathering and computations were supported by the Development Research Center of the International Bank for Reconstruction and Development. The results were written during a year in which the author held a Ford Foundation fellowship at the Center for Advanced Study in the Behavioral Sciences.

† The author is indebted to Leopoldo Solís for having provided access to the resources of the Departamento de Estudios Económicos, Banco de México. Helpful comments on successive drafts were received from: Bela Balassa, Gerardo Bueno, Yves Franchet, Louis Goreux, Donald Keesing, Janos Kornai, Mordecai Kurz, Saúl Trejo R., and Thomas Vietorisz. The drafts were typed carefully and cheerfully by Maureen Seymour. All computational aspects—including programs for matrix generation—were handled by Richard Inman with the assistance of Enrique Novelo Berrón. The specific facts, methods of analysis, and conclusions are the sole responsibility of the author.

[1] Much the same experience is reported in Bruno (1966, pp. 343–45). Apparently, in both these numerical models, there was insufficient indirect substitution via international trade to avoid knifeedge behavior of the shadow price with respect to the exogenously specified availability of labor skills.

have turned away from regarding labor skills as a demographically given primary factor of production. Much like Correa and Tinbergen (1962); Spiegelman, Baum, and Talbert (1965); Adelman (1966); and Bowles (1967); the current version of DINAMICO includes endogenous time-phased activities for upgrading unskilled into skilled manpower. Also included are activities for capital-labor substitution in agriculture and for short-run substitution between skills. Our calculations suggest that Mexico is approaching the end of the labor-surplus phase of her development, and that capital-labor substitution could become increasingly important.

With the exception of labor, the dynamic multisector linear programming model (for short, DINAMICO) follows along familiar lines. Among the standard ingredients are: a 15-sector current-account interindustry matrix, capital coefficients linking investment demands to capacity expansion in each of six future time periods, and alternative activities for trade-balance improvement.[2] In part, foreign exchange is viewed as an exogenously given primary resource—and in part, as an item for which there exist substitution possibilities. In addition to foreign-exchange earnings through traditional exports and tourism, the model allows for the possibility of exporting manufactures from high-cost "infant" industries. It is supposed that foreign exchange is also available through capital inflows—one portion on concessional terms and another portion through direct private foreign investment.

Altogether, the programming matrix contains some 300 constraint rows, 400 activity columns, and 4,000 nonzero coefficients. At this size, numerical optimization did not prove to be a bottleneck. The model evolved during a two-year period of experimentation. With a continuing series of improvements in the basic data, there were six successive versions of the "basic case." Eventually, a special-purpose program was written to generate the matrix and to facilitate data revisions.

2. ALTERNATIVES TO THE BASIC CASE

For ease in future reference, we define the "basic case" to be the one described in memoranda 71-9, 71-12, and 71-13.[3] Table 1 contains a list of the eight alternatives to be evaluated here. These eight cases refer to alternative formulations of DINAMICO's constraints on the primary factors of production: foreign exchange and labor. Also considered are alternatives to the maximand adopted for the basic case: aggregate consumption, subject to a "gradualist" constraint on the time path and a target annual growth rate $g = 7$ percent. The eight alternatives are examined one at a time—neglecting interactions between them.

The individual alternatives stem not only from different value judgements as to what is desirable, but also from different practical judgements as to what is

[2] It is assumed that the reader is already familiar with standard references on dynamic numerical planning models, e.g., Adelman (1966); Chenery and MacEwan (1966); Bruno (1967); Eckaus and Parikh (1968); Bruno, Dougherty, and Fraenkel (1970); and Murakami, Tokoyama, and Tsukui (1970).

[3] These reports are available upon request to the Development Research Center, International Bank for Reconstruction and Development, 1818 H Street, N.W., Washington, D.C. 20433. Eventually, they will appear as chapters in *Multi-Level Planning: Case Studies in Mexico*.

TABLE 1
ALTERNATIVES TO THE BASIC CASE

Assumptions Underlying the Basic Case	Alternative Assumptions	Identification Number of Alternative Case
Maximand: aggregate consumption, subject to gradualist restriction and annual growth target $g = 7\%$	Maximand: same except growth target $g = 6\%$	1
	Maximand: same except growth target $g = 8\%$	2
	Maximand: discounted consumption	3
	Maximand: terminal consumption	4
Initial differential of 30% between domestic costs and foreign-exchange earnings from high-cost manufactured exports	Initial export cost differential = 50%	5
Direct private capital inflows (FDP) restricted to an average of 5.0 and a maximum of 5.5 billion pesos in any one year	Same average rate, but—except for the initial and terminal years—no limit on inflows (FDP) in any one year	6
Includes constraints on the supply and demand for labor skills	Labor constraints eliminated	7
Allows for capital-labor substitution in agriculture through activities KA^t	Doubled marginal productivity of labor in agriculture, thereby doubling cost of activities KA^t	8

politically or technically feasible—e.g., one policymaker will say that the basic case is altogether too pessimistic in projecting the subsidy required for promoting manufactured exports; another will say that we have been too optimistic on this score. Case 5 permits us to check for the indirect implications of these alternative views. Similarly, through case 6, we may examine another aspect of the foreign-exchange constraints—the year-by-year limits on the inflows of foreign private capital.

A priori, it might be supposed that alternatives 5 and 6 would have a significant effect upon the GDP growth rate. Similarly, one might have anticipated sizable macroeconomic effects from such alternatives as: (1) and (2), changing the annual growth target to 6 or 8 percent; or (3), changing the maximand to discounted consumption; or (4), changing the maximand to terminal consumption.

Under each of these alternatives—when taken one at a time—it turns out that the 1968–1980 optimal annual GDP growth rate varies only between 6.8 and 7.1 percent. The output growth rates for individual sectors also tend to be insensitive to the variations considered under cases 1–6. The effects are concentrated upon a comparatively small number of primal variables: the amount of capital-labor substitution within agriculture, the inflows of foreign capital, and the marginal export activities for trade-balance improvement.

It is not until we turn to cases 7 and 8—those involving the labor constraints—that the alternatives become radically different. Case 7 is calculated as though the marginal productivity of labor in Mexican agriculture were zero, as though there were no social costs of rural-urban labor transfer, and as though the social product foregone by creating human capital were also zero. With the labor-surplus hypothesis carried to this extreme, all labor constraints may be neglected. The marginal productivity of physical capital would rise to 30–33 percent per year —virtually identical to the incremental ratio of aggregate output to physical capital. This also means that the 1968–1980 optimal annual GDP growth rate would be 7.6 percent, and that each sector's output requirements would be increased correspondingly.

From the viewpoint of income distribution, perhaps the most significant alternative is case 8. Here the labor constraints are reintroduced. It is supposed that long-term credit is made available to the agricultural sector on more favorable terms than heretofore, and that this policy is pushed far enough so as to double the marginal rate of substitution of capital for unskilled agricultural workers. The macroeconomic and foreign-trade effects are not sizable, but the income distribution then shifts significantly in favor of unskilled labor.

For our quantitative comparison of alternatives, the results are summarized in Tables 2 through 7. (Further details are to be found in the computer listings. These are available for inspection in the author's office.) Tables 2 through 7 are arranged as follows:

Table 2. Macroeconomic results

Table 3. Resource gap—financial flows

Table 4. Foreign-exchange projections, 1980

Table 5. Efficiency prices of foreign exchange and foreign aid

Table 6. Gross production levels, 1980

Table 7. Employment, efficiency wages, and labor income, 1980

TABLE 2
MACROECONOMIC RESULTS
[billions of 1960 pesos]

Case Identification	CON'		SAV'		INV'		GDP'		mps, 1968–80 $= \dfrac{SAV^A - SAV^O}{GDP^A - GDP^O}$	Annual GDP Growth 1968–80
	1974¹	1980²	1974¹	1980²	1974¹	1980²	1974¹	1980²		
0 Basic case	303.6	445.8	81.9	136.8	81.9	128.2	385.5	582.6	26.3%	6.9%
1 g = 6%	308.1	448.8	78.3	123.9	78.3	115.2	386.4	572.7	23.0	6.8
2 g = 8%	298.9	441.9	89.0	150.2	89.0	142.6	387.8	592.1	29.6	7.1
3 Discounted consumption	298.9	442.6	90.7	152.3	91.8	144.7	389.7	594.9	30.0	7.1
4 Terminal consumption	295.8	434.4	89.4	148.8	86.5	145.4	385.2	583.2	30.0	6.9
5 50% export cost differential	303.1	444.6	81.3	136.3	81.3	127.6	384.4	580.8	26.3	6.9
6 No annual limits on FDP'	303.7	446.0	83.2	143.2	87.6	125.5	386.8	589.2	27.7	7.0
7 Labor constraints eliminated	316.6	478.4	89.5	146.6	89.5	137.9	406.1	624.9	26.0	7.6
8 Doubled capital-labor substitution rate	300.2	437.3	86.1	132.3	86.1	123.6	386.3	569.6	26.0	6.7

¹ Period t = 2.
² Period t = 4.

TABLE 3
RESOURCE GAP—FINANCIAL FLOWS[1]
[billions of 1960 pesos]

Case Identification	Foreign Direct Private Capital Inflows, FDP^t						Less: Interest and Profit Remittances on Direct Private Capital Inflows of Prior Years					
	'71 1	'74 2	'77 3	'80 4	'83 5	'86 6	'71 1	'74 2	'77 3	'80 4	'83 5	'86 6
0 Basic case	5.0	5.5	5.5	5.5	3.5	5.0	−4.9	−7.5	−10.4	−13.2	−16.1	−17.9
1 $g = 6\%$	5.0	5.5	5.5	5.5	3.5	5.0	−4.9	−7.5	−10.4	−13.2	−16.1	−17.9
2 $g = 8\%$	5.0	5.5	3.5	5.5	5.5	5.0	−4.9	−7.5	−10.4	−12.2	−15.1	−17.9
3 Discounted consumption	3.0	5.5	5.5	5.5	5.5	5.0	−4.9	−6.5	−9.3	−12.2	−15.1	−17.9
4 Terminal consumption	0	0	0	2.4	5.5	5.0	−4.9	−4.9	−4.9	−4.9	−6.1	−9.0
5 50% export cost differential	5.0	5.5	5.5	5.5	3.5	5.0	−4.9	−7.5	−10.4	−13.2	−16.1	−17.9
6 No annual limits on FDP^t	5.0	9.9	9.3	0.8	0	5.0	−4.9	−7.5	−12.7	−17.6	−17.9	−17.9
7 Labor constraints eliminated	5.0	5.5	5.5	5.5	3.5	5.0	−4.9	−7.5	−10.4	−13.2	−16.1	−17.9
8 Doubled capital-labor substitution rate	5.0	5.5	1.3	3.2	5.5	5.0	−4.9	−7.5	−10.4	−11.0	−12.7	−15.6

Case Identification	Plus: Concessional Capital Inflows Less Interest, $FC^t - INFC^t$						= Resource Gap, $RGAP^t$					
	'71 1	'74 2	'77 3	'80 4	'83 5	'86 6	'71 1	'74 2	'77 3	'80 4	'83 5	'86 6
0 Basic case	2.4	2.0	.9	−.9	−2.9	−4.7	2.5	0	−4.0	−8.6	−15.5	−17.6
1 $g = 6\%$	2.4	2.0	.9	−.9	−2.9	−4.7	2.5	0	−4.0	−8.6	−15.5	−17.6
2 $g = 8\%$	2.4	2.0	.9	−.9	−2.9	−4.7	2.5	0	−6.0	−7.6	−12.5	−17.6
3 Discounted consumption	2.4	2.0	.9	−.9	−2.9	−4.7	0.5	1.0	−2.9	−7.6	−12.5	−17.6
4 Terminal consumption	2.4	2.0	.9	−.9	−2.9	−4.7	−2.5	−2.9	−4.0	−3.4	−3.5	−8.7
5 50% export cost differential	2.4	2.0	.9	−.9	−2.9	−4.7	2.5	0	−4.0	−8.6	−15.5	−17.6
6 No annual limits on FDP^t	2.4	2.0	.9	−.9	−2.9	−4.7	2.5	4.4	−2.5	−17.7	−20.8	−17.6
7 Labor constraints eliminated	2.4	2.0	.9	−.9	−2.9	−4.7	2.5	0	−4.0	−8.6	−15.5	−17.6
8 Doubled capital-labor substitution rate	2.4	2.0	.9	−.9	−2.9	−4.7	2.5	0	−8.2	−8.7	−10.1	−15.3

[1] By year and period.
Period $t = 1$:1971. $t = 3$:1977. $t = 5$:1983.
        $t = 2$:1974. $t = 4$:1980. $t = 6$:1986.

TABLE 4
FOREIGN EXCHANGE PROJECTIONS, 1980
[billions of 1960 pesos]

Case Identification	Imports	Merchandise Exports, at Producers' Prices, Z_i^4									
		$i^1 =$ 1	2	3	4	5	6	7	8	9	10
0 Basic case	41.13	4.90	3.78	.54	5.80	.98	.62	2.07	.29	.72	2.18
1 $g = 6\%$	38.95	4.90	3.78	.54	5.80	.98	.62	2.07	.29	.72	2.18
2 $g = 8\%$	43.27	4.90	3.78	.54	5.80	.98	.62	2.07	.29	.72	1.80
3 Discounted consumption	43.87	4.90	3.78	.54	5.80	.98	.62	2.07	.29	.72	2.18
4 Terminal consumption	43.11	4.90	3.78	.54	5.80	.98	.62	2.07	.29	.72	2.18
5 50% export cost differential	40.37	7.77	3.78	.54	5.80	.98	.62	2.07	.29	.72	2.18
6 No annual limits on *FDP*	41.15	4.90	3.78	.54	5.80	.98	.62	2.07	.29	.72	2.18
7 Labor constraints eliminated	43.25	7.77	3.78	.54	5.80	.98	.62	2.07	.29	.23	2.18
8 Doubled capital-labor substitution rate	39.71	4.90	3.78	.54	5.80	.98	.62	2.07	.29	.72	2.18
Exogenously specified upper bound, $Z_i^0(1 + e_i)^{12}$		7.77	3.78	.54	5.80	.98	.62	2.07	.29	.72	2.18
Exogenously specified lower bound, $Z_i^0(1 + e_i)^{12}$		4.90	2.36	.45	2.88	.58	.31	0.66	.12	.23	0.56

[1] i = item.

TABLE 4 (*concluded*)

Case Identification	Exports of High-Cost Manufactures, at Producers' Prices, $\sum_{t=1}^{4} ZM^t$	Foreign Exchange Earnings, at Market Prices		Resource Gap. $RGAP^4 =$ Imports $- ZA^4 - ZT^4$
		Merchandise Exports,[2] ZA^4	Tourism, ZT^4	
0 Basic case	12.01	39.14	10.63	−8.64
1 $g = 6\%$	10.13	36.96	10.63	−8.64
2 $g = 8\%$	13.34	40.23	10.63	−7.59
3 Discounted consumption	13.48	40.83	10.63	−7.59
4 Terminal consumption	9.21	35.90	10.63	−3.42
5 50% export cost differential	8.26	38.12	10.89	−8.64
6 No annual limits on FDP^t	19.84	48.19	10.63	−17.67
7 Labor constraints eliminated	4.84	33.60	18.29	−8.64
8 Doubled capital-labor substitution rate	10.84	37.78	10.63	−8.70
Exogenously specified upper bound, $Z_i^0(1 + e_i)^{12}$	—	—	18.29	
Exogenously specified lower bound, $Z_i^0(1 + \varepsilon_i)^{12}$	0	—	10.63	

[2] ZA^4 = merchandise exports, at market prices.

.8658 ZA^4 = merchandise exports, at producers' prices = $\sum_{i=1}^{10} Z_i^4 + \sum_{r=1}^{4} ZM^r$.

.1125 ZA^4 = commerce margins on merchandise exports.

.0217 ZA^4 = service margins on merchandise exports.

TABLE 5

EFFICIENCY PRICES OF FOREIGN EXCHANGE AND FOREIGN AID

Case Identification	1960 Pesos Worth of Maximand[1] per Thousand 1960 Pesos Worth of Item				Efficiency Price of Foreign Exchange Relative to Price of Tradable Manufactures		"Own" Rate of Interest on Foreign Exchange, 1974–80. Annual Rate
	Foreign Exchange (rows $[F^t]$)		Foreign Aid (rows $[FGAP^t]$)				
	1974[2]	1980[3]	1974[2]	1980[3]	1974[2]	1980[3]	
0 Basic case	72.40	24.72	72.40	24.72	1.15	1.15	20%
1 $g = 6\%$	77.07	26.17	77.07	26.17	1.15	1.15	20
2 $g = 8\%$	74.41	20.55	61.85	25.98	1.16	1.13	24
3 Discounted consumption	547.92	238.20	759.36	333.96	1.13	1.13	15
4 Terminal consumption	373.61	290.17	1,284.79	892.21	1.02	1.20	4
5 50% export cost differential	82.08	29.92	78.49	29.92	1.28	1.35	18
6 No annual limits on FDP^t	71.31	27.22	62.97	27.22	1.05	1.21	17
7 Labor constraints eliminated	130.91	24.61	130.91	24.61	1.17	1.17	32
8 Doubled capital-labor substitution rate	53.59	22.96	53.59	22.96	1.13	1.17	15

[1] Except for cases 3 and 4, the maximand is CON^t, and the units of measurement of efficiency prices are therefore identical. In case 3, the unit of measurement refers to discounted consumption; in case 4, to terminal consumption.
[2] Period $t = 2$.
[3] Period $t = 4$.

TABLE 6

GROSS PRODUCTION LEVELS, 1980, BY SECTOR

[billions of 1960 pesos]

Case Identification	Agriculture (1)	Mining (2)	Petroleum (3)	Food (4)	Textiles (5)	Wood (6)	Chemicals (7)	Nonmetallic (8)
0 Basic case	74.6	8.6	39.0	112.8	54.8	22.6	54.8	14.9
1 g = 6%	73.3	8.4	38.3	112.0	54.6	21.9	53.7	14.0*
2 g = 8%	76.3	8.8	39.5	112.9	54.7	23.1	55.6	16.0*
3 Discounted consumption	76.2	8.9	39.7	113.3	54.8	23.3	55.9	16.1*
4 Terminal consumption	74.4	8.8	38.9	108.5	53.4	22.6	53.6	15.9*
5 50% export cost differential	77.4	8.5	38.8	110.9	54.4	22.3	53.8	14.9
6 No annual limits on FDP^a	76.5	8.7	39.5	118.1	55.8	23.3	57.4	15.2
7 Labor constraints eliminated	80.0*	8.8	41.3*	115.7	58.7*	23.6	56.1	15.9*
8 Doubled capital-labor substitution rate	74.0	8.4	38.0	110.1	53.6	21.9	53.2	14.4

Case Identification	Basic Metals (9)	Machinery (10)	Construction (11)	Electricity (12)	Commerce (13)	Transportation (14)	Services (15)
0 Basic case	37.0	100.1	59.1	19.8	196.7	24.2	161.0
1 g = 6%	34.9	95.2	53.9*	19.4	193.9	24.1	159.1
2 g = 8%	39.1*	104.4	64.9*	20.2	199.1	24.2	162.1
3 Discounted consumption	39.6*	106.1*	65.4*	20.3	200.2	24.3	163.5
4 Terminal consumption	38.6	103.8	65.9*	19.9	196.3	23.8	161.3
5 50% export cost differential	36.3	98.4	59.9	19.7	195.5	24.1	160.4
6 No annual limits on FDP^a	38.1	101.8	58.5	20.0	198.2	24.3	161.5
7 Labor constraints eliminated	37.9	105.5*	65.4*	21.1*	210.2*	26.2*	170.3*
8 Doubled capital-labor substitution rate	35.7	96.7	56.8	19.3	192.0	23.6	156.6

NOTE: * Differs by more than 5% from level shown for basic case.

TABLE 7
EMPLOYMENT, EFFICIENCY WAGES, AND LABOR INCOME, 1980, BY LABOR SKILL CATEGORY[1]

Case Identification	Employment. ROL_s^4 (millions of persons)							Efficiency Wages, Annual Average Centered on 1980[2] (thousands of 1960 pesos per man-year of skill s)				
	Skill Category					Subtotal. 1–4	Total. 1–5	Skill Category				
	1	2	3	4	5			1	2	3	4	5
0 Basic case	.183	1.310	2.673	9.521	6.765	13.687	20.452	112.1	53.4	23.0	7.5	3.9
1 $g = 6\%$	.176	1.286	2.619	9.265	7.350	13.346	20.696	106.8	53.7	23.4	7.5	3.9
2 $g = 8\%$	.189	1.328	2.720	9.759	6.359	13.996	20.355	129.4	59.9	24.1	7.9	4.2
3 Discounted consumption	.191	1.339	2.741	9.836	5.996	14.107	20.103	75.9	41.8	17.7	8.2	4.8
4 Terminal consumption	.187	1.319	2.693	9.667	5.734	13.886	19.600	41.8	21.1	12.7	8.7	5.5
5 50% export cost differential	.182	1.305	2.661	9.467	6.884	13.615	20.499	111.6	52.0	22.9	7.6	4.0
6 No annual limits on FDP^a	.186	1.318	2.698	9.623	6.901	13.825	20.726	117.9	53.8	24.2	7.9	4.2
7 Labor constraints eliminated	.193	1.387	2.839	10.134	9.895	14.553	24.448	—	—	—	—	—
8 Doubled capital-labor substitution rate	.178	1.274	2.602	9.254	7.239	13.308	20.547	90.2	52.8	24.2	11.3	7.9

[1] Skill category $s = 1$: engineers and scientists.
   $s = 2$: other professional and technical workers.
   $s = 3$: administrative and clerical workers.
   $s = 4$: manual and sales workers outside agriculture.
   $s = 5$: unskilled agricultural workers.

[2] Average of efficiency wages for 1977, 1980, and 1983, normalized by dual variable for consumption goods.

TABLE 7 (concluded)

| Case Identification | Labor Income = Employment × Efficiency Wages (billions of 1960 pesos) | | | | | | Aggregate Consumption (billions of 1960 pesos) CON^a | Labor Income as Fraction of Aggregate Consumption |
| | Skill Category | | | | | Total, 1–5 | | |
	1	2	3	4	5			
0 Basic case	20.5	70.0	61.5	71.4	26.4	249.8	445.8	56%
1 g = 6%	18.8	69.1	61.3	69.5	28.7	247.4	448.8	55
2 g = 8%	24.5	79.5	65.6	77.1	26.7	273.4	441.9	62
3 Discounted consumption	14.5	56.0	48.5	80.7	28.8	228.5	442.6	52
4 Terminal consumption	7.8	27.8	34.2	84.1	31.5	185.4	434.4	43
5 50% export cost differential	20.3	67.0	60.9	71.9	27.5	248.5	444.6	56
6 No annual limits on FDP^b	21.9	70.9	65.3	76.0	29.0	263.1	446.0	59
7 Labor constraints eliminated	–	–	–	–	–	–	478.4	–
8 Doubled capital-labor substitution rate	16.1	67.3	63.0	104.6	57.2	308.2	437.3	70

3. ALTERNATIVE OBJECTIVE FUNCTIONS

Cases 1 through 4 all deal with the problem of welfare distribution between successive generations—near future versus distant future increases in aggregate consumption. Somewhat surprisingly, these different objective functions do not lead to great differences in the absolute levels of consumption during the early time periods. (See Figure 1 and Table 8.)

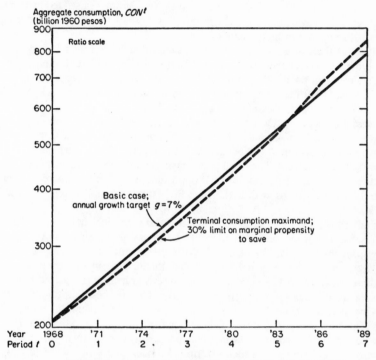

FIGURE 1   ALTERNATIVE TIME PATHS OF AGGREGATE CONSUMPTION

TABLE 8
AGGREGATE CONSUMPTION, CON^t: EFFECT OF ALTERNATIVE OBJECTIVES[1]
[billions of 1960 pesos]

	Case Identification	1968 0	1971 1	1974 2	1977 3	1980 4	1983 5	1986 6	1989 7
0	Basic case	208.8	251.4	303.6	367.5	445.8	541.8	659.3	803.3
1	$g = 6\%$	208.8	254.1	308.1	372.3	448.8	540.0	648.6	777.9
2	$g = 8\%$	208.8	248.7	298.9	362.2	441.9	542.2	668.7	828.0
3	Discounted consumption	208.8	245.3	298.9	363.5	442.6	542.5	692.7	848.6
4	Terminal consumption	208.8	245.9	295.8	359.5	434.4	535.9	700.1	857.6

[1] By year and period.
Period $t = 0$: 1968. $t = 3$: 1977. $t = 6$: 1986.
        $t = 1$: 1971. $t = 4$: 1980. $t = 7$: 1989.
        $t = 2$: 1974. $t = 5$: 1983.

For *cases 1 and 2*, the tradeoffs are examined through variations in the asymptotic target growth rate—still retaining the restriction that the time path be of the gradualist form with *increments* of consumption growing geometrically at the annual rate of g.[4] In case 1, for example, the target rate is reduced from 7 to 6 percent. This policy would make it possible to increase CON^1 from 251.4 to 254.1 billion pesos. Higher consumption levels would also be achieved during periods $t = 2$, 3, and 4, but lower levels during all subsequent time periods. Symmetrical effects are obtained when the target growth rate is raised to 8 percent. That is, case 2 provides lower consumption levels than the basic case during periods 1 through 4, but higher levels thereafter.

Although these alternatives differ from each other by less than 1 percent in the absolute levels of near-term consumption, they do have different implications for near-term fiscal policy. By lowering the annual growth target from 7 to 6 percent, the 1968–1980 marginal savings propensity is reduced from 26.3 to 23.0 percent. (Table 2.) This means lower taxes and lower prices on the products of public-sector enterprises. Over the long term, of course, this "soft" option leads to a lower aggregate growth rate and lower employment opportunities. Conversely, if the growth target is raised to 8 percent, the required 1968–1980 marginal savings propensity is 29.6 percent. The fiscal policy tasks would become correspondingly more onerous, but the 1980 employment opportunities would then increase from 13.7 to 14.0 million jobs within the four highest-paying skill categories. (See Table 7.)

In all cases, we have supposed that there are political constraints upon Mexico's fiscal policies, and that it would be infeasible to push the marginal savings propensity above 30 percent.[5] With the gradualist objective function (cases 0, 1, and 2), typically it turns out that the 30 percent savings limit is a redundant constraint.[6] When the gradualist objective function is replaced by that of maximizing discounted consumption (*case 3*) or terminal consumption (*case 4*), the savings constraints become critically important. Without them, the time path of aggregate consumption is exceedingly erratic from one period to the next. *With* a 30 percent upper bound upon the marginal propensity to save, then—even under a growth-maximizing criterion such as terminal consumption—there are no sharp discontinuities in the optimal consumption level between two successive periods. When the savings constraint is operative, the specific form of the objective function has little effect upon the optimal values of the primal variables.[7]

For numerical evaluation in case 3, we have taken 15 percent as the annual discount rate on future consumption,[8] and have retained 7 percent as the annual

---

[4] For the properties of the gradualist consumption maximand—and its relation to postterminal growth—see Hopkins (1969) and Manne (1970).

[5] For the statistical base period 1960–1968, the marginal savings propensity was 23.2 percent.

[6] In case 2, the 30 percent limit on the domestic savings propensity is binding only during periods 2, 3, and 4. Even during these periods, the shadow prices are quite low for the savings constraints, rows ($GSAV^t$).

[7] The optimal dual solution *is* sensitive to differences in the objective functions. For example, it turns out that the 1974–1980 "own" rate of interest on foreign exchange is 15 percent per year in case 3, and 4 percent in case 4. (See Table 5.)

[8] In principle, the consumption discount rate is a subjectively determined parameter—one that expresses the social rate of time preference. It is sheer coincidence that the same numerical value has been employed as for the cost of foreign private capital.

target for postterminal growth. Case 4 has the identical constraints as case 3, but a different objective function. Like a "turnpike" growth model, the maximand is CON^7, the level of aggregate consumption reached during the terminal year. Despite the difference in appearance, it can be shown that there is a close relationship between the objective functions considered in cases 3 and 4. The latter may be viewed as a special case of the former—a limiting case obtained by lowering the discount rate sufficiently. With this interpretation, the objective functions of cases 3 and 4 have the identical structure—that of discounted consumption. The only difference is that the consumption discount rate is 15 percent in case 3, and that it approaches 7 percent in case 4. The numerical results (Table 8) imply that the optimal solution is insensitive to variations in the discount rate within a rather wide range—7 to 15 percent per year. With this form of model, apparently the upper bound on the marginal savings rate has far more influence upon the optimal consumption path than does the subjectively determined time discount rate.

4. FOREIGN EXCHANGE

In the basic case, it turns out that the efficiency price of foreign exchange is 1.15—taking the domestic producers' price of tradable manufactures as the numéraire. Before advocating that 15 percent is therefore an appropriate tariff rate or export subsidy or adjustment in foreign-exchange parity, it is essential to check through the reasoning that led to this numerical result. In DINAMICO, one of the least reliable econometric components is the marginal cost of export earnings. The basic case was set up as though there were no limits upon the export of "infant" high-cost manufactures. It is supposed that the domestic cost of these products will exceed the foreign exchange earnings by 30 percent at the time that the manufactured item is first exported, and that this cost differential will drop to zero through the experience acquired during an 18-year period.[9] As an alternative, case 5 is calculated as though these marginal export items will have an initial cost disadvantage of 50 percent rather than 30 percent. We continue to suppose that it will require 18 years of experience before the cost differential can be eliminated.

Case 5 makes little or no difference in the macroeconomic results (Table 2), the pattern of foreign capital inflows (Table 3), the aggregate requirements for imports (Table 4), the gross production levels (Table 6), or the employment levels (Table 7). From the viewpoint of overall reliability of DINAMICO, it is fortunate that the principal effects of this parameter change are concentrated upon a small number of variables: the commodity composition of exports (Table 4) and the shadow price of foreign exchange (Table 5). It becomes optimal to reduce the 1980 exports of high-cost manufactures from 12.01 to 8.26 billion pesos, and to offset this loss of foreign exchange through an increase in agricultural exports. Associated with this shift in the direction of comparative advantage, there is a shift in the

[9] Presumably, in order to provide a financial incentive for the export of high-cost manufactures from individual enterprises, it would be necessary to provide export subsidies. Such subsidies might take a number of forms—either outright or in the form of permission to import raw materials and equipment duty free. (Mexico is not a member country of GATT [General Agreement on Tariffs and Trade].) With any of these measures, there are administrative difficulties—but no more so than in the case of existing import restrictions. The principal difference between an import tariff and an export subsidy is that one provides an inflow of pesos to the treasury, and the other generates an outflow.

shadow price of foreign exchange. It no longer remains 1.15, but increases to 1.35 in 1980—still taking the price of tradable manufactures as the numéraire. Case 5 also means that foreign aid would have a higher marginal productivity than in the basic case.[10]

Case 6 provides an instance of interdependence between the optimal time path of capital inflows, the shadow price of foreign exchange, and the composition of exports. Here we have eliminated the year-by-year limits on the private capital inflows FDP^t ($t = 2 \ldots 5$), but have retained the overall constraint that the average inflows are not to increase above the 1971 rate. Case 6 has little effect upon the macroeconomic results or the gross production or the employment levels. The effects are concentrated upon the sources and uses of foreign exchange. It now becomes optimal to allow exports to lag and to incur a sizable foreign-exchange deficit during periods 2 and 3, then to push up the level of high-cost manufactured exports to 19.84 billion pesos in period 4 (1980), and to run a sizable foreign-exchange surplus (17.67 billion pesos) in that year. Associated with this shift in the time pattern of exports, the shadow price of foreign exchange would rise over time—from 1.05 to 1.21 between periods 2 and 4 (1974 and 1980, respectively). This also means that the marginal productivity of foreign aid would be lower during period 2 and higher during period 4 than in the basic case. (See Table 5.)

From case 6, we cannot conclude that year-by-year constraints on foreign capital inflows are essential in a model of this type. Other devices may also be employed to avoid sharp discontinuities in the time pattern of exports. Among such devices are: an upward-sloping supply curve of foreign capital, a downward-sloping demand curve for exports, or a recursive programming constraint on the rate of growth of exports.[11] Among these alternative devices, the simplest to estimate is the year-by-year limit on private capital inflows. For the basic case, this has the disadvantage that the upper bound is an effective constraint during the early time periods, and that the unknowns FDP^t appear to be predetermined. It does not happen, however, that the upper bound is always an effective constraint during the initial time periods. For examples, see cases 2, 4, and 8 in Table 3.

5. EMPLOYMENT AND INCOME DISTRIBUTION

For *case 7*, the labor constraints have been eliminated. This makes it possible to achieve a significantly higher aggregate growth rate, higher output rates in

---

[10] Except for cases 3 and 4, the 30 percent limit upon the marginal savings propensity is not a critical constraint. Except for these cases, therefore, it makes little or no difference whether the impact of additional foreign aid is measured through the shadow price of the foreign exchange rows (F^t) or through the resource gap rows ($FGAP^t$). Cases 3 and 4 are typical of the "two-gap" phenomenon. There, foreign aid has considerably more leverage than foreign-exchange earnings alone. For further discussion of the two-gap model, see the interchange between Chenery and Strout (1968) and Fei and Ranis (1968).

The shadow price of the domestic savings rows ($GSAV^t$) may be read off from Table 5 here. In all cases, this equals the difference between the shadow price of rows (F^t) and ($FGAP^t$). To prove this proposition, refer back to the coefficients of the resource gap activity $RGAP^t$ and of the concessional foreign aid activity $\overline{FC^t}$ in Table 4, memorandum 71–13.

[11] Let Z_i^t denote the exports of item i during period t, and let e_i denote the maximum feasible rate of growth of this item between periods $t - 1$ and t. Then a recursive programming constraint on exports would be written: $Z_i^t \le (1 + e_i)Z_i^{t-1}$. See Day (1963); and Bruno, Dougherty, and Fraenkel (1970).

Note that a recursive programming constraint refers to *pairs* of unknowns, but that the export bounds in DINAMICO are imposed upon individual unknowns.

individual sectors, and greater employment opportunities outside traditional agriculture. (See Tables 2, 6, and 7.) It has already been noted that a zero shadow price for labor implies a high shadow price for capital. Almost equally dramatic are the implications for comparative advantage in foreign trade. With a zero shadow price for labor, it becomes optimal to set agricultural exports and tourism earnings at their upper rather than their lower bounds, and to place less dependence upon high-cost manufactured exports. (See Table 5.)[12] Case 7 is included here for the sake of completeness—not because we believe that it provides a realistic basis for projections.

Increasingly, Mexican policymakers are directing research toward the sources of inequities in income distribution. There is strong evidence that, along with the increase in average incomes, the extent of inequality worsened between 1950 and 1963. (During those years, the Gini coefficient of inequality increased from 0.50 to 0.55.) In part, this problem arises from interregional differences in development—and from imperfect labor mobility between regions. In 1965, for example, the 8 highest-income regions accounted for 30.3 percent of the total population, and produced 11,075 pesos per capita. The 17 lowest-income regions, with 43.8 percent of the population, produced only 2,417 pesos per capita. (Source: Navarrete [1970, p. 41 and Table 8].)

Not only regional but also occupational differences are a significant source of inequalities. During each of the years between 1950 and 1967, in industry and services the per capita output exceeded that in agriculture by a factor of approximately 5:1. Even within agriculture—despite the post-Revolution policies of agrarian reform and land redistribution—the pattern of development has been "dualistic." In the irrigated districts of the north, farming is commercialized and produces high economic returns. Elsewhere—in the central plateau and in the south—subsistence agriculture is hard pressed to keep up with the demographic pressures. (See Solís [1970, pp. 148 and 291].)

DINAMICO is too highly aggregated to be helpful in analyzing the detailed regional aspects of income inequalities and labor mobility. *Case 8* is focused on only one dimension of the tradeoff between aggregate growth versus equity in income distribution. As proxy measures for these concepts, we have taken aggregate consumption and labor's income share, both as of 1980 ($t = 4$). By measuring labor's income at efficiency wages, we have, in effect, adopted the view that money transfer payments could not be large enough to achieve a significant redistribution of real income between social classes. (If money transfers could be made sufficiently large—and transfers entailed no loss in productive efficiency—the question of a growth-equity tradeoff would not arise.)

Case 8 has been constructed as follows: Suppose that public infrastructure investments are made available for the benefit of the smallholders in the densely populated central and southern centers of Mexican agriculture. These investments might take the form of extension services, roads, tractors, irrigation, and land

---

[12] Rather than suppose that the marginal productivity of labor is zero in all skill classes (case 7), it might have been worth exploring a less extreme version of the labor-surplus hypothesis. Suppose, for example, that the only change in the basic case had been to assume that unskilled agricultural labor has a zero or a low marginal product. It would then be optimal to shift the composition of foreign-exchange earnings—setting agricultural exports at their upper bounds and reducing the exports of high-cost manufactures.

leveling. To the extent that the aggregate demand for agricultural products is inelastic, these investments might have to be made at the expense of northern agriculture. It is possible that this would lead to a loss in economic efficiency, but that nonetheless—from the viewpoint of income distribution—this would prove to be a desirable shift in investment policy.

For case 8, it is supposed that this reorientation of agricultural policy is pushed far enough so as to double the marginal rate of substitution of capital for unskilled agricultural workers.[13] It turns out that this would have a significant

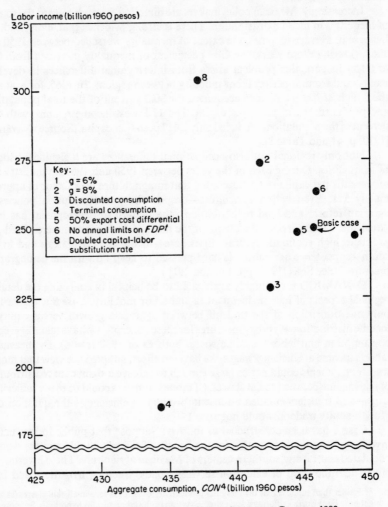

FIGURE 2   INCOME DISTRIBUTION VERSUS AGGREGATE GROWTH, 1980

[13] For the basic case, at a point of time y years after 1960, it is assumed that it would require $15(1.02)^y$ thousand pesos of capital to replace one unskilled agricultural worker. For case 8, this marginal rate of substitution is instead taken to be $30(1.02)^y$.

effect not only upon the efficiency wage of agricultural workers, but also upon that of unskilled urban workers. (See Table 7 and Figure 2.) Other policy measures would also affect labor's share, e.g., case 2, where the target annual growth rate is raised to 8 percent. None of the alternatives, however, would exert as pronounced an effect upon income distribution as would this shift in the direction of agricultural investments. In 1980, this would make it possible to double the income of unskilled agricultural workers—from 26.4 to 57.2 billion pesos at 1960 prices. Total labor income would increase from 249.8 to 308.2 billion. The loss in aggregate consumption (from 445.8 to 437.3 billion pesos) might well be worth the gain in equity from such a policy.

REFERENCES

Adelman, I., "A Linear Programming Model of Educational Planning: A Case Study of Argentina," ch. 14 in I. Adelman and E. Thorbecke, eds., *The Theory and Design of Economic Development* (Baltimore: Johns Hopkins Press, 1966).

Bowles, S., "Efficient Allocation of Resources in Education," *Quarterly Journal of Economics*, May 1967.

Bruno, M., "A Programming Model for Israel," ch. 12 in Adelman and Thorbecke, eds., *op. cit.*

———. "Optimal Patterns of Trade and Development," *Review of Economics and Statistics*, November 1967.

Bruno, M., Dougherty, C., and Fraenkel, M., "Dynamic Input-Output, Trade and Development," ch. 3 in A. Carter and A. Brody, eds., *Applications of Input-Output Analysis* (Amsterdam: North-Holland, 1970).

Bueno, G., "The Structure of Protection in Mexico" (Colegio de México, 1970).

Chenery, H. B. and MacEwan, A., "Optimal Patterns of Growth and Aid: The Case of Pakistan," ch. 6 in Adelman and Thorbecke, eds., *op. cit.*

Chenery, H. B. and Strout, A. M., " 'Reply' to a Comment by Fei and Ranis," *American Economic Review*, September 1968.

Correa, H. and Tinbergen, J., "Quantitative Adaptation of Education to Accelerated Growth," *Kyklos*, fasc. 4, 1962.

Day, R., *Recursive Programming and Production Response* (Amsterdam: North-Holland, 1963).

Eckaus, R. S. and Parikh, K. S., *Planning for Growth* (Cambridge, Mass.: M.I.T. Press, 1968).

Fei, J. C. H. and Ranis, G., "Foreign Assistance and Economic Development: Comment," *American Economic Review*, September 1968.

Harberger, A., "Techniques of Project Appraisal," in M. Millikan, ed., *National Economic Planning* (New York: National Bureau of Economic Research, 1967).

Hopkins, D. S. P., "Sufficient Conditions for Optimality in Infinite Horizon Linear Economic Models," Technical Report No. 69-3 (Operations Research House, Stanford University, March 1969).

Manne, A. S., "Sufficient Conditions for Optimality in an Infinite Horizon Development Plan," *Econometrica*, January 1970.

Murakami, Y., Tokoyama, K., and Tsukui, J., "Efficient Paths of Accumulation and the Turnpike of the Japanese Economy," ch. 2 in Carter and Bródy, eds., *op. cit.*

Navarrete, I. M. de, "La Distribución del Ingreso en México: Tendencias y Perspectivas," *El Perfil de México en 1980* (Mexico: Siglo XXI Editores, 1970).

Solis, L., *La Realidad Económica Mexicana: Retrovisión y Perspectivas*, (Mexico: Siglo XXI Editores, 1970).

Spiegelman, R. G., Baum, E. L., and Talbert, L. E., *Application of Activity Analysis to Regional Development Planning*, Technical Bulletin 1339 (Washington, D.C.: U.S. Department of Agriculture, March 1965).

A SIMULATION MODEL OF THE MEXICAN EDUCATIONAL SYSTEM

ERNESTO SCHIEFELBEIN*
Center for Educational Studies, Mexico

SUMMARY

This paper describes a linear programming model designed to study the Mexican educational system and the effects of alternative educational policies on it. In the course of implementing the model, the principal educational statistical data were found to be inconsistent. In order to overcome these inconsistencies a Markov-type model was constructed to simulate the flow of students at the elementary- and secondary-school levels. By means of this and other information and subjective estimates (Delphi Method) of the remaining parameters, versions of the linear programming model were computed for different periods starting with 1970. The specification of the model has been completed and when estimates of the demand for human resources become available, it will be possible to use the model for analyzing decision-making problems involving uncertainty.

1. INTRODUCTION

There is increasing pressure to make decisions in a rational manner, especially when the decisions affect large groups of the population. With perhaps a certain lag relative to other sectors, this need is now being felt in the educational field. Educational authorities in different countries may differ in the goals which they hope to attain, but all want to reach them with a minimum of resources, that is, in the most efficient way.

In the last decade, there has been great interest in applying the analytical tools of economics to the educational sphere. Specialized literature on educational models is abundant, but the number of works that describe applications to real situations is very limited indeed. This is, perhaps, attributable to the complexities of the interrelationships which must be taken into account in making decisions about educational problems.

As in most social systems, education can only be partially controlled. The educator in an executive position cannot foresee all possible results of each alternative decision, because they depend on events that cannot be predicted ex ante with any degree of accuracy. In other words, the executive who directs the educational system encounters problems of the type known as decision-making under uncertainty.

2. OUTLINE OF WORK

When the Center for Educational Studies undertook the task of examining concrete proposals for action for the Mexican educational system, it had to grapple with these problems of uncertainty. Among the various procedures that could be utilized, the designing of a model capable of systematically exploring the

* The author is currently Director of the Interdisciplinary Research Program in Education [PIIE], Catholic University of Chile.

relevant alternatives was selected. They wanted to devise a tool that would make it possible to show in a simplified form the effects of the various policies which might be implemented in the Mexican educational system. In other words, instead of attempting to calculate *the* optimal solution, the aim was to insure that the executive was consistent in his "guesstimates" and that he at least evaluate the possible effects suggested by the calculations of the model.

Since the global model should be useful to the educational executives (assuming they are educators), requirements such as the following had to be met:
—the model should comprehend the whole system;
—the variables and parameters should have obvious significance for the educators (see Appendixes A, B, C);
—the model should make it possible to obtain results comparable to those habitually obtained;
—the internal effects of the alternatives should be considered, that is, the repercussions within the educational system;
—the variables determined in other activity sectors, outside the educational system should be considered exogenous;
—the results must be obtained the next day.

A fundamental assumption underlying all the work is that the model will be used within a planning context, that is, it will be used by planners who have an extensive knowledge of the situation represented by the model.

The characteristics of the model of the educational system depend on the availability of the data necessary for its implementation. A few preliminary checks of the statistics indicated some inconsistencies; it was necessary to eliminate them with the aid of a Markov-type model of the flow of students. Since the future use which can be made of this model will depend, in part, on additional studies (e.g., of human resources and construction), it can be said that carrying out the objective will involve a system of models that are mutually complementary. Only the global model will be described below in detail.

A special effort was made to determine transition coefficients that would be consistent with the other information used in the model; however, other parameters also need to be estimated with great precision. In any event, the nature of the problem tells us that it will never be possible to reach a complete definition of the situation. That is why the model has been designed without waiting for better sources, and assumptions have been made on qualitative aspects of the model. The Delphi method was used to obtain some of these.

In the first stage, described in this paper, the goal has been to adjust the model so that its functioning adequately represents the reality that will be modeled. In a subsequent stage, it will be possible to include the recently completed studies of human resources, to utilize information from the recent population census, and to make specific studies with the assurance that their results will be incorporated in a model which has been shown to function adequately.

3. GLOBAL MODEL OF THE EDUCATIONAL SYSTEM

The educational system is considered in this model as a structure within which the intensity of use of a certain number of educational processes must be determined. Each process, or activity, is defined as the result of rates, or quotients, of the annual inputs of certain factors and the generation of certain results in the corresponding period. Each activity corresponds to a different way of teaching or learning.

The educational system is defined in the model as an aggregate of activities which generate educated persons in each period. To educate by these activities, different resources are used, the supply of which is assumed to be known. The number of people to be educated depends upon economic and social demands which are considered to be exogenously determined.

It is assumed that the variables are continuous, that is, that each process can attain any level within a previously defined range if the corresponding factors (resources) are available.

The optimum of a solution corresponds to the maximum value that a given function can attain while all the restrictions established in the problem are respected. This function, which is utilized as a criterion for determining the optimal solution, is called the objective function. In this problem, both the objective function and the restrictions will be linear expressions.

4. GENERAL CHARACTERISTICS OF THE MODEL

In the process of forming persons with different levels of preparation (academic achievement), the educational system utilizes human resources (teachers, students, workers) and other resources (buildings, texts, transportation, and various monetary and nonmonetary expenditures) at relatively constant rates. In order to design the model, it will be necessary to assume that the educational technology implicit in these coefficients will be maintained at least at the level that would be predicted by historic trends.

Another important assumption refers to the influence that education and on-the-job training can have on the productivity of the workers. This will permit relating various types of training to the demand for graduates of the system. The specific form of these relationships will be discussed below.

For each of the periods considered, 65 variables were defined: 20 levels of education; 22 alternatives for increasing the technology of the system; 2 types of teachers; 3 types of school building; 5 types of on-the-job training; 7 levels of skill of labor; and 10 overflow variables defined to facilitate the study of the system's bottlenecks. Notwithstanding this level of aggregation, the model has 646 linear equations, 1,419 variables, and 4,573 elements in the matrix. In order to give a picture of the structure of the model, a tabulation of the equations is presented in Table 1.

Both the objective function and the relationships that define the system are expressed as linear functions, so that the formulation will constitute a special case of the well-known family of linear programming problems (see Appendix D). This will permit us to make use of the well-known properties of this set of problems.

In Table 1 numerous intertemporal relationships are described. They are obtained in part from a model of the flow of students. The students in each year depend upon those who existed the year before, in accord with rates of promotion, repetition, or dropout, and upon the new pupils who are integrated into the system

TABLE 1
SUMMARY OF THE EQUATIONS BY PERIOD

	Classification of the Equations			
Period	Identities (definitions)	Functional Relations	Limits (restrictions)	Initial and Terminal Conditions
Criterion		1		
1970	3	10	10	1
1970–1971	2	24	18	
1971	1	7	10	
1971–1972	5	24	18	
1972	1	7	10	
1972–1973	5	24	18	
1973	1	7	10	
1973–1974	5	24	18	
1974	1	7	10	
1974–1975	5	24	18	
1975	1	7	10	
1975–1976	5	24	18	
1976	1	7	10	
1976–1977	5	24	18	
1977	1	7	10	
1977–1978	5	24	18	
1978	1	7	10	
1978–1979	5	24	18	
1979	1	7	10	
1979–1980		21	18	
Totals	54	311	280	1

during the year. Other intertemporal relations correspond to the equations which determine the best alternative activities for increasing productivity, that is, the efficiency with which the system functions. Equations defining teachers and buildings required in each period constitute the rest of the intertemporal relationships included in this model. Time is considered as being discontinuous and the unit is one year of operation.

In describing the model, the following symbols are used:

—lower case letters: the initial letters of the alphabet are used as indexes or as stock variables; the last letters of the alphabet are used as vectors of activity levels, that is, variables;

—upper case letters: the last letters of the alphabet are used as matrices of variables; the upper case letters with a bar indicate the availability of resources (limits);

—lower case Greek letters: used as parameter vectors;

—upper case Greek letters: used as parameter matrices.

A summary of these equations and a definition of the nomenclature are presented at the end of this paper (see Appendixes A through D).

5. THE OBJECTIVE FUNCTION

It was pointed out that the model furnishes an optimal solution for each trial. The criterion for reaching each solution is the minimization of the operating expenses of the entire educational system in a certain number of periods, while at the same time observing the various conditions imposed by the model.

Differing from the normal usage of linear programming models, no attempt is made to reach a unique optimal solution. Computers make it possible to use the model to obtain families of solutions resulting from systematic changes of the parameters which reflect the assumptions on which each decision is based.[1] These changes make it possible to compute the effects of diverse educational policies on the educational system. In other words, the model, within the restrictions and the optimization criterion that define it, provides a set of solutions for any combination of information, functions, and assumptions which define a given educational system.

Among the solutions computed by the model, it is possible for the executive to select some, on the basis of subjective criteria, which represent a relative optimum, so that he can examine these combinations of assumptions with greater attention. In this manner, the model will help the executive in making decisions in a sphere in which it is very difficult to measure the results.

In the general design of the model in its present form, it is assumed that expenses are discounted at the initial moment. This makes it possible to examine the use of an annual flow of resources. Market prices can be assumed to be constant since marginal variations in the amount of resources used constitute a small fraction of the market value of these goods and there exists a specific restriction that prevents the use of more teachers than those available.[2]

The simpler the projection, the better—especially when it is not possible to establish with clarity the tendency of change. That is why it seems acceptable to use an objective linear function. It is necessary to examine the assumptions each time that a solution which is considered optimal is reached in order to verify whether, in this case, a different function might have been able to change the result substantially.

In accord with what has been stated above, the objective function of the problem would be the following:[3]

$$(1) \quad C = \sum_t \alpha_{1t} p_t + \alpha_{2t} x_t + \sigma_t \bar{y}_t + \beta_t y_t + \gamma_{1t} r_t + \gamma_{2t} q_t + \delta_t v_t + \psi_t u_t + \varepsilon_t w_t$$
$$+ \pi_t z_t$$

If the meaning of each term is examined (see Appendixes A, B, and C), it will be seen that the expression to be minimized is nothing more than the sum of the operating costs (exclusive of teachers) of the kindergarten level (preprimary); plus the operating costs of the rest of the system; plus the expenses of attending to the children with serious problems before their entrance into the primary level; plus the costs of remedial courses and individual attention to those who need it; plus the social costs of children failing to enter the system on time; plus the social costs for premature dropouts; plus the costs of building new capacity for the various levels; plus the remuneration of teachers who work in the entire educational

---

[1] The selection of values can be made using the Monte Carlo method.

[2] In those solutions in which a rapid change in the inputs per pupil can be inferred, it will be necessary to estimate, subjectively whether the assumption of a linear cost function is met.

[3] Descriptions of the variables and coefficients appear in Appendixes A, B, and C.

system; plus the costs of on-the-job training; and plus the costs for resorting to extraordinary procedures to reach a feasible solution despite the restrictions established by the system's functioning.

The last set of variables enter into the solution solely when it is the only way to reach solutions, since, because of the high cost associated with them, the routine of computation tries all the rest of the variables first before letting these special variables enter; whenever a special variable does appear in the solution, it is a signal that there is some bottleneck in the system which must be uncovered.

The objective function assumes that both existing levels of expenditures for students and their prices will be maintained. Even if the prices are not affected by the quantities demanded by the educational system (with the exception of the demand for educators, which, in turn, depends on the levels of remuneration of the labor market), in a model with a ten-year time horizon it can be assumed that prices may have important variations, but clearly these cannot be foreseen in the base year.

6. The Restrictions

The algebraic expressions and the definitions of the variables and parameters appear in Appendixes A through D. Although the study of equations suffices for understanding the internal logic of the model, the comments below will facilitate identification of the purpose of each equation in the overall functioning of the model.

Equation (2): calculates the total current operating expenses of the regular educational system for each year and avoids letting these total current expenses exceed the current budget of this year. The variables and parameters correspond to those of the objective function. In order to avoid infeasibilities due to the budgetary restriction, a variable is included which, because of its high cost, only enters the solution when it is impossible otherwise to comply simultaneously with the budgetary restriction and the other restrictions of the model. It should be pointed out that equation (2) includes the costs of increasing the efficiency of the system in the future by means of consideration of the $\bar{y}$ variables lagged up to four periods.

Equation (3): calculates total capital expenditures required for the replacement of installed capacity or for the addition of new capacity, in each year, without exceeding the budgeted total for the period. If there is flexibility in the budget, it would be possible to combine this equation with the previous one, or to introduce variables which would permit the transfer of the budget surplus on capital account to the current budget.

Equation (4): calculates enrollment of year t as a function of the enrollment of the previous year and of those who enter the first grade of primary education. The transition coefficients between the two consecutive periods represent the technology of the system. This equation considers the possibility of improving the technology by means of two alternative processes. It is possible to improve the results by making students with problems enter the preprimary level ahead of schedule, or to attain this objective by giving them remedial courses, that is, special treatment, until the problems which impede their normal intellectual development are resolved.

Equation (5): defines enrollment in the preprimary course as the sum of students who require attention in kindergarten, before entering the first year of primary school, in order to avoid failures at the outset of their school life.

Equation (6): limits the annual increases of educational technology to a percentage of total enrollment in each grade in the following year. The resulting figure represents the maximum annual improvement in the efficiency of the system (more promotions or fewer dropouts) which can be attained given the conditions (especially costs) defined in the model for reaching these objectives. The allowed percentage by which the technology of the system can be raised is fixed subjectively by the Delphi Method.

Equation (7): calculates the total supply of personnel that is incorporated in each level of labor and compares this total with the labor demanded. The demand estimate is partially exogenous since, internally, consideration is given to the requirements for the replacement of persons who succeed, by means of accelerated schooling, in passing to a more highly skilled level, as well as to teachers needed in each level. This equation makes it possible to use the surpluses produced in the various qualification levels on the qualification levels immediately lower, where this personnel is included in the corresponding total supply.

Equation (8): calculates the total number of primary and secondary teachers that are needed to take care of students who are enrolled in the regular and remedial courses. It compares this total with the supply of teachers determined in equation (9) and it forces this supply to be equal to, or larger than, the number required. When the minimum level of supply is determined in this equation (supply equals demand), the minimum number of teachers to be trained in the period is also determined in the following equation. In this version it is established that supply and demand are equal in each period, but it would also be possible to define the relationship lagged by one year.

Equation (9): defines the total supply of teachers as the sum of the survivors of the previous period (who have not retired from exercising their profession) plus the teachers trained in that period. However, the teachers trained in the period increase the personnel requirements because they are included in total manpower demand (equation (7)).

Equation (10): calculates the space requirements (buildings) of the students enrolled in the regular educational system. It compares this total buildings requirement with the total capacity of the previous period, increased by the investments of the same period; and it establishes that the capacity must be equal to, or greater than, the requirements. When the minimum requirement is determined in this equation (capacity equal to demand), in the following equation the minimum square meters of building space that must be constructed in the period is determined. The relations between supply and demand could be planned with a lag of one or more periods in order to take into account the time the construction will take. In this version, nonetheless, no lag has been considered.

Equation (11): defines the total capacity available in the period as the sum of the available capacity in the previous period (reduced in accordance with an average rate of depreciation) plus the additions to capacity that are produced. If it is possible to establish how far in advance construction must be initiated, one can consider one or more periods of lag in the pertinent variables.

Equation (12): establishes that a certain proportion of the students of the preprimary level must remain at least two years in that level in order not to have learning problems later on. In the implementation of the model, this equation has only been used to establish that these levels grow by at least a 10 percent annual cumulative rate, given the low proportion initially expected. In utilizing this equation for its original purpose, it is necessary to return to the Delphi Method when appropriate studies are not available.

Equation (13): establishes that the first preparatory grade must grow from period to period. However, in order to prevent this restriction from generating an impossible solution, a variable is included which, because of its high cost, only enters the solution where it is impossible for the model to find any other method of matching the required enrollment in the first grade while satisfying the other restrictions imposed by the model.

Equation (14): establishes certain minimum activity levels for the regular educational system in each period. In implementing the model, this restriction is used only as an initial condition for the first grades in the first period. This equation has great usefulness in establishing initial and terminal conditions of the model which permit a true representation of the reality which is being modeled. These conditions require, usually, flexible functional relationships for their adequate definition.

Equation (15): determines the total number of youths within an age cohort who remain outside the system each year. This number is calculated as the difference between the total number of students enrolled in a certain level of the system and the total number of youths of the age which is normal for that level. This equation facilitates the representation, in the model, of the effects of various policies intended to reduce the number of youths who are marginal to the system in some of the age groups.

Equation (16): determines the dropouts from the first levels of the system. In these levels, it is very difficult to find measuring devices to evaluate the academic achievement of those students. Therefore, the large number of dropouts ought to be attributed to the teachers' expectations. That is why in the model the total number of premature dropouts is designated as one of the possibilities for massive increase in the efficiency with which the regular school system operates.

Equation (17): establishes that the number of pupils in the seven-year-old cohort, which is entering the first year of primary school, must be at least equal to that of the previous period. In this way the social imperative of not reducing the input capacity of the system in any period is represented. If desired, a coefficient could be included by means of which the input capacity would grow at least at the rate of increase of the total population, or of the respective cohort.

Equation (18): establishes a minimum activity level of institutions providing accelerated manpower training. In this way, one can assure the availability of a group of highly qualified instructors and of an operating organization, even though at a minimum level (its cost will correspond, basically, to fixed costs, that is, those that would not vary with changes in volume of activity), which could be easily expanded in the future if circumstances so demand.

7. Estimation of the Parameters

As was pointed out earlier, preliminary examination of the data revealed certain inconsistencies. The tasks of refining the model and of gathering adequate data were carried out simultaneously. A special study was made of those transition rates for which the historic values were seriously questionable.[4] In this way, it was possible to use these rates in the first versions of the model. For the other parameters, the best available data were used, as well as subjective estimates—using simplified versions of the Delphi Method—to complete the information needed in the design of the model.

The information used in the version described in this paper is presented in Tables 2 through 6. It is hoped that, in this way, it will be possible to verify the model's validity by comparing these figures with those available from other sources. Given their provisional nature and limitations of space, the sources for each table are not described.

It can be observed that, for example, the student-teacher relationship used in the model is 37, whereas the historical relationship is approximately 46. There is no intention of absorbing the difference in the ten years which the model considers; rather, it is maintained as a constant throughout the exercise. It is evident that if a better understanding of the educational policy about the student-teacher ratio is achieved, it can be easily represented in the model. A similar treatment was employed for school buildings used in multiple shifts. In order to simplify the problem in this case, the initial (theoretical) capacity was calculated in accord with the numbers per student which will be used in the period. Therefore, the total numbers for capacity which appear in Table 2 exceed reality by a large margin.

Regarding costs per student and teachers' salaries, it was estimated that the annual rate of increase would correspond, approximately, to the discount rate which exists in the Mexican market. Therefore, the initial prices were held constant for the entire period.

8. Testing the Model

Given the nature of the model, no systematic procedure for testing the model could be used. Only the quantitative aspects were tested, comparing actual figures for the 1962–1968 period with the model outcome for the same period. The results are presented in Table 7. The actual figures included in the 1962–1968 period were not used for estimating the transition parameters.

The fit for the primary level is relatively good. All discrepancies between the model's estimates and reality do not exceed 3.2 percent except for three cases in which errors reach −5.7 percent in 1963, +6.3 percent in 1966, and +4.2 percent in 1968. Given that the rates were estimated by adjusting continuous curves so that they would preserve historical tendencies, it can be concluded that these discrepancies are not significant. It might be considered that the differences denote deficiencies in the gathering of statistical data. It is evident, however, that certain tendencies exist among the differences. Initially the estimates tend to be smaller, while during the last years the situation is reverse. This type of error could

[4] E. Schiefelbein, "Un modelo de simulación del sistema educativo mexicano," *Revista del Centro de Estudios Educativos*, Vol. 1, No. 4, Mexico, 1971.

TABLE 2
VALUE OF THE PARAMETERS IN THE BASE YEAR

Symbol	Description	Value
ϕ_1	Student-teacher ratio at the preprimary level	0.027
ϕ_2	Student-teacher ratio at the primary level	0.03
ϕ_3	Student-teacher ratio at the secondary level	0.071
ϕ_1^i	Student-teacher ratio in primary-level remedial courses	0.05
ϕ_2^i	Student-teacher ratio in secondary-level remedial courses	0.1
θ_1	Square meters per student in the preprimary and primary level	1.85
θ_2	Square meters per student in the secondary level	4.5
θ_3	Square meters per student in the upper level	10.0
η	Maximum annual increment through better technology	0.10
$\bar{v}_1$	Square meters of initial capacity at the primary level	17,370,000
$\bar{v}_2$	Square meters of initial capacity at the middle level	6,770,000
$\bar{v}_3$	Square meters of initial capacity at the upper level	1,950,000
$\hat{w}_2$	Minimum annual activity in accelerated formation at level two	20,000
$\hat{w}_3$	Minimum annual activity in accelerated formation at level three	10,000
$\hat{w}_4$	Minimum annual activity in accelerated formation at level four	5,000
$\hat{w}_5$	Minimum annual activity in accelerated formation at level five	2,000
$\hat{w}_6$	Minimum annual activity in accelerated formation at level six	2,000
ψ_1	Annual cost per full-time teacher at the primary and preprimary level	493
ψ_2	Annual cost per full-time teacher at the middle level	1,420
α_1	Current costs per preprimary student (without teaching salaries)	181
α_{21}	Current costs per primary student (without teaching salaries)	91
α_{22}	Current costs per student of the first middle cycle (without teaching salaries)	760
α_{23}	Current costs per student of the second middle cycle (without teaching salaries)	1,366
α_{24}	Average costs per university student (1st to 4th year); including salaries	8,668
α_{25}	Average cost per 5th year university student; including salaries	9,000
α_{26}	Average cost per 6th year university student; including salaries	10,000
δ_1	Square meter cost of construction in the primary level	580
δ_2	Square meter cost of construction in the middle level	850
δ_3	Square meter cost of construction in the upper level	1,250
σ	Cost of entering students at the primary level	200
β_1	Cost of remedial work, primary	100
β_2	Cost of remedial work, first middle cycle	800
β_3	Cost of remedial work, second middle cycle	1,400
β_4	Cost of remedial work in the 1st to 4th year of the university	9,000
β_5	Cost of remedial work in the 5th year of the university	10,000
β_6	Cost of remedial work in the 6th year of the university	15,000
γ_1	Social cost of failure to enter at the proper time	26
γ_2	Social cost of premature dropout	26
ε_1	Cost of formation in the work of the first level	30,000
ε_2	Cost of formation in the work of the second level	20,000
ε_3	Cost of formation in the work of the third level	60,000
ε_4	Cost of formation in the work of the fourth level	20,000
ε_5	Cost of formation in the work of the fifth level	10,000
π	Cost of special variables	100,000

be corrected by increasing the number of trials in the Markovian model mentioned above.

The fit for the general secondary school is less good. In the lower cycle, differences do not exceed 10 percent, except for five cases concentrated in the years 1963 and 1964. In the higher cycle, in contrast, in several cases differences of 20 percent are reached, including some major ones in the last grade for several years. The great loss of students which occurs along the way until the middle level is reached means that one works with figures which can vary rapidly from year to

TABLE 3
VALUES OF THE LIMITS OF THE RESTRICTIONS IN EACH YEAR

	Budget Available		Manpower Requirements (thousands) by Years						Number of 7-year-old Children (thousands)
Year t	Current Budget C	Capital Budget K	7 to 9 Years W_2	10 to 12 Years W_3	13 and 14 Years W_4	15 and 16 Years W_5	17 Years W_6	18 Years and Over W_7	P
1970	10,700	1,300	200.0	75.0	17.0	4.0	6.0	3.0	1,537
1971	11,450	1,390	210.0	90.0	18.0	4.7	7.1	3.5	1,583
1972	12,250	1,487	248.0	97.0	21.0	12.0	8.4	4.1	1,631
1973	13,108	1,591	293.0	105.0	25.0	16.0	9.9	4.8	1,680
1974	14,025	1,702	346.0	113.0	30.0	20.0	11.7	5.7	1,730
1975	15,006	1,821	408.0	122.0	35.0	24.0	13.8	6.7	1,782
1976	16,056	1,948	481.0	132.0	41.0	28.0	16.3	7.9	1,835
1977	17,180	2,084	568.0	142.0	48.0	32.0	19.2	9.3	1,891
1978	18,382	2,230	670.0	153.0	65.0	36.0	22.7	11.0	1,947
1979	19,669	2,386	790.0	165.0	66.0	44.0	26.8	13.0	2,006

TABLE 4
RATES OF PROMOTION BY LEVEL IN EACH YEAR

	Rates of Promotion by Level																
Year	1	2	3	4	5	6	7	8	9	10	11	12	13	14	15	16	17
1970	.58	.66	.65	.64	.62	.55	.56	.60	.51	.62	.52	.66	.35	.48	.385	.365	.165
1971	.59	.68	.65	.64	.63	.56	.57	.61	.51	.62	.63	.65	.37	.49	.39	.39	.20
1972	.61	.69	.66	.67	.63	.57	.57	.61	.51	.63	.52	.65	.39	.50	.42	.40	.22
1973	.62	.70	.67	.68	.64	.58	.58	.62	.52	.64	.54	.66	.40	.51	.43	.41	.23
1974	.64	.71	.67	.65	.64	.59	.58	.63	.52	.64	.55	.67	.41	.52	.44	.42	.25
1975	.65	.72	.67	.65	.65	.60	.59	.64	.53	.65	.56	.69	.42	.53	.45	.43	.27
1976	.66	.72	.67	.66	.65	.61	.60	.64	.54	.66	.56	.70	.43	.54	.46	.44	.28
1977	.67	.73	.68	.66	.65	.62	.60	.65	.55	.67	.57	.71	.44	.54	.47	.45	.30
1978	.68	.74	.68	.67	.66	.64	.61	.66	.55	.68	.58	.73	.46	.55	.48	.46	.32
1979	.70	.74	.68	.67	.66	.64	.62	.67	.56	.69	.59	.74	.47	.56	.50	.47	.33

TABLE 5

RATES OF REPETITION BY LEVEL IN EACH YEAR

Rates of Repetition by Level

Year	1	2	3	4	5	6	7	8	9	10	11	12	13	14	15	16	17	18
1970	.38	.25	.25	.25	.28	.30	.24	.23	.26	.23	.23	.24	.45	.42	.55	.60	.585	.05
1971	.37	.24	.26	.26	.28	.30	.23	.24	.25	.22	.24	.22	.43	.41	.51	.56	.54	.05
1972	.37	.24	.26	.25	.28	.30	.23	.24	.26	.22	.23	.22	.42	.40	.49	.54	.52	.05
1973	.34	.23	.26	.25	.28	.30	.23	.24	.25	.21	.21	.21	.41	.39	.47	.52	.49	.05
1974	.33	.23	.25	.25	.28	.28	.28	.22	.24	.20	.20	.20	.40	.39	.45	.50	.48	.05
1975	.32	.22	.25	.24	.27	.28	.22	.22	.23	.19	.19	.18	.39	.38	.43	.48	.45	.05
1976	.31	.22	.26	.25	.27	.27	.21	.20	.23	.18	.18	.17	.38	.37	.41	.46	.43	.05
1977	.30	.21	.25	.24	.27	.27	.21	.19	.22	.17	.18	.16	.37	.36	.39	.44	.41	.05
1978	.29	.20	.24	.24	.26	.26	.20	.18	.21	.16	.17	.15	.36	.36	.37	.42	.39	.05
1979	.27	.20	.24	.24	.26	.26	.19	.17	.20	.16	.15	.14	.35	.35	.35	.40	.37	.05

TABLE 6

DROPOUT RATES BY LEVEL IN EACH YEAR

Dropout Rates by Level

Year	1	2	3	4	5	6	7	8	9	10	11	12	13	14	15	16	17	18
1970	.04	.09	.10	.11	.10	.15	.20	.17	.23	.15	.26	.10	.20	.10	.065	.035	.25	.95
1971	.04	.08	.09	.11	.09	.14	.20	.15	.24	.16	.23	.13	.20	.10	.08	.05	.26	.95
1972	.02	.07	.08	.08	.09	.13	.20	.15	.23	.15	.25	.13	.19	.10	.09	.06	.26	.95
1973	.04	.07	.07	.07	.08	.12	.19	.14	.23	.15	.25	.13	.19	.10	.10	.07	.28	.95
1974	.03	.06	.07	.10	.08	.13	.20	.15	.24	.16	.25	.13	.19	.09	.11	.08	.27	.95
1975	.03	.06	.08	.11	.08	.12	.19	.14	.24	.16	.25	.13	.19	.09	.12	.09	.28	.95
1976	.03	.06	.07	.10	.08	.12	.19	.16	.23	.16	.26	.13	.19	.09	.13	.10	.29	.95
1977	.03	.06	.07	.10	.09	.11	.19	.16	.23	.16	.25	.13	.19	.10	.14	.11	.29	.95
1978	.03	.06	.08	.09	.08	.10	.19	.16	.24	.16	.25	.12	.18	.09	.15	.12	.29	.95
1979	.03	.06	.08	.09	.08	.10	.19	.16	.24	.15	.26	.12	.18	.09	.15	.13	.30	.95

TABLE 7
ESTIMATES OF ENROLLMENT BY COURSE FOR THE PERIOD 1962–1968

Grade	1962			1963			1964		
	Estimated	Actual	% Error	Estimated	Actual	% Error	Estimated	Actual	% Error
Primary:									
First	2,272.5	2,272.5	0.0	2,333.9	2,360.0	1.2	2,377.3	2,416.9	1.6
Second	1,282.3	1,282.5	0.0	1,361.5	1,361.0	0.0	1,458.1	1,453.6	0.4
Third	970.2	868.6	0.1	1,025.5	1,043.5	1.8	1,105.9	1,098.2	0.7
Fourth	678.0	678.4	0.0	746.9	751.4	0.6	803.8	810.4	0.8
Fifth	504.0	508.2	0.8	565.7	576.5	1.9	614.1	627.4	2.1
Sixth	401.0	401.0	0.0	423.0	448.9	5.7	509.0	495.4	2.8
Secondary:									
First	168.7	167.8	0.0	203.4	182.5	11.5	201.6	199.3	1.1
Second	122.0	122.1	0.0	147.5	132.8	11.2	177.1	150.1	18.1
Third	90.7	91.4	0.8	109.8	103.3	6.2	131.9	118.0	11.8
Fourth	49.5	48.8	1.4	59.0	63.0	6.4	72.1	77.1	4.0
Fifth	36.9	37.2	0.8	37.5	50.0	25.0	44.4	49.6	1.1
Sixth	6.5	4.5	44.7	9.6	10.5	8.6	13.6	12.7	7.1
University:									
First	111.8	110.0	1.6	127.8	115.7	10.5	125.8	127.4	12.5
Second	68.1	60.5	12.5	73.3	61.6	18.9	80.7	70.9	13.8
Third	37.9	37.9	0.0	45.1	43.8	2.9	48.2	45.3	6.6
Fourth	20.8	15.6	32.4	22.9	17.9	27.8	25.8	19.5	32.3
Fifth	9.7	8.6	12.8	13.5	11.1	21.6	14.6	11.2	30.2
Sixth	5.3	2.8	88.5	5.8	3.0	93.1	6.4	2.8	–

TABLE 7 (continued)

Grade	1965			1966			1967		
	Estimated	Actual	% Error	Estimated	Actual	% Error	Estimated	Actual	% Error
Primary:									
First	2,393.4	2,399.3	0.3	2,455.2	2,521.9	2.6	2,486.9	2,542.3	1.3
Second	1,558.2	1,536.8	1.4	1,588.0	1,615.1	1.7	1,686.2	1,715.0	1.9
Third	1,191.2	1,166.9	2.1	1,308.2	1,276.4	2.5	1,365.4	1,374.4	0.6
Fourth	891.4	873.5	2.1	961.5	959.8	0.2	1,064.9	1,050.4	1.4
Fifth	683.6	683.2	0.1	794.2	747.8	6.3	833.1	818.6	1.8
Sixth	541.1	551.1	1.8	595.7	602.7	1.2	677.5	658.7	2.8
Secondary:									
First	233.7	231.0	1.2	249.3	253.4	1.6	271.8	269.9	0.7
Second	180.7	171.7	5.2	199.7	195.5	2.2	211.7	208.2	1.7
Third	157.1	138.8	13.2	164.2	154.3	6.4	178.1	170.0	4.8
Fourth	87.9	80.2	9.6	106.4	87.6	21.5	115.9	97.9	18.4
Fifth	54.8	64.1	14.5	67.8	66.2	2.4	83.6	74.3	12.5
Sixth	20.1	22.5	10.6	27.2	31.1	12.5	39.8	30.6	30.0
University:									
First	140.6	152.4	7.7	146.0	151.2	3.4	154.5	49.2	—
Second	78.9	84.7	6.8	83.4	85.1	2.0	84.2	30.0	—
Third	51.4	47.9	7.3	49.2	52.0	5.4	49.5	16.7	—
Fourth	26.5	21.4	23.9	26.1	22.7	14.9	23.8	2.5	—
Fifth	15.6	12.5	24.8	15.0	11.8	27.2	14.0	0.8	—
Sixth	5.4	2.4	—	3.9	2.5	—	3.6	0.1	—

TABLE 7 (concluded)

Grade	Estimated	1968 Actual	% Error
Primary:			
First	2,464.8	2,530.4	3.0
Second	1,811.0	1,738.4	4.2
Third	1,480.8	1,438.5	2.9
Fourth	1,140.1	1,122.0	1.6
Fifth	914.8	886.8	3.2
Sixth	715.6	713.3	0.3
Secondary:			
First	302.3	278.9	8.7
Second	224.9	225.7	0.3
Third	188.7	185.8	1.6
Fourth	127.6	108.1	14.4
Fifth	94.2	87.7	7.1
Sixth	57.6	39.0	48.8
University:			
First	168.7	158.5	6.4
Second	85.1	91.1	6.8
Third	49.1	79.0	38.1
Fourth	22.1	30.2	26.6
Fifth	12.1	3.0	–
Sixth	3.3	3.0	–

NOTE: The percentage of error is equal to the quotient $\frac{\text{Estimated}}{\text{Actual}}$.

SOURCE: The estimated figures are computed from the model (see text). The actual figures have been estimated by the Center for Educational Studies.

year. This partially explains the deficiencies of the fit. One should remember, at the same time, that the middle-level rates were not fitted through the simulation model, since at this stage all attention had to be given to the primary level. Analysis of the differences leads to the conclusion that it would be possible to improve the fit in the middle level of the educational system substantially by a certain number of additional trials in the model.

The situation for technical education is similar to that of the general secondary system. It can be observed, in this case, that the figures for 1967 reflect a failure in the statistical information, since an abrupt decline in enrollment of all courses is produced. As in the previous case, a part of the remaining discrepancies could be eliminated by means of simulation of new sets of rates.

In all cases, however, it can be asserted that the observed margins of error in the various transition rates are narrow. They would involve an increase or decrease of less than 5 percent in each of these rates. This, in turn, makes it possible to determine that a large underestimation exists in the repetition rates calculated on the basis of the available continuous statistics on repeaters. Although the repetition rate for the first year in 1965 is reduced to 35 percent, it is still considerably greater than the figure of 21.1 percent which appears in the continuous statistics. However, some evidence exists that repetition would be higher than 40 percent.

In any case, the objective of the model was to provide not accurate forecasts, but a tool for thinking of as many secondary effects as possible. The model is not solved in order to get *the* solution to be implemented, but to obtain families of solutions (sensitivity analysis) according to alternative sets of assumed policies.

When the model is used, for example, to study the possible effects of eliminating actual repetition of 40 percent of the first-grade enrollments, all the structure of the system must be changed. It follows that most of the historical relations are distorted. It makes no sense, therefore, to attempt a more detailed validation of the model.

9. Usefulness of the Model

As has been pointed out earlier, only the first stage of work has been completed. The model has been computed for different periods and its satisfactory functioning has been verified. It has been possible to confirm that in using the model for more than six periods, computation time tends to increase excessively, reaching close to one hour for each solution. In the future, it would probably be useful to reduce the size of the model.

For the time being, use of the model to represent the effects of the various alternative policies is not intended, since first the quality of certain estimates will have to be improved, especially those which refer to demand for manpower with different grades of qualification. It is known that work is being done along this line. It is probable that the data will soon be available to permit proper use of the model. The tabulation and analysis of the population census carried out in 1970 could, for example, clarify some important data, such as the values of the transition rates.

In the results of preliminary versions, it can, nonetheless, be pointed out that given the high rates of repetition, the model tends to include in the solution the activities of on-the-job training and of technological improvements. These activities represent alternatives to the regular system that have considerably higher annual costs per student than the regular system. The remedial classes cost almost three times as much as the regular ones, and four times more than the regular classes of preprimary school. Nevertheless, when computing the relative efficiency of the activities in terms of graduates, remedial classes are preferred. These results show the necessity of revising the data used and, should they be adequate, the desirability of modifying actual teaching practices.

Another indirect result of this first stage of the program lies in pointing out the need of concentrating efforts in collecting and analyzing a fairly limited number of statistics that would appear to be key ones in the decision-making process in the Mexican educational system. This concentration of effort should permit us to count very shortly on having the necessary information.

Once the revised version of the parameters is available, it would be desirable to use a model with five annual periods plus a terminal period of five years in order to reduce computer time and to keep a ten-year time horizon. This solution would maintain the ability to study the long-term effects of decisions that affect the system's day-by-day operation.

Using the model to show the repercussions of various policies on the variables included, it will be possible to construct transformation curves among different "products" of education, or to calculate constant cost curves among the various activities which generate these products.

Mention is always made of the desirability of considering secondary effects in evaluating educational projects, but actual computation is not frequently done. The frame of the model, nonetheless, permits computation of the reduction in costs which would be gained in the future because of the improved technology generated by the investment of the plan. The present value of the planned solution can be compared with the actual costs. The difference in the cost of using traditional techniques permits the calculation of an implicit discount rate which can be compared with the corresponding rates of other alternative projects.

Each time that results are found which have positive or negative characteristics of special interest, it will be possible to create work groups commissioned to study the problem in depth. The members of the group would have at their disposal, as a starting point for their work, the set of interrelationships that generated the model's results and that call for special attention. Their critical analysis would permit an in-depth study, at times with a creative approach, of the problems facing the system.

It should be remembered, in concluding this section, that the work already done confirms that "models cannot replace the executive or planner." The model does not constitute a sufficient basis (although it is a necessary one) for making decisions. Its main utility lies in checking intuitions, confirming the consistency of the assumptions, inspiring new solutions by computing unforeseen results and, quite importantly, in forcing explicit definitions of the essential elements that influence the decision. The model cannot be used mechanically. The solutions of the model can only be interpreted in light of a thorough understanding of the total situation into which the particular aspect being examined with the help of the model is being inserted.

It should be pointed out that the proposed model has certain features which differentiate it from previous models. It includes alternative methods of giving education, that is, various educational technologies; and it offers the possibility of assigning social costs for students not covered by the system, as well as for students who drop out prematurely. As in previous models, this one can consider the relations between regular education and on-the-job training, and the minimum levels of education subjectively desirable; and it can provide indications, through shadow prices, of the critical points which reduce the efficiency of the system.

10. CONCLUSIONS

The construction of models makes it possible to obtain results both in the design stage and in the utilization of the model as a manipulable representation of reality. Although some partial conclusions have been described in the previous sections, it is worthwhile to present here a general conclusion.

In designing a model of the Mexican educational system, it was possible to discover inconsistencies. The major problem appeared in the magnitude calculated for repetition rates, compared with the continuous statistics. It is mentioned in several available studies that the repetition in the first grade of Mexican primary school would be approximately 30 percent; but when this rate was used in the model, results were obtained which differed appreciably from reality. Later, the conclusion was reached that the repetition rate is greater than 40 percent. This result leads to the suggestion of the advisability of carefully revising educational policy, since it means that the attendance of at least one-million Mexican children is wasted in the first grade of primary school alone, with a loss of more than five hundred million pesos.

Testing the functioning of the model made it possible to concentrate efforts on collecting a relatively reduced set of statistical data. It would be possible to emphasize, on this ground, the statistics which facilitate the rationality of decisions, rather than those giving global orientations of the system.

In order to overcome traditional excuses of lack of statistics on the qualitative aspects of the educational system, recourse was had to the subjective judgement of experts. For this reason very simple versions of the Delphi Method were used. This procedure can also be considerably refined in the future in order to examine the possible effects of policies which would involve fairly large innovations in the functioning of the system.

The computations of the model showed that feasible solutions were obtained under the restrictions specified. No comments have been made about the numerical results, since the results of the studies of manpower now in progress still have to be incorporated into the model. At this time, it may be mentioned only that alternative activities to the system of regular education are included in the solution. As the inclusion of these activities in the solution involves a considerable cost per student, it is inferred that the regular system operates at an extremely low efficiency level (small percentage of graduates).

It is imperative to allocate resources, in the initial periods, to increasing the efficiency with which the system operates. There would not be any educational policy that would have greater importance than reducing the repetition in the first grades of the system. It is evident that if one out of every two children repeats the first grade, these children will be taking up space in the first grade in the following year, instead of having progressed a grade in their studies.

As in other models of equal size and complexity, it is possible to ascertain that the executive cannot foresee all the secondary effects of his decisions. In this sense a model such as the one described in this paper permits the person who sets the policy of the educational system to have systematic assistance in evaluating the possible effects of his decisions. The model cannot replace the executive in charge of the system, but it appears to be a necessary tool to improve the rationality of the system.

The time for running this type of model is fairly large and its initial conclusions must be considered more as suggestions for verification than for their value in themselves. The conference represents an excellent opportunity to confront the present formulation with the ideas of the other participants.

APPENDIX A: DEFINITIONS OF THE VARIABLES USED IN PERIOD t

The following variables are defined in the order in which they appear in the equations.

p Column vector (2×1) of the activity levels p_j. Each activity level represents the number of children attending in the jth preprimary level.

x Column vector (18×1) of activity levels x_j. Each activity level represents the number of students at level j of the regular educational system (primary, secondary, and university).

$\bar{y}$ Column vector (4×1) of activity levels $\bar{y}_j$. Each activity level represents the number of students promoted to the jth educational level (in excess of historal trends) thanks to a preparatory course for entering the first year of primary school. The activity level of these variables shows the increase, with respect to the number of students who are usually promoted to grade j, necessary to match the set of restrictions, that can be attained with minimum cost.

y Column vector (18×1) of activity levels y_j. Each activity level represents the number of students promoted to level j (in excess of the historical tendencies of promotion) thanks to remedial attention to their learning problems.

r Total number of children who cannot enter the first grade of the educational system in the period in which they become seven years old.

q Total number of students who drop out from the first three levels of the system due to deficiencies in the quality of the education that they receive, or because their family forces them to work.

v Column vector (3×1) of activity levels v_j. Each activity level represents the number of m^2 built in period t for the jth educational level.

$\bar{u}$ Column vector (2×1) of activity levels u_j. Each activity level represents the additional number of teachers that have to be trained (in the regular system or on-the-job) to satisfy the requirements of the jth educational level.

w Column vector (5×1) of activity levels w_j. Each activity level represents the number of workers, trained on-the-job (including teachers trained on-the-job), with the jth quality level.

z Column vector (10×1) of activity levels z_j. Each activity level represents an overflow variable that, because of the high cost assigned to it in the objective function, only enters the solution when a feasible solution cannot be obtained in another manner.

s Total number of children who enter the educational system in the period that they have their seventh birthday.

In addition to the variables that are defined in each period t, the following variable is used as a result of the objective function which simultaneously considers the total amount of time included in the model.

c The present value (discounting to the year one) of the operational expenses (of all levels) of the educational system, during t periods, necessary to satisfy all restrictions that are described in the text. The expenses include current expenses as well as those of the investments necessary to enlarge the system's capacity to match the restrictions specified.

APPENDIX B: DEFINITION OF THE COEFFICIENTS USED

α_1 Row vector (1×2) of coefficients α_{1j}. Each coefficient represents the current annual costs per student in the jth preprimary level.

α_2 Row vector (1×18) of coefficient α_{2j}. Each coefficient represents the current annual costs per student in the jth level of the regular educational system.

σ Row vector (1×4) of coefficients σ_j. Each coefficient represents the annual monetary costs per student (promoted in excess of the historical trend) of the jth educational level. This vector reflects the cost of anticipatory attention to those students who would have problems in entering the first grade of primary schools without previous training.

β Row vector (1×10) of coefficients β_j. Each coefficient represents the annual current cost of avoiding the repetition of a pupil in level j by having him attend remedial courses. It reflects the cost of introducing better technologies in the system in order to improve the promotion rates of the corresponding level.

γ_1 Social cost for each student who cannot be accepted by the school system when he reaches the normal age for entry. Initially, it is estimated at a very reduced value. It is included in the model with the aim of being able to represent in the future the effects of assigning various values to this parameter.

γ_2 Social cost per student who drops out unnecessarily during the first years of the system. Initially, a very reduced value is assigned to it. It is included to study, in the future, the effects of changes in the value of this parameter.

δ Row vector (1×3) of the coefficients δ_j. Each coefficient represents construction costs per m^2 in the jth educational level.

ψ Row vector (1×2) of the coefficients ψ_j. Each coefficient represents the annual costs for a teacher who works in the jth level.

ε Row vector (1×5) of the coefficients ε_j. Each coefficient represents the annual costs per worker who has been trained on-the-job for the jth level.

π Row vector (1×10) of the coefficients π_j. Each coefficient corresponds to a fairly high number, in order to avoid, if possible, having the corresponding variable remain in the solution.

Z Diagonal matrix (18×18) of the dropout rates ζ_{1j} of the jth level of the educational system.

H Diagonal matrix (18×8) of the coefficients η_j. Each coefficient represents the maximum increase in the number of promotions from the jth educational level (educated guess).

Λ Matrix $(n \times n)$, with ones in the diagonal above the main one and zeros in the remaining elements. The product of this matrix and a column vector is a vector, element j being the element $j + 1$ of the multiplied vector. The last element of the new vector is zero.

λ_η Column vector $(n \times 1)$ each of whose elements is 1.

M Diagonal matrix (18×18) of the coefficients μ_j. Each coefficient represents the proportion of the total number of students who drop out from the jth educational level and who join the labor force.

ρ Row vector (1×18) of the coefficients ρ_j. Each coefficient represents the minimum percentage of the enrollment of the preprimary school level who have to remain in that level for two years.

Φ Diagonal matrix (18×18) of coefficients ϕ_{1j}. Each coefficient represents the number of teachers per student in the jth educational level. Each coefficient is defined as the reciprocal of the student-teacher relation.

θ Diagonal matrix (18×18) of coefficients θ_{2j}. Each coefficient represents the number of m^2 per student in the jth educational level.

Ω Matrix (18×18) of transition rates. The elements ω_{ij} of the matrix correspond to the transition rates at the jth level. The elements $\omega_{j+1,j}$ correspond to promotion rates from the jth level to the level $j + 1$. The dropout rates remain included in the matrix M.

I Row vector (1×3) of coefficients i_j. Each coefficient represents the annual depreciation rate on buildings.

APPENDIX C: DEFINITION OF THE AVAILABLE RESOURCES AND OF THE LIMITS

$\bar{C}$ Maximum budget available for year t.

K Maximum capital budget available for year t.

P Number of children (population) aged seven in the period.

$\bar{U}$ Column vector (2×1) of coefficient $\bar{u}_j$. Each coefficient represents the number of teachers who teach in the jth educational level at the beginning of the initial period.

$\bar{V}$ Column vector (3×1) of coefficients $\bar{v}_j$. Each coefficient represents the number of m^2 available at the beginning of the initial period for the jth educational level.

W Column vector (7×1) of coefficients w_j. Each coefficient represents the number of workers (including teachers) required in the jth educational level in the period.

$\hat{W}$ Column vector (5×1) of coefficients $\hat{w}_j$. Each coefficient represents the minimum number of workers that have to be trained on the job in the period in order to maintain an activity level which permits expanding the operations up to the superior (maximum) range of the following period (educated guess).

APPENDIX D: DEFINITIONS OF EQUATIONS AND INEQUALITIES

(1) $$\text{Min}: C = \sum_t \alpha_1 p + \alpha_2 x + \sigma \bar{y} + \beta y + \gamma_1 r + \gamma_2 q + \delta v + \psi u + \varepsilon w + \pi z$$

(2) $$\alpha x_t + \beta y_t + \beta y_{t-1} + \beta y_{t-2} + \psi u_t + \varepsilon w_t - z_t \leq \bar{C}_t$$

(3) $$\delta v_t \leq K_t$$

(4) $$\Omega_{t-1} \chi_{t-1} + s_{t-1} + \bar{y}_{t-1} - \Lambda \bar{y}_{t-1} + y_{t-1} = x_t$$

(5) $$p_t = \bar{y}_t + \bar{y}_{t+1} + \bar{y}_{t+2} + \bar{y}_{t+3}$$

(6) $$\bar{y}_t + y_t \leq H_t x_{t-1}$$

(7) $$M_t Z_t x_t - \bar{y}_t - y_t - w_t - \Lambda w_t - h + \Lambda h + \bar{u}_t - \Lambda \bar{u}_t + z_t \geq \bar{w}$$

(8) $$\Phi_1 x_t + \Phi_1' y_t = u_t$$

(9) $$\bar{u}_t + \Upsilon u_{t-1} = u_t$$

(10) $$\theta x_t + \theta' y_t - v_t - i V_{t-1} = \bar{V}$$

(11) $$v_t + i V_{t-1} = V_t$$

(12) $$x_{1,t-1} + x_{2,t-1} \leq \rho x_{1,t}$$

(13) $$x_t + z_t \geq x_{t-1}$$

(14) $$x \geq \bar{P}$$

(15) $$s + r \geq P$$

(16) $$Z_t x_t - q_t \leq 0$$

(17) $$s_t \leq s_{t+1}$$

(18) $$w - z \leq \hat{w}$$

INTERNATIONAL TRADE PRICES AND PRICE PROXIES

IRVING B. KRAVIS

University of Pennsylvania and National Bureau of Economic Research

AND

ROBERT E. LIPSEY

Queens College and National Bureau of Economic Research

THE PRICE VARIABLE IN THE ANALYSIS OF TRADE FLOWS

Since Tinbergen's pioneering article on the measurement of elasticities of substitution in international trade of a quarter century ago,[1] there have been many studies designed to measure the relationship between changes in relative prices and changes in relative exports. It is in keeping with the spirit of these inquiries to observe that the increase in their quantity is attributable to changed supply and demand conditions. The demand for knowledge of price-quantity relationships in international trade has increased with the growing interdependence of nations, especially since governments often wish to influence trade flows for balance of payments or other reasons. The supply curve for such studies has also shifted outward, mainly as a result of the advent of the computer. A multiple correlation involving three or four independent variables required a substantial investment of man-hours when Tinbergen's article first appeared. Today, once the data are in hand, a computer can, in a few seconds, produce many equations, each involving different combination of the independent variables.

We are still, however, a long way from being able to assess in a quantitative fashion the influence of price and the other determinants of trade flows. The problems that confront us are, in part, a lack of understanding of the identity of all of these factors and of the relationships among the factors that we have been able to identify. There are also problems posed by the lack of appropriate data on prices and on other influences on trade.

Virtually all of the analytical work on international trade using prices as an explanatory variable has been based on unit value or wholesale price data, rather than on the actual international transactions prices which would be appropriate to the analysis of trade flows.

Both wholesale prices and the export unit-value indexes have at times given seriously misleading impressions of relative price movements in comparisons between U.S. and foreign price changes. Indexes of each type, as prepared by different countries, cover different commodities and are calculated by different methods. As a result, when either type of index for one country is compared with the corresponding index for another country, an apparent relative-price movement might be only a consequence of differences in the weighting of identical price movements. Furthermore, the unit-value indexes, including those published by the U.S. Department of Commerce, can change when the composition of exports or imports shifts, even though all prices remain the same. Wholesale prices avoid

---

[1] Jan Tinbergen, "Some Measurements of Elasticities of Substitution," *The Review of Economic Statistics* (August 1946).

this defect but include many list prices which may not reflect even domestic transactions prices and, being domestic prices, may not reflect fluctuations of prices in international markets. Changes in transportation costs, in the nature and extent of government intervention, and in other aspects of market imperfections, make it possible for the spreads between home and export prices to change.

In a recently published National Bureau of Economic Research study, the authors offered price indexes specifically designed for use in the analysis of international trade.[2] The new indexes are based on actual transactions prices or offers, not list prices or unit values, refer to international rather than domestic sales, and are combined using the same commodity weights in each country. Other innovations involve shifting the job of selecting commodities to be priced from the collecting agency to the reporter, the use of multiple regression methods to measure the prices of complex products such as aircraft engines and ships (many of which are usually omitted from price indexes), and the calculation of relative price levels as well as relative price changes.

The main purpose of the National Bureau study was to demonstrate that a wealth of data on actual international-trade price movements and price levels in private and government files could be collected by a sufficiently intensive effort, and to develop methods for tapping these sources and combining the data into overall measures for commodity groups and for the country as a whole.

The data were used to prepare "indexes of price competitiveness" which measured the changes in relative prices for each pair of countries, usually at the four-digit Standard International Trade Classification (SITC) level,[3] and these were aggregated, using world-trade weights.

Because our resources were limited and our objectives largely methodological, the resulting indexes are not very extensive in their coverage. They refer to five periods within the years 1953–1964 (1957/53, 1961/57, 1962/61, 1963/62, and 1964/63) and cover trade in machinery, transport equipment, metals, and metal products. Indexes were calculated for the United States, the United Kingdom, Germany, and to more limited degrees, for Japan and the Common Market as a whole. The range of products was determined both by their substantive importance in trade (about half the exports of the main industrial countries) and by the variety of competitive situations covered, from pig iron and its nonferrous equivalents to highly differentiated, technologically sophisticated products.

In addition to these indexes, it should be mentioned that Germany and Japan produce official export price indexes, which are more appropriate than wholesale prices and unit values for use in the analysis of international trade, although a close examination of the individual series in these indexes raises some puzzling questions—particularly with respect to the Japanese indexes.

[2] Irving B. Kravis and Robert E. Lipsey, *Price Competitiveness in World Trade*, New York, NBER, 1971.

[3] The index of price competitiveness is $[(P_t/P_{t-1})_F]/(P_t/P_{t-1})_U \times 100$ where P refers to prices, t to a time period, F to a foreign country and U to the U.S. It was usually formed by dividing the time-to-time price change for the foreign country by that of the U.S., but in some categories it was derived from the change in the place-to-place price comparison—i.e., $[(P_F/P_U)_t]/(P_F/P_U)_{t-1}$. The latter method was employed particularly for custom-made goods, for which place-to-place price comparisons could be obtained from bid data, while time-to-time data for any given country were difficult to obtain.

In the present paper we examine, more closely than we were able to do before, the relationship between changes in international prices on the one hand and changes in wholesale prices and export unit values on the other. Secondly, we compare the results of using international price indexes in the analysis of trade flows with those obtained from using indexes based purely on wholesale price data. For this purpose, we interpolated and extrapolated the National Bureau indexes for Germany and the U.S. covering five intervals within the 1953–1964 period, so as to convert them into annual data for the period 1953–1968.

THE RELATION OF INTERNATIONAL PRICE CHANGES TO CHANGES IN WHOLESALE PRICES AND EXPORT UNIT VALUES

Because international price data have not been available for most countries, time periods, and commodities, studies of international trade in which prices are required have used various proxy variables, chiefly domestic wholesale prices and export and import unit values. Since we have now accumulated a body of data on international price movements, it is useful to compare our indexes to the widely used proxies in order to estimate the effects of discrepancies between them on the conclusions from past and future work in this area.

It is not obvious how such comparisons should be made. Wholesale price indexes are frequently published in groups which do not match trade classifications, even when they have the same or similar names. Thus, an analyst who uses published data directly is almost always, to some extent, comparing price changes for one group of commodities with quantity changes for another group. A comparison of one of these published domestic price indexes with international price indexes might then only reflect the degree of misclassification of commodities.

Even if classifications are made comparable, wholesale price indexes are aggregated with domestic production or consumption weights. Differences between domestic and international weights, and differences between one country's weights and another's, will enter comparisons with international prices. Differences in the list of specific commodities covered will also lead to discrepancies between the two indexes.

In the volume *Price Competitiveness in World Trade* (Chapter 8), we compared international prices, wholesale prices, and export unit values at the two-digit SITC level. In order to test the influence of differences in weighting, and to insure that we would not be basing our judgments on the effects of weighting differences, we calculated our own indexes for wholesale prices from data for individual commodities, aggregating them using both domestic weights and the same international-trade weights as in our international price indexes. To test the influence of coverage differences, we also calculated indexes for only those products covered in both international and wholesale price indexes.

In brief, the results were that there were substantial differences between domestic wholesale and international price indexes, particularly during periods of rapid price change. Moving from domestic to international weights for wholesale prices usually, but not always, improved the degree of agreement between the two series, but left fairly large differences. Adjusting further for differences in coverage produced some improvements, especially in the case of Germany, but no gain, or even a worsening of the degree of agreement in the case of the United States and of the United Kingdom. Not only were the wholesale price movements different, but in the United States, and especially in the United Kingdom, they were biased upward relative to international prices. The most probable explanation for the discrepancies remaining after these adjustments is that international price movements differed from domestic price movements even on the individual commodity level. Unit values were even worse than wholesale prices as approximations to international prices.

When we used our internationally weighted wholesale price indexes in equations explaining quantity movements at a fairly aggregative level (two-digit SITC), we found that only for the United Kingdom was there a substantial difference between the equations using wholesale prices and those using international prices. When we fitted equations at the more detailed commodity level, however, the international price data performed considerably better, in general, in terms of explanatory power and of the significance of the elasticity coefficients.

Here we explore further the relationship between the detailed wholesale price indexes and the corresponding indexes from international price data. The question is of interest because wholesale price data continue to be the main readily available basis for estimating relative international price movements, and because efforts to improve on the frequently poor price coefficients calculated up to now naturally tend to turn toward disaggregation. The international price indexes we use for this comparison are those published in Appendix C of the *Price Competitiveness* volume, the indexes from wholesale prices are those of Appendix F, and the unit values are those of Appendix G. The four-digit wholesale price indexes are unweighted aggregates of individual series and the three-digit indexes are aggregates of the four-digit indexes with international weights. For purposes of the regressions discussed here all the indexes were put in the form of time-to-time changes, i.e. 1957/53, 1961/57, 1962/61, 1963/62, and 1964/63.

In addition to the calculations based on NBER data, we have performed similar tests using some U.S. export price indexes recently published by the Bureau of Labor Statistics for the period 1964–1970.

Are International and Wholesale Price Changes Alike?

Some idea of the typical discrepancies between the changes in international prices and changes in wholesale prices can be derived from tabulations based on data from the *Price Competitiveness* book. In 30 percent of the possible comparisons between international price changes (P_i) and wholesale price changes (P_w)[4] the difference between the two was greater than $4\frac{1}{2}$ percentage points.

Absolute Value of Difference Between P_i and P_w (percentage points)	Number of Cases	Percent of Cases
$>4\frac{1}{2}$	255	30.8
$1\frac{1}{2}$ to $4\frac{1}{2}$	266	32.2
$<1\frac{1}{2}$	306	37.0
Total	827	100.0

[4] P_i is the percentage change in international prices from one year to the next, and P_w is the percentage change in wholesale prices.

On the whole, when the direction of the price movement was the same in the two sets of data, the wholesale price movement was larger than that of international prices as often as it was smaller. However, the distribution of these differences was strongly related to the direction of price change.

WHOLESALE PRICE CHANGE
[number of cases]

	Same Direction as P_i				Opposite Direction from P_i	Total
	Larger in Absolute Value	Equal	Smaller in Absolute Value	No Change		
P_i positive	166	68	115	69	42	460
P_i negative	26	25	60	39	72	222
Total	192	93	175	108	114	682

When international prices were rising, wholesale prices rose by as much or more in half the cases, but when international prices were falling, the wholesale price changes equaled or exceeded them less than a quarter of the time. There was also greater agreement on direction when international prices were rising. Wholesale prices fell in less than 10 percent of such cases, while they rose in almost a third of the instances in which international prices declined.

Looking at the same data in a different way, if we accept the international price indexes as correct measures of international trade prices, we find that wholesale price changes were biased upward when international prices were unchanged or declining. That is, on the average, wholesale prices rose, or declined by less than international prices. When international prices rose, wholesale prices were biased downward. The upward bias was dominant on the average, however, despite the fact that international price increases were twice as frequent as decreases.

WHOLESALE PRICE CHANGE
[number of cases]

	Biased Upward	Equal	Biased Downward	Total
P_i positive	166	68	226	460
P_i zero	64	50	31	145
P_i negative	137	25	60	222
Total	367	143	317	827

Another way of measuring the similarity between the two price measures is by the correlation between them. Of course, the correlation can be high even when the two price measures are different if there is a systematic relationship between them, but a low correlation is an indication of dissimilarity unless the variance in both measures is low, which is not the case for the prices we are studying.

The results in Table 1 indicate that the correspondence between the two price measures is not close. The $\bar{r}^2$ are almost all below 0.5, whether we compare the two measures for all commodities, years, and countries combined, or for various

TABLE 1

REGRESSION OF INTERNATIONAL PRICE CHANGES AGAINST WHOLESALE PRICE CHANGES
[all commodities, countries, and years; and by country; year; SITC division; and
direction of price changes]

	b_{iw}[1]	t-Value	$\bar{r}^2$	Number of Observations
All commodities, countries, and years	.71	27.07	.47	827
By country				
United States	.69	24.69	.61	394
United Kingdom	.72	10.18	.48	114
Germany	.72	9.52	.30	206
Japan	.75	5.67	.22	113
By year				
1957/53	.55	9.30	.41	125
1961/57	.80	9.96	.42	138
1962/61	.73	8.95	.30	188
1963/62	.83	9.28	.31	188
1964/63	.75	8.92	.30	188
By SITC division (excluding Section 8)				
67 Iron and steel	.76	13.69	.54	162
68 Nonferrous metals	.85	8.22	.53	60
69 Other manufactures of metal	.59	8.03	.33	128
71 Nonelectrical machinery	.74	17.40	.64	170
72 Electrical machinery	.57	5.62	.21	113
73 Transport equipment	.69	7.52	.46	65
By direction of change in p_i				
p_i falling	.42	7.41	.18	254
p_i rising	.60	24.47	.51	573
By direction of change in p_w				
p_w falling	.95	10.18	.31	234
p_w rising	.66	19.96	.40	593

[1] From equation $P_i = a + b_{iw}P_w$, where P_i is the percentage change in international prices from one year to the next, and P_w the percentage change in wholesale prices.

subdivisions of the total—by country, commodity, year, or direction of price change. However, the wholesale price changes are related to international price changes, as we can see by the fact that the t-values for the b_{iw} coefficient are all statistically significant.

Among the comparisons for all commodity groups and periods combined, those for the United States show the strongest relationship; those for the United Kingdom also a fairly strong one; and those for Japan, a poor relationship. Taking all countries combined for individual periods, the $\bar{r}^2$ were all below 0.5.

A more detailed breakdown of the data in Table 2, separating them by country within each commodity division, shows a high correlation for the two U.S. price indexes in three divisions, and fair or poor results in the other three. For other countries, the relationship was much weaker. None of the $\bar{r}^2$ was as high as for some U.S. divisions, and many were quite low.

There is some ground here for saying that wholesale prices were somewhat more closely related to international prices in SITC 67 and SITC 71 than in SITC

TABLE 2
REGRESSION OF INTERNATIONAL PRICE CHANGES AGAINST WHOLESALE PRICE CHANGES
[commodity division by country][1]

SITC	Country	b_{iw}[2]	t-Value	$\bar{r}^2$	Number of Observations
67	United States	0.79	14.72	.79	59
	United Kingdom	0.75	7.60	.54	49
	Germany	0.45	0.99	0	20
	Japan	1.09	5.80	.50	34
68	United States	0.78	12.05	.83	30
	United Kingdom	0.53	1.94	.24	10
	Germany	1.31	4.28	.48	20
69	United States	0.52	6.54	.41	60
	United Kingdom	0.61	3.27	.25	30
	Germany	0.52	2.24	.15	23
	Japan	0.73	1.91	.16	15
71	United States	0.78	17.85	.75	105
	Germany	0.72	9.24	.63	51
	Japan	0.43	0.67	−.04	14
72	United States	0.54	4.64	.28	55
	Germany	0.82	2.54	.21	22
	Japan	0.49	1.67	.06	31
73	United States	0.23	1.35	.04	23
	Germany	0.49	5.11	.43	35

[1] Omitted countries are those with insufficient data.
[2] From equation $P_i = a + b_{iw}P_w$, where P_i is the percentage change in international prices from one year to the next, and P_w the percentage change in wholesale prices.

69 or SITC 72, a judgment similar to that one might derive from Table 1. The reasons for these differences probably vary from group to group. Nonelectrical machinery (SITC 71) showed few reductions in international prices—mostly fairly steady upward trends. Under relatively stable conditions or trends, the two kinds of prices may be expected to move more similarly. Some groups within electrical machinery (SITC 72), on the other hand, were subject to wide price fluctuations, severe international competition, and large discounts from list prices, and it is therefore not surprising that there were wide divergences between the two price measures.

It might be thought that these discrepancies between wholesale and international price measures are only short run in character, resulting from delays in announcing price changes, or in inserting them into the official or other price records. If that were true, they should average out over longer periods, and wholesale price changes should be similar to international price changes over periods of a few years, if not year by year.

This possibility is tested in the calculations shown in Table 3 where results for the three years, 1962/61, 1963/62, and 1964/63, are compared with those for 1964/61, taken as a whole. The results do not show much evidence that discrepancies are averaged out over time to a major degree. The levels of $\bar{r}^2$ increase more often than not as the periods are combined, but remain fairly low. The only really large

TABLE 3
REGRESSION OF INTERNATIONAL PRICE CHANGES AGAINST WHOLESALE PRICE CHANGES
[single years compared with three-year period]

	Single Years: 1962/61, 1963/62, 1964/63				Three-Year Period: 1964/61			
	b_{iw}	t-Value	r^2	Number of Observations	b_{iw}	t-Value	r^2	Number of Observations
All commodities, countries, and years	.80	16.30	.32	564	.82	11.67	.43	183
By country								
United States	.72	14.03	.44	253	.73	7.63	.41	83
United Kingdom	.38	1.81	.03	70	.46	1.87	.11	22
Germany	1.10	8.16	.33	136	.91	4.82	.34	45
Japan	.82	5.78	.24	105	.95	4.15	.34	33
By SITC division (excluding Section 8)								
67	.98	8.01	.36	112	.95	8.09	.65	36
68	.96	6.29	.52	36	.77	3.00	.42	12
69	.49	3.55	.12	84	.82	2.75	.20	27
71	.40	2.72	.05	116	.60	3.06	.18	38
72	.55	3.24	.10	85	.41	1.73	.07	28
73	.55	2.43	.10	44	.56	1.70	.13	14
By direction of change in P_i								
P_i falling	.70	9.22	.30	196	.71	5.95	.34	67
P_i rising	.53	9.52	.20	368	.42	5.28	.19	116
By direction of change in P_w								
P_w falling	.90	8.14	.25	196	.80	4.11	.21	60
P_w rising	.71	9.69	.20	368	.85	7.56	.32	123

improvement in the $\bar{r}^2$ is for SITC 67, in which the $\bar{r}^2$ for the period as a whole becomes 0.65, one of the highest in the whole set of regressions.

On the whole, the data do not support the idea that wholesale price changes are much more similar to international price changes for time spans longer than one year than they are for one-year periods.

Our international price data, and therefore the tests we report on them, are available only through 1964. However, the Bureau of Labor Statistics has begun to publish export price indexes for some types of machinery beginning with 1964, the last year of our data. These data can be used, in the same way as ours, to judge the relationship of wholesale prices to export prices.

These results are no more favorable to the proxy variable than the comparisons with the NBER indexes, as can be seen below. The $\bar{r}^2$ is very low, and the coefficient of b_{iw} is not statistically significant (partly because there are only twenty observations).

TABLE 4
REGRESSION OF U.S. EXPORT PRICE INDEXES (BLS) AGAINST U.S. WHOLESALE PRICE INDEXES[1]

b_{iw}	0.41
t-value	1.51
$\bar{r}^2$	0.06
Number of observations	20

[1] Four groups in SITC 71: 1965/64 through 1970/69.

This regression equation for 1964–1970 (Table 4) is almost identical to that for SITC 71 (the corresponding group) for the years 1961–1964, given in Table 3. The b_{iw} coefficient is 0.41 here, as compared to 0.40, and the $\bar{r}^2$ is 0.06, as compared with 0.05. These results suggest that there is no major discontinuity in the relationship to wholesale prices between the NBER international price indexes and the BLS export price indexes for the United States.

Are Changes in Unit Values and Changes in International Prices Alike?

A similar analysis can be made of data on U.S. export unit values. The results are even more unfavorable to the use of unit values as a proxy variable. As can be seen in Table 5, the $\bar{r}^2$ are all low, and hardly any of the coefficients are statistically significant. By this test, we would have to conclude that export unit-value changes are not only different from international price movements, but are almost totally unrelated to them.

Is the Measure of Price Competitiveness Sensitive to the Nature of the Prices Used?

The extent of errors in price competitiveness resulting from the use of proxy price measures cannot be inferred from the accuracy of a single country's price measures. For one thing, two incorrect price measures could yield a correct relative price measure if the errors in the two were identical in direction and magnitude. We therefore tested price competitiveness measures derived from wholesale price data in the same way that we examined the wholesale price series themselves.

TABLE 5

REGRESSION OF INTERNATIONAL PRICE INDEXES AGAINST INDEXES FROM U.S. EXPORT UNIT VALUES
[all commodities, countries, and years; and by year; SITC division; and direction of price change]

	b_{ie}[1]	t-Value	$\bar{r}^2$	Number of Observations
All commodities, countries, and years	.17	3.60	.06	192
By year				
1957/53	.19	1.56	.05	29*
1961/57	.12	0.69	−.02	34
1962/61	.004	0.03	−.02	43
1963/62	.01	0.09	−.02	43
1964/63	.04	0.65	−.01	43
By SITC division (excluding Section 8)				
67 Iron and steel	.26	3.44	.18	50
68 Nonferrous metals	.13	1.69	.09	20
69 Other manufactures of metal	.18	0.98	−.003	17
71 Nonelectrical machinery	.07	1.29	.02	41
72 Electrical machinery	.10	0.62	−.01	45
73 Transport equipment	.05	0.40	−.10	10
By direction of change in P_i				
P_i falling	.07	0.75	−.01	74
P_i unchanged or rising	.16	4.83	.16	118
By direction of change in P_e				
P_e falling	.02	0.09	−.01	85
P_e unchanged or rising	.16	2.65	.05	107

[1] From equation $P_i = a + b_{ie}P_e$, where P_i is the percentage change in international prices from one year to the next, and P_e the percentage change in export unit values.

Unfortunately we could not study unit-value measures in the same way, because we did not have the detailed data underlying foreign countries' unit-value indexes.

The results of these comparisons, for several groupings of the data, are given in Table 6. The $\bar{r}^2$ are all extremely low, none being above 0.08, but the coefficients relating the two price-competitiveness measures are all statistically significant. However, since the correlations are so low, it might be more sensible to treat the relation between the two competitiveness measures as almost random.

What conclusions can we draw from these comparisons about international trade demand or substitution elasticities estimated from wholesale prices or unit values? Errors in the measurement of prices affect not only the price variable, but also the quantity variable, because quantities are almost always estimated by deflating values by price indexes. Thus, errors in price measures cause equal and opposite errors in the quantity measures with which they are correlated. In the extreme case, where true price and quantity were not correlated at all with each other, or with the errors, the equation relating quantity to price change would essentially be reduced to a regression between the two sets of errors, producing an estimated elasticity of − 1, even though the true price elasticity was 0. A corollary of this conclusion is that estimated elasticity coefficients close to − 1 should not be taken very seriously, because they might easily represent only errors in the data.

TABLE 6
INTERNATIONAL PRICE COMPETITIVENESS CHANGES
[regression of measures derived from international prices against measures derived from wholesale prices; by country]

Coverage	Observations	b_{iw}[1]	t-Value	$\bar{r}^2$
All countries	419	0.29	4.71	.05
United Kingdom/United States	112	0.33	2.21	.03
Germany/United States	198	0.15	2.22	.02
Japan/United States	109	0.47	3.16	.08

[1] The coefficient b_{iw} is estimated from equations of the form $p_i = a + b_{iw}p_w$, where p_i is the percentage change in U.S. price competitiveness relative to a foreign country derived from international prices, and p_w is the corresponding index derived from wholesale prices.

Our comparisons here between proxy variables and international price measures certainly suggest that such errors are frequent.

Aside from random errors of this type, there are further effects of the systematic biases in wholesale price data. An important, and not unexpected, finding of the *Price Competitiveness* volume, in this connection, was that international price movements were more alike among countries than wholesale price changes. In other words, changes in international price competitiveness measures from international price data were smaller than those inferred from wholesale prices. This means that price and substitution elasticities derived from wholesale price data must be underestimated.

Similarly, the apparent upward bias of the wholesale price indexes described earlier must distort measures of elasticity. It presumably leads to exaggeration of the effect of price declines in some cases, and to incorrect signs in others when wholesale price measures move in the wrong direction, as they frequently do when international prices are falling.

ELASTICITIES OF SUBSTITUTION AS MEASURED FROM INTERNATIONAL AND WHOLESALE PRICE DATA

The NBER indexes, as already noted, covered only the years 1953, 1957, and 1961–1964. In order to increase the number of observations available for analysis, we have interpolated the various international price and price competitiveness indexes between 1953 and 1957, and between 1957 and 1961, and have extrapolated them from 1964 to 1968.

The interpolations between 1953 and 1961 produce hybrid indexes in which some part of the year-to-year price change is determined by the 1957/53 and 1961/57 movement of the indexes from international prices, as published in the *Price Competitiveness* book or derived from the same data. The indexes beyond 1964, however, are entirely dependent on the movements of the extrapolating series, and our contribution, aside from the selection of series to match earlier international price changes, is only the reweighting of each country's export or domestic price data by the same set of weights to make the indexes for different countries comparable.

In using the new annual NBER series to compare the utility of international price indexes in the analysis of trade flows with that of wholesale prices, it must be remembered that the comparison is not as sharp as we would like it to be, because the annual NBER international price series is an amalgam of true movements in international prices and of movements in wholesale prices. Also, it should be remembered that the wholesale price indexes that we use in this comparison are indexes that have been reworked in ways described in the *Price Competitiveness* volume[5] so as to make them more appropriate for the analysis of international trade; in this respect, they differ from the kinds of wholesale price data usually used for this purpose. It would be interesting to use our new annual indexes to compare the results they would yield with those obtained in some of the more widely cited studies of trade elasticities, but it is difficult for us to match the temporal and commodity coverage of these studies.

Our approach is to estimate the elasticity of substitution between U.S. and German exports in third-country markets. Our estimate of the elasticity is the coefficient b in an arithmetic relationship between the percentage change in relative quantities from one year to the next and the percentage change in relative prices. The relationship is:

$$(1) \qquad \left(\frac{Q_{G_t}/Q_{G_{t-1}}}{Q_{U_t}/Q_{U_{t-1}}} - 1 \right) = a + b \left(\frac{P_{G_t}/P_{G_{t-1}}}{P_{U_t}/P_{U_{t-1}}} - 1 \right),$$

where the Q's are export quantities to third countries; the P's are international prices; G, Germany; U, the United States; and t a particular time period. In what follows, we will write the bracketed quantity and price variables in (1) simply as q and p.

Export quantities were estimated by dividing trade values by country-weighted price indexes. Thus, there were two sets of German quantities, one corresponding to the German international price index and another to the German wholesale price index; and two sets of U.S. quantities, one corresponding to each of the U.S. indexes. The relative price variable was the index of price competitiveness (also described above), and there were also two versions of this, one based on the extrapolated and interpolated NBER indexes of international prices and the other on wholesale price indexes.

Each of the two sets of price and quantity data for each country could include as many as 90 observations for the 15 year-to-year changes between 1953 and 1968 for each of six SITC divisions included; in fact, the number was 88, since the 1954/53 price change for two of the divisions was missing.

First, we compare the results based on the original NBER international price series covering only five periods, equations (2) and (3), with those derived from the new annual series, equations (4) and (5). When this is done, we find, in Table 7, that the new data produce lower elasticities and somewhat lower $\bar{r}^2$s than the old, particularly a lower $\bar{r}^2$ than the old equation including a variable for time. That large difference in $\bar{r}^2$ is partly artificial, stemming from the fact that the use of some 4-year periods in addition to 1-year periods introduced wide variance in

---

[5] Kravis and Lipsey, *Price Competitiveness*, Chapter 8.

TABLE 7
EQUATIONS RELATING RELATIVE QUANTITY TO RELATIVE PRICE CHANGES
[6 SITC divisions pooled]

Equation Number (NBER data)	Coefficient of p^1	Constant^1	Time^2	Number of Observations	$\bar{r}^2$	S.E.	$\bar{q}$
NBER data:							
Original data							
(5 periods)							
(2)	−9.75	28.15		29	.21	67.69	26.84
	(2.9)	(2.2)					
(3)	−4.55	−37.43	+28.51	29	.60	48.02	26.84
	(1.8)	(2.4)	(5.3)				
Annual series,							
1953–64							
(4)	−2.67	7.54		64	.15	19.46	7.51
	(3.5)	(3.1)					
Annual series,							
1953–68							
(5)	−2.46	6.07		88	.16	17.61	6.81
	(4.2)	(3.2)					
Wholesale price data							
(annual series)							
1953–64							
(6)	−1.39	7.14		64	.07	19.83	7.40
	(2.3)	(2.9)					
1953–68							
(7)	−1.18	5.95		88	.05	17.80	6.48
	(2.5)	(3.1)					

[1] t-ratio in parentheses.
[2] Time variable set equal to 1 for 1-year periods, and to 4 for 4-year periods.

the quantity variable (as can be seen from the average q) which was then "explained" by the time variable.

While we have no means of choosing firmly among these and other explanations, a comparison between the results of equations (4) and (6), or between equations (5) and (7), using annual series for 1953–1964 and 1953–1968, respectively, seems to support the view that true international price indexes produce higher price elasticities and better explanations of quantity changes than do wholesale price data.

In the equations presented thus far, the explanatory power of the price variable taken alone is low, as we would expect both on theoretical grounds (since several important variables are omitted from the equation) and on the basis of our earlier finding that the substitution elasticity is not a constant but is affected by other variables.[6] Attention should be called also to the fact that while the first-difference forms of the variables in our equations produce much lower $\bar{r}^2$s than the more

[6] See Irving B. Kravis and Robert E. Lipsey, "The Elasticity of Substitution as a Variable in World Trade," in *International Comparisons of Prices and Real Incomes*, D. J. Daly, ed., Studies in Income and Wealth, Vol. 37, New York, NBER, 1972.

commonly used index-number forms, they avoid the severe problems of serial correlation that are often encountered.

Of course, the relative form in which the dependent and independent variables are cast (i.e., the percent change in Germany divided by the percent change in the United States for each variable) should obviate the need for some explanatory factors that would otherwise have to be taken into account. For one thing, if we have succeeded in comparing within each category identical or equivalent German and American goods, the income elasticity of demand confronting the exports of the two countries in any market should be identical. A variable reflecting growth of world income should not be significant except to the extent that Germany and the United States sell in markets which differ substantially with respect to the relation of their income growth to world income growth, or with respect to their income elasticity of demand for imports. Also, if the price changes in each country individually were substituted for the relative price change (i.e., Germany to United States), there should be no significant difference between the two individual-country price coefficients, although they should be opposite in sign, again except as differences in markets may affect the relationship.

In the light of these considerations, we have tried including individual-country price variables in our experiments as a check on the validity of our matching of price series. The results with respect to the 1953–1968 National Bureau series confirm our hypothesis about the equality of the coefficients for the individual-country time-to-time price indexes. For example,

$$(8) \qquad\qquad q = 5.30 - 2.10P_G + 2.18P_U,$$
$$ (2.6) \quad (3.6) \qquad (4.0)$$
$$\bar{R}^2 = 0.15$$

where q is the relative change in export quantities, P stands for a country's time-to-time price index, and G and U represent Germany and the United States, respectively. The wholesale series do not meet this test as well. The corresponding equation is:

$$(9) \qquad\qquad q = 4.51 - 1.01P_G + 1.83P_U$$
$$ (2.1) \quad (2.3) \qquad (2.8)$$
$$\bar{R}^2 = 0.07$$

The estimated elasticities are smaller and differ more from each other, and the $\bar{r}^2$ is lower.

Other Price Variables

We also experimented with other price variables and equation forms to allow for the possibility that the full response to a price change did not occur in the same year. Of these, equations using past changes in price did not produce good results and are not shown here.

Another approach to the possible lag in response is to compare price and quantity changes over a longer span than one year. The results, as can be seen from the following summary based on data for 1953–1968, suggest that longer than one year was needed for the full effects of price changes to work themselves out. However, a three-year span produced comparatively poor results. In each case, the equation based on NBER international price data suggested an elasticity more than twice that of the equations based on wholesale prices, and the $\bar{r}^2$, while not high, was also considerably better.

Equation	Length of Period (years)	Number of Observations	Elasticity of Substitution		$\bar{r}^2$	
			NBER	Wholesale Prices	NBER	Wholesale Prices
(10)	1	88	−2.5	−1.2	.16	.06
(11)	2	40	−4.4	−1.7	.20	.09
(12)	3	28	−1.7	−0.6	.09	.00

A very different way of getting at delayed reactions to price changes is to introduce into the equations price levels at the beginning of each period.

The price level variable, in a sense, incorporates all past price changes. If relative price changes always have their full impact upon relative trade flows within the year in which the price changes occur, there should be no relationship between the relative price level at the beginning of the period and trade changes during the period. In a world of perfect competition and instantaneous adjustment with no transfer costs, there could be no international differences in prices; indeed, there could be no international differences in price changes either. With transfer costs, there would be differences in f.a.s. export prices (which are what we measure), since competition would equalize c.i.f. prices at each destination. Even without these transfer costs, observed f.a.s. export prices could differ because of product differentiation—owing to real or reputed differences inherent in the appearance or performance of the product, or to nonprice factors, such as credit terms, speed of delivery, and presales and postsales service.[7] The net effect of all of these factors may be to establish an equilibrium position in which prices differ from one source of supply to another. Such price differences would have no relation to subsequent shifts in trade.

Sometimes, however, price-level differences represent disequilibrium situations in which purchasers, particularly of complex products, such as machinery, take a considerable time to respond to price differences. A number of factors work to cause such lags in response; among them are lack of knowledge, or the cost of obtaining it, uncertainty regarding the reliability of the supplier or the length of time he will remain in the market, reluctance to give up a satisfactory relationship with a supplier, a commitment to one type of machine because of previous purchases or stocks of spare parts, and official or private buy-domestic policies. When these factors are significant, we should be able to observe a shift in trade toward countries with relatively low price levels, quite apart from the impact of current changes in relative prices.

It turns out that when the price-level variable is added to an equation containing a variable for price change, its coefficient is almost always negative and

[7] See Kravis and Lipsey, *Price Competitiveness*, pp. 47–61.

often increases the proportion of the variation in quantity changes that is explained. An example is the equation based on 1953–1968 data shown below, first for the NBER series and then for the wholesale price series, with L representing the foreign price level relative to that of the United States.

(13)
$$q = 3.17 - 2.48p - 0.29L$$
$$(0.9) \quad (4.3) \quad (1.0)$$
$$\bar{R}^2 = 0.16 \qquad S.E. = 17.61$$

(14)
$$q = 2.79 - 1.25p - 0.31L$$
$$(1.0) \quad (2.7) \quad (1.5)$$
$$\bar{R}^2 = 0.07 \qquad S.E. = 17.67$$

The fact that L is not usually statistically significant suggests that it represents, as hypothesized above, a mixture of equilibrium and disequilibrium price-level differences. As in the earlier equations, both the elasticity coefficient and the $\bar{r}^2$ derived from international price data are twice as high as those from wholesale prices.

CONCLUSIONS

The conclusions that can be drawn from these comparisons of international price indexes and wholesale price indexes as alternative sources of the price variable in trade equations are:

1. International price movements are very different from movements in wholesale prices and unit values, and are not even related closely to those of these proxy variables. There is notably less association between unit values and international prices than between wholesale and international prices in the U.S. data which we have examined.

2. International price data produce higher elasticities of substitution than wholesale price data, at least in the case of German-U.S. exports to third countries for 1953–1968 for a limited, though important, range of products. The elasticities produced by the NBER annual data were roughly twice as high as those from the wholesale price data in a number of different formulations. Since the NBER data are themselves partly based on wholesale price data, the difference we find probably underestimates the downward bias in elasticity estimates from wholesale prices.

DATA PREPARATION FOR LATIN AMERICAN COMPARISONS OF CONSUMPTION*

HOWARD HOWE AND ROBERTO VILLAVECES

The Brookings Institution

INTRODUCTION

Effective empirical research depends on reliable data. In sample-survey work, considerable attention has been devoted to the prevention, detection, and correction of errors introduced in the survey process itself. However, there has been little explicit discussion of the problems in accurately transmitting information from the field interviews to forms suitable for statistical treatment. We attempt to focus attention on this question through discussion of data preparation for a major study of Latin American income and expenditure patterns.

The ECIEL[1] household income and expenditure study involves a large-scale body of sample-survey data. The collaborative nature of the study led to decentralized decision making in project design and execution. Computing played a fundamental role not only in the conventional processing of the data, but also in compensating for the organizational complications inherent in joint comparative work.

We establish a framework of technical criteria for the organization of a large-scale study. Project feasibility necessitated relaxation of the technical efficiency criteria at various stages in the project. Foremost among the organizational complications was the awkward position of a U.S. institution coordinating independent Latin American institutes in empirical research. Individual methodological preferences and opportunities for cost shifting contributed inefficiencies. The large size of the project magnified the effect of uncertainty.

We discuss in depth two major aspects of the data preparation: the conversion of national data to a common code for international comparability, and the data cleaning. This preparatory work entailed considerable computing effort. The data base was fully standardized to reduce the marginal cost of future comparative studies. Decentralization of the fieldwork necessitated greater attention to data scrutiny than would be the case with purely national studies.

We conclude with recommendations for efficiency in comparative survey studies and suggestions for improved reporting on current large-scale computing work.

* The ECIEL program is supported by funds from the Ford Foundation, the Interamerican Development Bank, and the Brookings Institution, in addition to local resources provided by the participating institutions.

We wish to thank Ximena Cheetham, Robert Ferber, Joseph Grunwald, Marcia Mason, Arturo Meyer, Philip Musgrove, and Robert Summers for their helpful comments and criticisms of earlier drafts of the paper.

[1] ECIEL is the Spanish acronym for Joint Studies on Latin American Economic Integration. The program is carried out by twenty independent research institutions in Latin America. The thirteen institutes participating in the income and expenditure study are listed in the Appendix. The Brookings Institution acts as coordinator.

ORGANIZATION OF THE STUDY

The data-processing system depended not only upon the research goals of the study, but also upon its organization. Understanding of the institutional context, in turn, requires some familiarity with the ECIEL program.

In 1963, several major economic-research institutions in Latin America joined in a common research program. They committed themselves to collaborate in comparative economic studies on Latin American integration and development, under the coordination of staff members of the Brookings Institution. The program's major objective was the preparation of professionally competent and relevant empirical studies. The strengthening of the economics profession in Latin America has been an important by-product of this cooperative effort.

Since 1963, additional research institutions have joined ECIEL. Twenty institutions from twelve Latin American countries currently participate in the program. The program is coordinated through twice-yearly seminars, attended by the principal researchers concerned with the ECIEL projects. The Coordinator provides methodological, technical, and administrative support. At the seminars, participants select and design studies, develop methodology and procedures, and resolve research and coordination problems. The seminar site rotates among the participating institutions in Latin America. Periodic visits by Brookings coordinating staff, consultants, and technical specialists from the institutes supplement the seminars. The income and expenditure study is one of four ECIEL studies currently under way.

As the foregoing discussion implies, the organization of the income and expenditure study was decentralized. The institutes participated in the research design from the inception of the study. Sample design and questionnaire design were carried out with the assistance of consulting specialists. The institutes assumed responsibility for the control and, in most cases, the implementation, of the field-survey work and data punching. The actual data processing was centralized to insure international comparability of the data. The Brookings Institution provided central processing facilities.

As a framework for discussing the tradeoffs in the data preparation, we cite three organizational criteria for efficient data processing: (1) uniform questionnaire; (2) centralized data processing; and (3) close linkage between the stages of the study. At all stages of the income and expenditure study, technical efficiency had to be balanced against feasibility within the context of the ECIEL program. Each of the criteria had to be relaxed in some measure.

Uniform Questionnaire

A uniform questionnaire facilitates efficient processing. International comparison is best attained by uniform definition of variables and common means of data collection. In the income and expenditure survey, however, country questionnaires differed substantially.

The Coordination provided an outline questionnaire core. Development of the actual questionnaire was carried out by the institutes. Some institutes had built up vested interests in particular approaches. The differences over collection focused on the diary method as opposed to the recall method. Each technique had committed proponents. In addition, the institutes were much more conscious of their unique national characteristics than of the wide range of regional similarities. They felt that the presence, or absence, of certain consumer items in each country necessitated country-specific expenditure categories. In this situation, adoption of a uniform questionnaire could have been accomplished in one of two ways, neither of which is attractive: imposition of a questionnaire by Brookings staff, or the direct supervision of questionnaire preparation in each country. It would have been politically unacceptable to impose a U.S.-designed questionnaire for large-scale application by independent research institutions in Latin America. Sensitivity to the second alternative would also have been high, and, in addition, the on-site supervision would have been prohibitively expensive.

To have insisted upon a common questionnaire at this stage of the study would, in all likelihood, have resulted in several countries dropping out of the study. Hence, in the interest of comprehensive coverage, the institutes were left to interpret individually the core outline and ex post means to attain comparability were adopted. The national data were transformed to a uniform international code. Essentially, commonality was attained by treating the data at a higher level of aggregation than in the questionnaire.

The increased cost due to the conversion step was relatively independent of the extent of the questionnaire differences. The major cost stemmed from simply allowing for the possibility of differences. Specification of the conversions cost more than their execution. Approximately four man-years of effort on the part of the coordinating staff were necessary to specify the variable-by-variable correspondences between each of the eleven questionnaire codes and the uniform international code. Granted the necessity of permitting different questionnaires, it is nevertheless important to recognize the consequent additional costs in time and resources.

Centralized Data Processing

Large economies of scale can be attained with centralized processing. Uniform treatment of the data, desirable in a comparative study and essential when different questionnaires were employed, is assured with centralized processing. Centralized processing also becomes more important if skill levels differ.

The institutes' capabilities for undertaking a study of this magnitude varied widely. Some had extensive experience in sample surveys, while for a few of the younger institutes, the ECIEL survey was a first experience. Capacities for handling a large data base were also disparate. While some institutes lacked facilities even for keypunching, others enjoyed a full complement of hardware, software, and experienced personnel. Technical support at the data-processing stage was necessary to strengthen the contribution of the less-experienced institutes.

The case for central processing is not all positive. In view of the training objectives of the ECIEL program, local processing would be desirable. The best way to advance Latin American research capabilities would have been to carry out all processing at the local level, with the technical guidance of consulting specialists. However, considering the standardization required by the comparative nature of the study, and the prohibitive cost of replicating the information-processing system eleven times, centralized processing was established as a technical criterion.

To a great extent, centralized processing was attained. After the study was under way, only three institutes felt that they could not export raw information for processing. In all three cases, the surveys had been carried out by government agencies in collaboration with the ECIEL institutes. Superficial similarities between the ECIEL survey and market surveys placed the institutes in a position vulnerable to criticism, albeit unfounded, for serving foreign commercial interests. Sensitivity to the potential for such criticism almost certainly played a part in the decision to process within the country.

Significantly, the countries carrying out the processing locally were among those best equipped with computing facilities. The processing system had to be adapted for use in those countries. Were the data-processing system fully automated, the only problem would have been modification of the programs to function at another installation. However, the processing system employed in the study involved considerable human-machine interaction. It was necessary to train researchers and assistants at the local level to use the data-processing system. It is doubtful that local personnel could have attained the expertise of a central processing staff benefiting from experience in processing other countries' data. The costs of local personnel, modification of the programs to run on a different system, and visits by programming specialists to set up the system, were considerable.

For the processing at Brookings, best results were obtained when institutes sent their programmer or researcher with the data. This provided the optimal combination of firsthand knowledge of the data, experience with the data-processing system, and use of the computer system for which the programs were written. The training objectives of the ECIEL program were also advanced by such arrangements.

Close Linkage Between Stages of the Study

Three main stages are relevant here: field survey, data processing, and analysis. Close linkage provides the intimate contact necessary to take into account the great externalities between stages. Indeed, in self-contained studies, a single organization normally has responsibility for all stages of the study. Often, the same group oversees each stage. The nature of the ECIEL study did not permit the overlap of personnel to attain close linkage. It was the task of the coordinating staff to orchestrate the various stages.

The impracticality of direct supervision of the fieldwork has already been discussed. Since the processing was centralized, it came under direct supervision of the Coordination. (Where processing was carried out locally, the system and programs were provided by the Coordination.) Appreciable coordinating influence could be exerted at the analysis stage. While the institutes were responsible for the analysis of their processed information, the Coordination provided technical assistance and consultation with recognized experts to insure high academic standards. Thus, the field survey was the only area where close communication was not attained.

Extensive data checking was undertaken to reinforce the relatively loose linkage between the field-survey and data-processing stages. Seven kinds of checking, undertaken in two stages, accomplished extremely close scrutiny of the data:

Stage I. Mechanical consistency: (1) sequence check; (2) nonnumeric characters; and (3) embedded blanks.

Stage II. Substantive consistency: (4) valid codes; (5) valid quantitative values; (6) logical and arithmetic consistency; and (7) extreme value test.

This checking was a relatively costly procedure; it constituted a major portion of the data-preparation work.

THE DATA BASE

The ECIEL household income and expenditure study constitutes a benchmark for inter-American comparisons in the consumption sector. The study is based on

TABLE 1
CHARACTERISTICS OF THE SURVEYS

Country and City	Total Population (millions)	Number of Observations	Number of Intervals	Panel	Date of Survey
Argentina	23.6				
Buenos Aires	7.7	1,398	4	Yes	4/29/69; 7/15/70
Bolivia	4.7	1,295			
La Paz	0.5	695	4	No	12/2/67; 5/30/69
Cochabamba	0.3	600	4	No	12/2/67; 5/30/69
Brazil	88.2	2,428			
Rio de Janeiro	4.2	1,006	4	Yes	5/20/67; 9/20/68
Porto Alegre	0.9	706	4	Yes	5/12/67; 5/30/68
Recife	1.1	716	4	Yes	7/26/67; 5/10/68
Chile	9.4				
Santiago	2.4	3,379	4	Yes	9/15/68; 9/30/69
Colombia	19.8	2,949			
Bogotá	2.0	798	4	Yes	2/10/67; 4/30/68
Barranquilla	0.8	727	4	Yes	2/10/67; 4/30/68
Cali	0.8	634	4	Yes	2/10/67; 4/30/68
Medellín	1.0	790	4	Yes	2/10/67; 4/30/68
Ecuador	5.7	1,994			
Quito	0.5	934	4	Yes	5/26/67; 11/14/68
Guayaquil	0.7	1,060	4	Yes	6/17/67; 12/14/68
Mexico	47.3	5,070	1	No	4/68
Mexico, D.F.					
Guadalajara					
Monterrey					
Paraguay	2.2				
Asunción	0.3	566	2	Yes	9/70
Peru	12.8				
Lima	2.4	1,357	4	No	2/15/68; 2/15/69
Uruguay	2.8				
Montevideo	1.2	1,135	4	Yes	8/20/67; 8/17/68
Venezuela	9.7	2,123			
Caracas	2.1	948	1	No	10/15/66; 11/15/66
Maracaibo	0.6	1,175	4	Yes	6/19/67; 3/10/68
Total number of observations		23,694			

large-sample cross-sectional surveys in twenty-one urban centers in all eleven LAFTA[2] countries. In most countries the surveys covered four quarterly intervals; the surveys of all the countries were carried out between 1966 and 1971. Approximately 24,000 interviews on 19,000 independent households (the difference represents repeat interviews of panel households) were obtained. Table 1 provides a detailed breakdown of the sample sizes by city and the survey dates.

Scope and Objectives of the Study

Knowledge of consumption patterns in Latin America is quite sparse. For example, the national accounts of most Latin American countries estimate private consumption as a residual. This approach does not constitute reliable measurement. Neither does it provide an indication of the composition of private consumption. The ECIEL study seeks to establish base-point national consumption studies. Specific comparative research topics include:

(1) allocation of family budgets by type of expenditure;
(2) price elasticities of demand for particular goods;
(3) income and expenditure elasticities;
(4) income distribution by level and type of income;
(5) estimation of cross-sectional consumption functions;
(6) international comparison of the determinants of consumption expenditures and investigation of the relevance of existing differences for the economic integration of the region;
(7) expenditure weights for price indexes; and
(8) estimates of household saving.

Many of these topics are relevant for intracountry comparisons by city and socioeconomic class, as well as for international comparisons.

Common Code

A typical questionnaire contains between 800 and 1,000 variables. The international code to which all country data are transformed contains 1,283 variables. A great many expenditure categories of the questionnaires are collapsed into aggregated variables in the common code. The common code also establishes a number of subtotals and dummy variables in addition to the original information.

Socio-demographic Data

For each member of the consumption unit, the following information is available: sex, age, marital status, education, occupation and occupational status, and relationship to the head of the unit. For income earners, sector of employment and income are also included. Limited migration information (number of years in city and previous place of residence) exists for the head of the unit and spouse.

Considerable information is available for the dwelling: type of dwelling, number of rooms, utility services, ownership status, rent (actual or imputed), and mortgage payments.

[2] The Latin American Free Trade Association (LAFTA) comprises Argentina, Bolivia, Brazil, Chile, Colombia, Ecuador, Mexico, Paraguay, Peru, Uruguay, and Venezuela.

TABLE 2
CLASSIFICATION OF EXPENDITURE DATA AND INCOME DATA

Expenditure Data: Major Groups and Subgroups

1. Food and beverages:
   - 1.01   Dairy products
   - 1.02   Cereals
   - 1.03   Meat and poultry
   - 1.04   Seafood
   - 1.05   Vegetables
   - 1.06   Fruits
   - 1.07   Fats and oils
   - 1.08   Sweets
   - 1.09   Tea, coffee, and hot beverages
   - 1.10   Alcoholic beverages
   - 1.11   Other beverages
   - 1.12   Other foods
   - 1.13   Food and beverages outside the home
2. Housing:
   - 2.01   Own residence
   - 2.02   Other residences
   - 2.03   Maintenance
3. Household equipment and maintenance:
   - 3.01   Durable goods
   - 3.02   Non-durable goods
   - 3.03   Services
4. Clothing:
   - 4.01   Men's
   - 4.02   Women's
   - 4.03   Children's
   - 4.04   Other clothing
5. Medical care
6. Education
7. Recreation and cultural activities:
   - 7.01   Entertainment
   - 7.02   Reading material
8. Transportation and communication:
   - 8.01   Own transportation: purchase of vehicle (net outlay)
   - 8.02   Own transportation: current expenses
   - 8.03   Public transportation
   - 8.04   Telephone and other communication
9. Other consumption expenditures:
   - 9.01   Tobacco
   - 9.02   Personal care
   - 9.03   Entertainment
10. Taxes
11. Insurance:
    - 11.01 Social security
    - 11.02 Other insurance
12. Transfers, gifts
13. Miscellaneous non-consumption expenditures
14. Total expenditure $(1 + 2 + 3 + 4 + 5 + 6 + 7 + 8 + 9 + 10 + 11 + 12 + 13)$

Income Data: Major Groups

1. Wage income
2. Income from independent labor
3. Income from capital
4. Transfers
5. Transitory income
6. Unclassified income
7. Total income $(1 + 2 + 3 + 4 + 5 + 6)$

Income and Expenditure Data

A total of 500 expenditure items and subtotals are available in the common code. Initial international comparisons will be made at the level of 13 major groups and 34 subgroups. Table 2 describes the expenditure groups and subgroups.

In addition to individual earner's income, income of the unit as a whole is available by breakdown among 6 major functional sources. The sources are listed in Table 2. A distinction between monetary and in-kind income is also available.

International Comparability of the Data

The design criterion for the common international code was maximum comparability of the data, subject to maintaining a reasonable degree of disaggregation. In the face of differing national definitions, some variables lent themselves to transformations that permitted eventual comparison. For example, wide differences in the names of vegetables exist among countries. Many produce items are found only in one or a few countries. Despite these differences, quite good comparability was attained for total expenditure on vegetables across countries. However, differences in definition of some socio-demographic variables were not so readily overcome.

Comparability Through Aggregation

Aggregation was used to attain comparability of income and expenditure categories. An evaluation of the international comparability of the major categories of the income and expenditure data, based on the degree of coverage for the category provided by the items in the country questionnaire, indicates that very good comparability has been attained. Comparability at the next level of disaggregation for expenditures, the 34 subgroups, is also quite good; 90 percent of the subgroups had good to very good comparability.

Noncomparability

Other differences in definition could not be overcome at all. The most serious of these occurred in the socio-demographic data. Definition of the consumption unit varied considerably. Some countries employed the concept of a "secondary unit" to identify a semiindependent consumption unit—for example, married children living with the parents. Some used the "supplementary member" to account for persons who only shared food and/or room expenses. Treatment of domestic employees varied as well; some countries counted them and others did not. Countries distinguishing secondary units and supplementary units would tend to show fewer persons per consumption unit. Those counting domestic employees would show larger consumption units.

Comparisons based on per capita measures of consumption will require care on two accounts. The consumption pattern is susceptible to the type of person included or excluded. Domestic employees, working children, and so on, have expenditures quite different from those of a typical family unit. The inclusion or exclusion of these types of persons and their expenditures and income was systematic, depending on the concept of consumption unit employed. Furthermore, not all types of expenditure are readily distinguishable. If a person was not counted in the consumption unit, his expenditures and income would not figure in the questionnaire *insofar as it was possible to separate them.* Personal expenditures such as entertainment, clothing, and so forth, were not likely to be counted. Per capita expenditure on living space, durable items, and food, however, would be susceptible to distortion by variations in the count of persons in the unit.

In these instances there was no way to manipulate the information to attain comparability. Means of comparison must be employed which take account of the differences in definition. The differences in definition were somewhat systematic and not so numerous. They could possibly be handled by the use of dummies in multivariate analyses. There was no possibility, however, for ex ante transformations to gain comparability as with the income and expenditure data.

DATA PROCESSING

This section describes the data-processing system for the income and expenditure study. The first part sketches some principles applied in the design of the system. The second part describes the preparation of the ECIEL data for international comparisons.

Design Principles for Information Processing

It is useful to consider the design question not from the point of view of information supply but, rather, from the principle of conserving the attention of the researcher and the audience.

Information overload. Empirical research can be envisioned as a combination of data with analysis, given a set of hypotheses. As the quantity of data increases, the human attention required for analysis can become the bottleneck in the process. It is necessary to allocate attention efficiently among the abundant information sources in the data.[3]

Information overload, a superabundance of data relative to the available attention, aptly characterizes the data-processing context of the ECIEL study. At the research stage, the claim on attention increases with the number of variables. Even greater demands are placed on attention when the data are being handled for the first time. File structuring and data scrutiny precede any analysis. During data preparation, the requirements for attention are proportional to the number of observations as well as to the number of variables. To what extent are the human resources of the project capable of analyzing the voluminous output from a bank of twenty-four thousand observations?

Information condensing. In a situation of information overload, an information-processing system will reduce the net demand on human attention only if it absorbs more information than it produces.[4] To conserve the scarce resource of attention, the system must be capable of condensing information. The crucial

---

[3] Several views in this section draw on concepts presented by Herbert A. Simon, "Designing Organizations for an Information-Rich World," *Computers, Communications and the Public Interest,* Martin Greenberger, ed. (Baltimore: The Johns Hopkins Press, 1971), pp. 37–63.

[4] Simon, *op. cit.,* p. 42.

design question is how much and what kind of information it will allow to be withheld from the researcher. The information-processing system should not conserve attention at the expense of the still more salient need for relevance. Performance on this count distinguishes good system design from poor.

During data preparation, the analyst cannot and need not inspect each datum. The system should bring to the attention of the analyst only those data which are obviously erroneous, or those which have a high probability of being in error. Clearly, a tradeoff between accuracy and cost is being made here. The system design can be tailored to shift the balance either way desired.

In response to the decentralization of the fieldwork, the balance was swung toward accuracy in the data-preparation stage. For almost every type of error, the system provided as close scrutiny of the data as possible. Other factors beside the decentralization of the fieldwork reinforced the choice of this option. Any checking that was to be performed had to be done at this stage. The greater the lag between the survey and the checking, the more difficult it would have been to obtain the collaboration of the institutes in checking the original questionnaires.

To facilitate widespread use of the data, we chose to incur all of the fixed costs at this stage and minimize the marginal cost of future applications of the information. This involved the correction of all detectable errors at levels of disaggregation higher than the 47 expenditure subtotals and 6 income subtotals used for the initial international comparison study. Future studies will be feasible at a higher level of disaggregation with virtually no additional fixed cost.

Data Preparation

Figure 1 presents a schematic description of the information-processing system of the study. The units delineate functional steps rather than individual programs. At some points more than one function was performed by a single program. At other points, the intermediate analyses, for example, several programs were necessary to perform the appropriate tests. Not indicated in the diagram are several housekeeping programs used for manipulating the data.

Forms of data. Initially it was expected that the questionnaires could be precoded with cards punched directly from the questionnaire. This did not prove practicable because the questionnaire layout best for field use did not lend itself to keypunching. Consequently the data were passed to coding sheets and some minor conversions and aggregations were performed at this stage. The data were punched locally in all but two cases. They were then forwarded to Brookings for processing.

Stage I of data cleaning. Certain checks of the data were necessary to permit further processing. Cards were passed to tape as soon as possible; this was often done locally. We have had good results with transporting the data on tape and converting the tape for use with the Brookings computer. Disk pack was often used for storage of active data files at Brookings. Tape was used for archive storage of the data at key junctures (data as received, the final clean file, and so on).

Sequence check. Initially card images were checked for proper sequence. An observation in country-specific format occupied from 39 to 60 cards. If the errors in card order were obvious, they were corrected without consultation with the institute. If not obvious, a decision was made either to drop the observation

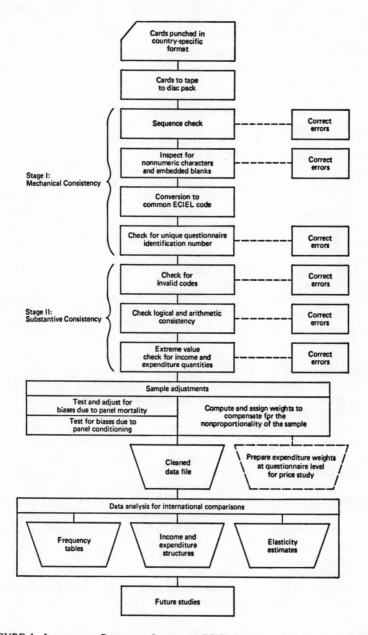

FIGURE 1 INFORMATION PROCESSING SYSTEM FOR ECIEL INCOME AND EXPENDITURE STUDY

permanently, to proceed with the good observations and process the others later, or to delay processing of the entire file until all possible observations were salvaged by checking with the institute. If the work schedule permitted, the last option was preferable. Special update programs replaced the card images in the file.

Nonnumerics and embedded blanks. These errors created different problems. Both were sought at the same time, however, because the programs were based on reading characters in A (alphanumeric) format. The ECIEL code is fully numeric. (Some institutes employed alphanumeric codes for variable formated observations. See below, *Conversion.*) For faster reading and calculating, I (integer) format was used as early as possible. Nonnumeric characters had to be removed because they would stop execution in this format.

Embedded blanks caused no such mechanical problem. They did, however, give a good indication that a field had possibly been slipped in keypunching. These errors would be found in no other way since, substantively, the blank was handled as a zero. Again, the institute performed double checks on the questionnaires to correct the erroneous data. Virtually all of these kinds of errors were salvageable because no questionnaire and coding sheet should have made it through field supervision checks with alphabetics or embedded blanks. Correction at this stage was executed with update programs capable of locating a given variable in a given observation.

Conversion. Original agreements specified that the institutes were responsible for providing the data in the format of the ECIEL common code. However, all of the institutes coded the data in questionnaire-specific form. Some institutes found the conversion beyond their means. In such cases, Brookings prepared the conversion program. Those institutes that did convert the data prepared conversion programs for use as part of the central processing. As discussed above, comparability of the income and expenditure data was obtained through aggregation. In principle, this solution was straightforward. However, several details complicated the conversion.

Variable format.—Most institutes employed a fixed location format for every variable in the country-specific format. This setup was the easiest to handle. However, some institutes used a variable format for the income and expenditure data. This arrangement involved one card for each datum; the format of each card was fixed. An identifying code specified the variable to which the datum corresponded. The number of cards varied with each record, depending on the number of responses obtained. Ostensibly, this format would reduce costs. Few cards are used when there are many zero data. If nonzero responses are expected on only a small number of all the possible data for most observations, this arrangement would economize on cards.

This system enormously complicated the conversion program. Greater conversion costs more than offset any savings on cards and punching. The identifying codes had to be compared with a library to specify the destination of the datum in the common format. The use of an identifying code doubled the opportunity for coding and punching mistakes to cause permanent error. The use of an alphanumeric code by one institute introduced further complication and opportunity for error.

Packed format.—Even in the case of fixed formats, suboptimal format design occurred. All institutes were concerned with reducing card costs. The common international code and format were being designed at a time when it was still expected that the institutes would be providing the data in common format. Thus, the pressure to reduce card usage influenced the design of the common code as well. As a result, the format was packed. Minimum necessary space was allocated to each variable. Adjacent variables thus had differing field widths. The local pressure for card reduction led to packed formats in the national formats as well. Thus, variable field-width formats were used at two stages. If the Coordination had known that it (rather than the institutes) would convert the data to common code, it would have been possible to employ a more efficient format design for the common code.

Variable field widths caused several difficulties. Indexing of variables was complicated. A fixed number of variables per card would have greatly simplified indexing. Varying the field width increased the opportunity for slipping fields during keypunching. Also, despite the extreme care that went into designing the common format, several field-width overflows occurred.

This complication exemplifies one kind of problem resulting from the organization of the study. Great externalities exist between steps in the data preparation. The manner in which costs were shared between the institutes and the Coordination offered many opportunities for cost shifting to the Coordination. As a result, overall project costs were somewhat higher.

Double counting.—The subtotals used in the questionnaires were not, of course, uniform across countries. All subtotal combinations could not appear in the common code. Insofar as possible, variables were mapped into the common code at maximum disaggregation. Lack of uniformity in the subtotals necessitated great effort to avoid double counting in the mapping.

Nonresponse.—Treatment of nonresponses was especially troublesome. Ideally, this problem should have been resolved in the field; the greatest amount of supplementary information was available at that stage. The time lag between fieldwork and central processing barred the possibility of obtaining any of the missing information detected at the checking stage. Perforce, missing data existed. They had to be given special treatment to permit the use of the existing information. A special code—the field filled with the digit 9—denoted nonresponse. The nonresponses had to be separated out of any computation performed with that variable.

For computing subtotals at all higher levels of aggregation, the missing datum was treated as a zero. (In tabulation and all subsequent computations, observations with missing data were excluded.) The error introduced in the subtotal by this approach depended, of course, on the relative magnitudes of the missing datum and the subtotal. This was not the same across expenditure categories. An individual food item, for example, was probably quite small in relation to the subtotal for food and beverages. An appliance, on the other hand, was likely to represent a significant portion of the subtotal for household equipment. However, the proportion of nonresponses relative to actual zero expenditures here was likely to be much lower than with a food item.

Since the nonresponses occurred at the questionnaire level, while the international comparisons were made at the level of the 47 major groups and subgroups, the nonresponse problem did not complicate the initial computations. Yet to preserve the possibility of working at the most disaggregated level in future research, the nonresponse codes and the consequent complications of checking for, and separating, the codes had to be borne throughout the data-preparation stage.

Stage II of data cleaning. At this stage, substantive errors were sought and corrected. In all cases, the questionable data were returned to the institute for double-checking. Substantive errors were more difficult to correct, because they may have been recorded as such in the questionnaire. In other words, the only error that could be corrected at this stage, as in Stage I, was a coding or punching error. If the datum was recorded erroneously in the questionnaire it was left as it was or changed to a nonresponse in the data file, depending on its "reasonableness."

Invalid codes and invalid values. Some data could be detected as erroneous by simple inspection. Qualitative data appeared in the file as numeric codes. The most obvious error was the use of a digit not designated for the particular variable. For example, the code for sex of household members was: 1—male, 2—female, and 9—no response. A datum of 0, 3, 4, 5, 6, 7, or 8 on this variable was invalid. A coded variable that employed all the digits could not, of course, be checked for this type of error.

Quantitative data covered a much wider range. Any number except a code (field filled with 9's—no response; field filled with 9's except 8 in the right-hand column—not asked in questionnaire) was a valid value. Expenditure and most income variables were nonnegative quantities. All variables that should have had positive responses only were checked to insure that no negative data appeared.[5]

Logical and arithmetic consistency. The interrelatedness between certain variables was exploited to check for erroneous data. If the data for the variables were not consistent with the a priori relationship, at least one of the data had to be erroneous.

A multitude of relationships existed among the socio-demographic variables. All possible logical relationships, approximately 50, were checked. Some typical relationships are presented as examples:

(1) children must be younger than the parents by at least 13 years;
(2) educational level must be consistent with age, i.e., a child cannot be recorded as having a university education;
(3) the number of persons must add up to the family size reported;
(4) both rent and mortgage payments cannot be reported for the same dwelling;
(5) expenditures can be made only for utility services (gas, electricity, and so on) installed in the dwelling.

Furthermore, all of the income and expenditure data were subjected to an adding-up check. Subtotals had to be greater than, or equal to, the addends. The greater-than inequality allowed for the possibility that the breakdown for certain expenditures was not known but the category total was known and reported. In

---

[5] This test was performed with a univariate distribution program. To test for negative values, the valid limits were established at zero and the maximum for the particular field width. The program output identified all observations having negative values. The program also divided the range between zero and the maximum valid value into twenty equal intervals and displayed the resulting distribution. The distributions proved to be helpful aids in interpreting the extreme value test (see below).

this case, the reported total exceeded the sum of the reported addends. In the consistency checks, nonresponses were handled as zero.

Although it would have been conceivable to check for consistency over time for those consumption units reappearing in the panel, such checking was not carried out. Problems in identifying family members (they might not be listed in the same order in each interview), possible changes in employment status, and defining "consistent" income or spending over time promised to make the check more costly than the benefits derived.

Extreme value test. As far as we are aware, this was the first time that regression methods were used in a checking procedure. This approach constitutes a considerable increase in the scrutiny with which survey data are reviewed on a large scale. Previously, the most detailed checks established valid ranges for expenditure quantities normalized by total expenditure. For example, all observations whose percentage expenditure on food did not lie between, say, 30 percent and 60 percent would be reviewed in detail. Other determinants of expenditure level were not taken into account.

The method employed here allowed for multiple explanatory variables for expenditure level of each of the 34 expenditure subgroups and 6 income subgroups. The test used a simple arithmetic regression model. The explanatory variables for each income and expenditure category were chosen on the basis of a priori notions of the determinants of spending and income. The advantage in employing multiple explanatory variables was the reduction in the number of observations brought into question. For example, if a household showed a high percentage expenditure on food, but the number of members was high, the high percentage was likely justifiable. With the regression test, this observation would not have been singled out for inspection. We desired a method that could rapidly scan the data file and identify "unreasonable" incomes or expenditure for further inspection.

Unreasonable in this case amounted to unreasonably high. We were concerned about errors which will bias the statistical estimates. They could be biased positively or negatively by observations with erroneously overreported or underreported expenditures and incomes. However, the danger from errors on the low side was less severe. Since income and expenditure items were positive, all negative quantities had been removed by checking. Errors were thus bounded on the low side (at zero) but not on the high side.

Up to this point in the data preparation, all erroneous data that could possibly have been detected were identified. This test, however, depended on the likelihood of a datum being erroneous. Only further checking with the questionnaire could confirm that it was a coding or punching error. There was latitude for a choice between certainty and cost. Absolute certainty on coding or punching errors would have required the inspection of every datum. Because we were seeking only extreme errors, we were able to focus attention on a relatively small number of observations.

The method compared the actual expenditure or income value with that predicted by the regression equation. It then identified all observations whose residual (actual value minus predicted value) lay more than three standard deviations away from the regression surface. Three standard deviations was an arbitrary choice. It was chosen to reduce the number of observations demanding human attention while picking out those erroneous values large enough to seriously bias parameter estimates.[6]

Only those observations having nonzero expenditures and incomes for the category in question entered the equation. We had no way of knowing whether they were correctly recorded as zero. We could not impose the condition that because a household had certain characteristics it *must* have made the expenditure or received the income. The presence of observations with zero for the dependent variable would have served no useful purpose and would have tended to confuse the interpretation of the regression equation.

The procedure gave very good results the first time it was employed on a data file of 2,949 observations from one country. In checking the 34 and 6 subgroups, 932 "extreme values" were identified. The percentage of observations identified per equation varied between 0.5 percent (food and beverages) and 2.6 percent (medical care). After double-checking on the questionnaires, 16 percent of the 932 extreme values were found to be errors introduced by coding or punching. The question remained of what to do with the "extreme values" that were not punching errors.[7] The easiest procedure was also the safest. Doubtful values were left as they were, unless they were extreme enough to bias the data.[8] Even if we were dealing with all "true" data, depending on the shape of the distribution of the residual, the 3 standard deviation test could have identified up to 11 percent of the observations as "extreme." In the first actual use of the test, none of the 84 percent of the observations inspected but not having punching errors were extreme enough to warrant replacement; they were all left as they were in the data file.

Few extremely low values were identified by the test. This was likely due to the fact that income and expenditure distributions are typically skewed to the right. Hence, more observations fell within 3 standard deviations on the low side than on the high side. If the variance of the residuals was high, the 3σ limit could fall below zero and *no* low values would have been detected (negative values had already been purged).

Sample adjustments. Up to this point, efforts were directed to correcting individual observations. Three possible sources of bias due to the sampling survey remained to be adjusted for: nonproportionality of the sample, panel mortality,

[6] If all the data were correct, up to 11 percent of the residuals could still have fallen outside 3 standard deviations. If in addition, the distribution of the residuals was approximately normal, as few as 0.3 percent of the observations may have fallen outside. Since the distribution of the residuals was likely to be unimodal with high contact, about 1 percent was a good guess for the proportion of valid observations lying outside the band. Working with a file of three-thousand observations, this would single out about 30 observations per equation for detailed inspection. From the point of view of information condensing, this is about all one would need to spot very serious outliers.

It is unlikely that as many as 30 observations would be an order of magnitude larger than the mean without our already having known about it. Univariate distributions of each subtotal were available at this stage. They were used in conjunction with the extreme-value test. If a large number of observations was noted at the high end of the distribution, it would have been easy to set the limit at 2 standard deviations for that particular variable and thereby scrutinize more observations with large values.

[7] Originally we speculated on the desirability of replacing the datum by the predicted value plus a random component. This procedure was rejected because it would have amounted to homogenizing some of the data (albeit to a small degree—less than 3 percent of the data) according to our a priori and oversimplified notions of the determinants of expenditure.

[8] "Extreme enough" would seem to be an observed value an order of magnitude larger than the mean of the dependent variable.

and panel conditioning. To date, only the nonproportionality adjustment has been carried out; the test and adjustments for the panel have not been completed. The sample adjustments are not particular to the ECIEL study; they are normally made on any survey data, regardless of the degree of decentralization of the fieldwork.

Nonproportionality. All sample data in this study had to be corrected for non-proportionality. The samples were designed to be stratified by income level with different sampling fractions employed. The most common method for adjustment involved the use of exogenous information on the distribution of income of the population. The income distribution resulting from the sample was used to determine appropriate weights to scale the sample data up to the population income distribution. These weights were assigned to the individual observations as a datum. Whenever a weighted mean was required, the computation programs brought in this datum as the weighting factor.

Panel mortality. As indicated in Table 1, eight of the eleven countries employed a panel. The panel is a subsample of families that was interviewed in each of the four intervals. Basically, the panel is used as a control group for variations in consumption through the year. If differential (by socio-demographic characteristics of the household) mortality occurred, the panel may not provide a good control basis. As a test, other subsamples were designated for once- and twice-interviewed families in different intervals. A series of χ^2 tests are performed to test for differences in composition of the subsamples and differential mortality in the sample over time. The cross-tabulation program written for ECIEL provides the χ^2 statistic for each table. Control variables checked here are size of household, employment status of head, age of head, and total income. If significant differences in composition of the panel subsamples across intervals are detected, differential weighting is applied to the observations to compensate.

Panel conditioning. The periodic reinterviews may make panel households more aware of their income and expenditures than they otherwise might be. As a result, they might have altered their spending or reporting practices to differ from those of comparable households being interviewed for the first time. The tendency for income and expenditure magnitudes to rise due to inflation further distorts the sample results over time. To test for panel conditioning, an analysis of variance is performed to determine significant variations in mean expenditure. The objective of the analysis of variance is to test for the significance of observed interaction between subsample and the control variable, and for the significance of the differences in mean expenditure among subsamples.

The control variables are: subsample number, quarter, and number of interview (first time, second time, and so on). Mean expenditures are to be tested for all 13 major expenditure categories (see above, Table 2). Three income variables—total income, wages, and income from capital—are also tested. The tests for panel mortality and conditioning have not yet been completed. Unlike panel mortality, conditioning effects are not readily adjusted for by weighting. The precise nature of the adjustment procedure for panel conditioning will be determined after initial tests are carried out.

Summary of data preparation. Throughout the data-preparation stage, it was necessary to balance accuracy against cost. For most checks, this amounted to performing, or not performing, the check. Such checks, by their nature, detected *only*, but *not all*, errors. It is evident from the descriptions of the checks that all errors could not be detected. The process only detected erroneous *and* inconsistent data. Data that were erroneous but consistent with the other information in the observation slipped through the tests. If a certain check was desired, it would focus attention on *only* errors, and all errors that were *detectable*. If such a check were deemed too costly for its contribution to accuracy, then *no* error of that type would be detected.

The extreme-value check differed in this respect; some of the extreme values may not have been erroneous. Within the boundaries of the test, it was possible to shift the balance toward inspection of more dubious information or toward economizing on human attention.

For data preparation as a whole, the balance was decided in favor of maximizing accuracy. This decision was largely made in response to the decentralization of the fieldwork. The desire to incur now as much of the fixed cost of data preparation as possible and to reduce the marginal cost of future studies complemented the decision to perform as many checks as possible.

The first two checks—sequence and nonnumerics—would have had to be performed in any study. They involved mechanical errors that would have involved nonsense processing in the first place, and interruption of program execution in the second. The check for embedded blanks was a good way to locate slipped fields in coding and punching. Its technical interdependency with the nonnumerics check permitted its incorporation at a relatively low marginal cost.

Determination of the point at which conversion was carried out involved subtle tradeoffs. To maximize the opportunity for uniform treatment of the data, conversion should be made as early as possible. On the other hand, certain kinds of errors—cards out of sequence and nonnumeric characters—had to be removed to permit conversion. Also, the earlier the checking was carried out, the closer to the source the error could be located, and backtracking through the intervening transformations was minimized.

Because of its technical interdependency with the nonnumeric check, the embedded-blank check was performed before the conversion. Since the socio-demographic data generally needed no transformation—their conversion mainly consisted of reformating—the location of the logical consistency check was not critical from the standpoint of backtracking. Conversion was located before the logical and arithmetic consistency checks so that these could constitute a double check on the conversion as well as a check on the data themselves. That is, the logical and arithmetic checks tested the reformating and the adding-up done by the conversion, in addition to the consistency of the data. This benefit compensated the backtracking necessary to locate errors in income or expenditure data at the questionnaire level. Since the extreme-value test was run on income and expenditure subtotals, it perforce had to be located after the conversion, even though corrections had to be sought at the questionnaire level.

One feasible check was not incorporated in the data-preparation system. A logical-consistency and extreme-value test of sorts was conceivable for the panel families interviewed more than once. These checks would have taken the form of imposing consistent behavior of a given household over time. The difficulty of defining consistency over time, and the low marginal benefits of the checks, resulted in their omission.

Invalid codes and invalid values did not have to be removed from a mechanical standpoint. Tabulations could have classified them as "other." However, they could have been numerous and a reduction in the effective sample size would have resulted. Furthermore, negative expenditure values could have seriously biased the statistical estimates.

Logical and arithmetic consistency were not essential from a mechanical point of view either. Again, however, such inconsistencies could have been numerous and could have adversely affected the results. Also, as noted above, these checks served as an effective double check on the conversion.

The extreme-value test was incorporated to prevent severe biases that would result from the presence of extremely large values not counterbalanced on the low side, due to the lower bound of zero. Here, however, it was possible to employ the principle of information condensing and reduce the number of observations requiring scrutiny. Only those values capable of severely affecting the results, and with a high probability of error, were inspected.

The nonproportionality adjustment was essential. The tests and adjustments for panel mortality and panel conditioning constitute a refinement attempting to adjust for effects in the interview process itself. This contrasts with the other tests in that they essentially discover errors introduced in the transmission of the information after the interview stage.

A review of the benefits of the extensive cleaning undertaken as part of the data preparation completes the summary. Even if all errors could not be detected by the data-cleaning system, the results of the cleaning probably give a good indication of the overall quality of the field response and coding operation. The number of undetectable errors in the data is probably highly correlated with the number of inconsistencies identified by the checking. Inconsistency rates can be employed as a rough indicator of the comparative quality of the data.

Prior cleaning and inspection will enhance the validity of the results of the comparative studies. The data will remain useful for a long time after the ECIEL international comparisons are carried out. Hopefully, the data will come to be used by a great many scholars for a wide variety of national and international studies. The data will have greater usefulness if accompanied by indications of their quality. Over the long run, the benefit from careful data preparation should exceed its costs.

CONCLUSION

On the basis of our experience, we can state a few technical criteria for micro-analytic survey work that should hold under most conditions. No attempt should be made to economize on the use of cards. This is the number one false economy for data processing. Data packing and coded free formats enormously complicate the later processing.

Alphabetic codes should be avoided. They complicate the input formating and then require cleaning checks to insure that they do not appear in fields where they do not belong.

Extra effort should be expended to solve nonresponse problems in the field. This measure is closely related to performing more consistency checks at the field level. In a joint study, the time lag between fieldwork and processing is great enough to preclude the possibility of correcting errors by return visit. The return visit is the optimal way to correct nonresponse and inconsistent information. The use of later automated checking does not obviate the need for good field checking procedures.

The benefits to permitting slight differences in questionnaire design are less than the costs of the additional complication. Difficulties due to differences in household terminology can be overcome with clarifying notes in the questionnaire. Often the solution is simpler; if a given item has a different name in another country, it can appear in the questionnaire under its local name. But it should go in the *same* location with the *same* code number as in other countries. The problem of nonexistence of certain items in household budgets or nonavailability is likewise tractable in a common questionnaire. Space for such items can be allowed in the format and the item blacked out in the questionnaire. The extent of differences in definition and nonavailability was overstated by the participants. The extra questionnaire space and cards due to a uniform questionnaire constitute the most expendable resource in a comparative study. These general criteria, however, are not sufficient guides for effective large scale microanalysis in either a national or comparative context.

The major consequence of these unforeseen factors was additional cost. Few coordination problems resulted in permanent impairment of the data. The data-preparation procedures have succeeded in overcoming most of the incompatibilities. The comprehensive coverage of the LAFTA region more than compensates for the additional costs necessary to obtain the participation of all countries. Indeed, the body of microanalytic data proceeding from the study promises to be the most compatible, comprehensive, and reliable yet assembled for Latin America.

Better information on costs could be generated in studies currently under way. We have attempted to identify and clarify the numerous aspects of large-scale information processing about which little information is currently available. We state a few open questions: How should the work be staged for optimum balance between machine and human resources? In how large increments should results be sought? (What portion of intermediate results are ultimately discarded?) What are the payoffs to data cleaning? (A reverse validation on uncleaned data would indicate how much the results differ.)

We would urge that additional resources be made available to individual research projects for the express purpose of investigating concurrently the computing aspects of the research. Such seed resources could draw out a body of organized methodological guidelines that would serve to improve the efficiency of large-scale economic-research computing.

APPENDIX

Institutes Participating in the ECIEL Household Income and Expenditure Study
Argentina: Centro de Investigaciones Económicas, Instituto Torcuato Di Tella, Buenos Aires.

Bolivia: Instituto de Investigaciones Económicas, Universidad Mayor de San Andres, La Paz.
Instituto de Estudios Sociales y Económicas, Facultad de Ciencias Económicas, Universidad Mayor de San Simón, Cochabamba.
Brazil: Instituto Brasileiro de Economía, Fundaçao Getulio Vargas, Río de Janeiro.
Chile: Instituto de Economía y Planificación, Universidad de Chile, Santiago.
Colombia: Centro de Estudios de Desarrollo, Universidad de Los Andes, Bogotá.
Ecuador: Instituto Nacional de Estadística, Quito.
Mexico: Centro de Estudios Económicos y Demográficos, El Colegio de México, México, D.F.
Paraguay: Centro Paraguayo de Estudios de Desarrollo Económico y Social, Asunción.
Peru: Centro de Investigaciones Sociales, Económicas, Políticas y Antropológicas, Universidad Católica del Perú, Lima.
Uruguay: Instituto de Estadística, Facultad de Ciencias Económicas, Universidad de la República, Montevideo.
Venezuela: Centro de Desarrollo, Universidad Central de Venezuela, Caracas.
Departamento de Estadísticas, Banco Central de Venezuela, Caracas.

THE USE OF THE COMPUTER IN HANDLING LARGE PRICE FILES: THE EXPERIENCE WITH A BENCHMARK COLLECTION IN LATÍN AMERICA

Jorge Salazar-Carrillo*

The Brookings Institution

Section 1

1. Introduction

Although the influence of the computer has permeated many fields of study, its use in price research has been rather limited, especially in international comparisons. This may be due to the nature of empirical work in this area; specifically, the number of observations handled and variables involved, which place such efforts between time series and surveys in terms of size and complexity.

Would a larger role for the computer in this field be beneficial? Could its present contributions be increased and how? As general background in answering such questions, an outline of some of the seemingly positive and negative aspects of the computer, as far as they are applicable to research projects in the area of prices, would appear worthwhile.

1.1 Positive Aspects

One of the potential advantages of computer applications lies in the quickness it allows in the processing, organizing, and cleaning of the data. This reduces the delay between the actual collection and the presentation of the final results.

Data processing and cleaning would appear to respond well to machine operations not only in terms of time, but also in the form of other cost reductions. Having the information readily available in well-organized tape or disk files, plus checking and editing by computer, appear to be the pillars of this greater efficiency.

Another apparently important factor on the credit side is increased accuracy in research operations. This advantage applies to all the stages of a project: from the cleaning and checking phase to the final manipulation of the data.[1]

An additional benefit is that computer operations necessitate that the data be arranged in a highly organized and explicit form, forcing the creation of files, banks, and other orderly information structures. This facilitates data retrieval, while encouraging efficient filing, which is central to accessibility of data to other researchers.

* The author is senior fellow with the Brookings Institution. He wishes to thank Joseph Grunwald for his continued encouragement, and Ricardo Martinez and George Plinio Montalván for general help. The author is also thankful to Philip Musgrove for his valuable comments, and to Stanley Braithwaite, Robert Ferber, Irving Kravis, and Richard Ruggles for advice on some aspects of the data processing operations discussed here. The views expressed in the paper are the author's and do not necessarily reflect those of the staff, officers, or trustees of the Brookings Institution. The research reported here has been mostly financed by Ford Foundation grants.

[1] This is partly compensated by the fact that some errors can be introduced in the computer handling of the data, as in keypunching and card reading.

The importance of rapid retrieval for research and experimentation is obvious. The availability of data files which are either easily transferable or accessible through computer linkups is also of great importance. This allows other researchers to use the data arising from a particular research project for other research purposes or for an alternative formulation of the same research goals.

The computer has no equal in its ability to undertake complicated and long manipulations of data. Computers permit experimentation with several alternatives, while previously cost considerations limited it to only two or three. For example, for large price files, the computer would permit the testing of the effects of different index formulas on the measurement of price change, at reasonable cost.

This characteristic, together with the fact that it provides rapid feedback, makes the computer quite amenable to hypothesis testing. Techniques which have relied heavily on these computer properties are those of economic simulation and sensitivity analysis.

1.2 *Negative Aspects*

On the other hand, computer applications could create problems. First of all, in the present state of computer technology, the additional burden of learning at least the basics of computer science and managing the computer aspects of research projects falls upon the researcher. For large projects, this task may be placed in the hands of specialists. However, these specialists must still be understood and controlled by the economist or statistician. This necessity may result in some waste in the use of human resources, as the attention of the researcher has to focus on matters in which his productivity is lower.

Second, the computer appears to diminish the independence of researchers, as they now have to rely heavily on the efficiency of their computer center. The alternative of buying computer services outside is sometimes open. However, just considering this possibility is rather time consuming, while again forcing the researcher into acquiring special skills not of his immediate interest.

Basically, as a result of communication problems with programmers, a large amount of research time has to be devoted to carefully checking computer output. In a relatively large number of cases, computer exercises end up being repeated. Facing these conditions, economists and statisticians frequently decide to learn programming, and end up by becoming their own programmers, a solution which negates specialization.[2]

SECTION 2

2. *Computer Operations and Price Research: An Illustration*

In the previous section, the advantages and disadvantages of the computer for price research have been discussed at a general level. It is now time to turn to a specific consideration of the potential use of computers in this area, and to

[2] Most of the difficulties introduced by the computer involve deficient communications. One of the most befuddling characteristics of computer operations is the extent to which its specialists persist in speaking "computerese," a complicated and confusing language extremely specific to their problems. Although every discipline is more or less affected by this problem, computer people seem to be more oblivious of the confusion this creates than are other specialists. This situation is particularly shocking because computer personnel basically serve other researchers, their output being more characteristically intermediate than those of other disciplines.

an examination of the ways in which its net contribution could be enlarged. This will be done first by way of a practical illustration, using a large benchmark survey of prices undertaken in Latin America in 1968.[3]

2.1 Purpose, Nature, and Scope of the ECIEL Study

It is necessary to enter a little bit into the purpose, nature, and scope of the ECIEL study of which the survey is part. For further reference two previous papers by the author should be consulted.[4]

The main purposes of the study are: (a) to construct an international price index for Latin America; (b) to determine purchasing-power parity rates for these countries; and (c) to estimate their gross domestic products in real terms. A secondary objective is the study of price and cost structures from the points of view of efficiency and trade (especially that among Latin American countries). Hopefully, such research will improve the understanding of integration and development in the area.

For the preparation of the basic estimates, the study required the collection of price and expenditure information. These were obtained in great depth and detail for 1968. The gathering of these data took place in all the countries involved under a common methodology and common procedures.

These estimates cover different categories of goods and services. They correspond to the main subdivisions of the gross domestic product, as calculated from the expenditure side. However, this paper will concentrate on the private-consumption sector, and particularly on the collection of private-consumer-goods prices.[5]

[3] Brookings undertook such research in collaboration with thirteen research institutions from Latin America. All these institutions participate in a unique research venture coordinated by Brookings under the acronym of ECIEL. ECIEL stands for the Spanish equivalent of Program of Joint Studies on Latin American Economic Integration. About twenty research institutions in Latin America participate in its several projects. For a fuller description of what ECIEL is, see Joseph Grunwald and Jorge Salazar-Carrillo, "Economic Integration, Rate Exchange and Value Comparisons in Latin America," in *International Comparisons of Prices and Output*, D. J. Daly, ed., New York, NBER, 1972. The ECIEL institutions participating in this particular study are: Fundación de Investigaciones Económicas Latinoamericanas (FIEL), from Argentina; Instituto de Investigaciones Económicas of the Universidad Mayor de San Andres and Instituto Nacional de Estadística, from Bolivia; Instituto Brasileiro de Economía of the Fundaçao Getúlio Vargas, from Brazil; Instituto de Economía y Planificación of the Universidad de Chile, from Chile; Centro de Estudios sobre Desarrollo Económico (CEDE) of the Universidad de los Andes, from Colombia; Instituto Nacional de Estadística, from Ecuador; Centro de Estudios Económicos y Demográficos of El Colegio de México, from Mexico; Centro Paraguayo de Estudios de Desarrollo Económico y Social (CEPADES), from Paraguay; Centro de Investigaciones Sociales, Económicas, Políticas y Antropológicas (CISEPA) of the Universidad Católica del Perú, from Peru; Instituto de Estadística of the Universidad de la República del Uruguay, from Uruguay; Banco Central de Venezuela and Centro de Desarrollo (CENDES) of the Universidad Central de Venezuela, from Venezuela.

[4] See Joseph Grunwald and Jorge Salazar-Carrillo, *op. cit.*, and Jorge Salazar-Carrillo, "Price, Purchasing Power and Real Product Comparisons in Latin America," *Review of Income and Wealth*, Series 19, No. 1 (March 1973), pp. 117–132.

[5] The reasons for choosing these goods for the illustration attempted here are:
   (1) It is by far the most important sector, covering about 75 percent of gross domestic expenditures in the countries in question.
   (2) The size and complexity of the information gathered in this sector makes it more amenable to computer handling and thus better for illustrative purposes. The number of observations per item, as well as the number of items, are much higher in the private consumption sector. Moreover, each price is identified as to quality, type of store in which it was collected, and the income stratum of the shoppers using the store. Not as much information was sought in connection with the rest of the prices in the survey.

There were 416 items included in the price sample for private consumption. Three qualities were priced in each item, adding up to 1,248 individual products. As an average, about seven or eight price observations were to be collected for each quality.[6] Thus, the maximum numbers of observations a country was expected to report came to about 9,000. Yet, a much smaller number were actually reported in the end, due to unavailabilities, price controls, poor fieldwork, and so on.

The level of disaggregation attempted was quite ambitious. For example, private consumption was ultimately divided into more than 100 subcategories. As to geographic coverage, it is important to note that not all the Latin American countries were included, the collection being restricted to the LAFTA (Latin American Free Trade Association) countries.[7]

Up to now, the work on prices has concentrated on the most important city in each nation.[8] However, the relationships will be adjusted to correspond to the nation as a whole by way of the regional price-index information available in the various countries.

2.2 *The Preparation, Execution, and Coding of the Benchmark*

The survey was prepared carefully; many months of work with the price indexes, national accounts, expenditure surveys, and so on, of the LAFTA countries were put in before the testing of alternative LAFTA baskets began. After a common basket was chosen and specified, the uniform methodology and procedures were set down. The final phase before the execution of the survey called for some testing, and for the training of supervisors and interviewers. All this was basically coordinated by Brookings.

A standard questionnaire was used in all countries. In fact, the price collection took place during the same month (May, 1968). To insure comparability in the goods selected for pricing, these were carefully specified. The same specifications were used in every country. Furthermore, a coordinating commission traveled to all countries in order to select (with the help of each collaborating institution), among all those varieties, brands, and models that complied with the specifications, those that were comparable in the different countries.

After the survey was completed, the data were given a thorough checking by the field institutes. When the corrections suggested by these verifications were done, the information was coded by the institutes. For this, the uniform coding sheets prepared at Brookings were used. Such a coding approach provides the first illustration of the application of computer operations in the price survey.

Although the Brookings Computer Center had been in existence only a short time by early 1968 and was, therefore, still facing some organizational problems, the decision was made to try to benefit as much as possible from its potential contribution. Thus, it was felt that in order to record and organize the data to be sent by the institutes as efficiently and cheaply as possible, it was convenient to homogenize the whole operation by distributing standard coding sheets to all institutes. These would then be filled out and sent in by every collaborating institute.

---

[6] The number differed among the major categories.

[7] See footnote three for a list of countries.

[8] With the exception of Ecuador, where both Quito and Guayaquil were covered.

Most importantly, these coding sheets were to be designed so as to streamline their keypunching.

This solution seemed to have various advantages. First, it removed the inefficiency involved in having to work with diverse types of coding sheets. Second, it speeded up keypunching, as well as making it less prone to error.[9] Third, having the data on cards made it easier to reap the potential benefits of certain computer operations.[10] Fourth, homogeneous data listings could be generated with ease, facilitating the verification and cleaning of the survey at Brookings.

On the other hand, some problems could be foreseen in adopting this approach. Misunderstandings could be expected in the field, as a result of which the coding sheets might not be filled out properly. Also, for certain institutes, country-specific procedures would have been preferable for several reasons.

In the end, the experience with this solution was somewhat mixed. Some institutes, because of various problems, failed to send the uniform coding sheets or did not fill them out properly. Then, inconsistencies were found between the information coded and that included in the questionnaires. Still, for the great majority of the institutes, no major problems were encountered, and the use of the coding sheets appears to have realized its expected gains in efficiency. The computerization of the study right from the beginning appears to have been beneficial for the study, in general, and for the initial phases of registering and checking the information, in particular.

Thus, in price studies across countries or regions, the uniformity of data-sources (principally coding sheets, but also questionnaires and field verification forms) seems worthwhile. However, it might be necessary to spend considerable time in examining the particular situation of every country or region before preparing these sources. Then, explaining the standard forms to supervisors, interviewers, verifiers, and coders, as well as training them in their use, would probably be essential.

2.3 *The Revision of the Coding Sheets*

The questionnaires used in the price collection and the standard forms utilized in checking the fieldwork were also sent to Brookings by the institutes.[11] The need for checking the coding work done by the institutes was firmly established by a cursory examination of these forms, in conjunction with the coding sheets. This set the stage for the next step in the data-handling process (see Figure 1).[12]

This step provided another opportunity for the application of computer methods. Given that the three data sources contained the same basic information, it was possible to establish a correspondence among them without much difficulty.

---

[9] It should be made clear that unlike most empirical research efforts in the area of prices, in this project an attempt was made to record and save the original price observations.

[10] To wit: the processing of the data could be expected to be fast; its organization explicit and well defined; and the information it conveyed ready for varied types of statistical analysis.

[11] Copies of these materials were returned to the institutes in case further field verification became necessary.

[12] At this point, it may be convenient for the reader to go over the various data-handling operations performed in the study, which are shown in Figure 1. Many of them will be discussed later on. Still, a review of such a chart may help the reader grasp the direction and objectives of the processing, cleaning, and editing operation performed, as well as their interconnections.

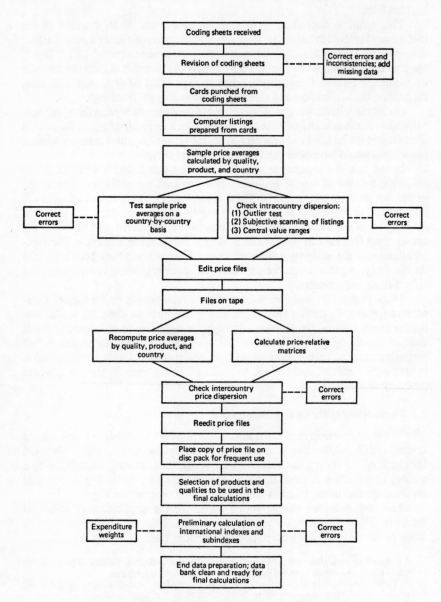

FIGURE 1 DATA HANDLING OPERATIONS IN THE ECIEL PRICE SURVEY

Using such correspondence, the data from each source could be keypunched and a program written to spot those cases in which they did not coincide. A review of the different data-sets could establish those cases in which the values in the coding sheets should be considered questionable.[13] If considered appropriate, the coding sheets would be edited at that point; if not, additional field verifications would be performed.

However, in this case, consideration was given to alternative ways of determining if such discrepancies existed. In particular, the possibility of checking the presence of such inconsistencies by hand was thought to be appealing. After close study, this technique was deemed superior because:

1. The keypunching of the three data-sets was found to be quite costly. This was partly determined by the facts that each data-source was organized somewhat differently, and that even for the same form (questionnaires, coding sheets, field verification forms) there were dissimilarities among countries.

2. At the time such checks were required, keypunching involved serious delays at the Brookings Computer Center.

3. With the use of the traditional procedures, the two steps involved in the revision of the coding sheets (scanning for discrepancies and determining their causes by checking the various sources) could be combined into one.[14]

2.4 Checking Price Averages Within Each Country

After the inconsistencies in the data had been corrected and other errors and omissions in the coding sheets were taken care of, the information included in them was punched into cards. If field verification was still pending in connection with the revision of the coding sheets, provisions were made to incorporate into cards any possible corrections or inclusions as soon as they came in. From these cards, computer listings were prepared for further checking. These listings showed the country, income stratum, type of store, and quality level corresponding to each particular price observation (see Table 1 for an illustration).[15]

The next step in the data-handling system called for average prices for each product and quality to be calculated. These averages were then contrasted with two independent sources: the average prices extrapolated from the 1960–1962 ECLA (Economic Commission for Latin America) survey and the average prices used in the calculation of consumer price indexes in the cities surveyed.[16]

A correspondence was first established between the items and qualities in the ECIEL [Joint Studies on Latin American Economic Integration] study and those in the ECLA survey and in the various consumer-price-index baskets in LAFTA. For those items and qualities found to be similar, the corresponding prices were compared. Whenever wide discrepancies occurred, the products in question were scheduled for closer examination. The specifications of the items in the different surveys were checked again. Those whose definitions were found to be somewhat

---

[13] The information contained in the coding sheets was considered the most credible, because these were supposed to be filled in after the preliminary field checking had been completed.

[14] The second step had to be done by hand anyhow.

[15] These listings were regularly updated as new data came in.

[16] See U.N., Economic Commission for Latin America, *A Measurement of Price Levels and Purchasing Power of Currencies in Latin America, 1960–62.* E/CN.12/653. 1963.

TABLE 1

EXAMPLE OF COMPUTER LISTINGS GENERATED FROM CARD DECKS, 1968 ECIEL BENCHMARK, LAFTA COUNTRIES

Country Code	Type of Store Code	Income-Strata Code	Product Code	Superior Quality	Intermediate Quality	Inferior Quality	Questionnaire Number
01	1	03	1111013	380.00	–	280.00	3
01	1	01	1111013	410.00	320.00	280.00	1
01	1	03	1111013	350.00	260.00	220.00	2
01	2	03	1111013	320.00	320.00	260.00	4
01	2	03	1111013	–	260.00	270.00	5
01	3	01	1111013	390.00	350.00	320.00	6
01	3	03	1111013	450.00	350.00	280.00	7
01	3	03	1111013	450.00	320.00	300.00	8
01	1	03	1111013	240.00	200.00	200.00	3
01	2	03	1111013	260.00	240.00	160.00	4

diverse were not checked further. For the rest, the ECIEL averages were verified by referring back to the original sources and by requesting additional field research when necessary. In the end, the card decks were updated to reflect the changes introduced in this process.

Most of this checking could have been undertaken by computer; however, traditional hand-calculation methods were preferred. Nonetheless, the computer was used as an aid in some of the tasks involved. The information conveniently printed and summarized in the computer listings, as well as the computer-calculated price averages, was central to the hand methods used.

The characteristics of the tests conspired against a more intensive use of the computer in this case. Before the average prices could be compared to each other, their similarity had to be established. Computer operations were not amenable to this kind of work, as an evaluation of the compatibility of the various specifications was required.

Furthermore, only the ECIEL price information was organized in a fashion that would make the application of computers straightforward. The consumer-price-index information and the ECLA extrapolations were provided in work sheets. Coding and punching these into cards would have been required before computers could be used.

Then, even though products with dissimilar specifications were to be screened out as a first step, some differences were bound to remain which could validly cause price discrepancies. Thus, any machine test comparing average prices from different surveys would be partially inconclusive anyhow and would need to be supplemented by subjective evaluation.

2.5 Checking Price Dispersion Within Each Country

2.5.1 Outlier tests. Unreasonable price averages can result from the influence of one or more extreme sample prices. It is important, hence, to check for price variation at the same time that the sample price averages are being questioned. Whenever such troublesome observations are detected, they could, depending on their causes, either be corrected, eliminated, or left standing. Some of the suspect price averages may be straightened out in this process.

Such dispersion checks were felt to be machine adaptable and a program was written to implement them. This program computes and prints the mean price for each product and country, as well as its standard deviation (see Table 2 for an example).

TABLE 2
SAMPLE PRINTOUT OF OUTLIER PROGRAM, 1968 ECIEL BENCHMARK (C = 2)[1]

Product Code	Mean (M)	Standard Deviation (S)	Lowest Value	Highest Value	M − C(S)	M + C(S)	Outliers
1111013	3.77	0.63	2.70	4.50	2.52	5.03	none
1111013	3.07	0.37	2.60	3.50	2.34	3.81	none
1111013	2.61	0.45	1.80	3.20	1.72	3.51	none
1111023	2.41	0.32	1.90	2.80	1.78	3.04	none
1111023	2.26	0.38	1.80	2.80	1.50	3.03	none
1111023	2.05	0.33	1.60	2.70	1.39	2.71	none

[1] C stands for an arbitrarily selected number used to define, together with the standard deviation (S), an interval about the mean (M).

In order to screen the outliers, or extreme values, the relationship between the mean and the standard deviation was used. The key question is how many standard deviations removed from the mean must a value be for it to be considered suspect? The rule to follow depends on the assumptions that can be made about the distribution function of the universe, as well as the size of the samples involved. When a normal or a t distribution can be assumed, it is known that the sample mean and standard deviation can be utilized to estimate confidence intervals, outside of which there is a low probability that the values found would belong to the same universe, or population, from which the rest of the sample is taken. Still, the selection of limits outside of which observations should be deemed suspicious is usually an arbitrary and subjective exercise.

In order to determine outlier values as *objectively* as possible, a procedure was used in which several confidence intervals were tested and, depending on statistical criteria, a particular one was chosen as the most appropriate. Intervals ranging from one to three standard deviations, at both sides of the mean, were experimented with. For this purpose, the program calculated the confidence intervals about the mean for a varied number of standard deviations. These intervals were printed out explicitly (see Table 2).

The results of the experimentation showed that confidence intervals between 1.5 and 2 standard deviations were the most reasonable from an objective standpoint. The program was then run again with the chosen values, with the prices falling outside the predetermined confidence intervals being printed out. These prices were then submitted to further tests in order to decide if they should be deleted from the sample.

Although operationally this test and the program that embodied it were quite successful, doubts about its practical and theoretical appropriateness were raised. To discuss them, it is important to remind the reader that three distinct qualities were surveyed for each of the items included in the survey, with at the most nine prices collected per quality.

Given that each quality could be considered as a separate product, the test was made to center on the dispersion of the price observations around the mean for *each quality*. When the outlier test was put to work, it was found that when observations fell outside the confidence intervals, there were usually one or, at most, two of them. Moreover, a superficial examination of the computer listings seemed to indicate that the observations spotted were not necessarily erroneous, while on the other hand, many irregularities had been missed by the test.[17]

The fact that commonly one, and rarely two, observations were flagged by the outlier program was implicit in the statistical methods used. With nine observations at the most, and with confidence intervals set around the 90 percent level, this is what would be expected if Student's *t* distribution is assumed.[18]

Another difficulty with this computer-oriented test was that in those cases in which the whole set of prices should have been suspect, rather than just one or two of them, the anomaly was usually missed completely. In particular, a very high dispersion about the mean might be a reason for which to be suspicious of the whole set of prices for a particular quality and country or, at least, of a substantial portion. Yet, in the outlier test such high variance would widen the interval within which acceptable observations could lie, and the problem might not be spotted.[19]

A further problem with the test was that its design was based on distribution functions that have been well studied, but that do not seem applicable when dealing with small price samples. Moreover, the distributions that seem to be appropriate vary according to category (e.g., different distributions would fit foodstuffs and services). In many cases the prices were distributed according to what could be considered a modal distribution. This was especially the case for categories affected by price controls.[20] In other cases, something approaching the normal curve would hold.

2.5.2 Objective outlier tests or subjective evaluations procedures? At the start of this data-handling stage, the criticisms leveled against *subjective* tests for detecting extreme values appeared quite convincing. Because of this, a determined effort was made toward the application of *objective* cleaning procedures that were unbiased in the selection of cutoff parameters. Yet, it has been seen that such outlier tests are subject to other troubles.

In sum, the computer-based outlier tests seemed to be useful for a preliminary checking of price dispersion but could not be considered definitive. Thus, the next step in the data-preparation process was the design of dispersion checks that would not be affected by the kinds of problems considered above.

[17] In some cases the outliers reflected the fact that the prices had been classified in the wrong quality slot (a price for rice, for example, being classified as superior rather than intermediate quality). On other occasions they were due to an inconsistent classification of brands or varieties (brand X toothpaste being considered sometimes as intermediate, and other times as inferior, quality). At other times, the unit of measurement was the source of trouble, with prices actually referring to units different from those specified. Finally, a number of mispunches were found, as well as prices that, even though screened out, appeared to be perfectly possible.

[18] In theory, one observation out of ten should have screened out in this case.

[19] If the observations are widely dispersed, but rather evenly distributed about the mean, the average price would remain largely unaffected. Thus, the irregularity may not be picked up by way of other checks.

[20] Under these conditions, an outlier might be perfectly valid. For example, all prices, except the ninth one, may be the same. The very low dispersion can easily frame such a price as an outlier.

It seemed that to comply with such requirements, the tests had to be based on a detailed examination of the computer listings.[21] The method finally adopted commenced with an examination of the price arrays for each quality, item, and country, as shown in the computer listings. A main objective of such scanning was to discern the dispersion patterns present in the data. As pointed out above, modal or quasi-modal distribution functions appeared to be prevalent, with a number of prices coinciding or closely grouped around a modal value. Once the appropriate central values were determined, ranges could be established around them, following some dispersion criterion.[22] The prices falling outside these limits would be considered suspect. The range was arbitrarily defined as *one-third* above or below the central value. This criterion provided a stiffer price dispersion test than the outlier program did.

The checking of computer listings, determination of central values, and the setting out of acceptable ranges were done with the aid of an assistant and a calculator. Once it was decided to go ahead with a detailed examination of the computer listings, the central-value ranges could be determined without much more work. For this reason, and also due to the flexibility required in the application of the various types of central-value ranges, the computer was not involved in the procedures.[23]

Thus, although conceivably the determination of the central value and its range could have been done by computer, the advantages that machines could bring were outweighed by flexibility requirements, and by cost considerations.[24] Another contributing factor was the circumstance that communication problems with the computer center were at their peak during the period in which these checks were required.

2.6 The Editing of the Price Files

Based on the tests described in the previous section, and on the checking of the sample price averages, a substantial number of prices were reclassified, adjusted, or deleted. In other cases, new information was requested from the field.

After these changes were incorporated into the card file, new computer listings were prepared and sent to the field, together with the unedited listings. The institutes were asked to appraise the editing done and encouraged to suggest other changes. As a result, new pricing was undertaken, either for testing purposes or to fill gaps in the survey.[25]

When the listings were returned to Brookings, it was found that in the great majority of cases the collaborating institutes agreed with the tentative editing done.

---

[21] These were being partially scanned anyhow, as part of the price-average checks.

[22] The mode was most frequently selected as the central value. However, in certain types of distributions, the median made more sense and was used instead.

[23] It was found that the great majority of the extreme values screened the second time around were also due to mispunches, incorrect quality classification, inconsistent relationships between brands and qualities, and the use of units of measurement different from those specified.

[24] The advantage of the machine in these routines lies in its greater accuracy and speed, together with the fact that it forces you to define explicitly the criteria used and to apply them consistently.

[25] These new prices referred to the original date of the inquiry: May 1968. Outlets were asked to provide prices corresponding to that month and year, although in certain cases current prices had to be deflated.

The other suggestions received from the institutes were generally incorporated into the data file. In some cases, though, their suggestions were quite foreign to the homogeneous editing procedures followed at Brookings and/or contradictory among the various countries involved. For the sake of overall consistency, no changes were introduced in these cases.

After the revision of the coding sheets and the critical examination of price averages and outliers, the first phase of the cleaning process was over. In it, the aid of the computer was quite significant, but the basic operations were mainly done by traditional methods. The computer speeded up the cleaning operations by quickly and accurately processing, calculating, and printing relevant information from the price survey (computer listings, averages, standard deviations, and so forth). Although it might appear that the computer should have been used even more, the special conditions of the project made this unadvisable. Some of these factors were: collaboration with heterogeneous research institutions resulting in diverse and/or poor reporting of the fieldwork; very broad country coverage; the infancy of the Brookings Computer Center; and the fact that much of the data was needed for only one kind of checking operation, which generally was not enough to justify keypunching expenses.[26]

2.7 Analyzing Intercountry Price Dispersion

The updated data were then put on magnetic tapes, from which price averages were again calculated and printed (see Table 3). A single geometric mean for all LAFTA countries was also calculated after converting the average prices into dollars.

TABLE 3

A SAMPLE LISTING OF COUNTRY PRICE AVERAGES FOR PARTICULAR ITEMS AND QUALITIES,
1968 ECIEL BENCHMARK
[in dollars][1]

Product	Product Code	Country Code	Superior Quality	Intermediate Quality	Inferior Quality	All Qualities
Beef, first class	1111013	01	–	0.84	0.77	0.81
,, ,,	1111013	02	–	0.91	0.78	0.84
,, ,,	1111013	03	–	1.00	0.62	0.79
,, ,,	1111013	04	–	2.05	1.75	1.89
,, ,,	1111013	05	–	1.03	0.86	0.94

[1] The official exchange rates used for conversion purposes are taken from: International Monetary Fund, *International Financial Statistics*, Washington, D.C., 1969.

Two basic types of dollar averages were calculated: one, using the official exchange rates for conversion purposes; and the other, utilizing the ECLA purchasing-power parity rates corresponding to the private consumption sector.[27]

[26] An example of the computer-center problems that had to be faced was the way in which the editing and updating of the price file was conducted in the initial stages. These had to be performed on the cards, because of delays in writing an update program. This, in turn, resulted from the needlessly complex tape structure proposed by computer specialists for the data file.

[27] On the latter rates see U.N. Economic Commission for Latin America, *op. cit.* The ECLA rates were extrapolated to May 1968.

With this material, matrices of price relatives by quality and item were formed. The price relatives converted by way of the ECLA rates were used in checking intercountry price dispersion. These rates were utilized because they equalize the purchasing power of money over consumer goods in the countries involved, and therefore their effect on the price relatives for individual products could be considered to be neutral. In contrast, official or other kinds of exchange rates distort the dollar conversions and, thus, the price relatives.[28]

An example of such a price relative matrix for a few countries is given in Table 4. In that table, each row is the set of price relatives with the country in the stub as a base. The last row is headed by the overall LAFTA average and provides the price relatives of the various countries with respect to it. Each column presents the price relatives of the particular country heading it with respect to all possible bases.

TABLE 4

A SAMPLE OF THE MATRIX OF PRICE RELATIVES FOR BEEF, FIRST CLASS, FROM THE 1968 ECIEL BENCHMARK FOR LAFTA COUNTRIES

| Denominator | Numerator | | | | |
	Argentina	Bolivia	Brazil	Chile	Colombia
Argentina	1.00	1.04	1.05	2.53	1.54
Bolivia	0.96	1.00	1.01	2.42	1.48
Brazil	0.95	0.99	1.00	2.40	1.46
Chile	0.39	0.41	0.42	1.00	0.61
Colombia	0.65	0.68	0.68	1.64	1.00
LAFTA average	0.62	0.64	0.65	1.55	0.95

These computer-generated matrices, as well as the country price averages referred to earlier, were used to check intercountry price dispersion. The basic assumption behind such tests was that even though technologies, factor costs, demand conditions, economic policies, and so on, differ from country to country, the prices of particular products could not be very far apart.

A test was designed which operated on the price relatives, spotting wide deviations from the LAFTA average. Extreme price deviants were defined as those that were over twice, or below one-half of, the LAFTA average. However, further confirmation of the extremeness of these deviants was sought by looking at other relevant parts of the price-relative matrices. Moreover, a quick reference to the price averages provided additional indications about the plausibility of these outlying prices. In the end, many of the extreme prices were left in, some because they appeared justifiable, and others because their importance in total consumer spending was found to be rather low.

Although the first part of these checks could have been done by computer, the fact that the whole matrix of price relatives would probably have to be consulted later spoke against any such use of the machine. The computer was not found to be economically efficient in providing a quick scanning of a varying subset of the price-relative matrix.

[28] On this point, see Joseph Grunwald and Jorge Salazar-Carrillo, op. cit., pp. 242–248.

The main justification for scanning the matrix of price relatives is that it is difficult to determine by rigid rules which prices are actually deviants. Just one extreme observation can give rise to an irregular pattern of price relatives. It is necessary to look at various sections of the matrix, rather than just the row headed by the LAFTA average, in order to have a clear picture of the problem.[29] Unfortunately, the parts of the matrix which are relevant vary with the product in question.

Apart from these efficiency considerations, it was felt that if the alternative of writing an algorithmic program had been chosen, it would have taken longer. Furthermore, a sizable amount of effort and resources would be spent in communicating the operations involved to a programmer, and in checking his program and output.[30] On the other hand, one important advantage of computerizing such operations would be that it forces the spelling out of an explicit and consistent procedure for determining which prices should actually be mistrusted. However, the disadvantages outweighed the advantages in this case, and the whole series of tests were done by hand.

A list of prices to be verified in the various countries emerged from these tests. For such purposes, computer listings of the edited price files, together with information about the outlying price relatives, were sent to the institutes. About three-quarters of the suspected price deviants were changed in the verification process that ensued, with all price modifications referring back to May 1968. At the end, the price file was again updated to reflect these changes.

In all, the net contribution of computer operations appears to have been somewhat larger in this second phase of data managing, with the computations it performed and printed being central to the testing done. This seems to reflect the fact that once a reasonably clean price file has been created, the contribution of the computer to succeeding data-handling tasks is bound to increase. Two other determining factors were: (a) increased reliability in the operation of the computer center; (b) the experience gained by the research staff in the use of the computer.

2.8 *Cleaning the Other Variables*

Information on a number of qualitative variables was also collected in the ECIEL benchmark survey for 1968. These characteristics pertain to each of the prices obtained. The principal ones are:

    (a) name of the store;

    (b) type of outlet (e.g. supermarket, small grocery store);

    (c) income stratum of its clientele;

    (d) brand and model or variety of the item priced;

    (e) quality classification; and

    (f) unit of measurement.

---

[29] To clarify further, one or a few high price-relatives may make some others appear low. Determining where the problem lies in cases like these may require looking at several rows and columns of the matrix or even to fall back on the country price averages. It is interesting to note that only about 4 percent of the total amount of country price averages were considered questionable at this stage.

[30] An assistant working in the project would be expected to grasp the essence of the test in a relatively short period of time.

Evaluation of the quality classification given in the field has been dealt with in previous sections. Apart from the quality indicators, only two other price attributes were processed and cleaned to some extent: the type of outlet and the income stratum of its clientele. These data were kept in the price file referred to above.[31] The burden of verifying such data was basically placed on the institutes. The central coordinating unit at Brookings attempted to obtain missing information from the institutes and insisted on the verification of the data received. Computer listings were sent to the institutes at various times, partly with this objective in mind. Any editing done by the institutes, or any new information sent, was incorporated in the price file.

The response to such editing tasks was mixed. Some countries thoroughly cleaned the information on type of store and income stratum, while others did so partially. The main categories, like foodstuffs, clothing, and rent are quite complete. Others, like consumers durables and services, present some problems. In all, most of the data can be utilized if care is exercised.

A similar type of checking was carried out with the other information mentioned, even though these were not included in the price file. This was done principally because such data were useful in the process of cleaning the price information. Because of these needs, the cleaning of these other attributes was relatively successful. However, the information on brand or variety, unit of measurement, and name of outlet did not appear useful for other research purposes and it was not subjected to systematic editing.

2.9 The Calculation of Price Indexes

Once the data were clean, the stage was set for the calculation of index numbers and their evaluation.[32] Of the different index formulations considered, the Walsh index with geometric weights seemed to be the most appropriate.[33] This index is a geometric price-relative formulation which geometrically crosses the expenditure weights of the countries involved.

The consumer expenditure weights required will come from a parallel ECIEL study, which is also coordinated by Brookings. This study is based on consumer expenditure surveys in the most important urban areas in LAFTA.[34] Because the weights generated in that project were ready for only a few countries, an alternative set was required in order to proceed with the construction of preliminary price indexes. The information utilized by the Economic Commission for Latin America in their 1960–1962 study was used for this purpose.[35]

[31] Only a limited number of store types and three income strata were specified in the study. These were kept homogeneous across countries.

[32] Of course, the items and qualities to be used in the calculations had to be determined first. As mentioned above, 416 items were included in the price survey, with three qualities priced for each. About 30 percent of these 1,248 qualities had to be excluded from the computations, because of omissions, errors, unreliability, and other data problems. However, in terms of the items themselves the situation was much better, with only 3 to 4 percent omitted from the calculations, which is a pretty low rejection rate.

[33] The advice of Richard Ruggles was most helpful in reaching this decision. For a comprehensive treatment of this topic, see Richard Ruggles, "Price Indexes and International Price Comparisons," in William Fellner et al., *Ten Studies in the Tradition of Irving Fisher*, New Haven, 1967.

[34] See the paper by Howe and Villaveces that is included in this volume.

[35] See U.N., Economic Commission for Latin America, *op. cit.*

The computer was relied upon entirely in the calculation of the price indexes. It was asked to relate the matrix of price relatives with the expenditure weight scalars according to the Walsh index-number formulation. This formula could be written simply as:

$$\prod_{i=1}^{n} \left(\frac{P_{ij}}{P_{ik}}\right)^{W_{it}},$$

where P indicates prices, i are products and j and k countries, and W_{it} is the geometric average of the country weights for every product. Place-to-place indexes were calculated for overall private consumption and for more than a hundred of its major categories and subcategories.

Apart from their overall usefulness for research, these indexes and sub-indexes can be used for further checks on the data. This is especially the case with results at lower levels of disaggregation. In fact, some of the preliminary sub-indexes suggested that there were problems in some categories (e.g. tobacco products, fuel and utilities), with dispersion being much higher than expected. These were scrutinized by researchers from the collaborating institutes in one of the semiannual ECIEL seminars, and some rechecking was done in the field when necessary. This required a minor updating of the price file, which was done by computer at this point.

The results of these tests were generally positive. The index numbers and the country rankings generated seemed quite reasonable. The overall index and sub-indexes did not diverge widely from the ECLA results in 1960, and the country rankings were quite similar.[36] As these surveys were largely independent, it can be concluded that these studies tend to support each other, and that a high degree of confidence can be placed in their findings.

Aided by the computer, several recalculations of the Walsh price index have been undertaken after the checking was completed. The indexes for overall private consumption and its main categories have been presented and analyzed in two recent papers.[37] The indexes corresponding to the various subcategories have not yet been published.

Table 5 shows a price-index matrix for a particular subcategory (preserves) as an illustration of the format in which these results are available. Some of the countries, as well as the LAFTA average, are excluded from the sample matrix shown. The structure of this table is similar to that of the price-relative matrix presented above. Each row is headed by the base country, while each column is headed by the other country.

The same process has been adapted to comparisons between pairs of countries within LAFTA. However, the index formulations used are different. The traditional Laspeyres and Paasche index numbers were calculated in this case, together with their geometric mean: Fisher's Ideal Index. As an illustration, some results from the Venezuela-Colombia binary comparison are included here. It should be noted

[36] On these points see Joseph Grunwald and Jorge Salazar-Carrillo, *op. cit.*, pp. 265–273.

[37] See Joseph Grunwald and Jorge Salazar-Carrillo, *op. cit.*, pp. 265–275, and Jorge Salazar-Carrillo, "Price, Purchasing Power and Real Product Comparisons in Latin America," pp. 128–131. The results presented in these papers differ. The latter incorporates the latest updates of the price file. Also, the weights used in the first paper refer to 1960, while estimates for 1968 were utilized in the second.

TABLE 5
MATRIX OF INTERNATIONAL PRICE SUBINDEXES FOR PRESERVES FOR SOME LAFTA COUNTRIES,
IN 1968[1]

Denominator	Numerator				
	Argentina	Bolivia	Brazil	Chile	Colombia
Argentina	1.00	1.76	1.38	1.68	1.32
Bolivia	0.57	1.00	0.79	0.95	0.75
Brazil	0.72	1.27	1.00	1.21	0.95
Chile	0.60	1.05	0.83	1.00	0.79
Colombia	0.76	1.33	1.05	1.27	1.00

[1] The official exchange rates used for conversion purposes are taken from: International Monetary Fund, *International Financial Statistics*, Washington, D.C., 1969.

that these results, in contrast to those referred to previously, are final rather than experimental. This is because for these countries the weights used were taken from the ECIEL consumer-expenditure surveys.

In Table 6, both the Laspeyres and Paasche indexes for Colombia, with Venezuela as a base, are presented. This is done for overall private consumption and its major categories. As can be seen, the discrepancy between the Laspeyres and the Paasche is quite wide, with the Laspeyres being 63 percent above the Paasche for overall private consumption.[38] The Ideal Index of Fisher, a relatively unambiguous estimate of the price difference between these countries, is also shown.

TABLE 6
BINARY PRICE COMPARISONS BETWEEN COLOMBIA AND VENEZUELA FOR OVERALL PRIVATE
CONSUMPTION AND ITS MAJOR CATEGORIES, WITH VENEZUELA AS THE BASE (1968)[1]

Categories of Goods and Services	Laspeyres	Paasche	Fisher
Food	0.87	.66	.76
Beverages	0.59	.52	.56
Tobacco	0.42	.33	.37
Clothing	1.19	.70	.91
Rent	0.52	.43	.48
Utilities	0.35	.30	.32
Durables	1.20	.76	.96
Nondurables	1.01	.68	.83
Services	0.87	.36	.56
All goods and services	0.83	.51	.65

[1] The official exchange rates used for conversion purposes are taken from: International Monetary Fund, *International Financial Statistics*, Washington, D.C., 1969.

As can be seen, consumer prices in Colombia are about two-thirds those of Venezuela at the official rate of exchange. This varies by category, but Colombia's consumer prices are lower throughout if the Fisher formulation is used. This result is not surprising. In terms of private consumption, Colombia has relatively low

[38] This is ultimately determined by the inverse correlation generally existing between prices and quantities.

prices if compared with other Latin American nations, while Venezuela has the highest prices of the group.

It should be stressed that the computer was all important in this last data-handling stage. Not only did it allow for quick and accurate calculations, as well as numerous disaggregations, but it facilitated the computation and testing of alternative formulas. In terms of cost and efficiency, there were for all practical purposes no alternatives to the computer in the calculations phase, even though some of its general disadvantages were still present.[39]

Thus, the utilization of computers in this last step of data preparation was very heavy. All calculations were done with the help of computers. It would seem that it is in the calculation stage that computer operations enjoy their greatest comparative advantage.

SECTION 3

3. *Computer Use in the ECIEL Price Study and the Usefulness of Computers: An Overview of Benefits and Drawbacks*

The 1968 ECIEL benchmark involved large masses of data. These had to be processed, organized, checked, cleaned, and used for the computation of the varying number of estimates required in the study. The computer was the backbone of these data-handling tasks, with some of the operations involved being entirely computerized.

A definite pattern can be noted in the ECIEL study computer usage. At the beginning, when the data were being processed for storage and organized as a file, the computer was heavily relied upon. The degree of computerization was relatively less intense in the cleaning and editing stages, even though it picked up somewhat at the end. During the final measurement and estimation stages, virtually all of the work was done by machine. The pattern seems to be ultimately dependent on the characteristics of the data at each stage and/or the type of work to be done on them.

The experience gained in handling the data gathered in the ECIEL benchmark price collection has shown that some of the supposed advantages of computers (see section 1) do not necessarily materialize. The advantage of increased quickness and accuracy was to a large degree offset by the time researchers had to spend in verifying that the instructions had been well transmitted throughout the chain of command (senior researcher, junior researcher, programmer, computer). A very careful and time-consuming check of the output was also necessary. This can be a formidable task, given the tremendous masses of results that the computer generates in projects of this nature.[40]

The avowed quickness of the computer was found to depend on the operation being executed. The computer can process and organize large bodies of data in little time. Nevertheless, in other tasks it does not perform as efficiently. Moreover, in every task, the computer is limited by the fact that some of its components

[39] Communication problems still remained. Computer programs and the output they generated had to be screened extra carefully.

[40] On this point refer to the information overload concept developed in the Howe-Villaveces paper included in this volume.

may act as bottlenecks. In the present study, things like keypunching, card reading, programming, and so on, on occasion created major delays that prevented the efficient use of the machine, diverting some work to the traditional method of hand calculation.

One of the more substantial contributions of the computer to the project lay in the idea of a data bank. If computers were not available, the possibility of the ECIEL data being used for other research ventures, or by other researchers, would be much smaller. Computer operations make the researcher aware of the potentialities for further use of the information and enriches his overall research product. At the same time, the requirements of data banks place certain demands on data organization, forcing the development of an efficient file structure aimed at rapid data retrieval.

The major contribution of the computer to the experience described here was in performing the final set of calculations. The research phase of the study has not been completed yet, but it can be expected that because of its computational advantages, the computer will handle nearly all of the remaining operations. It is also foreseen that the computer will permit the use of the price data file for varied experimentation and hypothesis testing, well after the main results have been presented.

On the other hand, it must be recognized that the use of the computer was, in some respects, burdensome. From the start, a project deeply plagued by lack of manpower had to devote a substantial amount of resources to mastering the essentials of computer operations. Discussions and relations with programmers and other computer personnel seem to have taken a disproportionate amount of time. One important lesson stemming from the study is that for sufficiently large projects, it is preferable to hire programmers directly, rather than to rely on those employed at the affiliated computer center. This is to a large degree determined by the lack of service orientation on the part of many computer centers, which seem to have a tendency to become absorbed with systems problems, shortchanging the users in the process.

Other problems with computer use involve the partial loss of independence and difficulties in communications. The latter are more important in day-to-day operations, the former in the long run. Communication problems with computer personnel can be quite wasteful.[41] The experience of the study described was rather negative in this respect. Complicated theoretical systems were designed never to be put into use, while in other cases, computer-center programmers spent months with the project without producing results. This not only slowed down progress, but also affected computer usage by diverting tasks away from it.

Loss of independence seems to be potentially dangerous for projects with large bodies of data. Once a file has been registered at a computer center, and a set of data-management programs has been developed, a researcher faced with unsatisfactory computer operations has few options available. The data- and

---

[41] One interesting point that seems to hold frequently is that the more sophisticated the programmer, the more complicated his solution to simple problems. The first system designed to handle the ECIEL price data would have required $200,000 for its full development. Due to the author's insistence, a less complex system was made operational by a lower-level programmer, effecting considerable savings.

program-conversion problems implied, the costs of establishing new computer relationships, the difficulties of rationally considering the alternatives (buying commercial time or exploring other possible computer linkups) tend to bind him to the status quo.

SECTION 4

4. The Use of the Computer in Price Research: Final Conclusions

After considering and weighing both the beneficial and harmful consequences of the computer for the ECIEL price benchmark, it appears that the overall impact has been positive. However, the strict controls and restrictions placed on computer usage had much to do with this outcome.[42] An additional contributing factor was the realization that programs, computations, and results had to be meticulously checked. Finally, another determining element was the continuous effort made to improve the understanding of computer operations and to better communications with computer-center staff.

The main conclusion of this paper is that the use of computers in price benchmarks in particular, and in price research in general, would be quite advantageous and thus should be expanded. However, their net contribution is likely to be much larger if the qualifications discussed above are taken into consideration in planning the role of the computer in each project.

Another important point arising from the experience gathered in the ECIEL study is the observation that the use of the computer in each task is substantially affected by factors that go beyond the computer per se. The quality of the computer center being dealt with, and of the programmers helping out, are just two of these factors. Two additional elements are the researcher's experience in computer work and his ability to relate to computer specialists. Thus, if each task is considered as output, the input coefficients corresponding to computer services would probably vary substantially, depending on these factors. Thus, things like having programmers attached directly to the projects (rather than using those on the computer-center staff) and keeping open the possibility of switching to alternative computation facilities are well worth pondering by researchers in the area of prices.

There is reason to be confident that computer science and management will improve fundamentally in the years to come. In particular, the development and canning of cleaning and editing programs amenable to price research should be expected. An improvement in the management of computer aspects of research projects, together with greater emphasis on services and user needs, also seems likely.

Moreover, researchers can help achieve a more efficient utilization of the computer setup, particularly if they are working in the same field. This could be done by an agreement to specialize in different aspects of computer work and to share the results with one another, as well as by exchanging programs and other

---

[42] As has been seen, there was no blanket endorsement of computer usage in the project. Its advisability in each task was carefully examined, with the knowledge that the net advantage or disadvantage of computers over traditional methods varies greatly from one application to another.

computer information, so as to avoid the enormous duplication of effort presently prevailing. To implement this proposal, it would be necessary to ask programmers and computer centers to tailor their work so as to facilitate its transfer to other computer centers.[43]

Hopefully, the winds of change will blow in such directions, because deriving reliable, up-to-date results for studies of the nature described above can be accomplished only with the computer. Being able to use its capabilities more efficiently may open new research frontiers in the area of prices, in general, and for price benchmarks, in particular.

---

[43] A start could be made by encouraging linkages among computer centers on a selective basis.

THE COMPUTER IN INTERNATIONAL PRICE COMPARISONS*

ZOLTAN KENESSEY

United Nations, New York

INTRODUCTION

The use of the computer in handling large price files, the subject chosen for his paper by Jorge Salazar-Carrillo, is one of the new examples of the use of the computer in economic and social research. The use of the computer in this area—more specifically in the simultaneous handling of price files for a number of countries and with a view to computerizing a great deal of the work of comparing such prices—is rather novel not only in this region of the world, i.e. in Latin America. One has to remember that the pioneering effort in this field of research, the study undertaken in the Organization for Economic Cooperation and Development (OECD) by Milton Gilbert and Irving Kravis in the early 1950s, could not yet rely on the computer handling of large price files. Neither was the computer involved in price-data operations required for the comparison of the socialist countries performed in the late 50s and early 60s in the Council for Mutual Economic Assistance (CMEA). The earlier Economic Commission for Latin America (ECLA) study in this area was not computerized either. Indeed, there is little previous experience in the field; and among the few exceptions, the experience of the Ruggleses in the management and computer manipulations of the price data for Latin American countries should be mentioned.

The current situation is very different in this respect. All the efforts at international price comparisons carried out on any significant scale are now computer-oriented. The UN International Comparison Project, a cooperative undertaking carried out by the UN Statistical Office and the University of Pennsylvania, relies heavily on the computers in New York and Philadelphia in handling price data (and some other tasks involved in the comparisons). The comparisons of the Statistical Office of the European Economic Communities, which are undertaken in a coordinated manner with the UN International Comparison Project, are also computer-oriented. And, as one can see from the paper presented by Salazar-Carrillo (as well as that by Howe and Villaveces) to the present meeting, the comparisons concerning the countries of Latin America carried out by the Brookings Institution in cooperation with a number of research institutions of Latin America are also heavily involved in computer operations.

Before going into the details of the discussion it appeared helpful to remember that the use of the computer for this kind of international comparison is a novel feature in economic and social research. Following this introductory thought, the more detailed remarks on the handling of large price data files by computers is offered in the following order: the merits of the study; findings on the positive side with the use of the computer; negative experiences with the use of the computer; and a few remarks.

* Comments on the paper of Jorge Salazar-Carrillo appearing in this volume. The views expressed in this paper are those of the author and do not necessarily coincide with those of the United Nations.

1. THE MERITS OF THE STUDY AND ITS POSITIVE FINDINGS

The basic purpose of the present conference is well served by the report of Jorge Salazar-Carrillo, which can be considered as a very helpful, honest, and frank paper on some main issues of the use of the computer in this field. The paper does not try to becloud the issues; it depicts both the positive and the negative as experienced by Salazar-Carrillo and his colleagues at Brookings while carrying out this particular piece of research. Obviously some of the experience reported is subjectively based: nonetheless, it is both valuable and relevant to our understanding of the problems related to the use of computers, since such problems, in fact, can be both objective and subjective in nature.

In keeping with the objectives of the paper and the conference, one should refrain from a discussion of the economic assumptions or statistical methods of the investigation and should avoid reviewing the ECIEL [Program of Joint Studies on Economic Integration in Latin America] study in general. In this respect, one should only stress that everybody concerned should be pleased with, and indeed grateful for, the efforts of the Brookings Institution in this important field of investigation, carried out in cooperation with a large number of Latin American research institutions of the stature of the Fundación de Investigaciones Economicas Latinoamericanos in Argentina, the Instituto Brasileiro de Economia of the Fundaçao Getúlio Vargas, the Centro de Estudios sobre Desarrollo Económico (CEDE) of the Universidad de Los Andes and the Departamento Administrativo Nacional de Estadistica (DANE) in Colombia, and the Centro de Estudios Economicos and Demographicos of El Colegio Mexico. It appears of wider international significance that a sustained research and training effort of this kind became a reality in the Western Hemisphere.

Leaving aside the relative merits of the economic assumptions and the statistical methods chosen for the ECIEL study and the various methodological decisions taken in guiding the work (for example, the views described by Salazar-Carrillo in part 2.7 of his paper concerning "Analysing Intercountry Price Dispersions") and concentrating on the computer problems described by the author, the following remarks are in order.

The exposition of the major sequences of the data operations and related problems is generally quite clear. Figure 1 of the paper (p. 296) is especially helpful for understanding the various stages of the work and identifying the place of the computer operations in them.

The summary of the experiences gained is also well designed, particularly concerning the definitive pattern observed in the use of the computer in the ECIEL study. At the early stages of the study, when the data were being processed for organizational and storage purposes, heavy reliance was put on the computer. The degree of computerization was less intense in the cleaning and editing stages. During the final estimating stages, virtually all the work was done by machine.

It is one of the merits of the paper that it does not avoid dealing with the evaluation of the day-to-day, down-to-earth operations. As an example of this, reference can be made to the review given by Salazar-Carrillo on the possibility of using the computer to check the coded results of the price surveys, the original questionnaires, and the standard checking forms against each other for possible errors and discrepancies. On the basis of this review, it was decided not to use the computer for this task but to rely on research assistants aided only by desk calculators. The reasons for this decision were various, among them the bottlenecks in keypunching at the Brookings Electric Data Processing unit at the time.

In respect to the general findings of the study, it has to be underlined that Salazar-Carrillo's overall evaluation of the use of the computer is positive. He especially emphasizes those advantages of the computers in the handling of large price-data files which permit the computation of cross-country indexes on the bases of various index number formulas at reasonable cost.

2. NEGATIVE EXPERIENCES WITH THE USE OF THE COMPUTER

In many ways, the negative experiences of the ECIEL study are more interesting than the positive ones. Therefore, one should dwell on them somewhat longer. However, an attempt is made in these remarks to attach a somewhat different interpretation to a number of the negative findings than is offered by the author.

One of the negative experiences of the study is related to the test for detecting outliers in checking the dispersion of prices within each country. In this work, the assumption accepted by Salazar-Carrillo was that "unreasonable price averages can result from one or more extreme observations in the sample prices of a particular product." (In parentheses, one is tempted to observe that neither the researcher nor the computer is in very good shape when it comes to deciding what price averages are "unreasonable" ones.) In order to screen the outlying extreme values, the means and the standard deviations were used. For various reasons, this test did not prove to be tremendously helpful, and finally it was decided not to involve the computer in this operation.

There is no apparent reason to question the wisdom of this decision. It is quite possible that under the given circumstances, a noncomputerized procedure was actually preferable. But it is certainly less obvious whether the computer or the "circumstances" should be blamed for the difficulties.

The test was based on the relationship of the mean and the standard deviation, following certain assumptions concerning the distribution function of the universe and the size of the samples involved. With the estimation of confidence intervals it was hoped to arrive at "reasonable" limits, outside of which there was a low probability that a value observed would belong to the same universe as that from which the sample was generated. Obviously, the successful application of the test chosen depended on a number of factors, among them on the adequacy of the size of the sample. Unfortunately, the size of the sample compared to the universe of prices was small. So the question posed by the author in one of the subtitles of the paper, namely, "Objective outlier tests or subjective evaluation procedures? " (p. 300), loses very much of its apparent generality and relevance for judging the relative efficiency of computer operations for such purposes. Under improper conditions, the use of the computer will obviously be less than helpful both for such and many other operations.

Naturally Salazar-Carrillo is aware of the general requirements of good price samples. However, in part because of the pilot character of the project and due to certain—under the circumstances probably unavoidable—limiting factors, the price samples could not be very close to the ideal. The data obtained in the ECIEL price sample referred to particular segments of the reference year in time and to particular geographical segments—capital cities—of the given countries. Compared to the whole universe of prices (both in the dimensions of a whole year and with respect to the prices all over the countries and not only in their capital cities) the selection of prices was a relatively small sample of all the prices in any given country in the year of observation.

Therefore, while one need not question at all the wisdom of the particular decision in the ECIEL project to avoid the use of the computer in testing the irregularities in the price data, one can still doubt the validity of any implied or explicit generalization concerning the usefulness of the computer for such studies carried out under different circumstances.

It is interesting to note that on the basis of the ECIEL project, Salazar-Carrillo considers that once the price data are clean, the computer is essential to the calculation phase. Again, one should like to agree with him. Certainly after the data problems of an external character are eliminated, the efficiency of the computer operations should become much greater. Computers are not particularly helpful in eliminating external data problems and obviously, to avoid the proverbial "garbage in—garbage out" situation with the computer runs, a very considerable effort was required in the ECIEL project to improve the quality of the basic data before further manipulation was considered feasible. In a sense, the need for such efforts is completely unrelated to the computer, since whatever method of computation is chosen, reliable basic data are essential inputs for them. Whether manual computations or machine runs follow, this type of effort is indispensable. Unless one is willing to regret the discipline required by computer runs in data preparations and implicitly considers the computer as the "cause" of such efforts, some of the remarks in the paper are not to the point. In this connection, one may find problematic those references in the paper which voice complaints about the time spent on the computer applications in the project. Naturally, this is not to question at all the facts described or the subjective feelings of those involved. It is in the interpretation of these facts that a different view is offered.

For example, the paper points out that in terms of costs and efficiency "there were for all practical purposes, no alternatives to the computer in the calculations phase, even though some of its general disadvantages were still present" (p. 308). The main disadvantage appears to be that "the additional burden of learning at least the basics of computer science and managing the computer aspects of research projects falls upon the researcher" (p. 292).

While this may be quite true, it hardly justifies classifying the price thus paid in the research as a "disadvantage." To use an analogy, if one wants to operate an automobile, it is unavoidable to learn to drive. This is a process which takes time, usually there is some amount of frustration or anxiety involved in it, and it even costs money. Yet, it would not be very illuminating to say that compared to walking, driving had this particular "disadvantage." (Also while we don't remember it—learning to walk is not that easy either.)

At an earlier session of the conference, Sadowsky referred to the larger gap that exists in the social sciences between computer specialists and the researchers than that observed in the natural sciences. Part of his explanation of this gap was given in a reference to the greater tendency of the social sciences to be what he called "one man shows," as compared to frequent team performances in the natural sciences.

It would certainly not be justifiable at all to classify the ECIEL project as a "one man show"—and this is not to lessen the significance of the contribution of such key individuals in the project as Joseph Grunwald and Jorge Salazar-Carrillo. However the ECIEL project (which is really a group of projects beyond and over the price-data operations now being discussed) is clearly a very complex, very ambitious undertaking, and the resources available for it are not quite proportionate to the width and depth of the task.

The tasks of the ECIEL project are of such a complexity from an operational point of view that the limitations of private research institutions—even if allied with each other in a cooperative manner—are quite severe. This is not only a matter of the limitation of the resources available at the center of the ECIEL project. According to the experience gained in the UN International Comparison Project, a very crucial role has to be played by the national statistical offices in the development and carrying out of such projects. Almost invariably, such offices are in a much better position to carry out the heavy statistical burden involved in the work than even well-organized private research groups. (Howard Howe and Roberto Villaveces give some excellent insight into these problems in their extremely useful paper.)

3. Concluding Remarks

Depending on the task, the computer can be a reliable tool and ally of the single researcher, the research group, and the large institution. But obviously it can fail to serve any of them—at least, for certain tasks and under certain circumstances.

It is very likely that the efficient use of the computer in the handling of large price-data files may require a somewhat larger-scale operation than was possible in the ECIEL framework. But irrespective of whether this is the case in this particular instance, it may be helpful to recall certain simple economic relationships which are taught to all students in other contexts, but which are often not in the forefront of the thinking when consideration is given to the use of the computer in economic research.

Just as in everyday economic activities certain proportions have to be maintained in the combination of the various factors of production, the work in economic research should be considered subject to requirements of a similar nature. It would appear, for example, that the use of the computer in research is not dissimilar to capital inputs in production and that the combination of computer use with the other types of inputs (like the time of the researchers) involves a great deal of managerial-type decisions.

In any given research, obviously not every combination of the capital, labor, and management inputs will be optimal or even feasible. It is surprising that the use of the computer in economic and social research is rather seldom analyzed from this angle. The usual approach to the study of the global economics of the use of the computer in economic research is much simpler, and in fact it is often restricted to the comparative costs of computer operations and manual ones. Consequently, our knowledge of the economics of the use of the computers in economic research is less satisfactory than one would expect in the case of a profession dedicated to the optimal allocation and use of resources.

Therefore, one should be grateful that the National Bureau of Economic Research and its sister organizations in Mexico, Brazil, and Argentina found it possible to organize a conference to highlight these problems.

PRICE COMPARISONS FOR CALCULATING RATES OF EQUIVALENCE IN MEMBER STATES OF THE EEC, 1954–1970

SILVIO RONCHETTI AND GUY BERTAUD

Statistical Office of the European Communities

INTRODUCTION

Ever since it started its activities, the Statistical Office of the European Communities (SOEC) has devoted special attention to social problems and to comparisons of the standard of living enjoyed by workers in member states. The first surveys carried out in these fields date back to 1953, and the first comparison of real incomes of industrial workers in the coal and steel industry relates to 1954.

Of course, it is now accepted that the conversion of nominal incomes—expressed in national monetary units—into common units of account is only meaningful if the rates of equivalence used relate to the purchasing power in consumption. The application of the official rates of exchange would, in some cases, involve such distortions that the comparison would lose a great deal of its significance.[1]

It is mainly for this reason that the Statistical Office has undertaken surveys in the field of prices and family budgets in order to collate the basic data necessary to calculate rates of equivalence in purchasing power in consumption, also known as "economic parities." The characteristics of these surveys and the methods used are explained in a number of publications of the Office.[2] These brief notes are intended to give a survey of the experience gained by the Statistical Office over a long period in the field of price surveys and to underline certain methodological problems of particular interest.

The first survey of retail prices in member countries was carried out by the Statistical Office in the context of the work of the High Authority of the European Coal and Steel Community (ECSC) in 1954. This was a pilot project, retail prices in ECSC member countries being collated for the first time for a direct comparison at the international level. The cooperation of the national statistics institutes of the six member countries enabled a list of about 230 articles to be drawn up, covering most of the range of consumption, and defined in such a way that they could be separately applied to each of the centers surveyed.

The endeavor to secure comparability had led the Office to commission a single team of survey workers to survey the prices. The results of the 1954 survey, which have the merit of being the first Community experience in the field of prices, were published in *Statistical Information of the High Authority of the ECSC*.[3]

---

[1] Cf. Milton Gilbert and Irving Kravis, *Comparative Study of National Products and Purchasing Power of Currencies*, Organization for European Economic Cooperation, Paris, 1954.

[2] Cf., in particular, *Statistical Information of the High Authority of the ECSC*, July–August 1957; "Comparison of Real Incomes in the ECSC," *Studies and Documents*, Statistical Office of the European Communities; and "Real Incomes in the ECSC 1954–1958," *Social Statistics*, No. 2, 1960, Statistical Office of the European Communities.

[3] *Statistical Information*, July–August 1957.

The calculation of economic parities and the calculation of real incomes of workers in the coal and steel industries were the subject of a report from the Office in 1956.[4]

In 1958, the Office repeated the survey on retail prices, introducing important improvements both in methodology and in the list of items. On the latter point, the experience gained in the 1954 survey and the data obtained from a survey of family budgets of workers in the coal and steel industries[5] enabled us to draw up a list of items which, while being less extensive than that used in the first study, ensured wider representativeness of workers' consumption. This list, structured in a more balanced manner in order to take account of the distribution according to item groups, consisted of about 180 basic items.

The 1963 survey, the third in the series, was characterized by a fundamental extension of the scope of the survey. Indeed, while the 1954 and 1958 surveys had been designed to cover the sectoral field of the ECSC industries, the 1963 survey extended to all manufacturing industry and, because of this, covered the whole of the territory of member countries.

In 1966, the Statistical Office repeated the price surveys from a different viewpoint: while the previous surveys had stressed the socioeconomic aspect of the problem, the new surveys were designed within a more restricted framework, having the precise aim of bringing together basic data for the study of the problem of economic fluctuations and competition.

It was important at the beginning of the first decade of the existence of the Common Market to determine the development of prices in the countries, to follow their trends, and to endeavour to pinpoint the influence which the European Economic Community (EEC) had been able to exert on these phenomena. For these reasons, the price survey was limited to a number of particularly representative items of international trade; it was carried out only in department stores, and related to a few of the largest towns in the member countries. While the scope of the surveys was limited, their frequency was increased and a twice-yearly frequency (April and October) was adopted.

The results of the semiannual survey of retail prices were published up to 1968 in the *General Statistical Bulletin*.[6] Since 1968, the results of the April and October surveys have appeared in the *Studies and Statistical Surveys* series.[7] 1970 was a key year in the work of the SOEC, the survey program being fundamentally redesigned so as to pursue several objectives at the same time within a coordinated plan at the international level.

For 1970, the United Nations started a project for the comparison of the gross national product of a large number of countries throughout the world (United States, United Kingdom, Japan, India, and so on). This study, very ambitious in its scope, was of interest in connection with that part of the retail price survey relating to "household consumption," which constitutes one of the basic

    [4] "Comparison of Real Incomes of Workers in the Community Industries—ECSC," *Studies and Documents*.

    [5] "Family Budgets of ECSC Workers 1956–1957," *Statistical Information*, Social Statistics Series, No. 1, SOEC, Luxembourg, 1960.

    [6] See Numbers 4-1967, 9-1967, 3-1968 and 9-1968, SOEC.

    [7] See Numbers 6-1968, 3-1970 and 4-1970, SOEC.

elements of the UN project, capital formation and public consumption making up other constituent parts of the comparison.

Alongside the UN study, which first and foremost will be conducted at a Community level, the Office has undertaken its regular surveys on industrial workers' wages. Of course, the Office has included in its plan the task of making comparisons of workers' incomes, which were carried out several times in previous years.

Taking into account these two elements, and with the desire of pursuing the studies on prices from the point of view of competition, the Office redesigned the semiannual survey and instituted a survey plan which suited the threefold objective pursued.

The coverage of the survey was considerably extended:
(a) the list of products was increased to 600 articles;
(b) the number of towns surveyed was doubled, i.e. 50 centers; and
(c) all types of shops were taken into consideration.

In this way, it became possible to collect in a single operation the basic data required for the various studies undertaken from different viewpoints.

For 1970, the general survey was carried out, by way of exception, on a twice-yearly basis, the April survey being in the nature of a pilot project.[8]

Starting in 1971, the price survey will be annual and will enable indicators to be drawn up on the level of prices according to major item groups (food, clothing, and so forth). The calculation of economic parities can be carried out only every three years in relation to the wage surveys.

METHODOLOGICAL PROBLEMS

No complete and systematic methodological description will be given of the work of the Statistical Office of the European Communities on this question. This methodology—dealt with in publications already mentioned—is, moreover, a conventional and well-known one: average prices per item and per country are calculated within the framework of a list of articles and a certain field of observation. These prices are introduced into a Laspeyres formula, which gives, by means of double-weighting country A and country B, a double parity or fork of binary parities for each pair (A, B) of countries. An interesting solution has been devised for calculation purposes in order to observe the rules of transitivity in a highly synthetic system.

We shall therefore only deal with certain aspects of this work. For a part of it, the Statistical Office of the European Communities has undoubtedly supplied, thanks to several years of experience, a major positive contribution. For others, leaving aside realistic or ingenious approaches, the conceptual basis still remains a subject for reflection and discussion.

It may be said that from many points of view, the problems posed by international price comparisons (comparison in space) greatly resemble those encountered on a more conventional level in the compilation of price indexes (comparison in time). In both cases, something has to be said about lists, definitions, and

[8] See "Retail Prices in the Countries of the European Community," Statistical Office of the European Communities, Doc. No. 479/71.

questions of representativeness and numerous decisions must be taken, such as
what articles should be included, where and when the prices should be noted, and
who should carry out the surveys and how.

But a new criterion, that of comparability,[9] has created an additional difficulty
in this international work. The difficulties are all the more serious, owing to the
great number of countries in which the comparison is carried out; and to the fact
that these countries, or, more precisely, the consumers in these countries, differ
from each other from the point of view of standard of living or behavior.

It is easy to say, in the name of logic, what appears to be obvious—that the
prices to be taken into consideration are those observed on the basis of both
representative and comparable items. In reality, matters are more complex than
this, and it can often be seen that the two criteria are conflicting.

Indeed, comparability may be increased by making the definitions as narrow
as possible (in extreme cases, only taking into consideration quite specific branded
articles). But the danger of bias appears clearly here, since in the last resort, these
articles may only be representative of themselves.[10] Conversely, an article or
service considered highly representative in one or more countries, owing to a
heavy budgetary weighting or coefficient, may not have an equivalent in another
given country. Finally, by playing on the double constraint of comparability-
representativeness and intersecting the detailed tables of consumption structures
of the countries taken into consideration, it is possible to devise a list (or lists) of
reference items.

But first of all a decision in principle ought to be taken, a decision which
determines to a certain extent what will be done subsequently: must the list of
articles be standard for all countries? Can other, less rigid solutions be envisaged?
Indeed, in reality, since 1954 the Statistical Office of the European Communities
has always adhered to, and applied, the principle of the standard list. The argument
on which this decision is based is that although, owing to their geography and
history, the six countries still have distinct social and economic differences more
than ten years after the Treaty of Rome, it cannot be denied that there is more
conformity than nonconformity.

It is therefore possible to find a standard list of some one hundred goods and
services which will be satisfactory from the point of view of representativeness and
comparability, and to arrive at a listing accompanied by all the necessary definitions. Perhaps we may point out that the European experts in difficult cases prefer
to stress representativeness, adding opposite general definitions of items (e.g.
refrigerators, stoves, washing machines) the reference "most common makes."

This principle of the standard list has therefore been adhered to. It implies,
as a corollary, that an average price should be available for each item and for each
country, on account of the mechanism of the double calculation of the index with
the two available weightings. The absence of a single average price results in
elimination of the item for all countries.

[9] When trends in time are being measured, the comparability criterion is also encountered. In
most cases, the problem is solved very simply by strictly adhering to the same article in time. Everything
is, however, complicated when, in order to take account of technological progress, it is necessary to
break a series. The difficulties are then of the same nature as those discussed in this paper.

[10] The problem is to find them on the market. In some cases, the item may be so scarce that a search
for it strangely resembles a treasure hunt.

Although not frequently, this situation has arisen. At any rate, there is something artificial here due to the rigidity of the system, which might be corrected so as to give greater flexibility.

It is one of the questions presently being studied by the Statistical Office of the European Communities for forthcoming surveys: one could perhaps envisage movable lists of items which could be common to two, three, or four countries. But the two disadvantages of such a procedure are well known: first, the weightings, being closely linked to the structure of the list, also become movable; and second, the nontransitive character of the Laspeyres indexes thus calculated must be considered.

As already pointed out, a list of items should be drawn up within the framework of a precise nomenclature, containing figures for consumption functions. The important harmonization projects carried out by the SOEC for the national accounting systems of the six countries have enabled the SEC system to be used from the beginning (European System of Integrated Economic Accounts, a European version of the SNA: Revised System of National Accounts of the United Nations). The representativeness of the list of items could therefore be checked in a systematic and logical way.

In the field of the lists of items and weights, the problems being closely linked, progress from the first survey of 1954 is very important in all sectors: number of articles, representativeness, detailed knowledge of consumption structures. This progress is also largely due to the convergence in time, over seventeen years, of economic policies and attitudes of the six countries; and, of course, to the good results obtained in harmonizing all the other Community statistics.

In order to organize the survey in the field, the scope of the study having been clearly defined, a decision must be made as to the number and distribution of selling points at which prices are noted. This is a scientific problem, since the fluctuation of prices around their average value is rarely zero.

In the first Community surveys, taking into account their objective, it was not difficult to pinpoint on the map the most representative towns of the coal and steel producing areas, and to locate in these towns—after rapid inquiries with the competent local authorities—the stores largely frequented by workers and their families.

But in the surveys we conduct today, without wishing to unduly exaggerate the size of the problem, some difficulties are encountered and certain precautions have been taken. In fact, the rates of equivalence envisaged comprise all households in the countries (value of private consumption within the GNP) or all workers' households (wages). Thus, there is a problem to be solved in order to arrive at a correct, or at least unbiased, estimate of average national prices.

On the strictly conceptual and theoretical level, it can easily be seen how this problem can be set out: in a two-dimensional universe of selling points, i.e. the town and type of store. A proper surveying plan must be elaborated with stratifications taking into account the geographical region, the size of the town (population), and the size of the store (sales surface area).

Given the knowledge, or an estimate, of price variations between towns and between types of stores, it will thus be possible to work on representative samples or selling points (which, of course, would depend on the article studied), and to extrapolate the results for the country as a whole.

From a practical point of view, the problem poses itself in other terms. The variances between prices are not properly known; the tables giving the distributions of retail turnover over these different criteria are very incomplete or too aggregated. The only thing to be done—assuming that the size of the town and type of store (essentially the sales surface area) probably, and in a general way, have a certain correlation with the prices to be observed—is to distribute the network of observations in space, taking into account these two factors in a "quota"-type system.

This is a system currently applied by the SOEC. The prices noted are later weighted according to turnover (as in the Federal Republic of Germany) or are distributed from the beginning in a self-weighted system (Italy and the Netherlands, for example).

Finally, thanks to certain machine-processed data additional to the 1970 survey, we have new information on the dispersion structures of prices. Having measured certain variation coefficients, we can examine whether the distribution adopted can be maintained and whether any useful changes can be made in the number of observations, number of towns, and number of stores for future surveys.

Of course, the greater the variance between prices, the more care should be taken to distribute the sample in space. This risk does not seem to be serious for western Europe although, paradoxically enough, we are rather ill-informed in this field. However, it may be that for other countries the problem merits very close study.

There is little that can be said about the period during which prices are noted. Of course, these prices vary in time within the framework of a general, more or less rapid, increase and certain seasonal movements. It is sufficient to determine this period according to the calendar, taking into account administrative or practical considerations. For reasons which need not be discussed here, the Statistical Office and the six EEC countries prefer the spring or autumn periods. By applying the corrective coefficients drawn from the national price indexes, not to the prices themselves but to the parities at the end of the calculations, estimates corresponding to the year's average can be readily made.

The problem of the survey workers—indeed, the organization of the survey in the field—raises certain very interesting questions. Over a number of years, the Statistical Office has adhered to a system which seems logically foolproof: carrying out the survey in the six countries with the same team of international civil servants. The survey was staggered over six months. This decision was justified by the endeavor to provide, as effectively as possible, good conditions of comparability. But this method has now been abandoned. The operation has been decentralized within the six countries and even inside certain countries (France), which, of course, makes it possible to reduce considerably the time span of the work, and to carry it out over the whole area simultaneously.

But what about comparability under such conditions? Since the list of articles and corresponding definitions have been drawn up and defined over recent years within the framework of semiannual surveys on competition, everything gradually fell into place in the course of various meetings of the Working Party on Prices, a veritable club of national statisticians. It may be maintained that, thanks to the constant change of sample products, and thanks to the frequent and regular visits—organized on a rotating basis so that five countries were always the guests of one of the others—the system is now well established, and comparability problems only arise when new articles are included in the list.

The program of processing the gross results of the survey in the computer, i.e. all the elementary price data, must be carried out in several stages. The first consists of showing the average prices per article and per country. It has already been pointed out that for certain countries the calculation requires a weighting system which takes account of trade structures. These average prices are given in national currency and in dollars on the basis of the official exchange rates. Coefficients of variation of prices around their average and the number of readings are also available.

The next phase is the calculation proper. This means working out the price ratios P_A/P_B and P_B/P_A for each article and each pair of countries (A, B). Thus we get the elementary parities which, when weighted according to the Laspeyres formula, give binary parities.

It is quite possible not to explain these price ratios, and to be content with storing them for the calculation of indexes. But the Statistical Office has always insisted on presenting the tables of these ratios because of their statistical interest: one country being taken as a reference (denominator of ratios), we have five columns, each of which corresponds to another country (numerator of ratios), the articles being listed in rows.

As all the permutations of the reference country are guaranteed, we have the matrices of elementary parities, which are extremely interesting to examine and analyse. First of all, there is the value of an ultimate test, since deviating ratios immediately attract attention. There is also the scientific interest, since the column of price ratios can be treated like any statistical series. The coefficient of variation of these ratios is calculated, a very significant indicator [11] which reflects the resemblance or nonresemblance of the pair of countries studied. The development can also be studied over a period, starting from the first surveys, and certain convergence effects measured. Finally, to the extent that the list of articles included can be regarded as constituting a sort of sample drawn from the universe of goods and services, some idea can be formed of the effectiveness of the sample and the theoretical accuracy of the estimator of the final parity. It may be noted, in passing, that the fact that the coefficients of variation vary appreciably between pairs of countries may be an argument against the principle of the common list.

Having the price ratios at our disposal, we continue the aggregation and synthesis by calculating the matrix of Laspeyres indexes. We know that for n countries there are: $n(n - 1)$ indexes.

These results will obviously be presented on the most general level, i.e.: all articles × all countries. But other results will also be worked out for interesting subassemblies. A first family will be of the following kind: category of articles × all countries (on the basis of the SEC). The other, prepared for all articles, will enable parities to be calculated according to type of trading establishment (small

---

[11] The value of the coefficient of variation is generally between 20 and 40 percent.

stores and large stores), and according to town: all articles × towns; all articles × types of trade.

All these results will make it possible to compare and measure price levels, either within a country or between countries, for homologous assemblies, such as large towns and small stores. Thus, we hope to be able to organize future surveys in a better way and even to simplify them, thanks to a more rational distribution of fieldwork.

One the Laspeyres indexes have been calculated, the work is usually continued by also calculating the Fischer indexes [of which there are $n(n - 1)/2$].

Unfortunately, these indexes are not transitive, although the Fischer indexes are not far from being so. Frequently, this difficulty can be avoided by a star-shaped scheme of reference, with one of the countries (A), taken from the international comparison, considered "important" enough to be placed in the center of the whole system:

$$D \quad B$$
$$A$$
$$C.$$

A scheme of this type is not applicable to the Common Market countries. It was, therefore, necessary to consider these problems of transitivity, since $n(n - 1)$ indexes cannot be used for converting nominal wages into real wages, or at least give a distorted effect.

A method devised by an expert from the Statistical Office, Professor Van Ijzeren, has many advantages. It has been described at length both in the publications of the Central Statistical Office at The Hague and by those of the Statistical Office in Luxembourg. It is worth recalling that this is a calculation by iteration of a nonlinear system of n equations with n unknown factors, in which the parameters are shown by the Laspeyres indexes. The system is based on a very concrete tourist-type model and has a number of qualities: in particular, its lack of sophistication. This method will again be applied by the Statistical Office of the European Communities to the results of the November 1970 survey.

APPLICATIONS AND CONCLUSIONS

Before examining the extension of the calculation of economic parities carried out within the framework of the 1970 price survey, it seems worthwhile to stress once again the possibilities of analysis offered by this calculation. Indeed, the various series of parities mentioned in the preceding paragraphs permit a graduated approach to the problem of consumer prices and highlight the various facets of this complex phenomenon.

In the first stage, the analysis of the matrix of elementary parities leads to a comparison of prices at item level. This operation is of fundamental importance, owing to the fact that among other things, it provides concrete evidence as to whether the definitions of the different items were correctly interpreted on a Community basis. Where the elementary parities deviate, the corresponding basic prices will be checked to ascertain whether the abnormality is to be attributed to a real difference in prices or to a misinterpretation of the definition of the item concerned.

The successive aggregations provide a variety of information of a structural nature. A first aggregation will deal with all the items broken down according to type of trading establishment: on the one hand, department stores, multiple chain stores, supermarkets and hypermarkets, and consumer cooperatives; and, on the other hand, other retail stores. This calculation, carried out for the first time within the framework of the study of economic parities, will supply the basic elements required for a concrete examination of prices broken down by kind of trading establishment.

A similar aggregation, equally concerned with all the articles, and considering all types of stores, will serve to throw light upon the element "size of towns." The price survey, in fact, considers two types of population center: towns with a population of over one-hundred thousand and those with populations of less than one-hundred thousand.

On the other hand, a study of the dispersion of prices according to region is not intended, the number of towns considered being too small to ensure acceptable representativeness in such calculations. But within the framework of analyses of subassemblies, economic parities covering all types of trading establishments and towns will be calculated on the basis of main categories of articles: food, clothing, rent, furniture, services. It will thus be possible to undertake a comparison of partial parities with the general parity and to indicate any possible discrepancies.

Finally, the synthesis for all articles, all forms of trade, and all types of towns gives the general parity for the country as a whole, i.e. the number of monetary units which, in each country, provides the same purchasing power during a given period. It is the rate of equivalence of consumer purchasing power compared with the official exchange rate which enables the real position of each country to be determined in relation to the others.

For information purposes, while awaiting the results now being worked out for 1970, it has been found worthwhile to revert to the economic parities of 1958 and 1963 and the values extrapolated to 1966, the last year for which the calculation was carried out. The parities were expressed according to commodity in Belgian francs. (See Table 1.)

Continuing along the same lines, we again compared the binary economic parities with the official exchange rate for 1958 for the steel industry. In spite of

TABLE 1
RATES OF EQUIVALENCE OF CONSUMER PURCHASING POWER
[in Belgian francs]

Country		Steel Industry	Industry as a Whole	
		1958	1963	1966
Germany (F. R.)	1 DM =	11.70	11.70	12.00
France	100 Fr.F. =	11.37	9.70	10.10
Italy	100 L. =	7.82	7.95	7.80
Luxembourg	100 Fr.L. =	97.46	100.00	102.00
Netherlands	1 Fl =	15.45	15.20	14.50

the outdated nature of this calculation, the results seem particularly interesting, owing to the fact that for certain countries, divergencies from the official exchange rate are considerable and systematic between Belgium, on the one hand, and each of the other countries, on the other.

Table 2 points up the most important aspects of the problem. The disparity between the economic parities and the official exchange rate provides, first of all, an indication of the level of prices according to pairs of countries. We note, for example, that compared with the official rate of exchange, the level of prices in France was 4 to 11 percent higher than in Belgium. On the other hand, in the Netherlands the level of prices compared to Belgian prices, still compared with the official rate of exchange, was 13.5 to 17 percent lower.

TABLE 2
COMPARISON OF ECONOMIC PARITIES WITH OFFICIAL RATES OF EXCHANGE, 1958
[official rate of exchange = 100]

	West Germany		France		Italy		Luxembourg		Netherlands	
	DM	%	Fr.F.	%	L.	%	Fr.L.	%	Fl	%
Official exchange rate	8.404	100.0	840.0	100.0	1251	100.0	100.0	100.0	7.590	100.0
Economic parity:										
a. Belgian weights	9.088	108.2	933.2	111.1	1356	108.4	104.5	104.5	6.564	86.5
b. Weight of country indicated in column head	8.350	99.4	872.4	103.9	1172	93.7	102.0	102.0	6.323	83.3

As has been pointed out, the level of prices falls within a greater or lesser area of dispersion, which reflects the difference in the weighting scheme used for the calculation of binary parities; the more the weighting schemes of two countries differ one from the other, the greater is the area of dispersion.

It can be clearly seen from the table that the Benelux countries have the closest weighting schemes, while the greatest difference in consumption structure occurs between Italy and Belgium.

We can discern for 1958 three groups of countries having particular characteristics:

In the first group, represented by France, economic parities are lower than the official rate and the indexes fall below the base line representing the exchange rate.

The second group (the Netherlands) shows opposite characteristics, the parities being greater than the official exchange rate.

Finally, for the third group, which includes Germany, Italy, and Luxembourg, the economic parities do not deviate to a great extent from the official rate, even if the dispersion zone is large, at least for the first two countries.

We might conclude, therefore, that in 1958:

(1) the internal purchasing power in France was distinctly lower than the value attributed to it by the official exchange rate, and, consequently, the level of prices was higher than in the other countries;

(2) the level of prices was, on the other hand, particularly low in the Netherlands and the Dutch guilder had a purchasing power considerably greater than the official value; and

(3) for the other countries (Germany, Italy, and Luxembourg), as a general rule, we can say that the price level was more or less similar; it was lower than that of France and higher than that of the Netherlands.

We might finally point out that the financial measures taken in France toward the end of December 1958 have corrected the situation in that country, thus implicitly confirming the results of the SOEC survey.

The Statistical Office of the European Communities, continuing its work on wages in the manufacturing industry, plans to undertake a comparison of real wages of workers by using, as in the past, rates of equivalence of consumer purchasing power. Of course, these parities take into account the general characteristics peculiar to industrial workers. Thus, a series of rents was drawn up corresponding to the types of workers' housing.

With regard to the weighting scheme corresponding to the consumption structure, the Office plans to carry out tests to determine to what extent the results of the calculation are influenced by this element. Moreover, a more general calculation will be made in order to incorporate the SOEC's work into the wider framework of the United Nations study mentioned above. In this project, the parities used for the conversion of gross national products will be calculated on a broader basis than that of private consumption. The latter will always play a basic part, however, provided, of course, that it relates to the whole of the population. This is why it is planned to calculate a rate of consumer purchasing power applicable to the population as a whole.

The results of this calculation, which will be made for workers, using the same principles as those discussed in the preceding paragraphs, will be integrated into a wider compilation which will feature parities relating to the formation of capital and public consumption. We shall thus arrive at the "equivalences of purchasing power" laid down for the first time twenty years ago by Gilbert and Kravis,[12] and which were used again on new bases by the UN study.

It remains for us to stress a final application which concerns the restructuring of the forthcoming price surveys planned by the SOEC. The drawing up of various series of parities—according to types of stores, size of towns, groups of articles—will provide a very intricate documentary basis for the organization of annual consumer price surveys. In other words, it will enable forthcoming investigations to be restructured according to a less pragmatic scheme than that hitherto used.

Moreover, the documentation available to the SOEC would make it possible to carry out a scientific study on variance analysis. This study, which would obviously be the ideal basis on which to tighten up the price surveys from the statistical point of view, would require a major effort on the part of the SOEC and would probably not be available for a considerable time.

---

[12] Cf. Gilbert and Kravis, *op. cit.*

INDICATORS OF PROTECTION AND OF OTHER
INCENTIVE MEASURES*

BELA BALASSA

Johns Hopkins University and the International Bank for Reconstruction and Development

AND

DANIEL M. SCHYDLOWSKY

Harvard University

This paper reports on research by the authors in deriving indicators of protection and of other incentive measures in Latin American countries. It describes methods of estimation by the use of computers and presents the major results obtained so far. It further examines possible future developments in using simulation models and in evolving "policy packages" for the developing countries.

1.

Following earlier efforts (Barber, 1955), the concept of effective protection received considerable attention after the publication of papers by Balassa (1965), Corden (1966), and Johnson (1965). These contributions reflect a dissatisfaction with models of international trade and protection which do not allow for trade in intermediate products. Thus, it has been pointed out that resource allocation and the protection of particular activities is affected not only by the nominal rate of protection on the product itself, but also by nominal rates on traded inputs and by the share of value added in the product price. The effective rate of protection captures these influences as it involves estimating the margin of protection on value added.

The effective rate of protection is conventionally estimated in a partial equilibrium framework under the following assumptions: zero substitution elasticity between material inputs and primary factors, constant returns to scale, infinite foreign elasticities of demand (for exports) and supply (of imports), absence of distortion in product and in factor markets, and no transportation costs. If substitution elasticities are zero, effective rates are expressed as the percentage excess of domestic over foreign value added.

(1) $$Z' = T'(I - A)(I - \widehat{1'A})^{-1} = T'(I - A)\hat{V}^{-1},$$

where Z = column vector of effective rates of protection;
T = column vector of nominal tariffs;
A = matrix of direct input output coefficients for domestic and imported inputs at world prices; and
$I - \widehat{1'A} = \hat{V}$ = diagonalized matrix of value-added coefficients at world prices.

* Portions of this research were supported by the Development Research Group through funds made available by the Agency for International Development, the National Science Foundation, and the Ford Foundation. The views expressed are those of the authors and are not necessarily those of the sponsoring agencies.

Since effective rates are always greater (smaller) than nominal rates on the product itself if the latter exceed (fall short of) average nominal rates on intermediate inputs, the variability of effective rates always exceeds that of nominal rates. It also follows that the greater are the differences in nominal rates of protection on products and their inputs and in the share of value added among industries, the greater will be variations in effective rates of protection as compared to nominal rates.

The additional information provided by the effective protection concept, and hence its practical usefulness, thus depends on the extent of interindustry differences in nominal rates and in value-added shares. This explains the importance of the use of effective rates in developing countries and, particularly, in the countries of Latin America where nominal rates vary to a substantial extent. In several of these countries, nominal rates range from less than zero (this will be the case for commodities subject to export taxes) to 150 to 200 percent.

We have assumed so far that transportation costs are nil. Under this assumption, all goods would be traded so that only production costs at the last stage of fabrication would be relevant, and effective rates could be calculated by utilizing (1). However, in reality, a variety of goods are not traded because the cost of transportation makes this prohibitive. Such "nontraded" goods generally include electricity, gas, water, banking, insurance, domestic trade and transportation, and other services. They are used as inputs in the production of traded goods.

The treatment of nontraded inputs will depend on the objective of calculating the effective rate of protection. If this is designed as a measure of the incentives provided to particular industries, we need to estimate the increase in the cost of nontraded goods to the producer that results from protection. In turn, if the effective rate of protection is used to estimate the cost of protection, the cost of nontraded inputs to the national economy should be included with the direct cost of processing. The former objective is served by applying the so-called Balassa method; and the latter, by employing what has come to be called the Corden method.

The Balassa method assumes infinite elasticity of supply of nontraded goods, so that protection-induced increases in the prices of traded commodities used directly and indirectly in producing nontraded goods are assumed to be shifted forward. The Corden method, too, assumes forward shifting of increases in these prices, while including direct and indirect value added in the production of nontraded goods with value added in processing.

In the practical application of the two methods, the input-output coefficients for nontraded inputs are divided into two parts: (a) material goods used directly and indirectly in producing nontraded goods and (b) value added expended directly and indirectly in the production of nontraded goods. This calculation is effected by using a semi-input-output method which involves utilizing elements of the matrix of direct and indirect value added and material input coefficients for nontraded inputs, without further partitioning the material inputs used in the production of nontraded goods. It is apparent that the difference in the formulas used for estimating the effective rate of protection under the Balassa and Corden methods is that the former includes, and the latter excludes, in the denominator of the equation, the cumulated value-added elements of nontraded inputs.

(2) $$Z'^B = T'[I - A_t - RA_{nt}][I - \widehat{1'A_t} - \widehat{1'A_{nt}}]^{-1},$$

(3) $$Z'^C = T[I - A_t - RA_{nt}][I - \widehat{1'A_t} - \widehat{1'A_{nt}} - \widehat{1'R_wA_{nt}}]^{-1},$$

where the superscripts indicate the Balassa and Corden methods respectively,

A_t = direct coefficient matrix for traded inputs;

A_{nt} = direct coefficient matrix for nontraded inputs into traded commodities;

R = total coefficient matrix of material inputs into nontraded goods; and

R_w = total coefficient matrix of domestic value-added inputs into nontraded goods.

The effective rate of protection calculated by using the Corden method can be reinterpreted as measuring the direct domestic costs of earning and saving foreign exchange. In turn, the so-called Bruno ratio shows the total (direct plus indirect) domestic cost of earning and saving foreign exchange by combining the cost of domestic fabrication at all stages of processing (Bruno, 1965). It is calculated by dividing the sum of direct and indirect domestic value added by net savings in foreign exchange, which latter is defined as the difference between the world-market price of the product and the world-market value of imported inputs used directly and indirectly in domestic fabrication.

(4) $$B' = W'[I - A]^{-1}[\hat{P} - \widehat{N'(I - A)^{-1}}]^{-1},$$

where V = column vector of value added per unit of output at world prices.

W = column vector of domestic value added per unit of production at domestic prices;

P = column vector of international prices per unit of production; and

N = column vector of imported inputs per unit of production.

Thus, while the effective rate of protection is estimated by the use of the semi-input-output method, the estimation of the Bruno ratio involves using a full input-output method. It can easily be shown (Balassa-Schydlowsky, 1968) that the latter is equivalent to the weighted average of effective rates at various stages of fabrication, the weights being world-market value added at the different stages.

(5) $$B = 1 + V'Z[I - A]^{-1}[V'(I - A)^{-1}]^{-1},$$

where V = column vector of value added per unit output at world prices.

Calculations of effective rates of protection and the Bruno ratio are customarily made at the existing exchange rate. However, this rate reflects the structure of protection itself and, in order to estimate net rates of protection and the cost of protection to the domestic economy, calculations need to be made at the exchange rate that would obtain under free trade. In practice, this involves adjusting the results obtained at the existing exchange rate for the difference between this and the free-trade rate.

2.

In the research project on "The Structure of Protection in Developing Countries," calculations of effective protection and the cost of protection were made, among others, for Brazil, Chile, and Mexico (Balassa, 1971). In the following, we briefly report on these results; in all cases, estimates adjusted for the difference between the existing and the free-trade exchange rates are shown.

The system of protection in all three countries is characterized by discrimination in favor of the manufacturing sector and against primary activities. However, the extent of this discrimination is substantially greater in Chile and in Brazil than in Mexico. This is shown by the fact that net effective rates of protection on manufacturing activities averaged 68 percent in both Brazil and Chile, as against 16 percent in Mexico.

Brazil and Chile also show much variability in effective rates of protection, indicating that the incentives provided to individual industries differ to a considerable extent. Nevertheless, a definite pattern emerges in the two countries; we observe an escalation in the level of protection from lower to higher levels of fabrication. Nominal and effective rates tend to be the lowest on construction materials, followed by intermediate products at lower levels of fabrication, machinery, intermediate products at higher levels of fabrication, and consumer goods (Table 1).

TABLE 1
NET NOMINAL AND EFFECTIVE RATES OF PROTECTION IN MANUFACTURING INDUSTRIES
[percent]

	Brazil (1966)		Chile (1961)		Mexico (1960)	
	Nominal Rates	Effective Rates	Nominal Rates	Effective Rates	Nominal Rates	Effective Rates
Construction materials	41	47	−1	−2	−12	−7
Intermediate products I	52	66	−9	1	12	26
Intermediate products II	1	1	30	54	15	27
Nondurable consumer goods	89	115	81	124	15	19
Durable consumer goods	64	98	10	30	37	77
Machinery	48	58	14	18	18	27
Transport equipment	2	2	2	2	16	26
Manufacturing total[3]	55	68	26	68	14	16

SOURCE: Bela Balassa, *The Structure of Protection in Developing Countries* (Baltimore: Johns Hopkins University Press, 1971), p. 56.
[1] Included with intermediate products I.
[2] Included with consumer durables.
[3] Includes processed feed.

The escalation in the structure of protection also explains the fact that in both Brazil and Chile effective rates tend to exceed nominal rates by a substantial margin. These differences, in turn, are relatively small in Mexico, where the extent of escalation of nominal rates of protection is small. Moreover, in part because of competition from smuggling, nominal rates on nondurable consumer goods do not exceed those on their inputs, and effective rates are, in fact, lower than nominal rates.

While protection encourages import substitution, export industries are penalized by export taxes, tariffs on their inputs, and the overvaluation of the exchange rate, as compared to the free-trade situation. The extent of discrimination against export industries is again substantial in Brazil and Chile, while it is small in Mexico; net rates of effective protection of export industries averaged −36 and −27 percent in the first two countries, and −5 percent in the third. Apart from discrimination against export industries, the system of protection in the three countries also involves a bias against exporting in import-substitution industries. This is because, until recently, the protection of sales in domestic markets did not have its counterpart in subsidies to exports, and thus domestic sales were more profitable than export sales.

The extent of the bias against exporting is measured by calculating the percentage excess of domestic value added in import substitution over that obtainable in exporting. In Brazil and Chile, this ratio exceeded 100 percent in most manufacturing industries; i.e. to compete in export markets, producers would have had to operate with a value added less than one-half of that obtainable in producing for domestic markets. In turn, relatively low tariffs on imports limited the extent of the bias against exporting in Mexico.

Discrimination among economic activities involves a cost to the national economy, since resources are reallocated from low-cost to high-cost industries. In Brazil and Chile, there are even instances when protection makes the domestic production of commodities profitable in industries where value added at world-market prices is negative; i.e. the world-market value of intermediate inputs exceeds that of the product itself. This may be due to the monopolistic position of the seller of parts and components, their high transportation costs, the waste of materials, the unsuitability of the countries' resource endowment for the production of the commodity in question, or may simply be the result of the allocation of resources brought about by protection, as shown by Guisinger (1969).

Negative value added at world-market prices provides extreme cases of the cost of protection. On the national-economy level, this cost was estimated following a method developed by Bergsman (1971): by separating protected industries into two groups, depending on whether they can be expected to disappear or to continue under free trade. The saving in costs in the first group of industries was considered an improvement in static (allocative) efficiency; in the second group, production costs were assumed to decline to competitive levels under free trade. In the latter case, the estimates are presumed to represent the dynamic costs of protection resulting from the use of backward and small-scale methods in the confines of protected domestic markets. In addition to the static and dynamic costs of protection, its consumption effects, terms-of-trade effects, and the increased costs of exports under free trade were also estimated. The resulting net cost of protection is shown in Table 2 as a percentage of the gross national product. It appears that this cost was the greatest in Brazil (9.6 percent) and in Chile (6.2 percent), and was relatively small in Mexico (2.5 percent).

These results are useful in indicating the extent and the cost of protection in the three Latin American countries. They were further utilized to show the relationship between the structure of protection and economic growth in these countries. The comparisons are favorable to Mexico where relatively low levels of protection and the low extent of discrimination against exports seem to have favored economic growth, while high protection and discrimination against exports hampered growth in Brazil and Chile (Balassa, 1971, Chap. 4).

While estimates of effective protection, adjusted for the difference between the existing and the free-trade exchange rate, indicate the increased costs of processing allowed by protection in Latin American countries, the total cost of

TABLE 2
THE "COST" OF PROTECTION IN INDIVIDUAL COUNTRIES
[percent of GNP]

	Brazil (1966)	Chile (1961)	Mexico (1960)
Static (allocative) cost of protection of import substitutes[1]	0.6	1.4	0.6
Dynamic cost of protection of import substitutes[2]	9.5	9.6	2.2
Consumption effect[3]	0.1	0.6	0.1
Terms-of-trade effect[4]	−0.5	3.5	−0.3
Cost of increased exports under free trade[5]	−0.2	1.9	−0.1
Net cost of protection	9.5	6.2	2.5

SOURCE: Bela Balassa, *The Structure of Protection in Developing Countries* (Baltimore: Johns Hopkins University Press, 1971), p. 82.

[1] Excess costs plus above-normal profits and wages in industries that would not survive under free trade.

[2] Excess costs plus above-normal profits in industries that would become competitive under free trade.

[3] Consumer surplus on the increased consumption of imports.

[4] Reductions in export prices in the event of free trade.

[5] The rise of the cost of exports under free trade under the assumption that export industries are subject to increasing costs.

production in Latin America has also been raised by the high cost of intermediate inputs due to the application of protective measures. Comparing total costs or prices at the existing exchange rate, in turn, has given rise to what can be termed the "inefficiency illusion" of Latin American industry (Schydlowsky, 1971a).

Comparisons of domestic and foreign prices, made by translating the former into dollars at the existing exchange rate, are often used as evidence for the inefficiency of Latin American industry. But such comparisons are inappropriate for the problem at hand, since domestic prices are raised by tariffs and other protective measures on intermediate inputs, as well as by the overestimation of domestic value added at the existing exchange rate. Indeed, a substantial part of the observed price difference is due to the improper valuation of intermediate inputs and productive factors, so that after appropriate adjustments, inefficiencies in Latin American industries will appear to be much smaller than price comparisons at the existing exchange rate would indicate.

3.

Estimates of nominal and effective rates of protection show the impact on relative prices and value added of measures of protection. These include "price" measures such as ad valorem and specific tariffs, import surcharges, advance deposits for imports, export taxes and subsidies, and multiple exchange rates, as well as "nonprice" measures such as quotas, licensing, and exchange controls. In the study referred to above, all price measures were expressed in terms of ad valorem tariffs that are levied as a percentage of import value. In turn, in the case where imports are limited by quantitative restrictions, we calculated the tariff equivalent of these restrictions as the excess of domestic over foreign prices. Price comparisons were also made wherever tariffs are prohibitive.

Measures of protection are the principal incentives affecting the allocation of resources in Latin American countries. But other types of incentives including credit, tax, and expenditure preferences may also be applied and, for the producer, the combined effects of all incentive measures will be relevant. Correspondingly, in the research project on "Development Strategies in Semi-Industrial Countries," all quantifiable incentive measures are being considered. In the framework of this project, directed by Bela Balassa, studies dealing with two Latin American countries, Argentina and Colombia, are being carried out by Daniel M. Schydlowsky jointly with several associates.

Credit preferences may take the form of loans at preferential rates granted to particular industries for exports and import substitution, for domestic and foreign investment, and for investment in selected regions. The government may also establish interest ceilings for bank loans and may interfere with the allocation of credits by the banks. In turn, in the presence of interest-rate ceilings and credit rationing, unofficial ("gray," "black," or "street") credit markets may develop, with higher interest rates. The difference between the rates actually paid and that obtainable in the absence of governmental intervention, then, will express the extent of credit incentives in a particular situation.

In turn, a nondiscriminatory tax system would entail applying a value-added tax that is rebated on exports and imposed on imports. Such a tax could not, however, be taken as a norm for making comparisons with the actual tax system, since this would negate the government's prerogatives to fashion the tax system to serve income-distributional objectives. It appears more appropriate, therefore, to consider each tax individually and to calculate the extent of incentives due to the differential treatment of various activities, in the form of deviations from the average in tax rates, tax exemptions, depreciation provisions, and loan carry-forward regulations applying to particular activities. Indirect taxes on imports and wage taxes, too, will have differential effects.

Incentives to individual industries may also be provided through government-expenditure preferences. Some of these, such as preferential railroad and electricity rates, export-promotion efforts, or the financing of research in a particular industry, are relatively easy to quantify. Others may, however, benefit several industries and necessitate a division of the relevant expenditures among them. Yet others are general in character, and it will rarely be possible to calculate their incidence to particular activities. This conclusion also applies to the general economic "climate," including the efficiency of government administration, the prevalence of competition, and political and social conditions, in general. Taking account of quantifiable credit, tax, and governmental-expenditure measures makes it necessary to reformulate the effective rate of protection concept. This is replaced by effective rate of subsidy, which will indicate the net incentives provided to value-added activities. Similarly, the cost of protection concept needs to be reformulated to express the cost of all incentive measures to the national economy.

Just like the effective rate of protection, effective rate of subsidy calculations express the net effect of incentive measures as a proportion of value added. This will be the appropriate procedure as long as the productive factors, whose remuneration is included in value added, are available in fixed supply. In turn, if we abstract land and assume that capital is mobile internationally, effective protection should be calculated with respect to labor (Basevi, 1966). If, on the other hand, the labor supply is infinitely elastic in the relevant range, entrepreneurs can obtain labor at a constant wage rate, and the relevant indicator of net incentives will be the effective rate of subsidy to cash flow (Schydlowsky, 1967).

While the assumption of the infinite elasticity of supply of capital does not appear realistic in developing countries, the labor supply is often rather elastic. To take account of this possibility, in the research project referred to above, the effective rate of subsidy is calculated with respect both to value added and to cash flow.

Further considerations are introduced in the event of factor-market imperfections. The effective rate of subsidy will now be calculated differently, depending on whether it is to indicate the extent of incentives for the entrepreneur or the cost of incentives to the national economy. In the first case, we will calculate a private effective rate using market prices; and in the second, a social effective rate using shadow prices.

4.

Effective rate of protection analysis has direct application to the construction of systems of protection. In the absence of infant industry and optimal tariff arguments, externalities, and factor-market distortions not compensable by other policy measures, optimal allocation of resources requires equal and uniform effective protection for all productive activities, whether they be export producers or import substituters. Such a situation is achieved either by free trade and an exchange rate that equilibrates the market, or by its equivalent combination of exchange rate with uniform import duties and export subsidies.

A different policy problem arises when inelasticity of foreign demand or systematic differences in factor costs make it desirable to discriminate between different types of producers, say, traditional exporters and others. Tax/subsidy rates and the exchange rate should now be set so as to maximize foreign-exchange earnings from traditional exports, and to provide uniform effective protection to all other activities. In this case, the required nominal rates can be derived from the following formula:

(6) $T = (I - A_1')^{-1} V_1 z,$

where T = column vector of nominal rates;
   z = uniform desired effective protection, a scalar;
   A_1 = matrix of input-output coefficients excluding inputs of traditional export commodities, i.e. $A_1 + M = A$;
   M = matrix of inputs of traditional export commodities; and
   V_1 = column vector of value-added coefficients for activities other than traditional export ones.

If some group of activities yield external economies or are infant industries, it may be desirable to provide them with higher effective protection in order to bring private benefits into line with social benefits. In this case, the construction of the nominal tariff proceeds by defining a vector of desired effective protections,

Z, and then applying the following formula:

(7) $$T = (1 - A')^{-1}(\hat{V}Z),$$

where A = input coefficients of all activities;
V = value-added vector for all activities; and
$\hat{}$ = diagonalization.

Combining optimal tariff arguments with infant-industry protection or external economies requires taking into account differentiation or the tariff due to desired differences in effective protection and due to differential input intensity in inputs of traditional export commodities. The general formula applicable then becomes a combination of (6) and (7), as follows:

(8) $$T = (I - A_1')^{-1}V_1Z.$$

A more complex tariff construction problem ensues if the market prices of factors of production diverge from their shadow prices. Optimal allocation would now require equalizing the social effective rate of protection, i.e. the ratio of domestic value added at shadow prices to the value added at world prices. In the absence of other policy measures to offset the divergence between social and private prices, uniform effective protection at market prices will imply differential social effective rates of protection. Hence, optimal allocation requirements under these conditions require incorporating into the nominal tariff structure appropriate subsidy elements to cover the divergence between social and private costs. The nominal tariff structure incorporating the subsidy elements under the assumption of fixed factor proportions can be calculated as:

(9) $$T = (I - A')^{-1}[V'z + Ls_L + Ks_K + (1 - L - K)s_{1-L-K}],$$

where L = column vector of labor input coefficients;
K = column vector of capital input coefficients;
$1 - K - L$ = column vector of primary factor input coefficients of other than capital and labor; and
$s_L, K, 1 - L - K$ = scalars of subsidy or tax needed to equalize social and private factor costs.

Taking into account simultaneously optimal tariff arguments, infant-industry considerations, externalities, and subsidies to cover divergences between social and private costs, nominal tariffs should be constructed according to the following formula:

(10) $$T = (I - A_1')^{-1}[\hat{V}Z + Ls_L + Ks_K + (1 - L - K)s_{1-L-K}].$$

It should be pointed out that the discussion so far has assumed that tariffs are used exclusively for the purpose of optimizing the production structure, and the inclusion of considerations relating to the structure of demand complicates the analysis still further. On the other hand, the inclusion of noncompetitive imports subject to a revenue tariff can easily be accommodated by the addition of a term NT_n in the bracket on the right-hand side of equation (10), where N is defined as the matrix of coefficients of noncompetitive imports, provided A_1 is replaced by A_2, defined to exclude noncompetitive import coefficients from the matrix, i.e. $A_2 + N = A_1$.

It is very important to note that apart from the trivial case when uniform tariffs and export subsidies apply to all commodities, none of the tariff structures developed above yield a uniform nominal tariff, thus disproving the intuitively plausible notion that a uniform nominal tariff provides the desirable uniform effective protection. Uniform nominal protection will offer uniform effective protection only under the restrictive condition that there are no inputs of traditional export commodities into protected industries. For uniform effective protection (at market prices) to be optimal, however, it is also required that: (i) the desired infant-industry protection be uniform; (ii) external economies be uniform; and (iii) the subsidy required to equate market to social costs either be uniform or be provided through policy measures other than the tariff.

5.

Export promotion can also be analyzed in the context of an effective rate of protection framework. The antiexport bias in the tariff system arises usually from protection on inputs which is not compensated by an appropriate subsidy on the exports of the particular commodities, while such a subsidy is forthcoming for sales to the domestic market through the tariff on the output.

In the absence of export subsidies, the taxation of potential exports implicit in this situation can be derived directly from (1) by dividing effective protection into its two components: (i) increased revenue on sales due to the output tariff; and (ii) increased cost for inputs due to the tariffs on the inputs.

$$(11) \qquad Z' = Z'TV^{-1} - T'AV^{-1}.$$

The implicit taxation on potential exports is given by the second term alone. The discrimination in favor of sales to the domestic market is given in absolute size by the first element.

It naturally follows that a drawback system designed to put export producers on an equal footing with their foreign competitors should refund to producers the total implicit tax to which they have been subject, i.e. $T'AV^{-1}$. Traditional drawback systems, however, only refund the duties actually paid, not refunding any excess cost of domestically purchased inputs. Thus, if the input-output matrix is disaggregated into a matrix of domestic coefficients A_d, and a matrix of coefficients of imports A_m, we have:

$$(12) \qquad Z' = T'\hat{V}^{-1} - T'A_d\hat{V}^{-1} - T'A_m\hat{V}^{-1}.$$

Traditional drawback systems refund only $T'A_m\hat{V}^{-1}$ insofar as determinable. They still leave exporters subject to the implicit tax of $T'A_d\hat{V}^{-1}$ arising from excess cost of domestic inputs.

It should also be noted that neither a traditional drawback system, nor a generalized one refunding all implicit taxation, equalizes incentives between sales to the domestic market and to export markets. Even in the presence of such systems, a discrimination against export sales equal to exactly Z' will then remain.

In order to equalize the incentive to produce for the export market in comparison to the domestic market, net export subsidies for nontraditional products are necessary. These should be set equal to the rate of nominal protection in industries operating at full utilization of capacity. If exports would take place on the margin out of unused capacity or making use of economies of scale, subsidies covering marginal cost would suffice. In the latter case, however, a reduction of nominal import protection would be necessary to equalize the subsidization offered to domestic and foreign sales, but contraction of firms may then ensue as a result of total revenue falling below total cost.

The export subsidies involved are usually regarded as having a fiscal cost. In many developing economies where the raising of taxes is a difficult matter, such a fiscal cost is seen as a well-nigh unsurmountable barrier to the adoption of an export subsidy program. If domestic installed capacity is not fully used, however, export sales will generate an increase in the level of domestic income via the foreign-trade multiplier. In turn, a higher level of income implies an expanded tax base, which at constant levels of ex post tax incidence will yield additional fiscal revenue. Such new revenue may pay for part or all of the subsidy program, depending on the macroeconomic interactions involved (Schydlowsky, 1971).

The net fiscal cost of export subsidies in the presence of excess capacity in domestic industry has been worked out for Argentina in Schydlowsky (1971) on the basis of the following macromodel:

(13) $$P = P_0 + pV'X,$$

(14) $$M = \hat{m}X,$$

(15) $$E = E_0,$$

(16) $$G = G_0,$$

(17) $$X = AX + P + G + E,$$

and

(18) $$T = a'M + (t_d + t_i)'X,$$

where all symbols refer to column vectors; a prime denotes transposition; a circumflex denotes diagonalization; and where P = private total expenditure on goods of the different sectors at market prices; P_0 = autonomous private expenditure on goods of the different sectors; p = marginal propensity of the private sector to spend on the goods of the different sectors; V = gross value added at factor cost less direct taxes in the different sectors; X = output of the different sectors at market prices; M = imports of goods similar to those of the different sectors at CIF prices; m = import requirements at CIF prices of the different sectors per unit of output at market prices; E = export of the different sectors at FOB prices; A = matrix of domestic input-output coefficient; G = total government expenditure on products of the different sectors; T = fiscal revenue generated in the different sectors; a = ad valorem rates of import duty on the products of the different sectors; t_d = rate of direct taxation as a proportion of gross output in the different sectors; and t_i = rate of indirect taxation as a proportion of gross output in the different sectors.

Substituting equations (13), (14), (15), and (16) in (17), we obtain the equilibrium levels of output and income:

(19) $\qquad X = (I - A - pV')^{-1}(P_0 + G_0 + E_0),$

and

(20) $\qquad Y = V'X = V'(I - A - pV^{-1}(P_0 + G_0 + E_0),$

as well as total new fiscal revenue:

(21) $\qquad dT = (a'\hat{m} + t_d' + t_i')(I - A - pV')^{-1}dE.$

Introducing the export subsidies, we obtain:

(22) $\qquad dTn = (a'\hat{m} + t_d' + t_i')(I - A - pV')^{-1}dE^* - \lambda'dE^*,$

where Tn is the vector of net fiscal revenue; λ is the vector of subsidies, as a proportion of private sector revenue from exports plus subsidy; and E^* is the vector of private-sector income from exports and export subsidies.

TABLE 3
FISCAL EFFECT OF SECTORAL INCREASES IN EXPORTS

		Revenue per Peso of New Exports	Maximum Allowable Subsidy Unchanged Fiscal Balance (% FOB value)
1	Agriculture	0.713	248
2	Livestock	0.712	247
3	Forestry, hunting, and fishing	0.696	229
4	Mining	0.691	224
5	Fuel and electricity	0.632	172
6	Foodstuffs and beverages	0.704	238
7	Meat	0.716	252
8	Tobacco	0.883	755
9	Textiles	0.714	250
10	Clothing	0.698	231
11	Wood	0.678	211
12	Paper and cardboard	0.671	204
13	Printing and publishing	0.653	188
14	Chemicals	0.687	219
15	Rubber	0.634	173
16	Leather	0.725	263
17	Stone, glass, and ceramics	0.691	224
18	Metals	0.615	160
19	Steel	0.607	154
20	Vehicles and machinery	0.642	179
21	Automobiles	0.632	172
22	Machinery and electrical equipment	0.630	170
23	Other industries	0.689	222
24	Recovery materials	0.713	248
25	Construction	0.694	227
26	Commerce	0.736	279
27	Transport	0.650	186
28	Other services	0.720	257

SOURCE: D. M. Schydlowsky, "Short-Run Policy in Semi-Industrialized Economies," *Economic Development and Cultural Change*, April 1971, Table 9.

Table 3 shows the total resulting fiscal revenues per peso of new earnings from exports in different sectors of the Argentinian economy, as well as the corresponding maximum sectoral subsidy levels which can be paid without generating a net fiscal deficit.

An optimal export subsidy program can be derived by the use of a linear programming framework which maximizes income subject to constraints representing installed capacity, the balance of payments, and the fiscal balance. The latter two should be independent constraints in the system, since domestic demand is assumed to come from existing internal excess demand as well as from new exports. Indeed, new exports are determined in part by the needs arising out of domestic demand. In symbols, the linear program is to maximize ΔY subject to:

$$(23) \qquad (I - A)X + (I + d)M - IE - p\Delta Y = 0,$$

$$(24) \qquad X \leq K,$$

$$(25) \qquad -m'M - 1'M + e'E \geq 0,$$

and

$$(26) \qquad 1'X + a'M - g'E \geq 0,$$

where ΔY is a scalar denoting the increase in income; A, X, p, E, a, and m are as defined previously; M is a vector of competitive import activities; d is a vector of ratios of market to CIF prices; K is a vector of potential additional output through 100 percent capacity use; e is a vector of marginal revenue in export markets (i.e., price FOB export point); and g is a vector of export subsidies (covering total or marginal cost according to the purpose of the calculation).

The solution to this linear program will give: (i) the maximum level of income obtainable; (ii) the commodities exported and, hence, the marginal export subsidy required to achieve the optimum;[1] (iii) competitive imports required to overcome sectoral bottlenecks; and (iv) the net change in the fiscal situation originating in the move to full capacity utilization.

6.

Virtually the totality of empirical work in the effective protection area has been done in the partial-equilibrium context discussed so far. At the same time, it has been recognized from the outset (e.g. Corden 1966) that the analysis of protection requires a general-equilibrium framework. This section (based largely on Balassa 1971a) examines recent attempts to investigate the theoretical validity of the effective protection construct in a general-equilibrium framework.

The consequences of allowing for substitution between different primary factors and between primary factors and intermediate goods has been a particular subject taken up in the context of one-country, three-commodity general-equilibrium models. Furthermore, general-equilibrium models incorporate the effects on realized protection of changes in factor prices, and, hence, nominal

[1] In this model it is implicitly assumed that commodities will be differentiated for subsidy purposes to the same extent that a differentiation exists for tariffs or quotas on the import side. The discussion of the relative advantages of this and other alternatives in terms of allocation and administration would carry us beyond the scope of this paper.

protection will affect particular activities not only through changes in product prices but also through changes in factor prices. In turn, factor price effects are accentuated if we admit the possibility of input substitution (Tan, 1970), and certain definitional problems will also result (Ethier, 1970).

It is easy to show that in a three-commodity model the effects of protection on particular industries may not be appropriately indicated by the effective protection measure, even if substitution elasticities among inputs are zero. Thus, industry A, having a lower effective rate of protection than industry B, may still enjoy greater protection if it is complementary in factor use with unprotected industry C and thus benefits from a protection-induced decline in the prices of the factors of production it uses intensively.

The error possibilities due to the neglect of protection-induced changes in factor prices will depend on the magnitude of these changes relative to changes in the prices of products, including material inputs. In the simple two-country, two-commodity, two-factor model, the protection-induced changes in relative factor prices are greater in magnitude than the changes in relative product prices.

By contrast, apart from Corden's two-product model (1969) where factor-price effects cannot reverse the effects of protection of product prices, the practitioners of effective protection have implicitly or explicitly emphasized international differences in efficiency that fit the Ricardian framework. This would mean that, rather than protecting factors of production, countries tend to protect industries that have high costs because of the use of small-scale production methods (due to differences in scale), the application of inferior technology and organization (due to differences in technical and organizational knowledge), and the prevalence of X-inefficiencies (due to the failure to minimize costs for the technology applied).

Given the present state of knowledge (or rather ignorance) as regards the effects of protection on factor prices, it is fair to suggest that—other things being equal—the relative importance of factor-price effects will be the greater, the more uniform are levels of protection. With the wide variety of nominal rates of protection observed in most countries, it may be surmised then that the effects of protection on output and input prices tend to outweigh its effects on factor prices.

On the basis of available evidence on substitution elasticities among inputs, it would seem that this conclusion is not materially affected if we introduce the possibility of input substitution. But we now face the problem of defining value added and the effective rate of protection. Ethier (1970) suggests that the relevant definition will have to be couched in terms of marginal value added, leading to a rather complicated formula that might be difficult to measure empirically. However, Jones (1970) has shown that the value-added concept has a meaning even with substitution, and the usual definition can be applied.

Efforts to analyze the effects of protection in a multiproduct and perhaps multicountry world require, under the present state of the arts, a mathematical programming framework. If the production conditions can be specified and the demand structure written in functional form, the inclusion of tariff-collection activities with the corresponding expenditure vectors for government revenue allows the complete specification of a programming problem.

An early effort of this kind was undertaken by Schydlowsky (1966), in which the general-equilibrium effects of tariffs in a three-country, nine-commodity, three-factor world were explored. Production conditions in each country were assumed to be of the Leontief kind, in input-output table form; demand conditions were specified as being of constant elasticity in all prices and income in order to allow for adequate consumer substitution between commodities, while additivity of demand conditions was assured by an explicit constraint to that effect. Appropriate tariff-collection activities and government-expenditure proportions were specified. Finally, home and foreign goods were assumed to be imperfect substitutes, thus preventing complete specialization through the demand side. The problem was solved by nonlinear programming with a variant of the gradient method on data specified to represent three different kinds of countries in terms of factor endowments and production functions. The policy situations simulated included unilateral changes in tariff, multilateral reductions, and customs union.

A more recent effort by Evans (1968, 1970) applied linear programming to a growth model for Australia specifically including the effect of tariffs in the specification of the economy. Upper and lower bounds were imposed on some activities in the model, and expansion and contraction of sectors was not allowed to proceed instantaneously. Demand conditions were specified as linear expenditure functions, with limited substitution between commodities. Production conditions were linear.

Evans compared the result of his model with the prediction from effective rate of protection analysis and found a rank correlation of 0.63 between the effective rates thus measured and the estimated changes in resource flows (this result pertains to the model without growth constraints for particular industries). In turn, the rank correlation coefficient between effective rates measured, respectively, in a general-equilibrium, and in a partial-equilibrium, model was found to be 0.52.

These results cannot be used, however, to derive conclusions on the inappropriateness of effective rates as an indicator of resource allocation, or on the existence of substantial differences between estimates of effective rates measured in a general- and in a partial-equilibrium framework. To begin with, effective rates are supposed to indicate the resource-pull and resource-push effects of protection in Marshallian long-run, under ceteris paribus assumptions after all adjustments in capacity have been made. By contrast, Evans has used a medium-term model that permits the expansion of capacity but does not accommodate reductions in it. Correspondingly, industries which can cover variable costs under free trade would continue to operate at existing output levels. Indeed, there is no change in activity levels in nearly one-half of the industries in the model; and this, in turn, reduces correlation between effective protection and changes in activity levels. The correlation would presumably increase if the time span of the model were long enough to permit the depreciation of equipment; in which case, several of the industries in question would show a decline in output.

The correlation between effective protection measured in a general-equilibrium model and resource flows, as well as that between effective rates estimated in a general- and in a partial-equilibrium framework, are further affected by the assumptions made on maximization behavior, the form of the consumption and investment functions, the supply and productivity of labor, and prospective export demand. While such assumptions are necessary for the ten-year projection Evans made by the use of his medium-term model, such a model cannot answer the question about the effects of eliminating protection under ceteris paribus assumptions.

In a policy-analysis context, the use of general-equilibrium models with adjustments over time is promising but not yet operational. Major improvements are needed in the specification of production conditions, where efficient and inexpensive algorithms need to be developed to handle decreasing, as well as increasing, costs. On the demand side, functional forms must be found which satisfy the integratability conditions while allowing more variability in the own and cross price elasticities than currently available forms. Finally, a specification of the factor markets that allows for unemployment and stickiness in factor prices, in lieu of the now common but unrealistic assumption of a fixed factor supply and full employment, needs to be undertaken. With these innovations introduced and an ever increasing computational capacity, the level of disaggregation can gradually be increased to the point where policy analysis can be brought to bear on specific policies in tariff setting.

REFERENCES

Balassa, Bela, "Tariff Protection in Industrial Countries: An Evaluation," *Journal of Political Economy*, December 1965.

Balassa, Bela and Associates, *The Structure of Protection in Developing Countries* (Baltimore: Johns Hopkins University Press, 1971).

Balassa, Bela, "Effective Protection: A Summary Appraisal," in H. G. Grubel and H. G. Johnson, eds., *Effective Tariff Protection* (Geneva: General Agreement on Tariffs and Trade and Graduate Institute of International Studies, 1971).

Balassa, Bela and Schydlowsky, D. M., "Effective Tariffs, Domestic Cost of Foreign Exchange, and the Equilibrium Exchange Rate," *Journal of Political Economy*, May/June 1968.

Basevi, G., "The U.S. Tariff Structure: Estimate of Effective Rates of Protection of U.S. Industries and Industrial Labor," *Review of Economics and Statistics*, May 1966.

Bergsman, Joel, "Commercial Policy, Allocative Efficiency, and X-Efficiency," mimeographed, June 1970.

Bruno, Michael, "The Optimal Selection of Export-Promoting and Import-Substituting Projects," in United Nations, *Planning the External Sector, Techniques, Problems and Policies* (New York, 1965).

Corden, W. M., "The Structure of a Tariff System and the Effective Protection Rate," *Journal of Political Economy*, June 1966.

———. "Effective Protective Rates in the General Equilibrium Model: A Geometric Note," *Oxford Economic Papers*, July 1969.

Ethier, W. J., "General Equilibrium Theory and the Concept of the Effective Rate of Protection," mimeographed, 1970.

Evans, H. D., "A General Equilibrium Analysis of Protection: The Effects of Protection in Australia," Ph.D. dissertation, Harvard University, 1968.

———, "Effective Protection in a General Equilibrium Framework," mimeographed, 1970.

Guisinger, S. E., "Negative Value Added and the Theory of Effective Protection," *Quarterly Journal of Economics*, August 1969.

Jones, R. W., "Effective Protection and Substitution," mimeographed, 1970.

Johnson, H. G., "The Theory of Tariff Structure with Special Reference to World Trade and Development," *Trade and Development* (Geneva: Institute Universitaire des Hautes Etudes Internationales, 1965).

Schydlowsky, D. M., "Tariffs and National Income: A Policy Model," Ph.D. dissertation, Harvard University, January 1966.

———, "Effective Rates of Protection and Allocation of Resources in a Competitive Economy," mimeographed, 1967.

———, "Short Run Policies in Semi-Industrialized Economies," *Economic Development and Cultural Change*, April 1971.

———, "Latin American Trade Policies in the 1970's: A Prospective Appraisal," *Quarterly Journal of Economics*, May 1972.

Tan, A. H. H., "Differential Tariffs, Negative Value-Added and the Theory of Effective Protection," *American Economic Review*, March 1970.

ANALYSIS OF FOREIGN TRADE POLICIES BY MEANS OF A NUMERICAL EXPERIMENTATION COMPUTER MODEL, WITHIN THE CONTEXT OF ALTERNATIVE ECONOMIC DEVELOPMENT STRATEGIES FOR VENEZUELA

JUAN PABLO PEREZ CASTILLO, LOURDES YERO, AND LUIS LEAL*

Center of Development Studies. Central University of Venezuela

1. GENERAL PRESENTATION OF THE PAPER

This paper consists of a comparative analysis of foreign trade policies, by means of a numerical experimentation (or simulation) computer model, that represents the Venezuelan economy in terms of its structure, basic relations, and base-year information.

The paper is based on a more extensive work carried out at CENDES (Centro de Estudios del Desarrollo) over the past few years in comparing and evaluating the economic feasibility of two very different development strategies for the economy of Venezuela, called Consumption Style and Creative Style. The foreign trade policies studied here have been formulated in the context and conceptual framework of these two Development Styles; and much of what follows has been taken directly from that extensive work, including summarized descriptions of the Styles and their salient characteristics.[1]

The research on Development Styles directly and concretely deals with those problems which, for one reason or another, Latin American (and, in general, underdeveloped) countries, their technical planning offices, and their economic policymakers abstain from taking into consideration. Among these we find the following resistances or failures: to set national objectives in explicit detail; to give concrete shape to the global long-run framework containing the strategy pursued; to discuss in concrete terms the qualitative aspects of the quantitative indicators representing each alternative strategy and its corresponding goals; and to make the strategy and the policy instruments and hypotheses that it embraces logically consistent with the final objectives sought, by applying the available normative and feasibility criteria, which would lead to a comparative study of alternative strategies and, thus, to a choice that could then be considered rational (in the sense of giving some assurance of its compatibility with the future desired).

---

* Other members of the research group that collaborated with the authors are: José Belda and José Carantoña (research professors), Haleis Dávila and Dilcia Vásquez (assistants). Fabiola de Carantoña (secretary).

[1] Grupo de Modelos Matemáticos (Equipo de Desarrollo Económico y Modelos Matemáticos), *Estilos de Desarrollo: Análisis Comparativo de Políticas a Largo Plazo* (CENDES, Universidad Central de Venezuela, Caracas, 1971). Due to restrictions imposed upon the length of this presentation, the authors have been forced to omit important details presented at the Cuernavaca conference and contained, therefore, in the original Spanish version. These concern details of the most important numerical hypotheses and their explanations, the equations of the model pertaining to the determination of the balance of payments, a brief explanation of the computer program, and the detailed results of the final basic run of each Development Style, grouped in tables of the form of national accounts. In addition, some of the details of the policy experiments also had to be omitted. This information may be obtained directly from Juan Pablo Perez Castillo, director of the group.

The above-mentioned omissions actually mean that the process of economic and social development has been conceived more as an extrapolation of the present structural conditions and relations (a process which evolves in stages and with autonomous dynamics) than as a conscious process of social change and, above all, of structural change. On the other hand, it also means that development is being considered in relation to the situations and processes presented by other countries considered "more developed"; implicitly, or explicitly, one tries to be like those other countries, without questioning feasibility or the normative contents that are implicit in this approach.

This imitation of other countries may nevertheless run into serious difficulties insofar as the decisions taken may produce contradictory results, different from those expected or predicted (especially if a development path is followed implicitly and not explicitly). Such decisions may have a lasting effect, preconditioning the future, and generating still other sets of complementary decisions that may reduce even more the degrees of freedom available for independent action.

It is undoubtedly difficult to specify concretely the desired Development Style, including the corresponding social aspirations and goals; nevertheless, it does not seem to be acceptable to substitute for concrete specifications vaguely defined propositions concerning social instruments and structures. What we propose is the testing of different possibilities by means of the *numerical experimentation* method. The method consists of first defining the different strategies in quantitative terms, but making explicit the differentiating categories (including their value judgments and ideological contents), such as the degree to which the society is planning to satisfy the needs for goods and services of the different population groups; and then evaluating comparatively the social effort—in terms of the human, capital, and foreign resources required—by means of the usual economic indicators.

Two strategies (Styles) were chosen, each possessing some real interest or possibility, rather than being entirely abstract cases. The starting point is the Venezuela of 1966 and 1967; thus, the model had to be correspondingly debugged and tuned to the statistical information previously gathered, processed, and analyzed.

The qualitative description of each Style constitutes the necessary frame of reference to estimate its (quantitative) time path, to indicate the sets of economic policy instruments that are consistent with it, to allow for the setting of quantitative goals, and to evaluate the results (also quantitative) comparatively.

One may or may not agree with this description, since it also serves as a working hypothesis. What is important is that each Style requires interdisciplinary discussion for its description, as well as to determine its correspondence with the numerical values of the exogenous variables that represent goals, policy instruments, and technical and behavioral hypotheses. In this manner, the sociopolitical context has to be taken into account, whether one likes it or not. Both the initial quantification and the evaluation of its concrete results in the economic field call for considerable effort, since the correspondence between the economic and sociopolitical aspects is frequently not univocal. However, there is, in fact, no alternative if what is sought is to implement a development strategy with some degree of rationality and feasibility.

Perhaps an example may clarify what has been stated in the previous paragraph. Most certainly, it is relatively simple to achieve consensus on some general proposition defining minimum levels of consumption for different population groups. But it will be considerably more difficult, if not extremely so, to achieve agreement as to the concrete specifications of those minimum levels in terms of individual components, their relative weights, and the policies to be implemented in order to achieve the goals.

Regardless of the many techniques and social experiences available to solve this type of problem, there always will be a margin of uncertainty; and it is precisely this margin that may be made explicit with this method. Once the values are tentatively fixed, based on the knowledge one has, the range of the variations may be limited and the sensitivity of the results may be examined by experimenting with different values. In a similar manner, one may proceed to set other groups of numerical values (the technical coefficients, for example).

2. THE PRODINGR MODEL

The PRODINGR Model, a numerical experimentation (NUMEX) model[2] for computers, was used for the comparative study of the Development Styles. It describes the economic system of Venezuela, simulating the economy as it is usually conceived. The economic system is divided into 19 productive sectors (which represent a greater disaggregation than what is generally used by the institutions that study the Venezuelan economy), each of which is divided, in turn, into three subsectors, or subdivisions, called "techniques."

The sectoral subdivision is based on specific criteria for each sector. In some sectors, particularly the industrial, the techniques reflect the average size of the productive units, measured by the volume of employment per unit; in others, as in agriculture and transportation, the techniques represent different forms of social or institutional organization, or define real subsectors. In still others, they reflect differences in technology.

Occupations are presented in a double classification, according to level of education (and thus skill) and according to type of occupation. Debts are also subject to a double classification, by type of creditor and by the conditions of each type of loan.[3]

In order to simplify understanding the PRODINGR model, it may be divided into two blocks, or submodels, which, however, are integrated and executed simultaneously. The first block (the PROD submodel) produces for each year the results of economic activity on the production side, including the technico-economic requirements for the different sectors and techniques. It deals basically with the following aspects of the economy: product and production, investment and capacity, foreign trade (exports and imports, and so on), employment, and intermediate input requirements. The second block (the INGR submodel) produces the other aspect of the productive process, from the point of view of the earning and use of the incomes generated and their consolidation in terms of a national

[2] For a detailed explanation of the method, see the bibliography listed at the end of Chapter III of the book cited, *Estilos de Desarrollo* [*Development Styles: Comparative Analysis of Long-Run Policies*].

[3] For a detailed listing of the classifications see the Appendix.

accounting framework: wages and salaries, interest and rent, depreciation, taxation, income distribution, and expenditures on final consumer goods. The results of the calculations performed by the model are then summarized in the familiar national accounts, including the family, enterprise, government, and capital accounts.

With the output obtained from the model calculations, it is possible to analyze the economic policies that are embraced in a development plan in terms of their consistency and feasibility.

According to the method of numerical experimentation, the conceptual model of the economic system (with the characteristics mentioned in the previous paragraphs, in our case) is converted into a series of equations in mathematical language, which are then translated to a computer language (in the PRODINGR case, FORTRAN) to be used in a computer (middle-sized in our case, an IBM 360-50). The model is basically exogenous; that is, almost all of the variables depend not on endogenous relations that serve to explain their behavior in time, but rather on rates of change, coefficients, and parameters that are introduced from "the outside," as data or information for the model, in the form of time series. The introduction of these exogenous values in the sequence of the calculations results in specific combinations of rates and coefficients. These exogenous time-series values represent the set of hypotheses, or theories, that are to be tested and tried out. Each of these combinations of values results in an output, a "run" of an experiment, as a function of the exogenous values introduced and processed by means of the same formal calculation scheme. The results of each run could be interpreted as a different theoretical model, comprising the behavioral relations introduced as data by the "user."[4]

The "output" of each experiment consists of annual results. Following a sequential, step-by-step calculation process, beginning each time with the previous year, already calculated, the model may extend its calculations into time for as many years as the time series of exogenous data introduced permits. These yearly results are organized into tables that may combine several years of the same run or several runs for the same year; in addition, plotting facilities are available which graph any variable selected. This whole process is automatically included in the run of the model. At his discretion, the user may select the tables, variables, or graphs that are to constitute the output.

It is, then, a model designed to provide a formal accounting framework, such that, in a rapid and precise manner, it is possible to try out different policies related to different time paths for a considerable number of variables of the economic system—without losing sight of the system as a whole; while at the same time, being able to detect inconsistencies, bottlenecks, imbalances, and so on among the many policies to be tested, in relation to the various aspects of the economy. This paper seeks to demonstrate that with this type of NUMEX model, and in our case, the PRODINGR, the above-mentioned objectives are achieved.[5]

---

[4] The term user refers to the researcher who designs the run and introduces the data he wishes to try out.

[5] For a more complete demonstration, consult the book cited, *Estilos de Desarrollo*.

3. Basic Characteristics of the Numerical Experimentation Model

In as great a degree as possible, theories about the behavior of the economic system have been left out. The purpose was to design an accounting framework as neutral as possible, in the sense of enabling the analysis of two substantially different patterns of development for any given country. The economic laws usually expressed in terms of endogenous mathematical relations have been replaced by explicit hypotheses about the future behavior of the most frequently used parameters in economic analysis, such as the coefficients for capital, labor, national and imported input requirements, final consumption, and so forth.

However, it must be admitted that the model has a theoretical basis, at least at two distinct levels. In the first place, there is an a priori criterion regarding what is important and what is not. To describe the economic system, a specific set of variables was selected over another one equally acceptable. In the second place, although in most cases the equations are of the accounting type or identities, in a few cases they contain a certain amount of theory, but expressed in very general terms. One may take as an example the calculation of investment requirements in Sector S, Technique T, for Period P.[6]

$$IBF(S, T, P) = CP(S, T, P)*[QQP(S, T, P + 1) - QQP(S, T, P)].$$

The relation simply states that investment is equal to a certain capital coefficient $CP(S, T, P)$ times the expected increase in production. At first glance, a naive linear relation is suggested with a gestation period of one year. This is not so, however, since $CP(S, T, P)$ depends on time, and its value must be given exogenously every year. It does have definite theoretical content, but this comes given from the "outside." In other words, the relation between investment and production does not have to turn out linear over time, and it may differ among experiments. In short, in each experiment tried with the same model, it is possible to have a different investment function given exogenously through the data; and the "theory" included in the model simply states that "investment is some general function of the increase in production." It is not even necessary to postulate a gestation period, although this is convenient from the point of view of computer programming.

It follows, then, that the substantive content of any theory is taken into account explicitly in the form of exogenous data expressed in time series of coefficients, parameters, and rates of change. The verification and confirmation of these numerical hypotheses remains outside the model; and it may be based on any type of reasoning, from mere intuition and consultations with experts to econometric estimates and historical extrapolations. In this manner, the methodology takes full advantage of the progress achieved by other methods, incorporating what is useful in each one. It is not exclusive of other techniques; instead, it is generalizing and complementary.

The computer model makes possible the confirmation and verification of the internal consistency, feasibility, and efficacy of the set of economic policies and

---

[6] The complete equation is of another form. Here, the assumption that there is no idle capacity nor depreciation is made only to simplify matters.

hypotheses concerning the future behavior of the economic system which is commonly labeled "development plan." Basically, it is an instrument that can be used to order, integrate, and analyze existing information so as to enable the evaluation of the implications and consequences of the hypotheses and goals of the implemented policies.

The equations have a clear and familiar meaning for. the researcher (or planner), and the analytical scheme they integrate is useful in discovering information gaps and critical areas for analysis; moreover, it forces the use of consistent concepts and dimensions.

The model is ambitious from the point of view of its scope and level of disaggregation, since it attempts to represent with great detail and in abstract form the relations of the economic system of a country. It is, therefore, more detailed than the usual models; although even greater detail would have been useful in the treatment of such problems as import substitution. This was not possible, however, because the necessary information was not available at the time; consequently, it remains a task for the future. In any case, the treatment given intermediate inputs was sufficient for the degree of detail considered in the conclusions.

Considerable work was necessary to tune up the model and adequately fit the data for the base year. Merely to adjust the initial year, more than 3,000 coefficients, parameters, and rates of change had to be elaborated, verified, and made consistent with each other. In addition, all this had to be done for the assumptions regarding their time paths into the future, to the year 2000.

Each run, or experiment, requires about 3,000 items of data per year; hence, for a thirty-four-year run, more than 100,000 numbers must be fed to the model (and this is especially true when alternative Development Styles are being studied). Since the problem, presented in such a manner, is almost impossible to handle, it was necessary to elaborate special routines that would give the option of presenting initial values and isolated points along the time paths of the variables, filling the gaps by linear interpolations between the numbers given.

An essential feature of the model, and of this technique in general, is its great flexibility and adaptability to changes in equations and relations among variables, as its use has suggested. In actual fact, the model has been continually modified and improved. Even as the final report was being prepared, the investment equation suffered successively two important changes, without producing any serious problem of adjustment or programming. As a result, it may be concluded that this model is never a finished instrument; it is under constant change and relatively easy to improve.

4. METHODOLOGY OF THE MODEL

Given the above characteristics of the model, the critical issues involving the use of this type of model concern the techniques of elaborating the input data and analyzing the output data. Two different problems arise.

On one hand, the exogenous data are not necessarily independent from each other, in the sense that the value of one variable in no way affects the value of any other variable. Actually, many variables are related although the nature of the relationships are often not known with reasonable precision; in such cases, these can be explicitly introduced into the model and experimented with.

On the other hand, the variables indicating at each iteration the state of the system do not correct the exogenous input data when imbalances appear. Thus, for example, the appearance of a deficit in the balance of payments does not affect the input data, nor such endogenous variables as the rate of growth of national income. The gap may continue to grow until the final year of the experiment run. This may be interpreted in different ways, but in the end it is the responsibility of the analyst to determine whether to consider the deficit tolerable and capable of finance, or to reject the experiment and change the assumptions.

There is an exception to the above rule, however. At the option of the analyst, the model may be made to correct automatically the sectoral supply-demand gaps by adjusting supply to its respective demand. In this case, the exogenous rate of growth of output for each sector is adjusted by a factor that depends upon its respective gap of the previous period. Since the assumptions affecting the rate of growth of supply are introduced independently of those affecting the rate of growth of demand (by sector), large inventories (positive or negative) may result and distort the analysis of other gaps and indicators. To avoid this, the automatic adjustment of the supply-demand imbalance was introduced in order to allow concentrating on such other output variables as unemployment, excess capacity, income distribution, savings, and so forth. This, of course, implies a specific value judgement about what is considered important and what is not.

Following is a description of the procedure used to deal with the problems cited above, for the comparison and evaluation of the Development Styles.

5. INPUT DATA

Taking into account the requirements raised by the quantitative expressions of the two Development Styles initially described in a literary and qualitative manner, as well as the obvious meanings of the many variables contained in the model, the exogenous input data were grouped into the following categories: initial values, goals, policy instruments, technical coefficients, and exogenous parameters.

The *initial values* describe the state of the system at the start of each run. Every calculation period, these values are updated so as to represent the current state of the system. Among the corresponding variables are included sectoral capital stocks, wages, exports, outputs, and labor productivities.

The *goals* describe the essence of each Development Style. Among the most important of these are the specific types of needs that are to be satisfied and distributed among the population in a certain way, which in turn are expressed in per capita consumption expenditures, by level of income and sector of origin, and are postulated for each Style at specific points in time. Among other goals helping to define each Style are the following: degree of economic independence of the Style with respect to the foreign sector, free time for creative and recreational leisure, health, education and skill composition of the labor force, housing, degree of political participation, and so on. Except for the last one, these goals may be expressed explicitly in numerical terms. Others, like the degree of participation in political decisions, can only be treated indirectly from the point of view of their possible effects on other variables.

The *policy instruments* are variables that may be controlled with greater facility than others. There is no precise definition for an instrumental variable; it is rather a question of degree. Given the goals, the range of instruments consistent with the goals and the manner by which they must be used are narrowed down. Within this range, they might even be ordered according to their implicit costs. The model contains an appreciable number of policy coefficients (most of the exogenous input of the submodel INGR is of this type). The intensity and way in which they are used will depend, in the final analysis, on the Development Style.

Finally, the *exogenous variables* are, in principle, all those parameters which are related to the technological structure (capital coefficients, intermediate and labor inputs) and are considered relatively more difficult to control, as well as expected to change rather slowly through time. The term exogenous as used here indicates the way the variables enter the model, but it also infers that these are variables which are not sizably affected by the state of the system, while it, in turn, is affected by them (for example, the price indexes for exports and imports).

6. OUTPUT DATA

The analysis of results was systematized, as in the case of the input data. The purpose was to organize a method to check the feasibility of the numerical hypotheses that constitute each Style, and to compare and evaluate them on that same basis. The output tables designed specifically for this work show clearly the physical and financial gaps that occur in the system as a result of the assumptions made.

Following is a list of the areas in which important *imbalances* can take place: balance of payments, human resources (unemployment, underemployment and demand-supply imbalances by occupational categories), installed productive capacity, government account, family account, enterprise (foreign, public, and private) account, and housing.[7]

7. DESCRIPTION OF THE DEVELOPMENT STYLES

Following is a description of the two socioeconomic Development Styles—which represent different social systems—delineating their salient features and exemplifying their differences concerning the foreign sector.[8]

The Style called CONS (for Consumption) receives its name from the generalized "consumerism" which characterizes the so-called mass-consumption countries with a high and diversified level of industrialization, which it seeks to reach by imitation and following the guidelines set by those countries. It is, therefore, a type of society in which private consumption is characterized by its diversification, sophistication, and constant renewal (the annual change in models of consumer durables is a typical example).

---

[7] Lack of space made impossible inclusion of the explanations of these gaps, their precise meanings, and forms of calculation. These may be found in the book cited, *Estilos de Desarrollo*.

[8] For detailed definitions, consult the publication cited, *Estilos de Desarrollo*.

In order to achieve this, the economy depends upon private enterprise. The State is fundamentally a mediator between the conflicting interests of labor and management, attempting to implement an economic policy which is, on the whole, more of the regulatory or complementary type than of the orientating or long-range type. It must guarantee the adequate supply of such basic services as public order, education, health, transport, and the material resources which in Venezuela are public goods (for example, natural resources, petrochemicals, basic metals), since this is considered indispensable for the efficient operation of the economy and is required by the private investor.

Since it seeks to imitate other countries, in particular their consumption patterns and habits, it is equally necessary that the Style organize its productive apparatus in a manner similar to those countries, employ the same modern technology (which will have to be imported), and, in general, guide economic activities by the traditional criteria of efficiency and profitability. This means that the CONS Style will try to adopt the technical, economic, and social conditions prevailing in the hegemonic and leading nations, even though they may be inconsistent with the internal possibilities and capacities determined by the development of the national productive forces. It means also that in attempting to take advantage of foreign creative endeavors, not necessarily adequately adapted, the material results of that creativity are also imported, in the form of capital goods, managerial capacities, organizational forms and norms, and so forth, so that foreign capital is stimulated, increasing its relative importance significantly—particularly in the most dynamic sectors of the economy.

The Style labeled CREA (for Creative) seeks to create an entirely different society: one that is economically, politically, and culturally creative and autonomous (but without attempting to reach self-sufficiency nor fostering isolationism). Its main objective is to free man from the alienation and subjection that characterizes the social system at present (Venezuela in the 1970s) by guaranteeing to the entire population the satisfaction of such basic needs as food, education, health and housing, and by realizing to a maximum the creative potential of that population.

Thus, another basic goal of this Style is the production of free time for creative leisure. This means that the present social structures and education will have to go through such profound qualitative changes as serve to produce, with the conscious and active participation of the workers, a significant increase in the productivity and efficiency of the productive apparatus in order to reduce substantially the "normal" work day.

In this society, it is expected that social participation will be generalized in the fixing of the social national objectives at every level of the decision-making process and in daily activities. It will have its own culture, critical and autonomous; and its own basic technology, which will be the product of the internal requirements generated by the development of the national productive forces.

The central role of the State, in its economic dimension, is to guarantee the fulfillment of the basic economic goals by conducting this activity directly. This calls for the socialization of the means of production in the basic sectors (in general, all large productive enterprises, but also those that provide such services as education, health, transport, finance, and information). The remaining sectors may be left in private hands, so that the relative weight of the private sector will be essentially complementary, and smaller than its initial relative importance or its role in a more traditional Development Style.

Foreign capital tends to disappear from the economy, but gradually, because it is contradictory with the objectives of this Style. As a result, most of the foreign-exchange requirements will have to be directly generated by exports, and considerably reduced; but it does not rule out the possibility of obtaining technical assistance, such as by renting the services of experts or the technical know-how of other nations.

8. FINAL BASIC EXPERIMENTS

Following is a very brief summary description of the results of the national development policies that were simulated for their evaluation in the more extended work cited, since the analysis of the Development Styles proper is beyond the scope of this paper although essential to its comprehension.

In that work, a first pair of experiments (called initial runs) directly assumed the hypotheses without prior corrections for methodological compatibility or feasibility (intentionally), with the object of demonstrating the concrete application of the technique used and, in general, the use of computers in the analysis of long-run development policies with a mathematical numerical-experimentation model. These experiments brought forth inconsistencies and problems that had to be corrected in subsequent runs, culminating with a second set of experiments (called policy runs). These, in turn, showed that all of the problems could not be corrected by means of changes in the policy variables (especially those relating to CONS), thereby indicating that some of the target variables had to be changed. Consequently, a final pair of experiments was put into effect (called final basic runs), which are the final results of attempts to close all of the important gaps, especially by changing the basic target variables representing per capita consumption expenditures for each of the four levels of income and seventeen sectors.

For purposes of this work, which is limited to the evaluation of foreign-trade policies, it is important to point out that these policies were conceived within the framework of alternative national development strategies. For each strategy, there is a corresponding set of policies regarding exports, imports, foreign capital remittances abroad, and the like; hence, there is a corresponding set of values reflecting rates of change, coefficients, and time series.

A. The Consumption Style

The final basic experiment for CONS (204) shows that regardless of its corrective efforts, this Style is unable to bring its unemployment rate within tolerance (17 percent, rising to 31 percent if the underemployed are included) and is equally unrealistic in terms of its external disequilibrium (a balance of payments deficit on current account amounting to 76 percent of its exports and a service charge on its foreign debt amounting to 79 percent of its exports).

This type of dependent society must be discarded as a plausible future prospect, because it seems unable to succeed. The technology it is forced to import constitutes a significant drain of foreign exchange and is capital-intensive biased; and it is unable to imitate the production and consumption patterns of the hegemonic nations. The regressive nature of the distribution of income keeps the market so small and skewed that consumption gaps arise, reaching intolerable levels that are impossible to correct. Moreover, the consumption patterns, in turn, call for production patterns that are inconsistent with the system's financial and physical (human resource) capacities.

B. The Creative Style

By contrast, CREA does not show serious imbalances in its final basic run (206), although it does present a series of issues that are difficult to evaluate. This Style is based on the search for an original social project, generating and utilizing its internal possibilities of development by means of profound structural changes in the socioeconomic system and in the organization and distribution of resources. However, the success of this Style depends upon changes in the power structure, which are not capable of being analyzed and evaluated with the model.

The set of assumptions that constitute the strategy of CREA leads to the elimination of unemployment and to an overly large balance of payments surplus. In addition, the consumption patterns established provide for a development process that is harmonious, proportional in its economic relations, and considerably autonomous as regards foreign influence. Yet, a great deal depends upon the system's possibility of generating (and materializing) sufficient creative leisure and producing foreign-exchange-saving technology via exports and import substitution. Nonetheless, this Development Style shows a possibility of success, at least from the point of view of economic rationality.

9. SENSITIVITY EXPERIMENTS

For purposes of this paper, several experiments were made based on the final basic runs, in order to measure the sensitivity of the balance of payments and other indicators to changes in key relevant assumptions. In the case of the CONS Style, under the criterion of placing it in the most favorable conditions, the assumptions regarding three groups of variables were modified: the growth of industrial exports, the effective utilization of industrial productive capacity, and the import substitution of capital and intermediate goods by industry. In other words, new assumptions were quantified with the predominant intention of overcoming the bottleneck presented by the balance of payments.

To avoid unnecessary programming difficulties, it was decided to apply the values assumed for these same variables in the CREA Style (final basic run 206). This in no way means that it was thought CONS could be made feasible and realistic via the CREA assumptions. The application of the values pertaining to CREA was done solely to simplify the preparation of the experiments and of the new sets of numerical input data; it does not necessarily imply that they are consistent with the conception of the CONS strategy.

Hence, industry exports (for five sectors) were made to grow at a higher rate (at an average of 4 percent) over the thirty-three years of the run (207), rather than the 3 percent of the basic final run (204); industrial excess capacity was reduced by the year 2000 to 8 percent (208) from the 24 percent of the final basic run; and total imports were reduced 20 percent (208) by the year 2000, by accelerating the rate of import substitution.[9]

In a similar fashion, sensitivity tests were made of the CREA strategy by applying to the same sets of variables the values that had been previously adopted for CONS in its final basic run (204). In other words, and for the same reasons stated above, the Creative Style was placed in less favorable conditions regarding industrial exports, industrial excess capacity, and industrial import substitution by giving these variables the values they had in the final basic run of the Consumption Style.

Thus, the average rate of growth of industrial exports was reduced from the 4 percent of the basic run (206) to 2.6 percent (209),[10] industrial excess capacity was raised to 25 percent (210) from the 8 percent of the final basic run, and total imports were increased 27 percent (210) for the year 2000.

A. Industrial Export Policies

The object of the first pair of runs was to measure the direct and indirect effects of export demand upon the Venezuelan economy, as conceived in each of the two development strategies. As was pointed out, the CONS strategy was modified by assuming a very successful industrial export policy, while a not so successful policy was assumed for the CREA strategy. Table 1 summarizes some of the most important results (see also Tables 4 and 5) and shows that, by the year 2000, export revenues increase by 43 percent in the former and decrease by 40 percent in the latter, relative to their respective basic runs.

As might have been expected, the larger demand for industrial products in CONS does not significantly alter the unemployment rate and produces a decline in the balance of payments deficit of reduced importance. On one hand, industrial enterprises are capital intensive (particularly the larger ones, which are the exporting industries in the model) and, therefore, have a relatively low employment-generating capacity. On the other hand, these enterprises are technologically dependent (so that their investments have high import coefficients) and absorb large sums of foreign capital (so that their profit remittances abroad are significant). Thus, a successful export policy, of and by itself, is shown to be incapable of solving the two basic problems posed by the Style.

Regarding the Creative Style, the reduced demand for industrial products does not generate significant unemployment, because industrial enterprises are similarly capital intensive and technologically advanced. However, since technological independence has supposedly been achieved and foreign capital is considered unnecessary, the impact upon the balance of payments is somewhat reduced—to the extent that only a small deficit is produced in spite of a 40 percent fall in export revenues.

---

[9] For the detailed results, see the tables given below. The inclusion of a table with the numerical hypotheses and policy changes was not possible, due to limitations of length. These may be found in the original Spanish version and in the book cited, *Estilos de Desarrollo*.

[10] This growth rate of total exports is lower than that of the final basic run of CONS due to differences in the assumptions regarding nonindustrial exports (agriculture, petroleum, iron), which were not altered in these runs.

TABLE 1
RESULTS OF THE INDUSTRIAL EXPORT POLICIES
[year 2000]

	Final Basic Runs		Policy Runs		Percentage Changes	
	CONS (Run 204)	CREA (Run 206)	CONS (Run 207)	CREA (Run 209)	CONS (From Run 204 to Run 207)	CREA (From Run 206 to Run 209)
Export policy						
Total exports[1]	35,036	50,890	50,169	30,783	+43.2	−39.5
Results						
Total imports[1]	30,341	31,387	34,479	27,409	+13.8	−12.6
Gross domestic product[2]	254,566	317,536	265,101	303,252	+4.1	−4.5
Balance of payments on current account[1]	−23,057	16,299	−12,510	−1,355	−45.7	−108.0
Unemployment[3]	1,641	−27	1,443	240	−12.1	−988.0
Gross fixed investment[2]	58,970	66,756	64,287	63,117	+9.0	−5.5
Foreign capital services:						
as % of GDP	15.2	0.2	13.6	1.3	−10.5	+550.0
as % of exports	110.5	1.5	71.7	12.7	−35.0	+746.0
Foreign debt:						
as % of GDP	125.1	2.8	98.5	15.5	−21.3	+454.0
as % of exports	908.5	17.4	520.3	152.4	−42.7	+790.0
Manufactured product:						
as % of GDP	20.8	23.5	22.0	21.7	+5.7	−7.7

[1] In millions of bolivars (Bs 4.50 = $1.00) at current international prices.
[2] In millions of bolivars at 1966 prices.
[3] In thousands of persons.

B. *Industrial Import Substitution and Idle-Capacity Utilization Policies*

The second pair of experiments consisted of assuming successful and not very successful policies regarding the replacement of intermediate and capital goods imports and the reduction of excess capacity in the same industrial sectors. Table 2 summarizes the results (see also Tables 4 and 5).

In the case of CONS, the new hypotheses signify large foreign-exchange savings, since the reduced investment requirements that have been assumed accentuate the decline in the import requirements also assumed. The external deficit thus falls 71 percent; however, this decline is insufficient to bring the service charges on foreign capital (including indebtedness) to acceptable levels. Unemployment also declines, but insignificantly.

On the other hand, while CREA continues to be economically feasible, despite the increased import and investment requirements assumed, the sensitivity of the Style is indeed notable. Imports rise by 27 percent and unemployment increases by 55 percent, while gross product is barely affected by 1 percent. Nonetheless, an external deficit is generated.

Table 3 gives the accumulated results of the joint application of the export, import-substitution, and excess-capacity policy assumptions. It therefore provides the net effects of those hypotheses upon such indicators as unemployment, balance of payments, and per capita income. Both strategies tested suffer significantly; nevertheless, the unrealistic and unacceptable situation presented for the year 2000

TABLE 2
RESULTS OF THE INDUSTRIAL IMPORT SUBSTITUTION AND IDLE-CAPACITY UTILIZATION POLICIES
[year 2000]

	Base Policy Runs		Policy Runs		Percentage Changes	
	CONS (Run 207)	CREA (Run 209)	CONS (Run 208)	CREA (Run 210)	CONS (From Run 207 to Run 208)	CREA (From Run 209 to Run 210)
Policies						
Total imports[1]	34,479	27,409	27,839	34,681	−19.3	+26.6
Industrial excess capacity[2]	23.5	8.3	7.3	25.1	−68.9	+202.4
Results						
Gross domestic product	265,101	303,252	267,823	299,632	+1.0	−1.2
Balance of payments on current account[3]	−12,510	−1,355	−3,614	−12,523	−71.1	−824.5
Unemployment[4]	1,443	240	1,350	372	−6.5	+55.0
Gross fixed investment[2]	64,287	63,117	61,625	65,222	−4.1	−3.3
Foreign capital services:						
as % of GDP	13.6	1.3	11.2	4.0	−17.7	+208.0
as % of exports	71.7	12.7	59.7	39.0	−16.8	+207.0
Foreign debt:						
as % of GDP	98.5	15.5	86.0	49.5	−33.0	+216.0
as % of exports	520.3	152.4	352.5	481.7	−39.3	+219.0
Manufactured product:						
as % of GDP	22.0	21.7	22.3	21.5	+1.4	−0.9

[1] In millions of bolivars (Bs 4.50 = $1.00) at current international prices.
[2] As percent of gross output: average for five sectors (4–8).
[3] In millions of bolivars at 1966 prices.
[4] In thousands of persons.

TABLE 3
RESULTS OF THE COMBINED INDUSTRIAL POLICIES: EXPORTS, IMPORTS, AND IDLE-CAPACITY
UTILIZATION
[year 2000]

	Percentage Changes	
	CONS (From Run 204 to Run 208)	CREA (From Run 206 to Run 210)
Policies		
Total exports	+43.2	−39.5
Total imports	−8.2	+10.6
Industrial excess capacity	−69.7	+226.0
Results		
Gross domestic product	+5.2	−5.6
Balance of payments on current account	−84.3	−176.8
Unemployment	−17.7	−
Gross fixed investment	+4.5	−2.3
Foreign capital services:		
as % of GDP	−46.0	−
as % of exports	−26.3	−
Foreign debt:		
as % of GDP	−47.3	−
as % of exports	−61.2	−
Manufactured product:		
as % of GDP	+7.2	−8.5

TABLE 4
CONS: Indicators of the Most Important Results of the Experiments

	Year 1967	Year 2000		
		Run 204	Run 207	Run 208
Per capita GDP (Bs at 1966 prices)	5,095	9,306	9,691	9,791
Average % rates of growth (1967–2000):				
of GDP	–	5.2	5.3	5.3
of exports—total	–	3.1	4.0	4.0
nonpetroleum	–	6.6	9.5	9.5
of imports—total	–	3.8	4.3	3.5
intermediate goods	–	4.0	4.3	3.5
capital goods	–	4.6	5.2	4.5
of labor productivity	–	1.9	1.9	1.9
Ratio of maximum to minimum sectorial labor productivity	92.5	58.4	58.3	58.4
Unemployment as % of labor force	6.1	17.3	15.2	14.2
Manufacturing as % of GDP	18.1	20.8	22.0	22.3
Urban underemployment as % of labor force	5.3	13.9	13.8	13.7
Gross fixed investment as % of GDP	19.3	23.2	24.3	21.9
Share of equipment in investment (%)	26.8	20.9	22.8	21.5
Share of imports in equipment (%)	92.9	83.6	83.8	75.0
Average monthly wage level (Bs at 1966 prices)	644	1,243	1,249	1,247
Share of labor in national income (%)	39.8	51.4	50.0	48.9
Average profits before taxes (% of gross income):				
Foreign enterprise	67.5	41.3	44.3	50.8
Public enterpise	8.8	15.3	17.5	19.4
National private enterprise	41.6	27.3	29.6	35.6
Distribution of families by level of income (%):[1]				
High (over Bs 3,000 per month)	8.8	2.2	2.2	2.2
Medium high (Bs 1,500–3,000 per month)	16.8	13.0	12.3	12.4
Medium low (Bs 500–1,500 per month)	44.7	61.9	61.1	61.2
Low (under Bs 500 per month)	29.7	22.9	24.4	24.2
Distribution of income by level of income (%):				
High	36.3	21.4	23.0	23.7
Medium high	26.9	23.0	21.3	21.3
Medium low	30.2	50.6	50.1	49.4
Low	6.7	4.9	5.6	5.6
Distribution of savings by level of income (as % of disposable income):				
High	32.3	58.2	62.4	64.1
Medium high	5.4	4.7	7.8	8.9
Medium low	−17.0	−10.2	−4.7	−3.7
Low	−44.5	−74.3	−54.9	−49.9
Housing deficit in the low and medium-low income levels (thousands of units)	700	455	473	462
Government deficit (+) on current and capital account (as % of total income)	−27.7	−3.8	−8.9	−11.9
Import coefficients (%):				
Total imports as % of GDP	12.7	8.2	9.0	7.1
Consumer goods as % of consumption	4.3	0.9	0.9	0.9
Intermediate goods as % of GDP	7.7	5.1	5.5	4.2
Capital goods as % of investment	23.9	16.1	17.6	15.2
Balance of payments deficit (−) on current account (as % of total exports)	+6.6	−76.0	−30.5	−8.8
Foreign capital services as % of exports	28.4	110.5	71.7	59.7
Foreign debt as % of exports	11.1	908.5	520.3	352.5
Trade gap (millions of Bs at 1966 prices)[2]	−3,633	+738	−9,739	−16,853

Note: 204 = Final Basic Run.

      207 = Export Policy Run. To the final basic run (204) have been applied the industrial exports assumption of CREA in its final basic run (206).

      208 = Import and Excess-Capacity Policy Run. To policy run 207 have been applied the industrial imports and idle-capacity utilization assumptions of CREA in its final basic run (206).

[1] The limits of the income levels shift through time according to the rate of growth of per capita gross income. [2] The trade gap is defined as the current account balance less net remittances abroad of profits and debt charges. It is favorable when it is negative.

	Year 1967	Year 2000		
		Run 206	Run 209	Run 210
Per capital GDP (Bs at 1966 prices)	5,095	11,608	11,186	10,954
Average % rates of growth (1967–2000):				
of GDP	–	5.9	5.8	5.8
of exports—total	–	4.0	2.6	2.6
nonpetroleum	–	10.5	7.5	7.5
of imports—total	–	4.0	3.6	4.3
intermediate goods	–	3.8	3.3	4.3
capital goods	–	5.1	4.7	5.2
of labor productivity	–	2.0	1.9	1.9
Ratio of maximum to minimum sectorial labor productivity	92.5	42.0	41.9	41.9
Unemployment as % of labor force	6.1	−0.3	2.5	3.9
Manufacturing as % of GDP	18.1	23.5	21.7	21.5
Urban underemployment as % of labor force	5.3	2.1	2.3	2.4
Gross fixed investment as % of GDP	19.3	21.0	20.8	21.8
Share of equipment in investment (%)	26.8	27.5	25.8	26.6
Share of imports in equipment (%)	92.9	67.5	67.2	75.1
Average monthly wage level (Bs at 1966 prices)	644	1,656	1,652	1,653
Share of labor in national income (%)	39.8	65.7	67.6	69.1
Average profits before taxes (% of income):				
Foreign enterprise	67.5	1.2	0.9	0.9
Public enterprise	8.8	32.1	29.2	25.4
Private national enterprise	41.6	35.7	34.1	25.6
Distribution of families by level of income (%):[1]				
High (over Bs 3,000 per month)	8.8	0.7	0.7	0.7
Medium high (Bs 1,500–3,000 per month)	16.8	6.9	7.4	7.4
Medium low (Bs 500–1,500 per month)	44.7	81.3	80.8	80.4
Low (under Bs 500 per month)	29.7	11.1	11.1	11.5
Distribution of income by level of income (%):				
High	36.3	2.0	2.0	2.3
Medium high	26.9	9.8	10.5	10.4
Medium low	30.2	82.1	81.9	81.6
Low	6.7	6.1	5.7	5.7
Distribution of savings by level of income (as % of disposable income):				
High	32.3	56.3	54.3	60.2
Medium high	5.4	33.6	30.3	29.7
Medium low	−17.0	20.5	17.9	17.2
Low	−44.5	−22.3	−37.2	−43.3
Housing deficit in the low and medium low income levels (thousands of units)	700	0	0	0
Government deficit (+) on current and capital account (as % of total income)	−27.7	1.9	6.9	13.1
Import coefficients (%):				
Total imports as % of GDP	12.7	6.9	6.3	8.1
Consumer goods as % of consumption	4.3	1.2	1.2	1.2
Intermediate goods as % of GDP	7.7	3.8	3.4	4.8
Capital goods as % of investment	23.9	16.2	15.1	17.4
Balance of payments deficit (−) on current account (as % of total exports)	6.6	40.4	−5.2	−48.0
Foreign capital services as % of exports	28.4	1.5	12.7	39.0
Foreign debt as % of exports	11.1	17.4	152.4	481.7
Trade gap (millions of Bs at 1966 prices)[2]	−3,633	−16,340	−200	+7,589

NOTE: 206 = Final Basic Run.

206 = Final Basic Run.

209 = Export Policy Run. To the final basic run (206) have been applied the industrial exports assumptions of CONS in its final basic run (204).

210 = Import and Excess-Capacity Policy Run. To policy run 209 have been applied the industrial imports and idle-capacity utilization assumptions of CONS in its final basic run (204).

[1] The limits of the income levels shift through time according to the rate of growth of per capita gross income. [2] The trade gap is defined as the current account balance less net remittances abroad of profits and debt charges.

by CONS in its final basic run remains basically unaltered in these sensitivity runs (see 210), while CREA becomes vulnerable and approaches the unacceptable point, as its rate of unemployment rises to 4 percent.

10. CONCLUSIONS

A. Methodological Results

Via the method of numerical experimentation, a computer program of a formal accounting system has been applied to the complex problem of economic and social development. In order to deal adequately with the problem, which has been conceived and handled in a manner different from the traditional approaches, it was necessary to design a methodology capable of dealing with the various aspects involved in the analyses and to devise a flexible and highly disaggregated mathematical instrument (the PRODINGR model).

The results obtained and the experience gained in the course of several years of intensive research clearly indicate that the method developed and the model built are instruments of great value and multiple uses, despite the important problems that remain but that are capable of solution.

In this respect, reference may be made to the degree of exogeneity of the model and its scarce theoretical (behavioral) content. The more exogenous it is, and thus the fewer endogenous relations (theories) it contains, the more the model performs as a mere accounting scheme of an economic system, and the greater the input data required. Moreover, the information required increases with the disaggregation of the model, which to a certain extent depends upon the objectives sought, the hypotheses to be tested, and the nature of the problems to be analyzed.

The input data present at least two crucial issues: the availability of the information required, in quantity and quality; and the need to make the data internally consistent so as to effectively represent the state of the system in the base year. A great deal of effort and coordination is necessary.

The output of data also presents problems of relative importance due to its magnitude. In this case, the output must be systematized to offer a minimum of consistent feasibility criteria, so as to simplify the analyses of experiments. Global or macroeconomic balance indicators are not sufficient; more specific sets of indicators are needed to arrive at a more profound evaluation of each experiment. Moreover, each experiment must be carefully designed in order to avoid a disproportionate rise in computation costs. In point of fact, it is only after the model user becomes thoroughly familiar with such a model that he will achieve a certain efficiency in the technique of numerical experimentation. This can be unduly delayed if the work is not performed by a coordinated team, taking advantage of the division of labor without losing the notion of the organic whole of the work.

Special subroutines can be very helpful in dealing with the input and output data. Thus, a program that translates raw data into the type of information fed into the model (coefficients, rates) greatly simplifies the debugging process and speeds the tuning of the model, also allowing experimentation by trial and error with unreliable or conjectural information. Similarly, it is convenient to have programs that process the output differently, thereby facilitating communication (and presentation) to persons not familiar with the model, computers, or economics. Bottlenecks in communications are not infrequently a great hindrance.

B. Policy Results

A first general conclusion of interest is that the two Development Styles studied show similar results regarding overall growth rates, although important qualitative differences may be observed in such aspects as income distribution, unemployment, savings gaps, and foreign-exchange requirements. In other words, the problem of economic development is not well stated if presented solely in terms of per capita income and its rate of growth as target variables, since the same rate of growth can have substantially different meanings in .terms of more concrete indicators or criteria that reflect with greater precision and fidelity the true significance of the process of development.

A second conclusion concerns the sensitivity of the strategies to the foreign-trade policies assumed. While CONS remained an unlikely possibility from the point of view of its internal conditions, particularly unemployment, in spite of the very favorable conditions assumed for the external sector; CREA remained feasible in terms of its internal conditions, although it became vulnerable in terms of the unfavorable foreign-trade assumptions adopted.

As regards CONS, its strategy is one of passive imitation of the achievements of the leading hegemonic nations, but without undergoing the profound structural changes that, in those countries, historically preceded their present situation. This seems to be contradictory in itself: an attempt at modernization without integrating all of the sectors and without the internal cohesion of all the forces generating a self-sustained process of modernization. While the consumption patterns of the leading countries are postulated as goals, the distribution of income engendered by the Development Style produces consumption gaps at the lower levels of the income pyramid; thereby indicating that large segments of the population become marginal and unable to participate in the market.

The CREA Style presents a different situation. Although it goes through profound structural changes and a revolutionary educational process, CREA must penetrate the world markets with new and competitive products, if it is to finance the import requirements generated by a 6 percent rate of growth without wasting its petroleum by exporting it crude and as a direct source of energy. Hence, an issue that arises concerns the optimum rate of growth or absorptive capacity of an economy like the Venezuelan, possessing abundant resources and attempting to adopt a specific style of development: what is the gestation period of the assumed changes; when can it begin obtaining the expected results?

Both Styles turned out to be rather unresponsive to changes in exports and imports, insofar as the share of the industrial sector in total production is concerned. This is not too surprising, in view of the relative unimportance of industrial exports; although the import content of manufactured products is rather large initially, and somewhat greater effects were to be expected. Obviously, then, this means that a more detailed and profound study of the problem is necessary before attempting to derive more concrete conclusions. But one fact does seem to hold true; namely, that Latin American countries (in particular those like Venezuela) should not expect definitive solutions to their problems from foreign-trade policies alone. Profound internal changes are required in order to overcome underdevelopment.

Furthermore, in both cases studied, a remaining issue concerns the consistency of the specific policy hypotheses tested with the general development strategies defined. In any case, to the results obtained nothing more should be attributed than what can be expected from long-run projections and analyses that are merely average indicators of approximate trends and situations.

It is reasonable to conclude, however, regardless of the style of development, that the social aspects of development are just as important as the technical-economic aspects. They interact and combine to establish the limits of the real internal possibilities of development and the feasibility or reality of the strategy adopted. Furthermore, it also seems to be fairly clear that foreign trade is an extremely important (strategic) variable in any style of development attempted, even in a country rich in resources such as Venezuela. And in this respect, it is significant to determine how to convert liquid foreign exchange into productive resources in a way consistent with a development program. Venezuela faces such a situation at present, although it does not have a clear and well-established development policy.

Finally, two additional conclusions stand out as interesting and plausible. The first of these refers to foreign capital, and the second to the thirty-three-year period of projection. In the case of foreign capital, it not only undoubtedly and excessively burdens the balance of payments with profit and service remittances abroad, but also seems to present an obstacle to the establishment of autonomous consumption (and so cultural) patterns and the eradication of technological and cultural dependence. Regarding the thirty-three years of the projection, these were barely sufficient to derive interesting conclusions; in fact, entirely different conclusions might have been derived from a shorter projection (say, twenty years or less).

11. Appendix

A. Sectoral Classification of the Model

Following is a list of the sectors comprising the PRODINGR. The number between parentheses refers to the International Uniform Classification of economic activities that applies to the sector. Each sector is subdivided into techniques, according to size or type of social organization involved.

1: Agriculture (0)
2: Petroleum (13, 32)
3: Mining (11, 12, 14, 19)
4: Foods and Beverages (20, 21, 22)
5: Textiles and Shoes (23, 24)
6: Other Consumer Goods (26, 28)
7: Intermediate Goods (25, 27, 29, 30, 31, 33, 34, 39)
8: Capital Goods and Vehicles (35, 36, 37, 38)
9: Housing Construction
10: Other Construction
11: Electricity, Water, and Urban Sanitation
12: Transport
13: Commerce and Finance
14: Other Services (82, 83, 85—except 821, 822, 823, 852, 853)
15: Recreation and Tourism (84, 852, 853)

APPENDIX TABLE
Classification of the PRODINGR Model by Sectors and Subsectors

Sector		Technique 1	Symbol	Technique 2	Symbol	Technique 3	Symbol
AGRO	(1)	Enterprises	EMPR	Land settlements IAN	ASNT	Subsistence	CNUC
PETR	(2)	Crude extraction	EXTR	Refining	REFN	–	–
MINR	(3)	Whole sector	UNIC	–	–	–	–
ALMT	(4)	Large industry	GNDE	Medium & small	PQMD	Crafts	ARTS
TEXT	(5)	Large industry	GNDE	Medium & small	PQMD	Crafts	ARTS
RCMO	(6)	Large industry	GNDE	Medium & small	PQMD	Crafts	ARTS
ITMD	(7)	Large industry	GNDE	Medium & small	PQMD	Crafts	ARTS
KPTL	(8)	Large industry	GNDE	Medium & small	PQMD	Crafts	ARTS
CTRV	(9)	Industrialized	INDA	Commercial not industrialized	TRAD	Self-help	AYPR
CTRP	(10)	Mechanized	MECN	Not mechanized	NMEC	–	–
ELEC	(11)	Whole sector	UNIC	–	–	–	–
TRSP	(12)	Cargo & storage	CARG	Passenger	PASJ	Communications	COMU
CMCO	(13)	Large & medium	GNMD	Small	PEQÑ	Street vendors	BUHO
SERV	(14)	Large & medium	GNMD	Small	PEQÑ	Not organized	NORG
ESPT	(15)	Large	GNDE	Small & medium	PQMD	–	–
SALD	(16)	Public	PUBL	Private	PVDA	–	–
EDUC	(17)	Public	PUBL	Private	PVDA	–	–
GBNO	(18)	Central government	CENT	States & municipalities	MUNI	Public service institutes	INST
VNDA	(19)	Whole sector	UNIC	–	–	–	–

NOTES: 1. The sectors (9, 3) (for S = 9, T = 3), (10, 2), (16, 1), (17, 1), (18, 1), (18, 2), (18. 3) are *public*, controlled by government.
2. The sectors (13, 3) and (14, 3) are called *not organized* due to their typical characteristics (street vendors, shoeshine boys, domestic servants, and so on).
3. The *mixed* sectors, which include the techniques 1 of S = 1 to 15, (2, 2), (9, 2), (10, 2), (12, 2), and (12, 3), are the best organized and contain foreign and public enterprises.
4. The *marketing* sectors are all sectors except VNDA, the *public* sectors, and the sectors *not organized*.

16: Health (822)
17: Education (821, 823)
18: Government Services (81)
19: Residential Property

B. *Labor Force Subdivision*

The labor force is classified into four levels of skills or training and four occupational categories.

Skills: Professionals and High Level Management
                     Technicians and Subprofessionals
                     Skilled Workers
                     Unskilled Workers

Occupations: Employers
                     Self-employed
                     Employees
                     Family Helpers

C. *Classification of Loans and Debts*

There are four types of loans, according to payment conditions regarding interest payments and terms.

Hard Loans (short term, averaging 3 months)
Semi-hard Loans (medium short term, averaging 1 year)
Semi-soft Loans (medium long term, averaging 3 years)
Soft Loans (long term, averaging 10 years)

In addition, three types of creditors are considered: foreign, domestic banks, and domestic non-banking sources.

D. *Distribution of Disposable Family Income*

Four levels of income account for the distribution of disposable family and personal income. The limits shift through time according to the rate of growth of per capita gross income.

High (over 3,000 bolivars per month, 1966 prices)
Medium High (between 1,500 and 3,000 bolivars per month, 1966 prices)
Medium Low (between 500 and 1,500 bolivars per month, 1966 prices)
Low (under 500 bolivars per month, 1966 prices)

SUMMARY OF THE CONFERENCE

RICHARD RUGGLES

Yale University and National Bureau of Economic Research

I think I might start by saying just a word about the purpose of this conference. It was meant to be exploratory in nature. What we were interested in exploring was the impact of the computer on economic and social research methods. The conference was purposely set up to be fairly wide-ranging. We chose as topics those areas in which the computer appears to be having a major effect. In order to achieve the objective, broad coverage was needed, and a number of examples within each of the various areas, to make sure that the range of work being done was fairly represented. The result of this approach was a large mass of papers and a diversity of subjects and participants, and we suffered through long sessions and long days. In this connection, I would like to thank not only the participants for their patience in enduring these long sessions, but also the translators, who had to listen to it all and to reproduce it when at times it didn't seem to make sense.

My presentation this morning is going to be a discussion of what this fishing expedition has netted—essentially a resume, or summary, of what I consider to be the high points. Now obviously this is my personal interpretation.

The conference started off with the session on government statistical systems. The purpose of that session was to ask where governments now stand with respect to computers. We would have liked to have had a wider representation of governments from Latin America, but this would have just lengthened the conference. The constraints of time meant that we had to start with just a few.

I think the history of the Brazilian experience as described by Kerstenetzky and discussed by Janes de Souza provided a very suitable point of departure for this conference. They explained how the new technology and the advanced hardware, superimposed on the old systems of procedure, inadequate staffing, and so on, resulted in the disaster of 1960, with no census forthcoming at all. But out of the ashes arose a new organization that was more centralized and that was based upon a computer bank of microdata. The new organization was set up to process the 1970 census, and we are told that within three to four months after collection of the data, tabulations were available. This, indeed, is a happy ending to what was originally a disastrous computer experience. I suspect that this experience has been repeated more often in both Latin America and the United States than we are willing to admit. Normally, these things are buried, but the Brazilian experience is so well known that there is no use burying it; it might as well serve as an object lesson.

The Mexican story as reported by Gleason was quite different. They started serious work on computerization for the 1970 census around 1968. They trained personnel, and they took over software already developed by the U.S. Census Bureau, gradually putting into operation techniques that were fairly well advanced but tried and true. The result was quite successful—a substantial improvement over the 1960 census. As Sourrouille pointed out, much of the success of this operation was due to the technology transfer in international cooperation.

With respect to the U.S. Census, Brown gave us a glimpse of, perhaps not 1984, but at least 1980. He pointed out that the computer was now trained to talk: it could hold press conferences on business and population, it could provide tract analysis for planners and local organizations, and it could even give congressmen profiles of their districts. There are really two implications in this: one is the ability of the computer to take statistical material and provide text, highlight important elements, do comparisons over time, or perhaps even provide comparisons between regions, all in nice words rather than in tables. But, and this is really much more important, an ability has been developed to define specific geographic areas and report on them, so that, essentially, the programs were adapted to yield data on regions defined in any way that might be desired. Ferran's point was that insofar as this procedure just saves time or improves public relations, it is not relevant to our present concerns; what we really need is better information for professionals.

Now, I think that the Census Bureau has actually sold itself short in this presentation of its work on geographic coding, because there are in it considerable implications for research. In fact, the Census Bureau has built for the United States a system called DIME, which stands for Dual Independent Map Encoding System. In this system, addresses are geographically coded so that they can be located by block face within a community (a block face is the area on one side of one street between two intersections.) Once given this coding system, data contained in other files of the city—for example, education statistics, health, police, fire—all can be merged and mapped onto block faces. This gives local planners and officials in local government the ability to analyze their own data about their city in relation to the demographic and social characteristics provided in the census data. Some two hundred and eighty cities now have the DIME system of geo-encoding. The Census Bureau provides to the cities all the necessary computer programs to take their local records and match them with the census records.

In all fairness, too, quite apart from the geo-encoding work, the U.S. Census is providing researchers with masses of information for social and economic research. The 1970 census will provide more than three-thousand tapes for research use. The Bureau is also creating a set of Public Use Samples, each of which is a 1-in-100 sample of the population, approximately two million individual households. There are six different samples containing different information in the set.

The paper by Fellegi and Goldberg describes the decision of Statistics Canada to keep their basic statistical information in the form of microdata. They are doing this because they have found that the ability to reprocess the microdata as needed gives them much more flexibility, making it possible to produce any required tabulations on demand. Also, they are finding that different kinds of economic analysis call for combining information in different ways, and this is only possible if the microdata are available.

The heart of the problem of preserving data in micro form, as Fellegi pointed out, and as Howe also recognized, is the editing that goes on in creating microdata files that are usable for a wide variety of purposes. Howe raised the question as to whether the editing did not in fact homogenize the data to a considerable degree. We will come back to this point because it was discussed a great deal during the conference, but part of the answer may be that the outliers may, in the aggregate, be of limited significance, and their correction may improve the usefulness of the data for microanalysis by making the data sets more consistent.

Fellegi also pointed out that Canada is involved in developing a central register of all companies and establishments, giving their industry totals and so on. I believe that in Canada at this moment, this register is held within the government, but it does help provide the consistency that is needed for classification of information from different sources. I understand that in the United States, the President's Commission on Federal Statistics is going to recommend such a system. Such a register would be a great help, not only to the various government agencies but to private outside research users.

Fellegi also stressed the tremendous need for generalized programming. I think that everyone who has been involved in computerization has been depressed at the rate of obsolescence of programming when different machines come along, or when different uses are made of data, or when different data sets are introduced. There is a great need for generalized programs to handle a wide variety of information. Statistics Canada has gone a great distance in this field.

Finally, Fellegi worried about the confidentiality problem and indicated that they were very careful in their custom processing and tabulation not to allow the use of the microdata to result in disclosure. They do give access to their microdata by allowing people to run programs on it so long as this does not result in disclosure. This same technique, incidentally, is being used in the United States by the Social Security Administration, by the Census, and by some other federal agencies.

Carlos Petit questioned whether a microdata basis for stastical systems was applicable to Latin America. Fellegi's reply was that he felt that it was. If the data is fragmentary, it is much easier to squeeze meaningful information out of a microdata set than it is to make a reasonable macrotabulation that could serve a wide variety of purposes.

This session, in general, shows that computer technology in governmental statistical organizations, both in Latin America and in North America, is moving very fast indeed. People are moving toward retaining information in its original micro form and then manipulating it as needed for specific statistical purposes. Governments, instead of publishing large tomes of tabulations such as census bureaus did for many years, are beginning to make machine-readable data available on tape. This opens up different kinds of research techniques to users. After all, I can remember keypunching some of the tabulations that used to come out of the census, and having the published tabulations available on tape is a far step forward in that it not only reduces the cost of using information but it certainly improves the quality as well.

The second session, on data banks and computer centers, was essentially an attempt to find out what their current status was. It is indeed unfortunate that we had no report from CLACSO [Latin American Council of Social Sciences], but we did have a very interesting report from CELADE [Latin American Demographic Center] that indicated that they hold a substantial sample of Latin American censuses. Now these samples are mainly demographic and were aimed at the study of fertility and migration; but, I think, one of the most interesting things about this data bank is the avenues which it opens up for comparative analysis of different countries in the area of demography. I would hope that at some later time they will add to their bank some of the other information aside from the purely demographic —such things as education and consumer budget studies—that we have heard of here. The interrelations among the demographic, social, and economic characteristics are important, and only by bringing this data together into a single data bank can its maximum potential be realized.

Domingo reported, with respect to computer centers in Venezuela, the existence of numerous computers, more or less modern. The major problem was a shortage of qualified personnel to use them. Rojas also agreed in this session that this was a major problem—that the large centers were more efficient, but the small ones were easier to start and control. I found these remarks particularly interesting because, not so many years ago, we, too, were starved for computer programmers, while now they're unemployed. This is not purely a function of economic recession; it is a function of the fact that the technology and training spread very fast. All of our graduate students practice programming; the undergraduates earn their money by programming—it is the sort of thing that people are picking up very rapidly. Part of the reason is that programming languages are becoming simpler, computers are becoming more powerful, and the problems at the applications level are not nearly as horrendous as they were a decade ago.

The question of the relation of large and small computers is also very interesting. I have been impressed at the small cost of hardware relative to other costs in running a computer center. The nonhardware costs of running a small computer center are almost as much as those of running a large computer center—you need your operators, your programmers on duty, your assistant programmers, and so on, in any operation. At Yale, we have had two or three computers and two or three staffs. It is not quite as bad as it might have been, because, theoretically, there is one head over them all—but even then, the waste of resources in essentially duplicate facilities of lower power is very marked indeed. In countries where there are shortages of both trained manpower and hardware, the sharing of facilities does seem to me to be a sensible approach, especially in the short run.

Perhaps paradoxically, in the longer run you can afford to have smaller computer centers rather than larger ones. The paper by Boschan on the NBER data bank gave us, I think, another view of things to come. The National Bureau data bank covers two-thousand time series on national accounts, financial data, and other economic data about the economy. A number of people have mentioned to me that they would just love to be able to sit down at those terminals and use that kind of information. I am always rather paralyzed by such an opportunity: there are such a variety of things to do, and everything I can think of seems so naive that I am somewhat stuck. On the other hand, the potentialities are tremendous. The NBER bank is in operating order; it is updated currently and there are some fifty commercial users, as well as five universities. The method of use is through interactive terminals and on-line storage of the data. At the present time, four computers are involved—two GE computers, a PDP-10, and a 360/67. There are different software packages on the different computers. One of the most sophisticated ones that is now available is the TROLL simulation system, which is up on the 360/67 computers at MIT and Yale. This is a rather interesting contrast with the Domingo and Rojas discussions of computer centers. Here you have a data bank without a computer center. As a matter of fact, the same terminal at the same place can reach different computer centers merely by using different telephone numbers. So it may well be that with interactive terminals, the actual location of the computer itself and even that of the computer center may become less relevant. Another problem that is bound to arise is that of cost. There are economies of scale; and once you have created a thing of this sort, in which the marginal cost of using the data (including the marginal computer cost) is so low, all red-blooded economists feel very unhappy if it is not made available as a free good. It is the old whether-the-bridge-should-have-a-toll problem.

Watts added another dimension to the discussion of the microeconomic data bank. He recognized the tremendous value of creating microdata sets, but he offered very sobering advice: he said to start small and develop competence with one body of data, to avoid the latest technology, to use a person-plus-machine approach, and to focus the data bank on specific needs and specific analyses. I am sure that if these rules were followed, one would not go wrong; and that had the Brazilians in their early stages thought in these terms, the disaster would not have occurred. But there is a kind of pessimistic flavor in all of this, which contrasts sharply with the achievements with the Survey of Economic Opportunity (SEO) Files, which Watts himself created. That SEO File is not designed for specific needs and specific analyses; it didn't start all that small; and it didn't develop competence necessarily with one body of data. The person-plus-machine approach didn't really work out there either. Let me give you just a brief history. The file was first turned over to Brookings, which engaged in extensive cleaning. It was then given to a firm called ASSIST for distribution, but this firm went bankrupt. I got my copy of the file from ASSIST, and it was never readable. From ASSIST, the file went to Wisconsin. In the meantime, some bootleg versions that were uncorrected had spread to the University of Georgia, Cornell University, and a number of other places. In order to get help, I went down to Georgia to get copies of their tapes, and we called Brookings up and got a little more help; it was chaos, but the point is that it worked. We have now bred, I think, four or five descendent generations which have gone to other users. I don't think that Harold Watts realizes the monster that he really created, or he would be more optimistic. At the present time, the SEO tapes are used for a wide variety of projects at the Urban Institute, Wisconsin, Yale, and other places. We have already had a number of theses started, using them in such areas as poverty, income distribution, unemployment, education, demography, and time-budget studies; and, of course, we have had a presentation here on their use in creating the MERGE File for tax analysis.

This reminds me that at a workshop on microdata held in Washington, D.C., a year ago, Okner presented some of the early results of his work on the MERGE File, and he had very much the Watts point of view—he was very pessimistic. At that time, he said, "I'd never do it again; you couldn't get me to do it." When I pointed out to him at this meeting that his paper had quite a different flavor, he said, "I got results." Perhaps, when Watts is closer to the end of his project, he may be happier.

Lebergott took a somewhat lighter view of this whole problem, indicating that, in the end, virtue would triumph. He also added another dimension that we have not discussed at all in this conference, but which I feel is probably one of the most important elements—namely, that the survey technique is not the only source of information. Administrative records—such as invoices, bills of sale, and things that result from the current operation of economic systems—provide very valuable bodies of data, which we should utilize; if these are gathered and linked and integrated, we will have types of data that are absolutely impossible to get from survey information. I have been particularly interested in the area of alternative sources of information on consumer expenditures, because I feel that there is a very real limitation as to what you can find out from people about their expenditures: they just don't know. They certainly don't know with respect, say, to brands and sizes. Not too long ago, a student of mine did an undergraduate thesis analyzing the load sheets of supermarkets for this purpose. These load sheets indicate wholesale price and retail price and the amount sold by each supermarket for some ten-thousand items, twice a week. The stores represented were located in both poverty areas and non-poverty areas, so that he could examine patterns of consumption and substitution from one item to another when prices changed in both poverty and non-poverty areas. Thus, I think that we are overlooking very valuable sets of information if we just think in terms of censuses and surveys.

After considering data banks, the conference shifted its focus from the processing, storage, and retrieval of information to the analysis of information. The Vargas paper pointed out that the model which they were developing was providing a framework for examination of data consistency and gaps. It is certainly too early to appraise this work because it is in midstream, but this paper emphasized the importance of the feedback from the model to the data, and from the data to the model. This is a very important point indeed. We will be coming back to it; and it will, I think, have major implications for the conclusions of the conference. In a sense, it reinforces Manne's point when he said that a model is a prisoner of the data. Well, it is only a prisoner if there is no feedback; but if there is sufficient feedback, and if the modelmakers either go out and get their data or manage to get other people to do it, they're not prisoners of their data.

The Okner and Pechman paper illustrated a completely different approach from that of a macromodel. What they were considering was the merging of two very different data sets that had some information in common. The object of the game was to map onto the one data set information from the other. The two files they used were the SEO File, which gives extensive demographic and social information about households, and the tax file, which is a sample of individual tax returns provided by the Internal Revenue Service. The idea was to produce a union of the two files which would have the desirable statistical characteristic of eliminating the bias in the selection of individuals which is inherent in the tax files, and which would provide a larger set of information than is available in that file. What is being done here reflects a very interesting and, in a sense, revolutionary idea: what we are trying to do is to create synthetic data sets of make-believe, but statistically valid, people or—if you want to put it another way—we impute to certain households information (perhaps on a stochastic basis) that seems reasonable, given our knowledge of that household. Now, this has two implications: first, it makes diverse samples very much more valuable, since it provides a method of merging the information in the samples; and second, it overcomes the problem of privacy because the people in this new synthetic sample do not really exist—it is just that the sample has the statistical characteristics of the data sets on which it is based. The validity of this procedure depends a great deal upon the overlap that is available in the two data sets.

As a national accountant, I can appreciate these problems very much, because the national accountants have been doing the same thing with macrodata all along. They essentially go to one source of data to get one type of information and to another source for another type. The various sources are seldom consistent, and the national accountants must make up their minds how to juggle them to bring them into consistency. As a matter of fact, Morris Copeland, in a recent communication, pointed out that we really should have statistical discrepancies in every account rather than just one, and there is much to be said for this.

There are biases in almost every set of data, and any imputation requires a theory of what is related to what. If you do not have a good understanding, you are going to mismatch data; and the intercorrelations among your variables will be very bad indeed. However this is not as difficult as it might appear, because there are several ways to find out about the intercorrelations among variables. For example, there is in the United States an unfinished study called LINK (not to be confused with the international project called LINK). This is a cooperative effort of the Census, the Internal Revenue Service, and the Social Security Administration, bringing together their records for identical individuals. Now, if this is done for just a sample, the principles of linkage can then be derived from this small sample and applied to other samples. Similarly, where difficulties arise in linkages, special samples can be collected which give more information about individuals, and this information can be used to develop theories of how linkages should be made. The payoff in the Okner-Pechman approach is that it yields income distributions with much richer social and demographic and income data than we have ever had before. The national accounts people in the Commerce Department have also realized this—this is not just an isolated gleam in Okner and Pechman's eyes. In the Bureau of Economic Analysis, Edward Budd is making a synthetic microdata set based on the Current Population Survey and the tax file, aligning it with national accounts. The income-distribution statistics in the future in the United States will be based upon such a microdata set. In the Brookings case, the use of the tax file for analysis of tax policy has been outstandingly successful. It has been so successful that the Internal Revenue Service has taken it over; they don't stir an inch without consulting the tax model to explore the implications of changes in the tax law upon receipts, distribution, who gains, who loses, and so forth.

A paper using a related technique but focused on different questions was presented by James Schulz. He undertook to simulate the effects of the social security system on the aged population in the future. He wanted to examine the income distribution of the aged population in the year 1980, given the present configuration of social security, private pension plans, and other savings that individuals might have. In order to do this, he created a life-process model which aged each person a year at a time, using a stochastic approach. For example, he first asked whether the person lived or died. To do this, he looked up in a mortality table the probability of death for a person of those characteristics and then drew a random number to apply that probability to the particular case. The basic data used was the Census 1-in-1000 sample for 1960, but a great deal of other information was added to this—information on labor turnover, unemployment, retirement, work status of the wife, mortgages, and other financial information—with the result that he was able to create an income statement and balance sheet for each household, adding savings in each year. The result of this analysis not only provided him with a distribution of income for the aged in 1980, given his initial institutional assumptions; but also, like most simulations, permitted sensitivity analysis to see how the income distribution changed with various changes in policy, or in assumptions, or in exogenous factors, and so on. Recently Schulz has extended this work to the social security systems of Austria and Sweden, applying their provisions to his base population. This allows him to appraise the effect upon his given population of alternative social security systems. This, of course, is very useful for revising our own social security system, and for getting some appreciation of how social security systems compare with each other. The basic principle in this work is applying the analysis to a set of microdata for households, household by household, and then tabulating the results at the end, or as might be said, running a census at the end of the period.

The paper by the Urban Institute group was along much the same line, except that the project it reports upon is much more ambitious. Rather than devising a special-purpose tool, the Urban Institute project views this technique of microanalytic models of household behavior as a general-purpose tool which can be applied to a wide variety of studies relating to economic and social problems of the household. One of the principal segments of the project was the demographic simulation of births and deaths and marriages and divorces. This microanalytic model is to be imbedded in a macro system of accounts which will provide an environment for the microsimulation of household behavior. I think that the methodological importance of this type of research is very great indeed. It is a long-range project—probably longer range than the people in it would like it to be—but it is very ambitious, very comprehensive, and tries to take an integrated approach to the whole of economic analysis in this particular area. It provides us with a tool for studying social problems—health, education, poverty—problems which our macromodels are not suitable for.

The final paper in this session, by Gamba, described a sectoral simulation of the Argentine beef industry. This was neither macro nor micro, but somewhere in between. It demonstrates that for particular sectors of the economy, partial simulation on a disaggregated basis may be very useful. I think Kresge's point that it would be interesting to explore this with the more recent simulation packages and to see how the results compare was extremely pertinent.

Next, we came to the session on macroeconomic models—the bread and butter of economists. De Souza and Monteiro gave an overview of seven different models for Brazil. Success was not claimed for any of them—there were major difficulties about the price-level problem—but the authors came, as everybody comes in this area, to the conclusion that what they needed was larger, more complex and sophisticated models.

The Klein-Beltran del Rio paper gave us one of those larger, more complex and sophisticated models. I think there were about 140 equations, with 40 of them behavioral, and some 46 exogenous variables. This model was not taken over from the models of developed countries directly. It recognized that for a developing country, special features are needed to take account of bottlenecks, the role of agriculture, the income distribution, internal migration, and the process of capacity creation. In the Mexican model especially, the special trade features with respect to the United States and the proximity to the United States are taken into account. The Klein model was of a long-term nature—not long term in the sense of time-period covered, but long term philosophically; it covered a four-year period, showing the output-price relationship which could be expected under deflationary policies and expansionary policies over the four years.

The Manne model was also on the Mexican economy. This paper, which is part of a much larger study, also presented alternatives—eight different alternatives —for Mexico, using a special model developed for this purpose. I was struck with the similarity of the results of these models, despite the fact that the models themselves were very different and were done by different people; this fact is indeed encouraging.

The Foxley model that was developed for Chile dealt with some 15 sectors and 115 variables. It was built with special emphasis on the copper sector, which has accounted for 70 percent of Chile's exports. The model was used to analyze the export subsidy and expansion policy.

The conclusion of this session was that the macromodel does provide a description of the economic system in a general, comprehensive way. Ranis pointed out that, obviously, different economists view these different models in different ways, and that there are widely differing views as to their suitability for handling a particular problem. Manne stressed the importance of information; he felt that were the information base different, his model would also be different. Denise Ford bemoaned the fact that the income distribution somehow got lost in macromodels, and I don't think that there was any specific suggestion as to how it might be introduced into them, although I am sure that the modelmakers are ingenious enough to do it. There was also the suggestion (and I believe a general conclusion) that the models themselves could be successfully expanded in a number of directions; that input-output could be introduced to take care of the production sector; that flow-of-funds information could be included to improve the treatment of the monetary sector; that short-term models could be related to long-term models; and that models in different countries could be linked with each other, as is being done in the LINK project.

The next session moved to demography, manpower, employment, and education. This was a much more heterogeneous session, which showed the wide variety of different uses of demographic information.

Lopes started out emphasizing the need for family data relating to the household, the family, and subfamily, and he presented some work in which he had united these concepts. It is actually very paradoxical; if you examine the microanalytic models of the Urban Institute, or of the other groups, it is so obvious that the household is of major importance that one wonders why it was never really taken into account in demographic information before. I think the reason is one of technology: prior to the computer, the head count was the most important thing, and tabulations were the major products. It is only now that we are able to examine the micro information; but certainly for microanalytic models, we need the household concept.

Grajal dealt with the short-term demand for manpower. This is a very pressing problem, not only in Venezuela but in places like the United States. We have problems of on-the-job training, locating areas of unemployment, identifying structural problems. But what is really fundamental here is not just the analysis of a few projections. There is a more fundamental problem of poverty, of the unemployable. I have the uneasy feeling that short-term unemployment is actually long-term unemployment in many of these countries, and that it cannot be cured by changing the level of economic activity of the system. We need more and better demographic models linked with macromodels to really approach the problem.

Schiefelbein studied the efficiency of the educational system in combining resources to serve educational needs and to provide the best educational payoff. He had considerable data problems in blending census material with education statistics, as happens wherever this is tried. But again I am impressed here with the potentiality of the microanalytic model in working on problems of this sort. The regional data which I mentioned in connection with the discussion of the census material is also very important here. Good regional information linked with social and demographic information would be very helpful.

Browning introduced into the conference an extremely interesting proposal for collecting life histories. The novelty of his approach was the idea of tapping the respondent's stream-of-consciousness, and in the context of a sequence of life events, to elicit as much information as possible. I feel that this is a richer area than one might think at first; however, I would like to direct attention to other bodies of data which we may not normally think of in this connection, such as social security records which link individuals over their lifetimes, showing who they work for and where they live, and are of great use for tracing the individual over a longer period of time. Over shorter periods of time, we have had references to the panel history which is being obtained at the Survey Research Center in Michigan, which interviews households continuously over a five-year period, getting a great deal of information on each household. The time dimension of households is something that we are going to need if we are going to drive the microanalytic models sensibly.

CELADE [Latin American Demographic Center] also presented a paper on the use of a computer for interrelating economic and demographic variables. Again, they emphasized the importance of household and family data. The data processing involved is not something to be taken lightly—it is a tremendous amount of material; but I think the point that computing isn't enough, that we need analysis, does deserve to be emphasized.

The conclusions that I would draw from this session are that there is a great deal of data already available in the social and demographic area, and even more problems; that this is a very fruitful ground for certain types of modeling, but that the modeling does need to be done if we are to relate the data to useful analytic procedures.

The session on international comparisons of income, consumption, and prices showed how the computer was used in this major research area. The paper by Kravis and Lipsey evaluated price data for international trade flows, using international prices, wholesale prices, and export prices. Their results showed that the price elasticities differ considerably, depending on which prices are used.

Arturo Meyer pointed out that although such results are interesting, you do not dare throw wholesale prices out because they appear to be invalid. I have long wanted to throw wholesale prices out, but no one has ever let me. From a data processing point of view, this sort of comparison would not really be possible to do except by computer. It involves many very detailed comparisons and many computations.

This is also true of the work that Ronchetti and Bertaud described with respect to the European Economic Community. Here there are some six-hundred prices with three-hundred-thousand items of data being analyzed. They used a national accounts frame, and tried to develop real-product measures. I would agree with Joel Popkin in this context that there are tremendous advantages in a data bank composed of original microdata, since it provides flexibility in the development of analytic strategies.

Jorge Salazar-Carrillo's account of the difficulties of computerization rings a familiar bell. Many of us have encountered problems similar to those which Salazar-Carrillo has so aptly described. It should be noted that even Salazar-Carrillo does not suggest that there is any practical alternative to forging ahead, in spite of the difficulties encountered. It is my own belief that the process is one of learning, and that the processing and analysis of data is not doomed to perpetual frustration, in which the individual is pitted against the computer. Kenessey's point was that probably one should take a broader view of the role of the computer in the research process. Perhaps by changing the procedures of operation, increased substitution of computers for individuals would be possible.

Howe's paper really was along the same line, telling about the preparation of the data for the ECIEL [Joint Studies on Latin American Economic Integration] budget-study project. This is again a very large volume of data—19,000 households with 800 to 1,000 variables per household, covering some 21 urban centers in 11 countries. This project encountered considerable problems of standardization at the level of the original data, but it was found that there were considerable advantages in central computer processing. Again this question of editing the data, and the elimination of outliers, was raised. Betancourt suggested, I think quite reasonably, that the outliers should be retained for two reasons: first, some analyses with the outliers included may be useful; and second, the strategy of editing may later be altered so that outliers are processed differently. I think that this point is very well taken; and, incidentally, the principle is also true in combining data sets. For example, if two data sets are combined which have different definitions of income, both should be retained. This makes it possible either to separate the data sets if desired, or to develop a different strategy of combining them, or to apply different hypotheses. This underlines the necessity for having extremely flexible computer technology, with records that are easy to read and open-ended so that information can be added.

The conclusion, I think, in this session was that price research on the scale reported on here could not be done without the computer. It is true that the early Kravis-Gilbert studies accomplished a tremendous amount without the present high-speed computers, but it is clear in these studies that computational limitations prevented them from doing things that they would have liked to have done. The same is true of the early Economic Commission for Latin America (ECLA) studies. Braithwaite in ECLA accomplished a great deal, but again the tabulations were strictly limited. I am particularly conscious of this because we computerized the basic ECLA data at Yale University, and we were able to do types of calculations that Braithwaite just could not do. He was not, for instance, able to compute Paasche and Laspeyres indexes; he was not able to develop more sophisticated weighting systems, or alternative weighting systems. The computer is really required for the large amount of computation involved in creating price indexes. This session also emphasized the importance of computer editing. The editing process has analytic implications, and these must be taken into account.

The last session dealt with international trade patterns and commodity markets. The Balassa and Schydlowsky paper was directed toward developing indicators of protection. This was an econometric analysis dealing with nominal rates, effective rates, and the effects of tax credits and government expenditures. While the results were very interesting, the authors themselves suggested the possibility of developing a wider framework of simulation models which would be concerned with this kind of analysis, as well as policy packages that could test alternative policies.

The Gomez-Sastry paper was an assessment of the UN trade projections for developing countries. Such projections are of obvious importance for both national and international policy. The basic approach here was the two-gap approach suggested by Chenery. Gomez felt that he obtained better results with a general international model than with the domestic models, which gave too high export estimates. There is in this area a very large problem of masses of data, minicountries, lack of consistency, and interdependence. I am sure that future work will go in the direction of linking various kinds of models. But I was particularly impressed at the quality of the projections that were made.

The Perez Castillo paper, on the evaluation of foreign-trade policies and economic-development simulation, really did not belong in this session; it was on simulation systems and belonged in the session devoted to macrosimulation models, but it is a far larger and more detailed paper than any that were presented in that session. Its function was to construct a general model for studying economic and social problems. It includes such things as income distribution and savings by income class. Projections were made for the year 2000 under different strategies. This is the sort of model which really gladdens the heart of a computer salesman; I am sure that the amount of time it must gobble up is horrendous. It is methodologically important because, as the authors point out, they started with an aggregated model and kept disaggregating it, and disaggregating it, and disaggregating it. It would have been useful for this paper to have been discussed in the simulation session in conjunction with the other models.

Luft's paper, also, did not really fit into this session. While he does study the effect of alternative trade policies on the Colombian economy, his, too, is a general model. It is an offshoot of a macroeconomic transport simulator model that was constructed for Colombia. What Luft did was to eliminate the transport segment and to add more policy variables. The result is a combination of a macroeconomic model and a more disaggregated simulation model. It is not probabilistic in nature, but has calibrated values. John Meyer pointed out the relationship of this model to the data base. It brought together large bodies of heterogeneous information from a great many sources, and was, in fact, responsible for creating a consistent set of data for the Colombian economy.

This session, although it was nominally on international trade, underlined the same conclusions which were reached in the previous sessions. It pointed out that general models of the economy are needed to evaluate policy and to make projections under different alternatives. The specific objectives of any given use determine the variants of models, the kinds of variables, whether various areas are disaggregated, or how the model is expanded and in what directions. Finally, it was, I think, agreed in this session that we need to link various models because of the basic interdependence of all economic and social activities.

As a conclusion to the conference as a whole, I came away with the following feelings: that the computer has drastically changed the technology of data processing, storage, and retrieval; that the increasing availability of data and the ability to use the computer have had very significant effects on research methodology; that the variety of micro- and macromodels and the techniques of simulation which were presented here have wide applicability and are intimately related to the improvement of the data base; that there must be feedback between the research work and the data base and between the data base and the research work; that the computer is already essential in many well-established areas—in demography, social research, price comparisons, and international trade. However, there were evident during the conference other currents besides these major formal conclusions.

A declaration was circulated expressing the strong feelings of many people that the relationship between producers and users of data was very unsatisfactory, that the technology of the computer, rather than improving this, had in fact worsened it, and that radical changes were needed. The most important change proposed was the introduction into central statistical offices of research groups who would utilize the data as it was being produced, so that the feedback between the research process and the collection and processing process would be closer. Also recognized was the tremendous need for international cooperation and, perhaps, multinational institutions which could effectively provide for the transfer of technology and know-how. I would add to this that it is not just computer technology that is really needed; it is the technology of economic-research methodology and social-research methodology, because you cannot divorce data processing and analysis from one another.

There was a further undercurrent in the conference that I personally was gratified to see. That was a feeling that despite all of our labors over the years, GNP is not necessarily the goal; that optimizing with respect to monetary transactions of one sort or another, or a transaction network, or perhaps even other macro measures such as unemployment, is not perhaps the ultimate end of our models. There are a wide range of social problems and social ills that somehow do not seem to have been attacked by the massive amount of computer work that economists are turning out. I do not know quite what the answer is, but I suspect that we probably should try to attack specific social problems more directly, and to develop analytic procedures that are more relevant to these problems. This same matter came up at the meeting of the International Association for Research in Income and Wealth in Sweden this past year, and an Irishman got up and said that as far as his country was concerned he did not think they could adequately measure welfare, but they could certainly measure important aspects of "illfare." Perhaps it is true that in our desire to take account of the systems effects and interdependence, and in our desire to get a measure of welfare, we have overlooked the problems which are not adequately reflected in the overall totals. Perhaps if we concentrate on what we can determine is wrong with societies, rather than trying to identify the optimal society, our approach might change.

In closing, I would like to reflect for a moment on the future. I feel that this conference has succeeded in opening the door to a whole wide range of problems concerned with the role of the computer in economic and social research. I personally am gratified at the methodological discussions that were held here, and I feel that this has encouraged more methodological divergence.

We are very grateful to IBM for their generous support for this conference. They gave it without any reservations whatsoever, and we have used it without reservations.

We are very happy, also, to announce at this time that IBM is continuing its support over the next five years. We would like to continue our cooperation with national and international research organizations in Latin America. We shall try to get some additional support from other sources so that we can hold workshops and conferences in various areas, and work together with other research organizations in this area on a cooperative basis over the next few years. I would expect that in the future we shall not have such a large or lengthy conference. This conference has been ideal for accomplishing its purpose, people have been very patient, the surroundings have indeed been lovely, and it has been most productive indeed, but I think that at the next stage a narrowing of the focus and perhaps smaller and shorter workshops might be in order. As to the particular areas which I feel show promise as topics for workshops, it is quite obvious that economic models and simulation techniques were some of the more exciting things in this conference. But I think we also need to give some direct attention to the development of microdata, macrodata, and statistical systems. We cannot depend purely on the discussion of models to cover data development, and, conversely, we cannot expect our discussion of data to cover the analytical problems. Finally, I also feel that we should recognize demographic and social research explicitly and, perhaps, try to concentrate on some of the "illfare" problems and see how they can be tackled, given the techniques of the computer and the availability of information.

LIST OF PAPERS PRESENTED

Session 1. *The Computer and Government Statistical Systems*
Electronic Processing of the Data of Mexico's 1970 Population Census
   RUBEN GLEASON GALICIA and collaborators, Direccion General de Estadistica, Mexico
Computerized Reporting of Census Data for Small Areas: A Promising New Technique for the 70s
   GEORGE H. BROWN, U.S. Bureau of the Census
The Statistical System of Brazil
   ISAAC KERSTENETZKY and A. C. OLINTO, IGBE, Brazil
The Computer and Government Statistics
   IVAN P. FELLEGI and SIMON GOLDBERG, Statistics Canada

Session 2. *Data Banks and Computer Centers*
The CELADE Data Bank
   JULIO MORALES, CELADE, Chile
Computer Centers in Venezuela
   CARLOS DOMINGO, Universidad Central, Venezuela
The NBER Times Series Data Bank
   CHARLOTTE BOSCHAN, National Bureau of Economic Research, USA
Micro-economic Data Banks: Problems and Potential
   HAROLD WATTS, University of Wisconsin, USA

Session 3. *Computer Simulation Models*
A Simulation Model of the Economy of Brazil
   THOMAS H. NAYLOR, Duke University, USA; MARTIN SHUBIK, Yale University, USA; MOACYR FIORAVANTE, Vargas Foundation, Brazil; and IBRAHIM A. S. IBRAHIM, Duke University, USA
Uses of Tax Files Combined with Field Surveys
   BENJAMIN OKNER and JOSEPH PECHMAN, The Brookings Institution, USA
Comparative Simulation Analysis of Social Security Systems
   JAMES H. SCHULZ, Brandeis University, USA
Microanalytic Simulation of Household Behavior
   HAROLD W. GUTHRIE, GUY H. ORCUTT, STEVEN CALDWELL, GERALD E. PEABODY, and GEORGE SADOWSKY, Urban Institute, USA
The Argentine Cattle Cycle—A Simulation Model of an Economic Sector
   JULIO GAMBA, Universidad de Buenos Aires, Argentina

Session 4. *Macroeconomic Models*
Development Models for the Brazilian Economy
   JANES DE SOUZA, Fundaçao Getulio Vargas, and JORGE VIANNA MONTEIRO, Pontificia Universidade Catolica do Rio de Janeiro, Brazil
Macroeconometric Model Building in Latin America: The Mexican Case
   ABEL BELTRAN DEL RIO and LAWRENCE R. KLEIN, University of Pennsylvania, USA

Economic Alternatives for Mexico: A Quantitative Analysis
ALAN S. MANNE, Stanford University, USA
Development Alternatives Under Conditions of Reduced External Dependence
ALEJANDRO FOXLEY, Universidad Catolica de Chile

Session 5. *Round Table on the Computer and Society*
Panel Members: JOHN MEYER, National Bureau of Economic Research and
Yale University, USA
SHERMAN MAISEL, Board of Governors of the Federal
Reserve System, USA
SANTIAGO FRIEDMAN, Organization of American States
GUSTAVO POLLITZER, Universidad de Buenos Aires, Argentina

Session 6. *Demography, Manpower, Employment, and Education*
The Use of the Computer to Generate Family Data Based on Information in
the Census of Population
VALDECIR F. LOPES, CELADE, Chile
The Short-Term Demand and Supply of Manpower
ALEJANDRO GRAJAL, Universidad Catolica Andres Bello, Venezuela
A Simulation Model of Student Flow in Mexican Education
ERNESTO SCHIEFELBEIN, Centro de Studios Educativos en Mexico
The Role of the Computer in the Processing of Life Histories
HARLEY BROWNING, University of Texas, USA
A Model of the Interrelations between Demographic and Economic Variables
ANGEL FUCARACCIO and CARMEN ARRETX, CELADE, Chile

Session 7. *International Comparisons of Income, Consumption, and Prices*
International Trade Prices and Price Proxies
IRVING KRAVIS, University of Pennsylvania, and ROBERT E. LIPSEY,
National Bureau of Economic Research, USA
Computing Aspects of Latin American Comparisons of Consumption and
Income
HOWARD HOWE and ROBERTO VILLAVECES, The Brookings Institution,
USA
The Use of the Computer in Handling Large Price Files
JORGE SALAZAR-CARRILLO, The Brookings Institution, USA
The Experience of the European Economic Community in Calculating Price
Comparisons
S. RONCHETTI and M. BERTAUD, Statistical Office of the European
Communities, Luxembourg

Session 8. *International Trade Patterns and Commodity Markets*
Indicators of Protection and of the Other Incentive Measures
BELA BALASSA, IBRD, and DANIEL SCHYDLOWSKY, Harvard University,
USA
A Preliminary Assessment of UNCTAD Trade Projections for Developing
Countries
JULIAN GOMEZ and V. K. SASTRY, UNCTAD

Alternative Policies of Foreign Trade and Economic Development Analyzed on the Basis of Numerical Experimentation
JUAN PABLO PEREZ CASTILLO, LOURDES YERO, and LUIS LEAL, Universidad Central de Venezuela

An Example of Computer Simulation of Economic Development: The Effects of Alternative Trade Policies on the Colombian Economy
HAROLD LUFT, Harvard University, USA

Session 9. *Summary Session*
Rapporteurs: RICHARD RUGGLES, Yale University and National Bureau of Economic Research, USA
AFFONSO PASTORE, Universidade de Sao Paulo, Brazil

INDEX OF NAMES

SUBJECT INDEX